'This volume arrives at a moment when psychology has grown increasingly estranged from the very experiences it once claimed to illuminate. Across its chapters, we are reminded that moral life cannot be reduced to compliance, calibration, or codified procedures. What emerges instead is a textured account of ethics as a matter of attention, relation, and aesthetic encounter. The authors take seriously the idea that beauty can unsettle us, that it can disrupt the sterile logics of self-optimization and invite us into forms of perception that resist abstraction. Rather than treating the aesthetic as decorative or indulgent, the book positions it as a condition for ethical responsiveness, for seeing the world and one another with care. In doing so, it gestures toward a psychology that has not forgotten how to wonder and that has room for what lingers unresolved.'

Justin M. Karter, *Ph.D., Boston College*

'For more than a hundred years, there has been an intense debate over which branch of philosophy could replace metaphysics as the first and most foundational way of knowing. Some have argued that ethics ought to take the place of primacy and be enshrined as our "first philosophy." Others, myself included, have championed the supremacy of aesthetics. With deftness and insight, the contributors to this volume demonstrate the proximity and reciprocity of the Good and the Beautiful in ways that their intellectual forerunners would no doubt have envied.'

Matthew Clemente, *Ph.D., author of Bacchus Agonistes: Metarealism and the Future of Art*

'*Aesthetic Ethics* is poised to become a landmark text, reminding us that being moved by beauty, form, and the sublime is no luxury but the very pulse of our personhood. The contributing authors reclaim the aesthetic as an inroad to moral imagination by illustrating how embracing our discarded, inferiorized aspects can ignite the exaltation and urgent vision needed to forge new possibilities for humanity.'

Zenobia Morrill, *Ph.D., William James College*

Aesthetic Ethics

Aesthetic Ethics: Towards A Moral Imagination seeks to challenge and expand the boundaries of how we conceive ethics and morality, proposing that beauty, sublimity and emotional resonances found in the realm of the arts are essential for re-imagining a more just and compassionate world.

This volume delves into how aesthetic experiences cultivate ethical sensibilities and a deepened responsibility towards others and the world around us. Through a blend of philosophical inquiry, psychoanalytic theory and humanities scholarship, the contributors examine the transformative power of the aesthetic on ethical wisdom and practices. The volume asserts that aesthetic experiences are not merely for hedonic pleasure nor detached contemplation, but are vital to developing a moral imagination capable of confronting the complexities of human existence and social engagement. The chapters in this volume propose that engaging with art, literature, music and culture opens capacities and re-imagines possibilities. Contributors utilize case studies, theoretical explorations and analysis of artistic expressions to argue for the aesthetic as a fundamental component in the cultivation of deepened ethical relations and, ultimately, societal change.

Aesthetic Ethics hosts the voices and scholarship of significant figures across disciplines, addressing questions at the intersections of aesthetic theory, ethical psychotherapy and the social order. Practitioners, as well as students and researchers of the humanities, the arts, politics, philosophy, psychology, psychosocial studies, sociology and social work alike, will find this an illuminating and revivifying read.

M. Mookie C. Manalili is Licensed Independent Certified Social Worker (LICSW) Psychotherapist, Professor and Researcher based in Boston, USA. He is completing his PhD in Pastoral Counseling and Psychology at Boston University. He is faculty at School of Social Work and Department of Psychology and Neuroscience at Boston College, and is co-leader of the Psychological Humanities Lab. He is also in a private group practice in Boston, MA.

David M. Goodman is Clinical Psychologist and Dean of the Woods College of Advancing Studies at Boston College, USA, where he also serves as Executive Director for the Center for Psychological Humanities and Ethics. Dr. Goodman is on the faculty in the Lynch School of Education and Human Development and in the Philosophy department at Boston College's Morrissey College of Arts and Sciences. He also has a private practice in Boston, MA.

Diana Boros is Professor of Political Theory in the Political Science Department at St. Mary's College of Maryland, the National Honors College. She is also affiliated faculty in the Women, Gender, and Sexuality Studies Program at SMCM. She has published books on the topics of art, public art, politics, and public space and is creator of the video podcast series "Hosting Art."

The Psychology and the Other Book Series
Series editor: David M. Goodman
Associate editors: Matthew Clemente, Brian W. Becker,
Donna M. Orange and Eric R. Severson

The *Psychology and the Other* book series highlights creative work at the intersections between psychology and the vast array of disciplines relevant to the human psyche. The interdisciplinary focus of this series brings psychology into conversation with continental philosophy, psychoanalysis, religious studies, anthropology, sociology, and social/critical theory. The cross-fertilization of theory and practice, encompassing such a range of perspectives, encourages the exploration of alternative paradigms and newly articulated vocabularies that speak to human identity, freedom, and suffering. Thus, we are encouraged to reimagine our encounters with difference, our notions of the "other," and what constitutes therapeutic modalities.

The study and practices of mental health practitioners, psychoanalysts, and scholars in the humanities will be sharpened, enhanced, and illuminated by these vibrant conversations, representing pluralistic methods of inquiry, including those typically identified as psychoanalytic, humanistic, qualitative, phenomenological, or existential.

Recent titles in the series include:

Hosting Earth
Facing the Climate Emergency
Edited by Richard Kearney, Peter Klapes and Urwa Hameed

A Phenomenology of the Alien
Encounters with the Weird and Inscrutable Other
Edited by Aaron B. Daniels

Aesthetic Ethics
Towards A Moral Imagination
Edited by M. Mookie C. Manalili, David M. Goodman and Diana Boros

For a full list of titles in the series, please visit the Routledge website at: https://www.routledge.com/Psychology-and-the-Other/book-series/PSYOTH

Aesthetic Ethics

Towards A Moral Imagination

Edited by M. Mookie C. Manalili,
David M. Goodman and Diana Boros

LONDON AND NEW YORK

Designed cover image: Getty Images

First published 2026
by Routledge
4 Park Square, Milton Park, Abingdon, Oxon OX14 4RN

and by Routledge
605 Third Avenue, New York, NY 10158

Routledge is an imprint of the Taylor & Francis Group, an informa business

© 2026 selection and editorial matter, M. Mookie C. Manalili, David M. Goodman and Diana Boros; individual chapters, the contributors

The right of M. Mookie C. Manalili, David M. Goodman and Diana Boros to be identified as the authors of the editorial material, and of the authors for their individual chapters, has been asserted in accordance with sections 77 and 78 of the Copyright, Designs and Patents Act 1988.

All rights reserved. No part of this book may be reprinted or reproduced or utilised in any form or by any electronic, mechanical, or other means, now known or hereafter invented, including photocopying and recording, or in any information storage or retrieval system, without permission in writing from the publishers.

Trademark notice: Product or corporate names may be trademarks or registered trademarks, and are used only for identification and explanation without intent to infringe.

British Library Cataloguing-in-Publication Data
A catalogue record for this book is available from the British Library

ISBN: 978-1-032-98328-8 (hbk)
ISBN: 978-1-032-98327-1 (pbk)
ISBN: 978-1-003-59810-7 (ebk)

DOI: 10.4324/9781003598107

Typeset in Times New Roman
by Apex CoVantage, LLC

Contents

Introduction: Aesthetic Ethics? Towards the Beauty of
Moral Imaginations 1
M. MOOKIE C. MANALILI, DIANA BOROS, AND DAVID M. GOODMAN

PART 1
Aesthetic Ethics as "Moral Attunement and Formation" 13

1 Can the Experience of Beauty Make Us Better People?
Thinking Otherwise About the Aesthetics/Ethics Connection 15
MARK FREEMAN

2 'Aesthetic Articulations': Toward a Poetics of Formation 29
A. TAIGA GUTERRES

3 Small Tears in Logic: The Power of Poetic Image and
Aesthetic Knowing 42
ROSS GORMLEY

4 Meaning and Morality: Shaping How the Light Shines In 58
MARILYN CHARLES

5 The Power of Art to Shape Our Ability to See: A
Phenomenological Reflection on Rembrandt's *Aristotle
With a Bust of Homer* 75
KAREN E. BOHLIN

PART 2
Aesthetic Ethics as "Responsibility and Attentive Witnessing" — 91

6 Mourning the Dying of the Unharmed Self — 93
   SANDRA BUECHLER

7 To Speak of Suffering: Art's Ethical Obligation — 101
   HANNAH LYN VENABLE

8 Psychoanalysis, Art, and the Vale of Soul-Making — 124
   MICHAEL PARSONS

9 How to Build the Other From Scratch After Its Destruction? — 155
   FRANÇOISE DAVOINE

10 Levinas, Decreative Hermeneutics, and Holocaust Testimony — 163
   ROBERT C. REED

PART 3
Aesthetic Ethics as "Political and Prophetic Action" — 179

11 Whom Shall I Walk With? Reflections of a Black(ish) South African Scholar in the North American Academy — 181
   LESWIN LAUBSCHER

12 Spoken Futurities: Poetry, Prophecy, and Psychology — 195
   MANÒN VOICE

13 Aesthetic Motivation in Religious Activism — 211
   BRANDON VAIDYANATHAN

14 The Beloved Community as Aesthetic Theory: Intimations From Josiah Royce, Martin Luther King Jr., and Erich Fromm — 233
   NAHANNI FREEMAN

15 Radical Empathy: Socially-Engaged Art as Democratic Tool — 256
   DIANA BOROS

Index — *268*

Introduction
Aesthetic Ethics? Towards the Beauty of Moral Imaginations

M. Mookie C. Manalili, Diana Boros, and David M. Goodman

Truth [ἀλήθεια] . . . Goodness [αληθής] . . . Beauty [αγαθός]. What does it mean to live a good life? Must the study of moral virtue in ethics be tethered solely to juridical, rational, or calculable logic? Is morality reducible to abstract principles, to rule-based obligations, or cost–benefit analyses of human action?

These questions haunt the traditional Western ethical canon, from Plato's dialogues to Kant's categorical imperative to Rawls' veil of ignorance. Implicit lines of reasoning shape a discourse where moral knowledge is often framed as duty, constraint, or consequence – typically prioritizing an agentic actor.

But what of beauty, of art – what of the aesthetic, the experience beyond words, the transcendent, the felt sense, the ineffable? What of cultures, traditions, and heritages where excellence does not go against logic but goes beyond it? What of the truths that abound not in the words of a poem but in its rhythms, in its obscurities? Or the triggering capacities of an intertwining melody and harmony to bring tears to our eyes despite every urge to resist? These moments of being "taken" or "swept away" or "overwhelmed" by art are usually accompanied by a physical component as well – we may shed tears, or start to sweat or tremble, or grow goosebumps, or feel a tightness in our chests or throats. These experiences are an essential and irresistible part of being human, and they can be deeply instructive in viewing ourselves and our world from an aesthetic distance (while we are "swept away"), one where we might see ourselves, and our relations to others, differently from the everyday. This shift can be vital to recognizing the interconnected and interdependent nature of human relationships and the related ethical possibilities. Reflecting upon Plato's notions that fair forms come from fair practices to fair notions, towards a sense of absolute beauty, C.S. Peirce (1931) renders the aesthetic as the font of wisdom: "*Logic follows ethics and both follow aesthetics*" (Peirce, 1931, p. 311).

So what of the abilities of art, poetry, and music not only to move but to transform, not only to delight but to call forth responsibility beyond oneself? The transformation that happens not merely in the coldness of reason but in the warmth of a heart touched or broken open. What of the power of aesthetic emotions to invigorate and form the imagination, encourage empathy, and incite just action?

This volume contends that aesthetics and ethics (too often estranged from each other in philosophical inquiry) must be brought into profound and constructive conversation. From the transcendental tradition of the ancients and moderns to contemporary engagements with phenomenology, psychoanalysis, and cultural critique, the aesthetic can be understood as an encounter with that which exceeds the merely functional – and we define art as a process that transforms material and experience, both with the capacity to draw us into contemplation, awe, and affective attunement.

To experience immersive beauty, to create or witness transformative art, is to be *arrested* and drawn beyond the everyday into a moment of heightened and transformative presence, where perception shifts and new possibilities emerge. Indeed, *"rebellious art also ends by revealing the 'We are,' and with it the way to a burning humility"* (Camus, 1954). The aesthetic emotions produced in these experiences with the sublime – joy, wonder, awe, bewilderment, despair – powerfully separate us from the mundane while simultaneously bringing us closer to that divine spark, the shared human experience.

What if ethics, too, requires this (aesthetic) attunement? What if the moral life is not merely a question of rational obligation but of *moral imagination* of perceiving the suffering of the other, of responding to injustice, of being moved by the world in ways that compel action?

The (Western Philosophical) Divorce of Ethics and Aesthetics

In the Western tradition, the relationship between ethics and aesthetics has long been fraught. Plato's *Republic* (Adam, 1907) famously banished the poets from the ideal city, fearing that art's capacity to stir emotions would destabilize rational order. And yet Plato's *Phaedrus* (Hackforth, 1972) describes the soul's ascent toward truth as an erotic longing – a flight toward beauty that is inextricably linked to the pursuit of the good. Kant distinguished between morality and ethics; furthermore, Kant separated these from the aesthetic: While ethics is governed by duty and reason, aesthetics is defined by disinterested pleasure. Kant also acknowledges in the *Critique of Judgment* (Newcomb, 2022) that the experience of the sublime – of nature's vastness, of art's transcendence – awakens in us a sense of moral dignity, a feeling of our place within a larger moral order.

This tension between ethics and aesthetics, between the rational and the affective, persists into the modern era. Analytical moral philosophy has largely relegated beauty to the domain of subjective taste and, thus, focused goodness on the universality of moral norms. This trend towards *etic,* universalizing virtues can miss the specific, unique *emic* virtues that sprout from the diverse soil of humanity (Sandage et al., 2008). Meanwhile, aesthetic theory has often detached itself from moral concerns, celebrating artistic autonomy and resisting the instrumentalization of art for ethical or political ends.

Thinkers from Aristotle (Everson, 1996) to Kant (Pluhar, 1996) to Nietzsche (Kaufmann, 1977) and Camus (O'Brien, 1991) have argued that it is human nature to desire undebatable answers and to yearn for a structured and knowable existence. Of course, Nietzsche and Camus did not believe in the "Truth" that Aristotle invested himself in but nonetheless believed that humans yearned (if ever fruitlessly) for it. Both Nietzsche and Camus expanded on this by arguing that we also inherently fear the chaos and unknowability both of the passions and of life (and its desired "meaning") itself. Indeed, the passions are less predictable and less able to be controlled, but they are rich with ethical and moral information.

Still, emotions and affect are often ignored, buried, derided, or devalued in most spheres of the wider society. Typically, these are split off through the relegation into the arts, forms of relational psychoanalysis, and other ventures sympathetic to affectivity. Emotions are, and have historically been, seen as the weaker and the more feminine in response to stimuli. The realm of the rational, or the masculine *logos* (reason and speech), has consistently emerged as the victor in discussions of human experience and choice, in society and our psychological fields. Anthropologically, human beings believe themselves to be the logical species [Latin: *homo sapiens*]. We are, it is so often argued, at our best when we act according to reason and at our most vulnerable when we act according to our passions.

For our current societies, the Western world tends to place the highest value on approaches to education and on vocations that most overtly rely on reason as a foundational support. Our societies might decry the display of emotions, especially in public, and seek coherence, order, and stability in all realms of life (or at least the appearance of this) to set ourselves up for presumed and perceived success. Thus, ethical choices are framed and understood as reason-based decisions and relegate emotional urges to the realm of the less vital, the not necessary.

However, especially in the current socio-political landscapes, emotions can (vitriolically) bend the very structures of a logical society. The warnings of Hobbes, Locke, Hume, and Rousseau ring forth, embedded even in how Western cultures organize society. While some Enlightenment thinkers worried about the "state of nature" in fear of humanity's "nasty, short, and brutish" tendencies (Hobbes & Missner, 1651/2016), others believed (similar to Freud) that pleasure/pain affected the "tabula rasa" of the mind and argued for emotive experiential education (Locke, 1689/1948). Later thinkers posited that emotions like compassion are the root of society and morality (Rousseau, 1754/2009) and took a more sentimental approach to ethics, noting that reason is bounded and enslaved by passions (Hume, 1740/2000). Whether the take on human nature is more cynical or more hopeful, several Enlightenment thinkers understood and warned/promoted the role of emotions in human societies.

Emotions are not only a critical part of the human experience, one that needs not be denied or repressed, but they are also profoundly universal among human beings and across cultures. While philosophers will debate the proclivities of human nature, it is clear that when we are overcome by the fullest of feelings, like the greatest joy or the deepest grief or an abject horror or overwhelming anger, we are feeling a connected experience. This encompassing humanness, this understanding that we all share a fundamental likeness, has been described in a multitude of ways by thinkers, poets, and musicians. Notable examples from philosophy include

Rousseau's concept of pitie (Cole, 1993), Marx's species being (Milligan, 1988), and Emerson's oversoul (2012).

While these concepts are notably distinct from one another, they also all characterize the power and importance of shared human experience, and all of the mentioned thinkers claimed that it was this experience, this understanding of the self in relation to all others, that was unique to humans. Rousseau argued that our first emotion is pitie, or compassion. Prior to reason, we feel an instinctual care for another of our species. Marx, in his early manuscripts, spoke of how one of the key ways that the modern capitalist structure alienates us from ourselves is by dividing us from our understanding of shared humanity (this recognition being species being). Emerson, in his famous essay of the same name, described the oversoul being a human consciousness or spirit that is inclusive of all, that guides as it unifies. These concepts illustrate a vital thread in philosophical thought that identifies a universal human experience, and an accompanying urge for justice, that is gleaned from the realm of the emotional, the spirit.

Ethics as Encounter: Amidst Otherness, Excellence, and Liberation?

If aesthetics and ethics are to be reconciled, the very nature of ethical responsibility might have to be re-understood. Here, Emmanuel Levinas (1979, 1981) offers an urgent provocation: prior to ontology and being, *ethics* calls. Before studying isolated ways-of-being (ontology), Levinas argues that our embeddedness with others (ethics) must come before this. Ethics is not first and foremost a matter of rational calculation or moral law but of *being confronted by the Other* – of encountering a face that calls me into responsibility. Not unlike how beauty beckons, the hungry, poor, migrant, widow, orphan, and stranger beckon me, rendering my first-person agentic "I" into the summoned and influenced third-person "me." Whether the call is ignored or answered, the call of the Other already, always abounds.

For Levinas (1979), the ethical relation is *an interruption*, a moment in which I am arrested, drawn beyond my own concerns, and summoned to respond to another's suffering. Is this not precisely what aesthetic experience makes possible? Is it not in poetry, in painting, in music that we encounter alterity – that we are drawn beyond the self toward a reality that resists totalization? "*This 'saying to the Other' – this relationship with the Other as interlocutor, this relation with an existent – precedes all ontology*" (Levinas, 1979, p. 48). Expanded and sharpened in his later works, Levinas notes that "responsibility for the Other, this way of answering without a prior commitment, is human fraternity itself, and it is prior to freedom" (Levinas, 1981, p. 116). Put poetically, Levinas notes:

> Love is only possible through the idea of the Infinite, through the Infinite placed in me, by the "more" that ravages and wakes up the "less," turning away from teleology, and destroying the time and the happiness [l'heure et le bonheur] of the end.
>
> (Levinas, 1998, p. 67)

Ultimately, the invitation of the Other is towards relationality, responsibility, and love – away from the pull of narcissistic solipsism. The aesthetic ethical pulls away from the self and towards relation, responsibility, and love for the Other.

Contrasting yet resonant, the tradition of *virtue ethics,* particularly along the Aristotelian line (Sachs, 2011; Anscombe, 1958; MacIntyre, 2013), reminds active agents that morality is not merely about following rules but about forming character. Virtue is *"the excellence that makes anything an outstanding specimen of its kind, especially well fitted to its end"* (Sachs, 2011, p. 212). In particular for humanity, human excellence [virtus, ἀρετὴ] extends not only in our rational capacities but towards our moral relationships with others. This formation of a way-of-being, this ethos, is not something to merely think through but something to enact, pulled by beauty and exemplars beyond oneself. We cultivate habits (like that of perception, amongst many others) and actions that shape us into who we are. Thus, to become an ethical agent is not simply to obey an external moral law, but to *literally see differently* – to allow habitus to re-constitute oneself in attentiveness, compassion, and justice towards the other. We do not just pass by or ignore others, oblivious to those who are suffering . . . we have the capacity to *see* them. And thus, to *be moved* and *to enact.*

And yet, how is such formation possible without the aesthetic? If virtue is shaped through lived experiences, through storytelling, through mythos, through artistic expressions, the images and metaphors that shape our moral vision, then aesthetics is not merely an accessory or auxiliary to ethics. It is its very condition of moral life.

These insights are deepened by *liberation psychologies* (Watkins & Shulman, 2008), which insist that ethical life cannot be abstracted from lived experience but from the concrete realities of oppression, trauma, and struggle. Born from the movements of Latin American liberation theology, thinkers such as Ignacio Martín-Baró (1996) argue that *ethos* must be embodied, historical, and aesthetic – that the imagination is not a luxury but a necessity for those seeking to resist dehumanization. For example . . .

> have we thought of looking at . . . clinical psychology from the standpoint of the marginalized? What would mental health look like from the place of a tenant farmer on a hacienda, or personal maturity from someone who lives in the town dump . . . or motivation from a woman who sells goods in the market?
> (Martín-Baró, 1996, p. 28)

What of the power of *testimonios,* of spoken-word poetry, of murals and sketches, of hip-hop, bachata, salsa, reggaeton, of stories amidst bread broken in the barrios? What of the ancient stones arranged in patterns to the stars, cathedrals painted with frescos and marred by wartime, and the living stones and sacred bones of folks who carry mysticism and prophecies towards justice in the *fronteras*/borderlands?

"When the heart is touched by direct experience, the mind may be challenged to change. Personal involvement with innocent suffering, with the injustice others suffer, is the catalyst for solidarity which then gives rise to intellectual inquiry and moral reflection" (Kolvenbach, 2008, p. 155). Indeed, folks even note that divinity and liberation can be found in prioritizing and attuning to the voices of the poor and marginalized [Spanish: *la opción preferencial por los pobres*] (Gutiérrez, 1973). Additionally, the liminal spaces in between offer newness. The exploration of *la frontera* [borderlands] as liminal spaces and *mestizaje* [mixed identities] offers dances beyond the rigidity towards resistance and transformation (Anzaldúa, 1987).

Across traditions, we find thinkers above and beyond who resist this divide – who insist that beauty and goodness must be intertwined, that the aesthetic is not merely ornamental but foundational to the ethical and the good life-worth-living – eudaemonia [ευδαιμονία] (Sandage & Hill, 2001; Fowers, 2005; Sachs, 2011, Goodman et al., 2021). If ethics without aesthetics becomes rigid and blind to the fullness of human experience, then aesthetics without ethics risks complicity with injustice. This volume seeks to resist both tendencies, arguing for an ethical imagination that is both a/effective and transformative.

Aesthetic Ethics: Towards A Moral Imagination

Whether through poetry, visual art, music, film, or the beauty of lived experience expressed, aesthetic experience disrupts habitual perception, calling forth new ways of seeing and being. It is in this disruption, this arrest, this irruption (Severson, 2019) that ethical possibilities emerge.

This volume emerges from such a resistance and invitation to foster moral imaginations. This book volume is arranged as a triptych, expanding aesthetic ethics into several directions . . . as "moral attunement and formation," as "responsibility and attentive witnessing," and as "political and prophetic action."

We (and our collaborators) develop and lend various supports to the argument that aesthetics is not an escape from the ethical but a mode of ethical engagement – one that expands the moral imagination and deepens our capacity for response.

Part 1: Aesthetic Ethics as "Moral Attunement and Formation"

This initial section explores how aesthetic experiences cultivate ethical sensibilities, shape moral imagination, and serve as a foundation for ethical responsiveness. Indeed, liberatory practices remind us that a newness emerges from engagement with alterity. *"To acquire new psychological knowledge, it is not enough to place ourselves in the perspective of the people; it is necessary to involve ourselves in a new praxis"* (Martín-Baró, 1996, p. 28). The five authors note in diverse ways how the beauty of poetic intelligence and artistic experiences invites a reconstitution of the person influenced.

Chapter 1: "Can the Experience of Beauty Make Us Better People? Thinking Otherwise About the Aesthetics/Ethics Connection": Mark Freeman begins by exploring our central question, exploring the ties of beauty towards the good life. He unpacks through poetic and articulate discourse how beauty fosters moral perception and ethical awareness through undivided attention, drawing on Simone Weil and Iris Murdoch. Through poetic philosophy that embodies what it signals, Freeman argues that undivided attention is at the very heart of the connection of aesthetics/ethics and that it requires "thinking Otherwise" about both the experience of beauty and the challenge of "becoming better people."

Chapter 2: "Aesthetic Articulations': Toward a Poetics of Formation": A. Taiga Guterres continues by exploring how aesthetic experiences – through art, music, and narrative – give voice to the ineffable and deepen moral understanding. Engaging with Charles Taylor, Mark Freeman, and Stefania Pandolfo, Guterres argues that aesthetic articulations are not merely expressions of beauty but practices towards a 'poetics of formation.' Between what is already-expressed and ineffable (beyond-expressible), these practices invite a movement towards creativity and newness – as the self interprets and articulates the world anew.

Chapter 3: "Small Tears in Logic: The Power of Poetic Image and Aesthetic Knowing": Ross Gormley argues that poetic and aesthetic knowing challenge rigid rationalism, opening alternative ethical possibilities. Through Dadaism, Hannah Arendt's theory of the banality of evil, and critiques of capitalist logic, he notes the differences of image and language – positioning image as even beyond-narrativity and beyond-language. Gormley explores how artistic and poetic images disrupt conventional meaning-making structures, inviting persons to create their own meaning apart from dominant narratives.

Chapter 4: "Meaning and Morality: Shaping How the Light Shines In": Marilyn Charles explores how metaphor and aesthetic experience shape ethical consciousness by offering an alternative to linear temporality. Drawing on Bion, Ricoeur, and Bachelard, she argues that poetic and aesthetic experiences create "vertical time," fostering moral authenticity, deeper self-reflection, and ethical responsiveness. Utilizing two clinical examples, she argues that the aesthetic can move one towards transformative elusive meanings – between primary process, the aesthetic vertex, and the call towards authenticity by the other.

Chapter 5: "The Power of Art to Shape Our Ability to See: A Phenomenological Reflection on Rembrandt's Aristotle With a Bust of Homer": Karen Bohlin concludes by exploring how aesthetic experience can cultivate moral perception and deepen ethical inquiry. Using a phenomenological approach, she argues that slow-looking and sustained engagement with art may refine our ability to see, shape our desires, and cultivate a more expansive moral imagination. By analyzing Rembrandt's composition, light, and symbolism, Bohlin demonstrates how art fosters contemplation, guiding us toward a deeper understanding of wisdom, legacy, and human aspiration.

Part 2: Aesthetic Ethics as "Responsibility and Attentive Witnessing"

This second section focuses on how art and aesthetics serve as sites of ethical witness, particularly in relation to trauma, suffering, and historical memory. For Levinas, "the ethical relation is not grafted onto an antecedent relation of cognition; it is a foundation and not a superstructure" (Levinas & Hand, 1987, p. 56; Orange, 2009, p. 79). The encounter and witness to the Other reconstitute the witness. The following five authors emphasize *attention, witnessing, and responsibility*, focusing on how aesthetics and ethics converge in trauma, memory, and suffering. Thus, we pivot towards interpretations of that which shapes (and breaks) the heart of whom the witness is being received by.

Chapter 6: "Mourning the Dying of the Unharmed Self": Sandra Buechler explores how poetry and literature help individuals process trauma and reconstruct a moral sense of self. Engaging with Simone Weil and Iris Murdoch, she argues that aesthetic experience fosters undivided attention, expanding ethical awareness and deepening a sense of responsibility and care. Poetry and literature provide pathways for healing beyond the abuse's inevitable legacy, pointing to a healing through art and beyond what-is.

Chapter 7: "To Speak of Suffering: Art's Ethical Obligation": Hannah Venable argues that art carries an ethical obligation to bear witness when language fails to express suffering. Drawing on Merleau-Ponty, Nietzsche, and existentialist thought, she explores how aesthetic expression makes grief, trauma, and injustice visible, offering both testimony and transformation. She notes how art refuses to soften reality while calling into action the reality of suffering, allowing the suffering not to be permitted but allowed to be borne.

Chapter 8: "Psychoanalysis, Art, and the Vale of Soul-Making": Michael Parsons connects psychoanalytic practice to aesthetic experience as a process of ethical and existential transformation. He argues that by creating space for the unknown and the poetic imagination, psychoanalysis, like art, fosters soul-making – an ethical engagement with interior life. Put simply, Parsons echoes the sentiments of John Keats in psychoanalysis, rather than merely a vale of tears and sorrow, a vale of soul-making – towards a spiritual encounter beyond transformation.

Chapter 9: "How to Build the Other from Scratch After Its Destruction?": Françoise Davoine explores how art and psychoanalysis reconstruct meaning and relationality after social rupture and historical catastrophe. Drawing on Lacanian and historical psychoanalytic traditions, she argues that survivors of extreme violence use creative expression to reclaim agency and restore ethical relations. The theme of "therapôn" is central – or a 'second in combat' and 'ritual double' in times of funeral duties, as the aesthetics of psychoanalysis echo forth in the transference. She notes that the rhythm of the epic reanimates the breath of life, as well as ritual theaters performed across the globe over the centuries, as patients try to reconstruct life from destruction.

Chapter 10: "Levinas, Decreative Hermeneutics, and Holocaust Testimony": Robert C. Reed applies Levinasian ethics and Simone Weil's decreative hermeneutics to analyze how art and testimony bear witness to trauma. Through Paul Celan's poetry, he explores how aesthetic experience disrupts fixed narratives, opening a space for ethical responsiveness and moral engagement with radical suffering. Reed argues for employing Weil's decreative attention as a hermeneutics that can lead to non-voluntary action on behalf of suffering others. An outcome far different from the experience of conscious motivation, non-willed action reflects the alterity or other-ness of the ethical encounter itself, leading to Levinasian phenomenology not as an intentional philosophical act so much as a hermeneutics in which non-willed action constitutes the ethical "interpretation."

Part 3: Aesthetic Ethics as "Political and Prophetic Action"

This final section explores how aesthetic experiences inspire social justice, cultivate radical empathy, and mobilize ethical action in political and communal life. Aristotle notes that we are political animals [Greek: πολιτιχὸν ζῷον, *zoon politikon*] and that human excellence [virtus, ἀρετή] cannot be divorced from actions within the polis, within community. These final five authors move toward the prophetic – social action and political aesthetics, showing how art might be used to mobilize justice, empathy, and communal transformation. Beyond attunement towards *whom* and beyond the descriptions and interpretations of *what-is,* we dare to hope for the *what-could-be* – which is the realm of the creative, the aesthetic.

Chapter 11: "Whom Shall I Walk With? Reflections of a Black(ish) South African Scholar in the North American Academy": Leswin Laubscher beautifully examines in heartfelt testimony and scholarly exploration . . . how identity, race, and historical memory shape an aesthetic and ethical reckoning with belonging and difference. Through a phenomenological and psychoanalytic lens, he argues that storytelling and philosophical reflection offer a means of resisting erasure and affirming ethical presence in the face of colonial and historical trauma. Laubscher shares and confesses the questions he asks of them and the sometimes insight they offer(ed) about what it is to negotiate Black and Brown life in a white world . . . about the question of the foreigner, a foreigner's question.

Chapter 12: "Spoken Futurities: Poetry, Prophecy, and Psychology": Manòn Voice transmutes spoken voice into written words, noting how poetry and prophecy function as ethical calls to justice and societal transformation. She notes that akin to psychological practice, in poetry, we learn to inhabit a safe space where we interrogate the wild and unknown layers of our consciousness. Drawing on James Baldwin and narrative therapy, she argues that poetic language reclaims fragmented identities and envisions alternative futures, revealing the transformative power of aesthetic expression in shaping moral consciousness. Through interwoven poetry of others and her own voice, Voice prompts the artists towards the prophetic, towards lighting a path towards the humane.

Chapter 13: "Aesthetic Motivation in Religious Activism": Brandon Vaidyanathan explores how aesthetic experiences generate ethical commitments to justice, particularly in religious social movements. Through historical case studies – including Martin Luther King Jr., Dorothy Day, the White Rose Movement, and Mahatma Gandhi – he argues that beauty provides "positive emotional shocks" that sustain long-term activism and collective action and invites future scholars to take on the mantle. Vaidyanathan connects social movement theory and aesthetic theory, identifying potential pathways for others to walk the road from beauty towards justice.

Chapter 14: "The Beloved Community as Aesthetic Theory: Intimations From Josiah Royce, Martin Luther King Jr., and Erich Fromm": Nahanni Freeman situates Martin Luther King Jr.'s vision of the Beloved Community within an aesthetic framework, linking it to the philosophies of Josiah Royce and Erich Fromm. She argues that artistic and prophetic expressions, such as sorrow songs and liberation theology, serve as aesthetic counternarratives to systemic injustice, sustaining social movements through beauty and moral imagination. Furthermore, she notes that revelation of divine love co-occurs with awareness of diaspora and the confined spaces that are transmitted intergenerationally for oppressed people. For Freeman, a beautiful invitation in authentic love is mounted, inviting a transformation through the Other and the pursuit of meaning.

Chapter 15: "Radical Empathy: Socially-Engaged Art as a Democratic Tool": Diana Boros sheds light on the political and ethical value of social practice art. This form of artmaking is inherently interactive and collaborative (as well as justice and care seeking) in that in place of a traditional viewing audience, there is rather the creation of an inclusive experience where the "audience" becomes participant, and that participation is an integral component of the work itself. She presents a vibrant argument that empathetic behavior can and should be taught, and employs "radical empathy" as the political expression of this – a habitual practice, done both deliberately and consistently, of imagining ourselves in another's situation when discussing contentious issues. She employs the aid of both aesthetic and democratic theory to argue that socially engaged artworks can play a key role in aiding the development of these political (and emotional) habits.

Conclusion: Beyond the Divide, Dialoguing Towards a Beautiful Justice

If ethics without aesthetics risks becoming rigid, abstract, and disconnected from the affective dimensions of human life . . . aesthetics without ethics risks becoming indulgent, detached, and complicit in the status quo. Rather than a divorce, we invite a dialogue. The aim is not right or wrong, nor even the unity of way. However, the aim is towards a beautiful justice that invites the hearts and minds of the many.

This volume seeks to move beyond this impasse, to imagine an ethics that is not merely about duty but about *responses* . . . not merely about deontological law but about *attunement* . . . not merely about knowing but about *imagination.*

For in the end, what is required of us is not merely to know the good but to *desire* it, to be moved by it as well as toward it, to be drawn by beauty and creative force into its orbit. Ethics, in this sense, is not only a matter of judgment but of perception – not only of reason but of *attention*. To attend to the call of the suffering Other. It is not simply about the capacity to make a just decision or choice but about seeing and feeling the plight of those victimized and marginalized, again and again. It is this caring, this attending – the attention demanded by art, by poetry, by the gravity of universal emotions, by the particularity of a patient's life story, by the beautiful fabrics of cultures, by the ineffable and the sublime – that this volume seeks to reclaim. In an era where ethical discourse is increasingly polarized, where moral imagination is stifled by bureaucratic rationality, possessive individualism, and technological alienation, the aesthetic offers a way forward. By creating new perspectives on the worlds around us, it offers both an alternative and an antidote to existing realities. Profound aesthetic experiences can engage a deep imaginative urge to see not-yet-tried possibilities and to consider what has not yet been. They call us to *see otherwise*, to *feel otherwise*, to *live otherwise.* Indeed,

> the face of the Other [French: L'Autre] at each moment destroys and overflows the plastic image it leaves me . . . To approach the Other in conversation is to welcome [their] expression, in which at each instant [they] overflow the idea a thought would carry away from it. It is, therefore, to receive from the Other beyond the capacity of the I, which means exactly: to have the idea of infinity.
> (Levinas, 1979, p. 38)

And in this call, an ethics of beauty – and a beauty of ethics – begins to take shape. To encounter beauty, to feel awe, to lose oneself in the creative moment is to be drawn outside of the self – away from the individual and towards the ever-elusive but ever-present universal. In this, we can enter into relation with that which is Other – with the unseen, the marginalized, the unattended to. We can thus perceive beyond the rigidity of what is ostensibly given, towards futures and timelines not solely our own but rather intertwined with all others.

Whether therapist, academic, patient, student, or any lover of goodness – we hope this volume, and the beautiful voices that give it life, invite you towards beauty to bring a more just world into being. May our hearts and minds, eyes and ears, all senses visible and invisible, our flesh and possibilities, attune to the call that beckons all around us. May we find beauty in each Other.

References

Adam, J. (Ed.). (1907). *The republic of Plato* (Vol. 2). Cambridge University Press.
Anscombe, G. E. M. (1958). Modern moral philosophy. *Philosophy*, 33(124), 1–19.
Anzaldúa, G. (1987). *Borderlands/la frontera: The new mestiza.* Aunt Lute Books.

Aristotle. (1996). *The politics and the Constitution of Athens* (S. Everson, Trans.). Cambridge, UK: Cambridge University Press.
Camus, A. (1954). *The Rebel*. Alfred A. Knopf.
Camus, A. (1991). *The myth of Sisyphus* (J. O'Brien, Trans.). Vintage.
Emerson, R. W. (2012). *The over-soul*. California: CreateSpace.
Fowers, B. J. (2005). *Virtue and psychology: Pursuing excellence in ordinary practices*. American Psychological Association.
Goodman, D. M., Sandage, S. J., Rupert, D., Manalili, M. M. C., Owen, J., Farchione, T., & Zanarini, M. C. (2021). The virtue of virtue for psychotherapy: Contextualizing and situating the conversation. In *Routledge international handbook of theoretical and philosophical psychology* (pp. 497–515). Routledge.
Gutiérrez, G. (1973). *A theology of liberation: History, politics, and salvation*. Orbis Books.
Hackforth, R. (Ed.). (1972). *Plato: Phaedrus* (Vol. 119). Cambridge University Press.
Hobbes, T., & Missner, M. (1651/2016). *Thomas Hobbes: Leviathan (Longman library of primary sources in philosophy)*. Routledge.
Hume, D. (1740/2000). *A treatise of human nature*. Oxford University Press.
Kant, I. (1996). *Critique of pure reason* (W. Pluhar, Trans.). Hackett.
Kolvenbach, P. H. (2008). The service of faith and the promotion of justice in American Jesuit higher education. In *A Jesuit education reader* (pp. 144–162). Loyola Press.
Levinas, E. (1979). *Totality and infinity: An essay on exteriority* (Vol. 1). Kluwer Academic Publishers.
Levinas, E. (1981). *Otherwise than being or beyond essence* (Vol. 3). Kluwer Academic Publishers.
Levinas, E. (1998). *Of God who comes to mind*. Stanford University Press.
Levinas, E., & Hand, S. (1987). *The Levinas reader*. Wiley-Blackwell.
Locke, J. (1689/1948). An essay concerning human understanding, 1690. In W. Dennis (Ed.), *Readings in the history of psychology* (pp. 55–68). Appleton-Century-Crofts. https://doi.org/10.1037/11304-008
MacIntyre, A. (2013). *After virtue*. Bloomsbury.
Martín-Baró, I. (1996). *Writings for a liberation psychology*. Harvard University Press.
Marx, K. (1988). *Economic and philosophical manuscripts of 1844* (M. Milligan, Trans.). Buffalo, NY: Prometheus.
Newcomb, T. (2022). *Critique of pure reason* (Vol. 7). Newcomb Libvraria Press.
Nietzsche, F. (1977). *The portable nietzsche* (W. Kaufmann, Ed. and Trans.). Penguin Books.
Orange, D. M. (2009). *Thinking for clinicians: Philosophical resources for contemporary psychoanalysis and the humanistic psychotherapies*. Routledge.
Peirce, C. S. (1931). *Collected papers of Charles Sanders Peirce*. Harvard.
Rawls, J. (1999). *A theory of justice*. Belknap Press (Harvard University Press).
Rousseau, J.-J. (1754/2009). *Discours sur l'origine et les fondements de l'inégalité parmi les hommes, suivi de La reine fantasque*. Prodinnova.
Rousseau, J.-J. (1993). *The social contract and the discourses* (G. D. H. Cole, Trans.). New York: Everyman's Library (Random House).
Sachs, J. (Ed.). (2011). *Nicomachean ethics*. Hackett Publishing.
Sandage, S. J., Cook, K. V., Hill, P. C., Strawn, B. D., & Reimer, K. S. (2008). Hermeneutics and psychology: A review and dialectical model. *Review of General Psychology*, 12(4), 344–364.
Sandage, S. J., & Hill, P. C. (2001). The virtues of positive psychology: The rapprochement and challenges of an affirmative postmodern perspective. *Journal for the Theory of Social Behaviour*, 31(3).
Severson, E. R. (2019). Levinas and the trauma of responsibility. *Research in Phenomenology*, 49(1), 119–125.
Watkins, M., & Shulman, H. (2008). *Toward psychologies of liberation* (Vol. 74). Palgrave Macmillan.

Part 1

Aesthetic Ethics as "Moral Attunement and Formation"

Chapter 1

Can the Experience of Beauty Make Us Better People? Thinking Otherwise About the Aesthetics/Ethics Connection

Mark Freeman

Preliminaries: Dubious Definitions and Contestable Conceptions

I think the answer to the question posed in the title of this chapter is radiantly clear: *Yes*. In claiming this, I am certainly not asserting that the experience of beauty *necessarily* makes us better people. Some aesthetes are haughty, self-absorbed jerks, and while it can plausibly be asserted that their experience has no doubt "rubbed off" in *some* way, there is no reason to assume, or posit, that this rubbing-off culminates in becoming morally better. Even the most beautiful paintings or symphonies or poems will not turn a sinner into a saint, or even just a tolerably decent person. How, then, might we understand the connection at hand? To begin, it would seem important to unpack some central terms in the question before us. What exactly is meant by "the experience of beauty"? And what is meant by "better people"? Fortunately for me, there *is* no fully agreed-upon definition of beauty, and the reason it is fortunate is that I have the opportunity to come up with my own. It is too soon to do so, though. So let us begin this exploration by getting some sense of the range of definitions and conceptions that are out there.

We can begin with that now-classic source of knowledge, Wikipedia:

> Beauty is commonly described as a feature of objects that makes these objects pleasurable to perceive. Such objects include landscapes, sunsets, humans and works of art. Beauty, together with art and taste, is the main subject of aesthetics, one of the major branches of philosophy.

This is pretty standard fare. But it is also problematic in a number of ways, including the idea that it is "a feature of objects" and that these objects are to be considered "pleasurable." So let us continue by turning to a fuller, more scholarly rendition, taken from Crispin Sartwell's (2022) entry from the *Stanford Encyclopedia of Philosophy*, concentrating mainly on the first of these two ideas. According to Sartwell, among others, "Perhaps the most familiar basic issue in the theory of beauty is whether beauty is subjective – located 'in the eye of the beholder' – or rather an objective feature of beautiful things." As he immediately goes on to note, rightly, neither of these stances, in their "pure form," is adequate. Put in (too) simple terms, the first, "objectivist," position, does not and cannot account for the great variability across time and space for what is taken to be beautiful. This doesn't mean that the objective properties inhering in objects are irrelevant; such properties obviously can be, and generally are, quite relevant. All it means is that insofar as the determination of beauty involves some measure of judgment and such judgment varies, considerably, there is no way to link the perception of beauty to objective properties alone.

As for the second, "subjectivist," position, suffice it to say that if beauty were to be considered wholly subjective, it would render the judgment of value essentially meaningless, such that there would be no reason whatsoever to consider any painting or poem or symphony (or whatever) any more beautiful than any other. That would be silly. A caveat is in order here too. That subjectivity is involved in the determination of beauty is obvious. I suppose this could be refuted through the old "What if a tree falls in the woods" question, but there is not much reason to go down that wooded path. The very idea of beauty entails perception and judgment and thus some measure of subjectivity – or, if not subjectivity, *experience*. Indeed, this would be so even if one subscribed to an objectivist perspective; we would just need to invoke the important distinction between objective and subjective experience – as, for instance, the Gestalt psychologist Wolfgang Köhler (1929/1970) did, the former referring to our experience of the dynamic properties of objects themselves, the latter to what is going on internally, perhaps by virtue of cultural values, what we bring to the encounter as individuals, and so on (Freeman, 2018, 2021a). In any case, the long and short of this brief excursion into "this most familiar basic issue in the theory of beauty" is that it is imperative to conceptualize the idea of beauty in *relational* terms – which is to say, in terms of that which exists in-between the purely objective and the purely subjective. There is, of course, much more to say about all this, but this will do for the time being.

Let us therefore turn to the idea of the "pleasurable." Presumably, this term cannot simply mean "that which makes us feel good," for there are plenty of phenomena that, arguably, deserve to be called beautiful that don't make us feel good at all. Along the same lines, it can't be taken to refer to what is "enjoyable" either. Some of Simone Weil's (1951/1973) thoughts about beauty strike me as particularly apt in this context. "The beauty of the world," she writes,

> gives us an intimation of its claim to a place in our heart. In the beauty of the world brute necessity becomes an object of love. What is more beautiful than the action of gravity on the fugitive folds of the sea waves, or on the almost eternal folds of the mountains?
>
> The sea is not less beautiful in our eyes because we know that sometimes ships are wrecked by it. On the contrary, this adds to its beauty. If it altered the movement of its waves to spare a boat, it would be a creature gifted with discernment and choice

and not this fluid, perfectly obedient to every external pressure. It is this perfect obedience that constitutes the sea's beauty.

All the horrors produced in this world are like the folds imposed upon the waves by gravity. This is why they contain an element of beauty. Sometimes a poem, such as the *Iliad*, brings this beauty to light.

(pp. 128–129)

Yes, of course; there are some phenomena, conventionally regarded as beautiful, that bring us pleasure: their "pleasing" qualities can indeed be enjoyable, make us feel good. "Such objects," we learned earlier, "include landscapes, sunsets, humans and works of art." We would hardly want to exclude these from the province of the beautiful. Nor, however, would we want to exclude the kinds of phenomena that Weil is referring to, which, while not conventionally beautiful, may nonetheless stir our souls and incite a more capacious regard for the world, in all of its wondrous, and at times disturbing, thereness. As Weil writes elsewhere (1952/1997), "The attitude of looking and waiting is the attitude which corresponds with the beautiful. As long as one can go on conceiving, wishing, longing, the beautiful does not appear. That is why in all beauty we find contradiction, bitterness and absence which are irreducible" (pp. 136–137).

It could be argued that Weil has gone too far in asserting that even the horrors of the world contain an element of beauty. The very idea and ideal of beauty would seem to be diminished from the perspective she is offering, flattened out. If even the horrific may be deemed beautiful, doesn't that imply that *everything* could be deemed so? Perhaps. But her claim, at least in my reading, is a more modest one, her primary aim being to expand our view and appreciation of those phenomena that bear within them "obedience" and necessity and that thereby transcend willful human choice.

Reimagining Beauty

Let me try to make some of Weil's ideas more concrete by turning briefly to the story of my mother, who died in 2016 at age 93 after a dozen or so years of dementia. Most of those who knew her would agree that she had been a beautiful woman, conventionally conceived. When she was younger, she looked like a Hollywood starlet. And much later, even after she had been diagnosed with dementia and had landed in an assisted-living facility, she was still striking. It came as no surprise, therefore, that when it came time to select a model for the yearly fashion show, she was the chosen one – graceful, elegant, lovely in the way of older women who somehow carry their years of beauty into their later lives. This sometimes left her wondering, painfully, how she had managed to land where she had, filled as it was with lots of withered, broken people. Little did she know that, in due time, she would become one of them.

Things changed. At one point, she began to wear the same clothes day in and day out. Her hair was often unkempt, scraggly. She started to shuffle as she walked. And later on, when her dementia was in full force, she would be missing teeth, and her face would be hollowed out. My mother had "partials," dentures that supplemented her remaining teeth, and she often found them annoying enough that she would "lose" them, probably by tossing them in the garbage. For a time, we replaced them. But that proved to be pointless – and unnecessary – at least to me and my family. But between her scraggly hair, missing teeth, hollow face, and her skin all scaly and mottled, suffice it to say that she was a far cry, visually, from what she had been a few short years before.

Not surprisingly, those who hadn't seen her for some time were often horrified at what my mother had become. "She was so beautiful, my sister," her elder sister, Shirley, said. "I can't bear to see her like this." Another sister proclaimed that my mother was effectively gone. "She left us a long time ago." As I put the matter in my (2021b) book, *Do I Look at You with Love?*, "They so wanted her to be what she had been before. And she wasn't. She had become something scarily *other*, and for some, it was a terrible shock to the system" (pp. 104–105). She was "the *othered*: an object, a thing, an *It*, as Martin Buber (1970) might put it – in this case, a once-beautiful woman now saddled with dementia, compromised, ostensibly emptied of her unique being" (p. 105).

She didn't have to become that, though. She didn't have to be othered and "uglied" in the way she was. And perhaps with the passage of time, she would have been more authentically seen, taken and appreciated for what she was, as someone "essentially other than myself" – as Buber (1965) put it,

> someone that does not have merely a different mind, or way of thinking or feeling, or a different conviction or attitude, but has also a different perception of the world, a different recognition and order of meaning, a different touch from the regions of existence, a different faith, a different soil.
>
> (pp. 61–62)

I do not wish to elevate myself above those who fled in the face of my mother's seemingly dreadful transformation, for it was no small challenge to behold her, and to be beheld by her, in her otherness. Indeed, I went on to confess,

> It took me some time to get there. Actually, I'm not sure what "getting there" could even mean. Beholding the other in her otherness without my own needs and wishes intruding? A worthy ideal. But I repeat: Easier said than done. The force of the ego is strong. And decay and death still remain, for many of us – actually all of us, I think, to a greater or lesser degree – alien, and frequently threatening, scary territory. Better to avoid it entirely, some would say. That's certainly what some people in my mother's life saw: no beauty there, only decay and death, only a faceless It.
>
> (Freeman, 2021b, p. 105).

My response to some of this: Their loss! They could have had their aesthetic – and ethical – horizons expanded but opted for remaining in the domain of the

Same: She is not that, not any longer; and so there is no more beauty. Am I deluding myself in wanting to expand these horizons? Actually, I'm not sure that's what I was aiming for. Indeed, following Weil, I wasn't "aiming," I wasn't wishing, for anything. Nor was I bemoaning what she no longer was. And with that, her beauty – or, more to the point, *beauty* – emerged.

Did I become a "better person" in the process? Well, yes, I think I did. But what can this possibly mean?

On Becoming "Better"

Entering this territory is, of course, risky. Who's to say what it means to become "better" anyway? I think there are some compelling ways of doing so – ways that lots (and lots) of people know but that continue to bedevil philosophers and the like. Was Jesus a better person than Hitler? Was Mother Theresa a better person than Donald Trump? (Yes to both.) Now, one can still argue about all this by trotting out all kinds of situations in which Adolf and Donald might actually be considered better (how kind they've been to their loyal followers!), but we wouldn't want to push this argument too far. In any case, rather than trying to defend the claim that there are better (and worse) people in some general way, let me turn my attention to the more modest claim that *I* became a better person – at least in some domains – during the course of my mother's dementia. And so I ask again: What can this possibly mean?

In Levinas's (1996) terms, I eventually became my mother's "hostage," captivated by her need and cry, by the nakedness and "destitution" of her face. As I explained in the aforementioned book (Freeman, 2021b),

> In the early years of my mother's dementia, I related to her more in terms of scripted and somewhat superficial obligations than authentic, ethical demands. I ought to go see her because that's what I'm supposed to do, I'd think. Or because I want to be a good son. Eventually, though, this would change; rather than continue to follow these banal scripts, I followed *her* – her lead, you could say.
>
> (p. 106)

Levinas (1999) speaks in this context of the "extreme urgency of the commandment . . . an urgency by which the imperative is 'dropping all other business'" (pp. 33–34). Another way of framing this urgency is to speak of "the priority of the Other" (Freeman, 2014). "Sure," I wrote,

> I can be hostage to my wife or my daughters or my friends or my new grandson, but with my mother, my being there for her had become a practice, a discipline. When I would go see her, she was the priority, through and through. Now that she's gone, some of that priority – and beauty – is gone too.

It's strange and somewhat tragic to think that we might require extreme circumstances, like dying mothers with dementia, to become the hostages about which Levinas speaks. But it may be so.

(p. 107)

One way I may, arguably, have become a better person, therefore, has to do with setting aside my own needs and preoccupations and being more responsive and responsible to her. Another way has to do with moving beyond "banal scripts" about how to be good and actually *being* good. Implicit in both modes of transformation is the centrality of *attention* – which, following Iris Murdoch (1970), embodies "the idea of a just and loving gaze directed upon an individual reality" (p. 33). The process can be unsettling: "Innumerable 'lookings' have discovered and explored a world which is now (for better or worse) compulsively present to the will in a particular situation, and the will is dismayed by the feeling that it ought now to be everything and in fact is not." Indeed, the result may be a kind of *angst* – in this case, a "felt discrepancy between personality and ideals" (pp. 37–38) – or, in Levinasian terms, a felt discrepancy between the urgency of the command and the impossibility of ever fully executing the desired response. I felt this acutely whenever it was time to leave my mother after a visit. If only I could be there, always and wholly. If only I could give her all the attention she warrants and needs. If only I could be perfect, truly and wholly *Good*. But I can't be; I can only be better than I was.

Returning to Murdoch (1970), who is herself drawing on Weil, "the ideal situation" we are considering

is to be represented as a kind of "necessity." This is something of which saints speak and which any artist will readily understand. The idea of a patient, loving regard, directed upon a person, a thing, a situation, presents the will not as unimpeded movement but as something very much more like "obedience."

(p. 40)

As Murdoch goes on to note – and here we can get a brief preview of the argument to come – "One of the great merits of the moral psychology I am proposing is that it does not contrast art and morals, but shows them to be two aspects of a single struggle" (pp. 39–40). What exactly is this struggle? It is nothing less than the capacity to behold reality in its fullest measure through the faculty of undivided attention. From this perspective, Murdoch continues,

Goodness and beauty are not to be contrasted, but are largely part of the same structure. . . . So that aesthetic situations are not so much analogies of morals as cases of morals. Virtue is *au fond* the same in the artist as in the good man in that it is a selfless attention to nature: something which is easy to name but very hard to achieve.

(p. 40)

Indeed.

To live the priority of the Other, I have suggested (Freeman, 2021b), requires a kind of self-emptying, a giving-oneself-over to the other person. Seen from one angle, the process entails a kind of diminishment: The responsive person "accepts to be diminished by concentrating on an expenditure of energy, which will not extend his own power but will only give existence to a being other than himself, who will exist independently of him." Self-emptying thus amounts to "the destruction of oneself. It is to deny oneself. In denying oneself, one becomes capable under God of establishing someone else by a creative affirmation. One gives oneself in ransom for the other" (Weil, 1951/1973, pp. 147–148). Seen from another angle, however, the process may be seen as entailing self-expansion, such that reality, now beheld in fuller measure, "gives back," as it were, a fuller, more responsive and responsible self (see Marion, 2002).

Let me continue with a few additional words from Weil. "The love of the order and beauty of the world is thus the complement of the love of our neighbor" (p. 158). Here is a nice statement of her position:

> We live in a world of unreality and dreams. To give up our imaginary position as the center, to renounce it, not only intellectually but in the imaginative part of our soul, that means to awaken to what is real and eternal, to see the true light and hear the true silence. A transformation then takes place at the very root of our sensibility, in our immediate reception of sense impressions and psychological impressions. It is a transformation analogous to that which takes place in the dusk of evening on a road, where we suddenly discern as a tree what we had at first seen as a stooping man; or where we suddenly recognize as a rustling of leaves what we thought at first was whispering voices. We see the same colors; we hear the same sounds, but not in the same way.
>
> (p. 159)

This is the kind of transformation that eventually took place when I saw my mother, and it is one way of thinking about the beautiful: "*the coming-into-being of the real*" (Freeman, 2021b, p. 109). Weil offers an important qualification in this context. "The beauty of the world," she writes, "is not an attribute of matter in itself" but is instead "a relationship of the world to our sensibility, the sensibility that depends upon the structure of our body and our soul" (p. 164). It also depends on our willingness to *welcome* reality – even if what is before us diverges, significantly, from our ordinary way of seeing things and the categories they reflect. Can we see without categories? Strictly speaking, probably not. But it may be possible to see beyond them – or, again, at least to see better – deeper, wider, more attentively – than we had before. It may not bring us pleasure or enjoyment. But it may bring us a feeling of truly *being there*, in relation. "That, at least, is how it would feel when I would go visit my mother and find her huddled and alone in her wheelchair, fragile, and in her own broken way, beautiful" (Freeman, 2021b, p. 110).

Beauty and Goodness

It is, of course, true that being her son played a role in my finding beauty in this way. I didn't, and couldn't, feel quite the same seeing others. Does this mean that, in the end, beauty *is* purely subjective, that it's just in the proverbial eye of the beholder? No; I think not. For one, it is quite clear that some phenomena – including, as we saw earlier, landscapes, sunsets, humans, and works of art – are deemed beautiful, and this is so even if they are not to everyone's taste. (The question of beauty and the question of taste, though not unrelated, are different.) For another, even though I have avowed that being my mother's son played a role in my beholding a dimension of beauty that had been unavailable beforehand (and that remained unavailable to others), I came to see (some) beauty in the others in her midst as well. They too emerged in fuller reality. Rather than being instances of this or that category – old, decrepit, dying – they became more of who they were. In Buber's (1970) terms, in place of an It, they became a Thou, beautiful in their way. One could still argue, of course, that I have taken the idea of beauty too far here, that I am imposing my own subjective view on some decidedly *un*-beautiful people, and that I am paving the way to a purely relativistic conception of the idea. But I don't think that's so. What I am doing, or at least trying to do, is decouple the idea from some of its more traditional meanings and thereby render it more capacious and inclusive. More beauty may be there in the world, waiting to be seen, than we tend to assume.

The question remains: *Can* the experience of beauty make us better people? Or maybe it's the other way around, such that by becoming better people – more attentive, more caring, more loving – we come to find more beauty in the world? Then again, we could, and probably should, follow Murdoch when she asserts that what we are ultimately considering are "two aspects of a single struggle." Perhaps by looking more closely at the nature of this struggle, we can gain some clarity on this vexing issue. As Murdoch (1970) notes, "Moral change and moral achievement are slow; we are not free in the sense of being able suddenly to alter ourselves since we cannot suddenly alter what we can see and ergo what we desire and are compelled by" (p. 38). Assuming for argument's sake that I did indeed become (modestly) better over the years, it wasn't because of some decision I made. "It wasn't about unfettered choice, and it wasn't about moral strength. Instead, it was about a kind of vulnerable welcome, in which, by degrees, I came to see and feel the beauty that was there" (Freeman, 2021b, p. 110). But how?

"How," Murdoch asks, "can we make ourselves morally better? *Can* we make ourselves morally better?" (p. 51) And again, if so, how? "(A)re there any techniques for the purification and reorientation of an energy which is naturally selfish, in such a way that when moments of choice arrive we shall be sure of acting rightly?" (p. 53). Sure? Doubtful. How about just better prepared? It is precisely at this juncture that Murdoch invokes beauty as a prime vehicle of what she calls *unselfing* (p. 82). By way of example:

> I am looking out of my window in an anxious and resentful state of mind, oblivious of my surroundings, brooding perhaps on some damage done to my

prestige. Then suddenly I observe a hovering kestrel. In a moment everything is altered. The brooding self with its hurt vanity has disappeared. There is nothing now but kestrel. And when I return to thinking of the other matter it seems less important.

(p. 82)

In a small way, Murdoch has become "better" through this very process. As she goes on to note, "It is so patently a good thing to take delight in flowers and animals that people who bring home potted plants and kestrels might even be surprised at the notion that these things have anything to do with virtue." They may be even more surprised that gazing at the face of an elderly woman with dementia also bears upon virtue. But it does. And so, she adds, does the work of art – or, to be more precise, the work of good or, better still, *great* art. This is because such art

> affords us a pure delight in the independent existence of what is excellent. Both in its genesis and its enjoyment it is a thing totally opposed to selfish obsession. It invigorates our best faculties and, to use Platonic language, inspires love in the highest part of the soul. It is able to do this partly by virtue of something which it shares with nature: a perfection of form which invites unpossessive contemplation and resists absorption into the selfish dream life of the consciousness.

(p. 83)

We could quibble with some of this; Murdoch gets a bit lofty in such passages, and some readers may find her a bit too comfortable talking about what great art is and does. And yet,

> Art gives a clear sense to many ideas which seem more puzzling when we meet with them elsewhere, and it is a clue to what happens elsewhere. An understanding of any art involves a recognition of hierarchy and authority. There are very evident degrees of merit, there are heights and distances; even Shakespeare is not perfect. Good art, unlike bad art, . . . is something pre-eminently outside us and resistant to our consciousness. We surrender ourselves to its *authority* with a love which is unpossessive and unselfish. . . . Art pierces the veil and gives sense to the notion of a reality which lies beyond appearance; it exhibits virtue in its true guise in the context of death and chance.

(pp. 85–86)

In a word, great art *arrests* us, and in so doing, opens up "aspects of our world which our dull dream-consciousness is unable to see" (p. 86).

Along the lines being drawn, Murdoch writes elsewhere (1999),

> (A)ny serious artist has a sense of distance between himself and something quite other in relation to which he feels humility since he knows that it is far more detailed and wonderful and awful and amazing than anything which he can ever

express. This "other" is most readily called "reality" or "nature" or "the world" and this is a way of talking one must not give up.

(p. 26)

This doesn't mean that art needs to be representational in the sense of depicting something other than itself; non-representational painting – certain modes of abstract expressionism, for instance – can be extraordinary in what they are able to disclose about the world. The same may be said of music, which is generally regarded as the least representational of the arts. Whether representational or non-representational, therefore, art can open up a world and allow it to be encountered in fuller, deeper measure.

My mother was neither a lovely hovering kestrel nor a great work of art. But her presence, her face, did come to perform much the same function: It arrested me; it stopped me in my self-ish, preoccupied tracks and thereby allowed me to become just a bit better, at least for a time: more in touch with reality, "a reality which lies beyond appearance" – or initial appearance; more responsive to her; more compassionate and loving. Don't get me wrong; I didn't become a saint! But when my mother was alive, I surrendered to the authority of her decaying beauty and did what I could to be there for her and with her. For the most part, I had no choice in the matter. Her face issued the command and I obeyed. And with that obedience, I grew into a better person for a while.

Earlier, I suggested that one way of speaking about the beautiful was as "the coming-into-being of the real." Taking this idea one step further, we can speak about the-coming-into-being of the real in a way that arrests us and, at the same time, *moves* us, such that we are led to a more welcoming, capacious way of being. This is not the beauty of fashion magazines. Nor, really, is it the beauty of the great work of art, the kind we might appreciate for its lovely colors or its wondrous harmony. It is the beauty of reality itself, which shows itself when our attention is called forth by what is *other*. The process takes time and practice. "To silence and expel self, to contemplate and delineate nature with a clear eye, is not easy and demands a moral discipline" (Murdoch, 1970, p. 63). In this context, practice doesn't, and can't, make perfect, just better.

What is it, then, that makes the appreciation of beauty and the process of becoming a better person of a piece? If beauty, as conceptualized here, entails encountering phenomena that arrest and move us – that indeed *unself* us – such that we are led to a more welcoming, capacious way of being, then becoming a better person is essentially built into the very process. Because some of those who came to see my mother couldn't find any beauty in her, they treated her like a thing, an It, an instance: whatever beautiful was, she was clearly not it. And only when her beauty could be seen could she emerge as a Thou – or, in different terms, the Other of Levinas rather than the other who has been othered.

Turning to Murdoch (1970) once more, she underscores the idea "that great art teaches us how real things can be looked and loved without being seized and used, without being appropriated into the greedy organism of the self" – and, in the case of persons, without being appropriated into this or that category and thereby nullified in their distinct, irreplaceable personhood. "This exercise of *detachment*" – which is to say, attentive beholding, drawn forth by the presence of what is *other* – "is difficult and valuable whether the thing contemplated is a human being or the root of a tree or the vibration of a colour or a sound." Beauty, in turn, "is that which attracts this particular sort of unselfish attention." And such unselfish attention, she asserts, is part and parcel of moral life. Indeed, she asserts, "true vision occasions right conduct. This could be uttered simply as an enlightening tautology; but I think it can in fact be supported by appeals experience." This is because "The more the separateness and differentness of other people is realized, and the fact seen that another man" – another person – "has needs and wishes as demanding as one's own, the harder it becomes to treat a person as a thing" (p. 64). Not impossible, mind you, just harder. *Beholding beauty and becoming better both entail the apprehension of, and fidelity to, the Other.*

But there is still more:

> If, still led by the clue of art, we ask further questions about the faculty which is supposed to relate us to what is real and thus bring us to what is good, the idea of compassion or love will be naturally suggested. It is not simply that suppression of self is required before accurate vision can be obtained. The great artist sees his objects (and this is true whether they are sad, absurd, repulsive or even evil) in a light of justice and mercy. The direction of attention is . . . outward, away from self . . . towards the great surprising variety of the world, and the ability so to direct attention is love.
>
> (pp. 64–65)

I don't know whether to fully follow Murdoch when she asserts that "true vision occasions right conduct." That seems a bit too . . . automatic. I also don't know whether to subscribe to her idea of "accurate vision." Is practicing fidelity to the Other a matter of "accuracy"? But the last thing I want to do here is diss Murdoch, for she has given us, or at least me, some extraordinarily valuable ways of answering the question this essay seeks to answer. In simple terms, again, the answer is a resounding *Yes*: The experience of beauty can indeed make us better people – especially, I want to emphasize, if we adopt the view of beauty proposed herein. But we are not just considering two "variables" in this context – the experience of beauty, on the one hand, and the process of becoming a better person on the other. No; what we are really considering, again, are two dimensions or moments of a single process, our being arrested by the beautiful being, at one and the same time the living embodiment of the priority of the Other.

Coda: Psychological Humanities and Ethics

I want to close this chapter with a somewhat audacious assertion: Beauty is, or ought to be, at the very heart of the psychological humanities; to the degree that it is, ethics will, as a matter of course and necessity, be right there with it. And in it. I am certainly not saying that everything that happens under the roof of the psychological humanities needs to be about beauty. That would be too imperious. But in keeping with what has been said thus far, a significant piece of the psychological humanities project ought to be oriented to both creating, and appreciating, things of beauty – that is, things that arrest and move us by virtue of bringing us closer to the real, in all of its variousness and multifariousness. For, in bringing us closer to the real – especially the realness of *persons* – we are also in the neighborhood of care and compassion. Neighborhood: the condition of being a neighbor rather than a faceless other.

For the most part, contemporary psychology has remained within the province of the faceless other. It aspires to be about everyone, but in so doing, cannot help but be about no one. And because it tends to be about no one, whatever ethical charge it might have had is immediately cancelled, rendered mute. Such psychology has its value; I wouldn't deny it. But it remains at an unbridgeable distance from the living, breathing, dying person and thus also at an unbridgeable distance from the ethical sphere. One can care for a group, a collective – the Palestinians, for instance, or the Israelis. But it is a distant and disembodied care, far afield from the flesh-and-blood person. So it is that "a single Anne Frank excites more emotion than the myriads who suffered as she did but whose image has remained in the shadows" (Levi, 1989, p. 56). Could psychology's privileging of the group over the person be a defensive maneuver, born out of its own discomfort with the radical alterity of the person and the feeling, and responsibility, that comes in tow? Of the terrible salience of Anne Frank, Levi continues, "Perhaps it is necessary that it can be so. If we had to and were able to suffer the sufferings of everyone, we could not live" (p. 56).

Levi is surely right about this. But psychology can do vastly better than it has in rising to the challenge of suffering the sufferings of others, and one significant way of doing so is through the path of beauty. Why create work that aspires toward a measure of beauty, as conceptualized herein, in the context of suffering? One very basic reason is that it will be more likely to evoke *feeling* – especially *compassionate* feeling for those in need – than the standard psychological fare tends to do. This suggests that a portion of the psychological humanities needs to be *artful* in what it does. Just as the beauty of a withered, toothless old woman with mottled skin may serve to arrest and move us through her sheer presence, so too with portrayals of the same insofar as they practice fidelity to the phenomenon at hand. Such portrayals can thus help alert us to what is most real and, in turn, deepen our attentiveness – and openness – to the dreadful beauty of human suffering.

Wendy Farley (1996) does well to supplement this perspective through her discussion of *eros*. "The beauty of beings," she writes, "is fragile and poignant. Eros is aroused by the exteriority and beauty of reality, but then chastened by its vulnerability. Compassion modifies eros, inculcating in it a necessarily ethical dimension" (p. 68). Eros, in turn, "reorients consciousness through a detachment from the ego and passion for the other, which in turn bring into view the beauty and, ultimately, the suffering of others. This awareness of the uniqueness, beauty, and suffering of others is the prerequisite for a turn from illusion to reality" (109). It is also the prerequisite for discerning *truth*. As Farley continues,

> The understanding of truth that emerges in these reflections is characterized by two opposite qualities. It is on the one hand a kind of realism: truth is a relation to realities that are not reducible to power, ideas, or transcendental structures of human consciousness. Truth has to do with actually existing beings whose existence is exterior to concepts, subjectivity, social constructions, or institutions of power. But the other side of this interpretation of truth attests to the hiddenness and vulnerability of reality. The predominance of illusion and domination in society suggest how thoroughly reality can be obscured and how radically it can be harmed.
>
> (p. 188)

Following both Murdoch and Weil, Farley goes on to highlight the centrality of attention and asserts that "Attentiveness to others in their distinctive reality and concrete needs enables one to understand them better, with greater complexity and profundity, and to become more adequately responsive" (p. 192), especially to their suffering.

The psychological humanities need not, of course, be restricted to the exploration of suffering. There is ample room for exploring other realities too. And yet, it may be that placing beauty at the heart of the psychological humanities bears within it an implicit commitment to placing suffering at its heart too. Yes; there are many ways of becoming better people. We can be kinder, nicer, more thoughtful and civil. We can become more attentive to reality and become better servants of truth. And we can be more welcoming of others in their separateness and differentness, as Murdoch had put it. All good. But beyond the sphere of these worthy virtues is the challenge of being responsive and responsible to those who call out, or cry out, in need. Following Levi, it will be imperative to recognize our limits in doing so, for the challenge is vast, infinite. An important feature of the psychological humanities is nevertheless to move in this direction. Doing so may serve to make the discipline of psychology a more beautiful and virtuous endeavor than it currently is.

References

Buber, M. (1965). *Between man and man.* New York: Macmillan.
Buber, M. (1970). *I and thou.* New York: Charles Scribner's Sons.
Farley, W. (1996). *Eros for the other.* University Park, PA: The Pennsylvania State University Press.
Freeman, M. (2014). *The priority of the other: Thinking living beyond the self.* New York: Oxford University Press.
Freeman, M. (2018). The sociocultural constitution of aesthetic transcendence. In J. Valsiner, & A. Rosa (Eds.), *The Cambridge handbook of sociocultural psychology* (pp. 351–365). New York: Cambridge University Press.

Freeman, M. (2021a). How does the world become ecstatic? Notes on the hermeneutics of transcendence. In R. Bishop (Ed.), *Hermeneutic dialogue and shaping the landscape of theoretical and philosophical psychology* (pp. 112–123). Routledge.

Freeman, M. (2021b). *Do I look at you with love? Reimagining the story of dementia*. Leiden, The Netherlands: Brill | Sense.

Köhler, W. (1929/1970). *Gestalt psychology*. New York: W.W. Norton.

Levi, P. (1989). *The drowned and the saved*. New York: Vintage.

Levinas, E. (1996). Substitution. In A. Peperzak, S. Critchley, & R. Bernasconi (Eds.), *Emmanuel Levinas: Basic philosophical writings* (pp. 80–95). Indianapolis, IN: Indiana University Press.

Levinas, E. (1999). *Alterity and transcendence*. New York: Columbia University Press.

Marion, J.-L. (2002). *Being given: Toward a phenomenology of givenness*. Stanford, CA: Stanford University Press.

Murdoch, I. (1970). *The sovereignty of good*. London: Routledge.

Murdoch, I. (1999). *Existentialists and mystics: Writings on philosophy and literature*. New York: Penguin.

Sartwell, C. (2022). Beauty. In E. N. Zalta, & U. Nodelman (Eds.), *The Stanford encyclopedia of philosophy* (Fall 2024 ed.). https://plato.stanford.edu/archives/fall2024/entries/beauty/

Weil, S. (1951/1973). *Waiting for God*. New York: Perennial Library.

Weil, S. (1952/1997). *Gravity and grace*. London: Routledge.

Chapter 2

'Aesthetic Articulations'
Toward a Poetics of Formation

A. Taiga Guterres

Dreams contain revelations of a repressed truth which can only appear under the mask of non-sense. It is in the non-sense [that] psychoanalysis looks for truth. And the gospel: wisdom in foolishness . . .
~Rubem Alves (2002, p. 14)

In short, art, in its form, unites the very same relation of doing and undergoing, outgoing and incoming energy, that makes an experience to be an experience.
~John Dewey (1932/1980, p. 48)

Preface

In the complexities of human experience, there exists a tension between what can be articulated and what resists articulation, between the clear and the opaque, the expressed and the ineffable.[1] This tension is not merely a limitation but an invitation – an opening to explore how meaning is created, shared, and transformed. The process of articulating our experiences, values, and aspirations is deeply formative, shaping not only our understanding of the world but also our sense of self and our capacity to engage with others. Yet not all phenomena yield easily to denotational clarity or explicit representation.[2] Many seek alternative modes of expression that embrace ambiguity, depth, and resonance.

Amid growing critiques of scientism and the dominance of purely empirical frameworks in psychology, scholars have sought to reclaim and expand the discipline's engagement with the human condition. Scholars such as Mark Freeman[3] and Thomas Teo[4] have called for a revival of the *psychological humanities* – a mode of psychological inquiry that foregrounds the existential, moral, and relational dimensions of human life. These scholars remind us that psychology, at its best, is not merely a science of behavior but a discipline deeply engaged with the complexities of being, challenging the assumption that measurable outcomes or explicit formulations are sufficient for understanding subjectivity, morality, and meaning. Instead, the psychological humanities emphasize the value of imaginative, critical, and narrative approaches to examining human experience. They remind us that not all aspects

DOI: 10.4324/9781003598107-4

of life can be quantified or neatly categorized and that the arts and humanities offer profound insights into the dynamics of subjectivity and the formation of self.

Building on this ethos, this essay examines what I will call aesthetic articulation as a critical and transformative practice. *Aesthetic articulations* – the creation of expressive forms that evoke, hold, or critique – extend the reach of psychological and moral inquiry into domains that resist denotational precision. By offering a space for resonance and ambiguity, these articulations illuminate how meaning is shaped in ways that transcend purely cognitive or denotational frameworks.

In a cultural landscape that often prioritizes clarity, efficiency, and empirical precision, the aesthetic invites us to dwell in complexity, ambiguity, and relationality. By offering an imaginal space for resonance, critique, and holding, aesthetic articulations engage the moral imaginary, fostering new ways of understanding ourselves, our values, and our place in the world. This inquiry into aesthetic articulation is not simply an academic exercise; it is an exploration of how meaning itself is made and remade, how we come to navigate the inarticulate dimensions of our lives and connect to the shared and contested moral frameworks of our time.

Through this lens, the *poetics of formation*[5] is not a retreat from critique or reality but a dynamic engagement with the tensions that define the human condition. It invites us to consider how the arts, language, and other expressive forms not only reflect our moral imagination but actively shape it, enabling us to confront the complexities of our lives with attentiveness, creativity, and care. By situating aesthetic articulation within this broader framework, this essay seeks to explore its transformative potential, offering a path to deeper understanding and more expansive modes of relating to the self, others, and the world.

Psychological Paradigms and the Limits of Denotational Clarity

Psychological research has long emphasized explicit communication and observable behavior as central to understanding the self and fostering relationships. Rooted in traditions of empiricism and behavioral science, this perspective aligns with the goals of clarity, reproducibility, and empirical verification. In some forms of therapeutic modalities, for example, denotational clarity is often seen as a gateway to self-awareness and healing. Patients are encouraged to 'name' their experiences, emotions, and thoughts as a way of gaining control over them and making them legible to themselves and others. Similarly, in psychometric research, standardized instruments rely heavily on explicit denotational responses – measuring specific behaviors, thoughts, or emotions as indicators of psychological states. This explicit and denotational focus has provided psychology with robust tools for diagnosis, intervention, and analysis.

While the emphasis on explicitness and denotational clarity has proven valuable, it has also relegated the tacit and ineffable dimensions of human experience to the margins of contemporary psychological practice. However, these dimensions have not been entirely absent from the field. Psychoanalytic and psychodynamic traditions, in particular, have long grappled with the unarticulated, the unconscious, and the tacit. Sigmund

Freud's (1919/1953) concept of the uncanny (*Das Unheimliche*) illustrates this focus, exploring the unsettling feelings that arise when something familiar becomes strange or reveals hidden depths. The uncanny, Freud argued, points to the repressed or unacknowledged aspects of the psyche, surfacing in ways that evade explicit articulation yet profoundly shape one's emotional and cognitive landscape. Similarly, Donald Winnicott's (1971) concept of the transitional space highlights the interplay between the tacit and the explicit in human development, emphasizing the creative and symbolic processes that mediate between internal states and external realities.

Anthropological frameworks provide further insight into the cultural dimensions of this issue. Psychiatrist and anthropologist Robert Levy's (1973) concepts of hypercognition and hypocognition reveal how cultural norms shape what is articulable and what remains tacit. Hypercognitive phenomena, as described earlier, are those for which a culture has a surplus of categories and terms, providing individuals with a rich vocabulary to describe and share their experiences. For instance, contemporary Western societies often hypercognize emotions like anxiety or burnout, offering extensive medical, psychological, and social vocabularies that facilitate recognition and articulation. These frameworks enable individuals to map their internal states onto shared cultural categories, creating opportunities for connection, discourse, and understanding.[6]

Conversely, hypocognition refers to the absence or scarcity of cultural categories for certain experiences, leaving them difficult to articulate or even recognize. Levy's ethnographic research in Tahiti exemplifies this dynamic – he observed that the Tahitians lacked a specific word for sadness. This absence of linguistic representation, Levy argued, reduced the "conscious accessibility" of sadness among the Tahitians, altering how the emotion was experienced and expressed (Levy, 1973, p. 324). In such cases, the lack of cultural scaffolding, or culturally available categories for experiences, can obscure certain phenomena, rendering them less visible in social and psychological contexts.

Expanding on Levy's ideas, Enfield and Zuckerman (2024) suggest that hypocognition does not necessarily denote the absence of an experience but rather its lack of cultural excavation and refinement. For example, in Tahiti, the absence of a term for sadness might not imply that the emotion is entirely absent but rather that it remains unshaped and unshared in public discourse. This dynamic highlights how cultural frameworks influence not only what we articulate but also how we engage with the tacit dimensions of our lives.

These insights align with anthropologist Webb Keane's (2003) work on semiotics, which critiques the psychological reliance on explicitness. Keane argues that communication is deeply embedded in cultural systems that shape meaning and perception. Signs and symbols mediate not only what we express but also how we understand ourselves and our world.[7] This perspective challenges the assumption that explicit articulation, through denotational clarity, is the sole or primary mode of understanding and suggests that the tacit and ineffable are vital to human experience.

The interplay between hypercognition and hypocognition reveals the limitations of a psychological paradigm that privileges denotational clarity. Even in hypercognitive cultural spaces, where rich vocabularies allow for detailed articulation, certain phenomena resist expression. For instance, emotions like alienation or transcendence may evade full articulation, even when extensive frameworks exist to describe them. These gaps underscore the importance of alternative modes of engagement – those that embrace ambiguity and seek meaning through relational, aesthetic, or symbolic practices.

While the prioritization of explicit articulation has yielded valuable insights, it has also narrowed the scope of what is considered legible and meaningful in human experience. This focus on clarity and denotation overlooks the tacit dimensions that shape identity, relationships, and one's imagination. By considering cultural frameworks like hypercognition and hypocognition alongside the semiotic affordances described by Keane and others, we gain a richer understanding of how human experience is mediated. These frameworks remind us that what remains unspoken is not merely a void but a fertile ground for deeper engagement, inviting us to expand our tools for understanding and articulating the ineffable.

Potency of Articulation

Articulation, as Charles Taylor (1989) suggests, is far more than a mechanism for achieving clarity or denotational precision; it is a transformative process of reaching toward and engaging with phenomena that shape our sense of self and moral imagination. In articulating experiences – whether to shape, express, or "make sense" of them – individuals actively shape their understanding of phenomena, cultivating a deeper relationship between their inner worlds and the external realities they inhabit.

Central to Taylor's framework is the concept of "strong evaluations," which refers to the qualitative distinctions individuals make about their values, experiences, and the good. Strong evaluations are not merely expressions of preference or utility but involve a higher-order reflection on what matters deeply – what constitutes a meaningful, good, or worthwhile life. These evaluations emerge through the process of articulation, as individuals grapple with their experiences and locate them within broader moral and existential frameworks. For Taylor, the ability to articulate such distinctions is not just a cognitive exercise but a deeply formative one, shaping one's moral imagination and sense of self.

This formative process unfolds as individuals engage with phenomena in ways that extend beyond the immediate or explicit. For example, encountering beauty, suffering, or love often evokes a need to articulate their significance, not merely to others but to oneself. In doing so, individuals are compelled to reflect on their values, their relationship to the world, and their aspirations. This act of articulation provides a sense of movement – both inward, toward greater self-awareness, and outward, toward a richer engagement with the world. It is through this movement that the self is not only understood but also formed, as articulation provides the scaffolding for personal and moral development.

Strong evaluations also enable individuals to create qualitative distinctions between different phenomena, allowing them to discern and prioritize what is significant. For instance, a person might reflect on their experience of joy or despair, not merely as fleeting emotions but as expressions of deeper truths about their life or relationships. Articulation helps translate these raw experiences into meaning, translating the ineffable into something that can be communicated, at least partly. In this way, strong evaluations are not static judgments but ongoing processes that allow for the refinement and transformation of one's understanding.

Moreover, this formative process underscores the relational potency of articulation, which has the capacity to cultivate either belonging or polarity. Articulating one's experiences often requires situating them within a shared cultural or moral framework, inviting dialogue and engagement with others' perspectives. In its most constructive form, this process fosters a sense of connection and shared humanity, enabling individuals to feel part of a collective while still affirming their unique perspectives. It is through this shared dialogue that articulation becomes a bridge, not only linking the individual to the collective but also creating spaces for mutual understanding and co-creation of meaning.

Yet articulation also holds the potential to delineate boundaries, amplifying distinctions that may lead to polarity or division. By naming and articulating differences in values, beliefs, or experiences, individuals and groups may emphasize separateness rather than connection. This dynamic reveals the dual nature of articulation: While it can be a tool for fostering inclusion and solidarity, it can also reinforce exclusion and discord. The relational power of articulation, therefore, lies in its capacity to navigate this tension, either drawing individuals closer together through shared meaning or accentuating divisions that challenge communal bonds. This dual potential highlights the critical responsibility involved in how articulation is wielded – whether to foster belonging or to navigate and reconcile polarities.

By fostering strong evaluations and qualitative distinctions, articulation provides a pathway for individuals to make sense of phenomena in ways that are deeply formative. It enables them to navigate the complexities of their inner and outer worlds, cultivating a sense of self that is attuned to the moral and existential dimensions of life. In this sense, articulation is not merely about describing reality but about shaping and reshaping it, offering a dynamic process through which meaning is continually created and re-created.

Aesthetic Articulations: Creating Resonance

While articulation fosters strong evaluations and provides a framework for engaging with moral and existential dimensions of life, certain phenomena elude the clarity and structure of denotational articulation. These moments call for what can be termed *aesthetic articulations* – expressive forms that transcend explicit meaning, prioritizing resonance and emotional depth over denotational precision. Through aesthetic articulations, individuals encounter and engage with experiences that resist categorization, embracing the opacity and complexity inherent in human existence.

Aesthetic articulations, as Mark Freeman's discussion of *poiesis* reminds us, are not limited to reflection or explication but involve an active and imaginative process of creation. Drawing on Paul Ricoeur, Freeman conceptualizes *poiesis* as a dual engagement: the constructive act of shaping meaning and the revelatory act of discerning what is present in the world (Freeman, 2017). Aesthetic articulations embody this dynamic interplay, as they construct forms – poetry, art, music, or gestures – that engage deeply with the structures of reality while also re-presenting dimensions of experience that often remain obscured (Figure 2.1). This process is not only an act of expression but also one of discovery, enabling individuals to encounter the ineffable through imaginative forms that resonate with their inner and outer worlds. Unlike denotational articulation, which seeks to map experiences to established categories or concepts, aesthetic articulations prioritize the resonance of lived experience. Denotational clarity, while offering utility and precision, carries the inherent risk of reducing experiences or phenomena to restricted meanings that fail to encompass their full dimensionality. When phenomena are distilled into explicit definitions or measurable frameworks, the richness of the experience – its ambiguities, nuances, and complexities – may be obscured or lost.

Yet the solution to this reduction is not found in obscuring meaning altogether but in cultivating resonance through aesthetic articulation. In this resonance lies

Figure 2.1 Clara Lieu, 2010, *Falling: No. 3*, lithographic rubbing ink. © Clara Lieu. Used with permission.[8]

the potential to hold and engage with the density of human experiences. Aesthetic articulations – through their embrace of opacity and polyphony – create spaces where multiple meanings can coexist, where the ineffable dimensions of experience are not confined but expanded. This openness invites a deepened engagement, enabling individuals to navigate the tacit and unarticulated aspects of life without the constraints of oversimplification.

Resonance, in this context, represents a relational and dynamic engagement with phenomena that transcends denotational understanding. It allows for an interplay between the self and the external world that neither demands explicit clarity nor confines itself to denotational boundaries. Charles Taylor discusses resonance as the felt sense of attunement between an individual and broader frameworks of meaning, a dynamic interplay where the articulation of experiences invites us into deeper understanding and engagement with our moral imagination (Taylor, 2007). This dynamic is not merely cognitive but profoundly embodied, as the signs we use – words, gestures, images – carry the capacity to resonate beyond their immediate denotation, creating spaces for aesthetic holding and relational depth.[9]

Moreover, the *poietic* nature of aesthetic articulations underscores their creative and relational dimensions. As Freeman argues, the act of making – whether through words, images, or gestures – is deeply tied to the act of meaning-making. Aesthetic articulations do not merely represent experiences; they actively shape them, offering individuals and communities a means of engaging with complexity and ambiguity. This creative process enables individuals to grapple with unarticulated or ineffable dimensions of life, offering a way to hold and transform their understanding of the world.

The relational dimension of aesthetic articulations further enhances their resonance. Operating within shared cultural or symbolic frameworks, these forms invite both personal reflection and communal dialogue. They offer a means of expressing experiences that resonate or challenge one's understanding of the broader human condition, fostering connection and deepening relational bonds. By situating individual expressions within collective narratives, aesthetic articulations create a poetics of formation that is as much about shared humanity as it is about personal growth.

In their opacity, aesthetic articulations resist reductive clarity, allowing individuals to engage outside of the bounds of denotational precision. This dual function of creation and revelation, as embodied in *poiesis*, highlights their transformative potential – not only as tools for personal understanding but also as vehicles for communal meaning-making and moral imagination.

Resonance as Aesthetic Holding

The formative potency of aesthetic articulations lies in their ability to hold the ineffable dimensions of human experience, offering a space for encountering and dwelling within phenomena that resist denotational clarity. This dynamic, which I will call *aesthetic holding*, creates an imaginal space where individuals can grapple with the density of their feelings, thoughts, and sensations, even when these cannot be fully articulated.

Lisa Stevenson captures this dynamic in her observation that people "do not always want the truth in the form of facts or information; we often want it in the form of an image. What we want, perhaps, is the opacity of an image that can match the density of our feelings. We want something to hold us" (Stevenson, 2014, p. 13). The opacity of such images – whether visual, metaphorical, or symbolic – provides a resonance that facts or denotational clarity cannot achieve. Rather than simplifying or reducing experience, these images create a space for engaging with complexity, allowing the unarticulated or tacit dimensions of life to surface and be encountered.

This capacity for resonance is not limited to the visual arts. It extends across diverse mediums of expression, including music, poetry, and narrative. These forms, through their ability to evoke rather than explain, function as vessels for emotional and existential densities. They provide a holding space where individuals can engage with their experiences in ways that honor their depth and nuance, fostering a sense of connection to the self, others, and the world.

Aesthetic Articulations in Practice: The Case of Ilyas

The concept of aesthetic holding finds vivid illustration in the work of Stefania Pandolfo, who examines the paintings of Ilyas, a Moroccan man living on the outskirts of Rabat. Ilyas experiences psychotic episodes, referred to as *mard nafsanī*, during which he enters an altered state of consciousness (*hala*) and transforms the walls of his empty apartment into vivid murals. These murals, which are later whitewashed by Ilyas himself, serve as both a personal expression and a liminal space for engaging with his psychological and emotional struggles.

Pandolfo (2018) describes these murals as "ontological intervals," spaces that blur the boundaries between visible and invisible realms, reason and unreason. Drawing on the works of Binswanger, Warburg, and Lacan, she situates Ilyas's art within a broader framework that can be seen as a form of aesthetic articulation, where the images he creates function as both a dialogue with his symptoms and a means of holding his inner turmoil. Motifs such as snake-monsters and trees of life, which draw on Christian and Islamic traditions, embody the complexity of Ilyas's experiences, intertwining cultural, personal, and existential dimensions. These images do not resolve Ilyas's experiences into denotational clarity but, instead, provide a space where their density can be encountered and held.

Through these murals, Ilyas navigates the liminality of his condition, engaging with the ineffable dimensions of his psychosis in ways that allow for both expression and transformation. The act of painting becomes a form of *poiesis*, where the creative process enables Ilyas to shape and make sense of his experiences, even as they resist full articulation. In this way, his art serves as a profound example of the potential of aesthetic articulations to hold, critique, and transform human experience.

Aesthetic Articulation as Critical Engagement

In addition to their formative and relational capacities, aesthetic articulations carry a critical edge that resists the constraints of established realities and denotational limits. Drawing on Herbert Marcuse's insights in *The Aesthetic Dimension* (1978), Freeman emphasizes that the liberating power of aesthetic forms lies in their ability to sublimate and re-present reality while simultaneously critiquing it (Freeman, 2024). As Marcuse argues, "The truth of art lies in its power to break the monopoly of established reality . . . to *define* what is *real*" (Marcuse, 1978, p. 9). This dynamic allows aesthetic articulations not only to stylize and reorder experiences in alignment with their form but also to expose and challenge dominant frameworks of understanding.

Central to this critical potential is the notion that aesthetic holding – the space created by a resonant opacity of experience – is not inherently comforting or affirming. While aesthetic holding may offer a sense of containment or resonance, it can also confront individuals with unsettling truths, provoking reflection and critique in ways that challenge their existing frameworks of understanding. Such articulations can command attention in ways that are not always welcome, surfacing tensions, ambiguities, or conflicts that disrupt comfort or certainty.

For example, the vivid murals of Ilyas, as analyzed by Stefania Pandolfo (2018), not only hold his personal struggles but also evoke broader cultural and existential tensions. His art, which incorporates motifs from Christian and Islamic traditions, engages with themes of reason and unreason, visible and invisible, self and other. These murals are not merely spaces of comfort or resolution; they provoke reflection on the boundaries of understanding, inviting both personal and communal critique of the frameworks through which his experiences are perceived.

Similarly, Paul Virilio's concept of the "phatic image" – a targeted image that demands attention – underscores the critical power of aesthetic articulations to disrupt complacency (Virilio, 1994). Such images, like the "face of the Other" described by Emmanuel Levinas, force confrontation with the ineffable, commanding a response that may involve discomfort or unease.[10] This dimension of aesthetic articulation reveals its capacity to challenge dominant modes of understanding, making visible what has been overlooked or repressed.

Through these acts of critique and confrontation, aesthetic articulations might invite individuals and communities to grapple with the unarticulated and tacit dimensions of life. They resist the reductive clarity of denotational articulation, offering instead a space for engaging with complexity, ambiguity, and the tensions that shape the human condition. In this way, they serve as bridges not only to resonance and holding but also to transformation and reimagination. By disrupting the taken-for-granted boundaries of reality, aesthetic articulations foster new possibilities for self-formation, moral imagination, and collective understanding.

Conclusion

At the heart of human experience lies a tension between the articulable and the ineffable, the seen and the unseen, the said and the unsaid, and perhaps unsayable. Yet within the ineffable lies a profound invitation – not to resolve or conquer but to engage, to be moved, and to respond. The signs we create, whether through words, art, or gestures, are not just expressions of understanding but acts of reaching toward the unknown or un(der)shaped experiences. They hold space for the opaque, the elusive, and the deeply personal dimensions of life that defy denotation yet resonate with our shared humanity. Aesthetic articulations remind us that understanding is not always about clarity or resolution but about creating spaces where the complexity of human experience can be held, encountered, and reimagined. Through their resonance, they offer pathways for self-formation, moral imagination, and critical engagement, allowing us to navigate the unarticulated and tacit dimensions of life with creativity.

These acts of *poiesis* do more than merely reflect or affirm; they challenge us to confront the boundaries of what we consider real, inviting us to reconfigure the contours of our understanding. Whether through the vivid murals of Ilyas or the evocative metaphors that hold our emotional densities, aesthetic articulations serve as bridges between the visible and the invisible, the individual and the collective. They resist denotational reduction and invite dialogue, creating opportunities for shared meaning and transformative growth.

The poetics of formation lie in this process of creation and engagement. Aesthetic articulations are not merely reflective; they are formative practices. They are potentiated to guide us in cultivating attentiveness to what resists articulation, fostering a relational engagement with the self, the other, and the broader world. Through these acts, we may find ourselves shaped – not by rigid categories or definitive answers but by the layered and nuanced interplay of resonance, ambiguity, and discovery.

Such engagements do not promise resolution or mastery; they invite us to inhabit the space of becoming, where meaning is shaped and reshaped through our encounters with the world. They remind us that understanding is not an endpoint but a continual and formative process – one that calls for attentiveness, humility, and the courage to explore beyond the limits of what we can easily grasp. It is in this space, perhaps, that we find not answers but the quiet, enduring possibility of transformation. In the poetics of formation, we are held not by certainty but by the expansiveness of imagination and the resonance of the ineffable.

As we continue to grapple with the tensions between clarity and opacity, articulation and silence, the denotational and the aesthetic, the question remains: How might we cultivate practices that honor the richness of human experience in its full complexity? This essay offers no definitive answers but suggests that the journey of articulation – whether through words, art, or other expressive forms – holds some promise of dwelling more deeply within our shared humanity. In this dwelling, we find not resolution but the enduring possibility of becoming.

Notes

1. Philosopher Diana Raffman outlines three forms of ineffability: structural ineffability, where unconscious structural representations influence conscious experience without being accessible for verbalization; feeling ineffability, which pertains to the sensory-perceptual nature of certain phenomena that cannot be fully communicated through language; and nuance ineffability, where features of experience are processed at such an early cognitive level that they remain untypeable or resistant to linguistic representation. These distinctions offer a nuanced lens for understanding why some experiences resist articulation, even in hypercognitive cultural environments, and highlight the interplay between tacit and explicit forms of engagement. See *Language, Music, and Mind* (Raffman, 1993) for further discussion.
2. By 'denotational,' I refer to the prioritization of explicit, referential meaning in communication – where language is expected to clearly map onto objects, states, or concepts in a manner that is readily verifiable and universally understandable. Denotational responses are those that focus on the propositional content of language, emphasizing clarity, precision, and direct correspondence between words and the phenomena they describe. In psychology, this denotational focus manifests in practices like psychometric testing, where responses are standardized and quantified, or therapeutic modalities that encourage clients to "name" their emotions and experiences as a step toward self-awareness and healing. While this approach has enabled significant advances in understanding and intervention, it often marginalizes the tacit, relational, and ineffable dimensions of human experience that are less amenable to direct articulation. Scholars such as Keane (2003) argue that communication extends beyond denotational clarity, encompassing broader semiotic and cultural processes that mediate how meaning is constructed and experienced.
3. Freeman's compelling vision for the psychological humanities represents a bold reimagining of psychology's scope and purpose. In his recent work, Freeman articulates a vision for psychology that not only complements scientific inquiry but also transcends its limitations by embracing the richness of the arts and humanities. While acknowledging the value of the scientific perspective in advancing the discipline, Freeman emphasizes that significant dimensions of human experience – particularly those marked by complexity, ambiguity, and aesthetic resonance – escape the reach of traditional empirical methods (Freeman, 2024).
4. Teo highlights the risk of neglecting psychology's foundational questions about the human condition, as the discipline has historically pursued scientific legitimacy at the expense of engaging with deeper existential and cultural concerns. Reclaiming subjectivity as a central focus, Teo advocates for a psychological humanities approach that integrates insights from diverse disciplines (Teo, 2017).
5. I borrow the terminology of 'poetics of formation' from Mark Freeman, who introduced the idea in a colloquium at Boston College on September 19, 2024. In it, he alluded to the formative potential of practices of *poiesis*. See his work on *Rewriting the Self: History, Memory, Narrative* (1993) and "Reaching Toward the Poetic" in *Toward the Psychological Humanities: A Modest Manifesto for the Future of Psychology* (2024).
6. In recent U.S. culture and literature, "trauma" has become a particularly salient example of hypercognition. The increased cultural availability and visibility of the term have made it easier to map a wide range of personal and collective experiences onto the category of trauma. This dynamic fosters greater attention to the nuances of traumatic experiences, encouraging further discrimination of phenomena to determine their alignment with the concept. For example, the widespread adoption of trauma-informed practices in education, therapy, and social work reflects both the accessibility of the term and its integration into cultural frameworks for understanding adversity and recovery. As trauma becomes more hypercognized, this heightened awareness invites new interpretations

and refinements of the term, broadening its application while simultaneously deepening its conceptual complexity. Importantly, this observation is not to suggest that such increased usage inherently dilutes or deepens the concept itself; rather, it highlights how the hypercognition of trauma shapes the processes through which experiences are interpreted, communicated, and integrated into cultural and personal narratives. Scholars such as Fassin and Rechtman (2009) have examined how the rise of trauma as a cultural keyword reshapes narratives of suffering, resilience, and identity, offering insights into both the affordances and limitations of this hypercognitive dynamic.

7 Enfield and Zuckerman (2024) explore how linguistic practices function as public semiotic moorings, tethering them to three semiotic processes of meaning-making: actions, statuses, and experiences. They argue that expressed signs operate on multiple levels, engaging a form of a community calibration of experience that guides people in co-constructing shared representations. They provide a helpful and succinct articulation of the development of the concept of signs, "A word is often thought of as a sign (or signifier; e.g., the sound of the word 'tree') paired with an object (or signified; the concept of a tree; de Saussure, 1916). But as intuitive as this seems, 'the pervasive twentieth century understanding of meaning – a sign stands for an object – is incorrect" (Kockelman, 2005, p. 233). Instead, meaning is grounded in a three-part semiotic process discovered by Peirce and elaborated since." (Enfield & Zuckerman, 2024, p. 556).

8 Clara Lieu, a visual artist and educator, describes her series, "Falling," as an engagement with her experience with depression. Lithographic rubbing ink, as she describes, is a dark, greasy medium that is akin to black tar. In a post about this series, she writes, "There is no erasing with lithographic rubbing ink, every mark is permanent" (Lieu, 2016).

9 Lacan's concept of the Real complements this understanding, emphasizing the dimensions of human experience that resist symbolization and remain ineffable within the frameworks of the Symbolic order (Lacan, 1978). Resonance, in a Lacanian sense, arises as we engage with these ineffable dimensions – not to master or control them but to allow their presence to shape our understanding. The Real is not fully assimilable within language, but its effects ripple through symbolic expressions, producing a resonance that speaks to the gaps and silences within our articulations (Lacan, 1977). In this way, aesthetic articulations provide a bridge, engaging with the unspeakable dimensions of human experience to invite formation rather than closure.

10 For Levinas, the face arrests us, compelling attention and ethical responsibility by its mere presence. As he notes, "The face is present in its refusal to be contained. In this sense it cannot be comprehended, that is, encompassed. It is neither seen nor touched – for in visual or tactile sensation the identity of the I envelops the alterity of the object, which becomes precisely a content" (Levinas, 1969, p. 194); see also Goodman (2012). Similarly, the phatic image demands engagement, but its scope extends beyond the human face to include paintings, objects, music, and other forms of aesthetic expression. These images, like the face, hold us in their grasp, inviting a relational and ethical encounter. While Levinas emphasizes the human and ethical dimensions of the face of the other, the phatic image broadens this arresting power to encompass the material and symbolic world, functioning as a semiotic and affective anchor that engages our moral imagination. By expanding Levinas's insight into the transformative potential of encounters, the phatic image highlights the multiplicity of ways we are called into relational and ethical engagement with the world. For more on phaticity, see Zuckerman (2020).

Bibliography

Alves, R. A. (2002). *The poet, the warrior, the prophet*. SCM Press.
de Saussure, F. (1916). *Cours de linguistique génerale*. Payot.

Dewey, J. (1932/1980). *Art as experience*. Perigee.
Enfield, N. J., & Zuckerman, C. H. P. (2024). Moorings: Linguistic practices and the tethering of action, status, and experience. *Current Anthropology*, 65(3), 554–576. https://doi.org/10.1086/730187
Fassin, D., & Rechtman, R. (2009). *The empire of trauma: An inquiry into the condition of victimhood* (R. Gomme, Trans.). Princeton University Press.
Freeman, M. (1993). *Rewriting the self: History, memory, narrative*. Routledge.
Freeman, M. (2017). Living in verse: Sites of the poetic imagination. In O. V. Lehmann, N. Chaudhary, A. C. Bastos, & E. Abbey (Eds.), *Poetry and imagined worlds* (pp. 139–154). Springer International Publishing. http://link.springer.com/10.1007/978-3-319-64858-3
Freeman, M. (2024). *Toward the psychological humanities: A modest manifesto for the future of psychology* (1st ed.). Routledge. https://doi.org/10.4324/9780429323652
Freud, S. (1919/1953). The uncanny. In J. Strachey (Trans.), *The standard edition of the complete psychological works of Sigmund Freud* (Vol. 17, pp. 219–252). The Hogarth Press. https://archive.org/details/freud-uncanny_001/
Goodman, D. M. (2012). *The demanded self: Levinasian ethics and identity in psychology*. Duquesne University Press.
Keane, W. (2003). Semiotics and the social analysis of material things. *Language & Communication*, 23(3–4), 409–425. https://doi.org/10.1016/S0271-5309(03)00010-7
Kockelman, P. (2005). The semiotic stance. *Semiotica*, 2005(157), 233–304. https://doi.org/10.1515/semi.2005.2005.157.1-4.233
Lacan, J. (1977). *Écrits: A selection* (A. Sheridan, Trans.). W. W. Norton & Company.
Lacan, J. (1978). *The four fundamental concepts of psychoanalysis* (J.-A. Miller, Ed., and A. Sheridan, Trans.). W. W. Norton & Company. https://archive.org/details/fourfundamentalc00laca/
Levinas, E. (1969). *Totality and infinity: An essay on exteriority*. Duquesne University Press.
Levy, R. (1973). *Tahitians: Mind and experience in the Society Islands*. University of Chicago Press.
Lieu, C. [claralieu]. (2016, September 28). *A figure sketch from 'Falling.'* Instagram. https://www.instagram.com/p/BK7NxKbB9sg/
Marcuse, H. (1978). *The aesthetic dimension: Toward a critique of Marxist aesthetics* (H. Marcuse, & E. Sherover, Trans.). Beacon Press.
Pandolfo, S. (2018). *Knot of the soul: Madness, psychoanalysis, Islam*. University of Chicago Press.
Raffman, D. (1993). *Language, music, and mind*. The MIT Press. https://doi.org/10.7551/mitpress/4120.001.0001
Stevenson, L. (2014). *Life beside itself: Imagining care in the Canadian Arctic*. University of California Press.
Taylor, C. (1989). *Sources of the self: The making of the modern identity*. Harvard University Press.
Taylor, C. (2007). *A secular age*. Harvard University Press.
Teo, T. (2017). From psychological science to the psychological humanities: Building a general theory of subjectivity. *Review of General Psychology*, 21(4), 281–291. https://doi.org/10.1037/gpr0000132
Virilio, P. (1994). *The vision machine*. Indiana University Press.
Winnicott, D. W. (1971). *Playing and reality*. Tavistock Publications. https://archive.org/details/playingreality00winn/
Zuckerman, C. H. P. (2020). Phatic, the: Communication and communion. In J. Stanlaw (Ed.), *The international encyclopedia of linguistic anthropology* (1st ed., pp. 1–5). Wiley. https://doi.org/10.1002/9781118786093.iela0311

Chapter 3

Small Tears in Logic
The Power of Poetic Image and Aesthetic Knowing

Ross Gormley

One: "The image of the human form is gradually disappearing from the painting of these times and all objects appear only in fragments," wrote the artist Hugo Ball in 1916 as he took refuge in neutral Switzerland during the First World War. "The next step is for poetry to decide to do away with language" (Trachtman, 2006). That same year, Ball publicly recited a poem using garbled language: "gadji beri bimba / glandridi lauli lonni cadori" Ball went on to call this trend in art Dada, or Dadaism, which, according to David Byrne's Broadway play *American Utopia* (as cited in Marth & Byrne, 2020) sought to use "nonsense to make sense of a world that didn't make sense." What didn't make sense for the dada artists was that for the first time, armies had new technologies capable of murder at a scale previously unknown or unimagined – and that these armies stemmed from the perceived rationality of Enlightenment-era European institutions, a rationality captured in G.W.F. Hegel's argument that the state is the actualization of rational freedom. It was, for the dadaists, a war fought under the pretense of reason and logic that was not logical or reasonable at all.

Perhaps a good counterpoint to the sense-making nonsense of Dadaism is Hannah Arendt's theory on the banality of evil, in which she profiles the architect of the Final Solution, Adolf Eichmann, while on trial in Jerusalem. Arendt's central claim is that evil is not defined by its typical associations – malice, cruelty, diabolical scheming – but rather results from the detached bureaucracy of institutions. Unable to finish high school or vocational training, evil, like Eichmann, was in fact boring and dull. Eichmann lacked the intelligence to think critically for himself. He shielded himself under the reputational prestige of various organizations. Stringing together stock phrases, he spoke in euphemisms and legalese. The citizens of Jerusalem perhaps expected a snarling and rage-filled man on the stand. Instead, they got someone whose boring demeanor belied the atrocity of the genocide he helped to orchestrate.

Joseph Conrad's novella *Heart of Darkness* captures a similar juxtaposition between detached workaday bureaucracy and evil actions against a marginalized population. The accountant hired to facilitate the Belgian Congo's ivory trade is described as the pinnacle of polish by Marlow, the novella's protagonist. "I saw a high starched collar, white cuffs, a light alpaca jacket, snowy trousers, a clean necktie, and varnished boots. No hat. Hair parted, brushed, oiled, under a green-lined parasol held in a big white hand. He was amazing, and had a penholder behind his ear," Marlow writes of the man. Against this exacting sartorial description, the reader encounters some of the more dehumanizing language used to describe the African natives (note too the loosening of the language from a concise listing of details to drawn-out, languid sentences): "They were dying slowly – it was very clear. They were not enemies, they were not criminals, they were nothing earthly now – nothing but black shadows of disease and starvation, lying confusedly in the greenish gloom. Brought from all the recesses of the coast in all the legality of time contracts, lost in uncongenial surroundings, fed on unfamiliar food, they sickened, became inefficient, and were then allowed to crawl away and rest. These moribund shapes were free as air – and nearly as thin."

For the prim and proper man, accountancy provided a means of corporal and moral separation, a necessary juxtaposition, it seems. "In the great demoralization of the land, he kept up his appearance," writes Marlow.

The lessons from this scene are not far from fiction; in the 1890s, Prudential Insurance Company hired a statistician to defend itself against the charge of racial discrimination after not offering to insure Black Americans. The resulting paper, "Race Traits and Tendencies of the American Negro," used statistical analyses to argue for the inherent inferiority of Black people, captured in mortality rates and standards of living – an early example of how the burgeoning field of statistics could achieve dehumanizing ends (Lepore, 2023).

Our present obsession with data science seems the inevitable apotheosis of the Enlightenment-era rationalism that the dada movement was reacting against. "The age of data is associated with late capitalism, authoritarianism, techno-utopianism, and a discipline known as data science, which has lately been the top of the top hat, the spit shine on the buckled shoe, the whir of the whizziest Tesla," writes Jill Lepore in her *New Yorker* essay "The Data Delusion" (2023).

There are many ways of knowing things, but capitalism has designated data and numbers as the supreme arbiters of truth. Consider even its intrusion into how we now consume art. Whereas art and taste were once – and largely still are, for now at least – in the province of human understanding, it is increasingly subject to data. The company Artfacts, for example, "harnesses power of data and technology to organise and understand the art market." Companies like Spotify use algorithms to create A.I.-tailored playlists for their users. With A.I. now capable of generating songs and music (e.g., "Heart on my Sleeve" by A.I. Drake), one can imagine a dystopian future in which A.I. analyzes the music market, writes a song it predicts will be a hit, and promotes it to the masses again using another A.I. system. (See Nick Seaver's book *Computing Taste* for more on this).

Much has been written on the effects of declining religiosity in America and abroad. Whereas religion used to provide humans with answers and certainty to the biggest questions – What happens when I die? How do I grieve the loss of a loved one? – our present culture of mass consumerism offers no such answers. In the languishing confusion born out of this uncertainty, data and numbers instead emerge as a kind of religion, offering certainty where there otherwise is none. Data becomes a means to an absolute truth, and it aligns part and parcel with an obsession with efficiency. Data has even come for the human body. Whereas we once placed immortality into mythos and religion, men like Bryan Johnson and Andrew Huberman now place immortality in data, attempting to optimize the human body. "Every decision about his health is made by specialized software and a team of 30 medical specialists who monitor and analyze data about his organs," writes Matteo Wong in a recent *Atlantic* article) (2024). Data emerges as a kind of newfangled panacea, a techno-optimism that promises to revolutionize every facet of life.

"What saves us is efficiency – the devotion to efficiency," writes the accountant character in *Heart of Darkness* in describing his work in the ivory trade (ironically, as hundreds die under his watch).

In this essay, I want to propose a means to dilute the tyranny of analysis and data. I want to provide a counterweight to logic, one resistant to interpretation. Call it poetic intelligence or aesthetic knowing, but it is best captured in an image.

Two: Much has been devoted to the image of a ship being hauled over a mountain. Werner Herzog's self-funded attempt to capture this image in his film *Fitzcarraldo* required the construction of two identical steamboat ships, which in turn required the construction of a ship wharf and a jungle camp to house the 1,100 laborers who would build the ships. The effort was notoriously plagued by inconvenience: A border war between Peru and Ecuador spilled into the camp, burning it to the ground; half the movie was filmed with Jason Robards and Mick Jagger before Robards fell ill and was barred by his doctors from again entering Peru, forcing Herzog to hire Klaus Kinski instead. Several deaths, two small plane crashes, an amputation, and the alleged exploitation of the indigenous people around the film set later, the film was done. All this because Herzog "had the feeling I should do something about a ship over a mountain" (Herzog, n.d.). The film itself then inspired Les Blank's making-of documentary Burden of Dreams and Herzog's book *Conquest of the Useless: Reflections from the Making of Fitzcarraldo* (Note "useless" as a synonym for "nonsense"; this is an art that purports no objective meaning or purpose). Aside from the obvious question – is Herzog a genius or a privileged lunatic who too readily gives over to his fever dreams? – I want to explore the power of image in aesthetics and its relationship to power and morality.

But first, it's worth considering image as a germ with the utility of transferring across a wide array of media. Genre labels in bookstores are convenient to sell and market writing but are useless in theory. Most pieces of writing are in some measure a combination of fiction, poetry, and nonfiction. Indeed, *Fitzcarraldo* was loosely based on a real-life Peruvian rubber baron whose life was further fictionalized and stylized by Herzog to fit into the constraints of a feature film. In addition, the whole plot of the story seems in service not to a character but to poetry: the image of a ship traversing a mountain. Watching the movie, one gets the sense that the whole plot is in service of the image itself, which is true for many great stories. In this sense, the plot is a vehicle for delivering images.

Each literary genre necessarily borrows from the other genres. Creative nonfiction (also called literary nonfiction) relies on poetry to imbue it with aesthetic beauty and verisimilitude while techniques from fiction structure the content into narrative form (e.g., Truman Capote's *In Cold Blood* being labeled a "nonfiction novel," the first coining of such a term). Fiction relies on real-world events for inspiration and depends on poetry to again imbue it with beauty and soul beyond mere plot structure. However, while poetry can be inspired by real-world events (e.g., documentary poetry) and can be structured as a fictional story (e.g., *Paradise Lost*), poetry is the only genre that can exist purely as poetry – a fact best captured in haiku and other image-rich poems. Take, for example, Ezra Pound's "In a Station of the Metro": "The apparitions of these faces in the crowd: / Petals on a wet, black bough." (Note that brevity alone is not criteria for a purely poetic image, as evidenced by Hemingway's famous flash fiction story: "For sale: baby shoes, never worn," which manages to fit a narrative of grief into six words.) Poetry, then, in that it is inevitably present in nonfiction and fiction, is a kind of building block – a kernel from which narrative can grow and wrap itself around. And an image is a kind of atom for that element of poetry. Image is narrative's smallest divisible part. "Images are not quite ideas; they are stiller than that, with less implication outside themselves. And they are not myth, they do not have that explanatory power; they are closer to pure story," writes the poet and critic Robert Hass (1984, p. 276). Images, too, according to Higginson and Harter (1985), result in a kind of "vicarious experience in which the reader pictures what the writer's words show, hears what they sound, feels what they touch" (p. 115).

The utility of compartmentalizing genres again falls away when considering the "truthiness" of nonfiction and fiction. Why is Tim O'Brien's *The Things They Carried* categorized as fiction over memoir? Why is Dave Eggers's *A Heartbreaking Work of Staggering Genius* – which opens with the caveat "this is not, actually, a work of pure nonfiction. Many parts have been fictionalized in varying degrees, for various purposes" – sold as nonfiction? Herzog, at first famous for his fictional films but later more widely known for his work in documentaries, tells Charlie Rose in an interview, "I do not make so much a distinction between documentaries and feature films. I stage them [documentaries]. And I stylize them. I'm not the kind of cinema verite who postulates you should be unobtrusive." But even for those fly-on-the-wall filmmakers who purport absolute neutrality in their filming approach, when documentary films shoot an average of eighty hours of film for every one hour that makes it into the final cut, the product resembles more of a fiction than the raw reality of whatever was filmed simply by elision. Condensing, shaping, cutting away – editing inevitably entails a degree of fictionalization. "The sense of meaning and continuity that is achieved through the storying of experience is gained at a price. A narrative can never encompass the full richness of our lived experience," writes Michael White and Epstein (1990), founder of the psychotherapeutic modality narrative therapy (p. 11).

To make this personal: In what is known as "parts-for-whole coding," we story only what is relevant to us and let all the rest of the raw, unfiltered experience fall away. For example, when we watch a movie or read a book, we mostly remember what is personally significant to us. And if it's significant enough, we may assimilate aspects of that film into our self-understanding. In that we inevitably self-edit, ignoring and eliding the vast sum of reality around us, we are more fictions than nonfictions – subjective truths in an objective world. Taken a step further, we become positive self-illusions, telling ourselves the narratives we need to hear in order to get along with our lives. Nevertheless, in this debate over "truthiness," what most writers seem to agree on is a fidelity to the creative and emotional truth of the matter. O'Brien (1990) captures this by writing, "I want you to feel what I felt. I want you to know why story-truth is truer sometimes than happening-truth" (p. 171). I want to argue that "story-truth" is best supported by poetic images. Writers often refer to this form of knowing as "aesthetic knowing" or "poetic intelligence." These non-analytical ways of knowing are wary of deconstructionism; they resist overt interpretation, in turn helping to promote a greater tolerance for ambiguity, the absence of contradiction, and a loss of identity in the consumer (Snyder, 2002).

All good works of literature can be placed on a continuum between poetic image and narrative. The question is what drives the story? What gives it the magical quality that allows a reader to engage with it? Literature structured around narrative can be obvious – the Stephen Kings and James Pattersons of this world who write for suspense, character development, and action. Literature structured around images can be less obvious. But some writers, eschewing traditional narrative structures, compose entire short stories by stringing together arresting images. Take, for example, Stuart Dybek's short story "Pet Milk." Originally written as a poem, the work morphed into a fiction story after further edits. It opens with a man drinking coffee with condensed milk, which occasions a flashback to the cans of Pet Milk he drank as a child at his grandmother's house, which in turn occasions a flashback to the heavy cream being poured into a cocktail in a bar he frequented with his first love in Chicago. The story is driven not by plot or suspense but by the aesthetic linkages of swirling cream. It is a kind of non-story story, and even without a formal plot, it manages to be an indelible bildungsroman. The story ends with the narrator and his first love sidling close together on a moving train:

> A high school kid in shirt sleeves, maybe sixteen, with books tucked under one arm and a cigarette in his mouth, caught sight of us, and in the instant before he disappeared, he grinned and started to wave. Then he was gone, and I turned from the window, back to Kate, forgetting everything – the passing stations, the glowing late sky, even the sense of missing her – but that arrested wave stayed with me. It was as if I were standing on that platform, with my schoolbooks and a smoke, on one of those endlessly accumulated afternoons after school when I stood almost outside of time simply waiting for a train, and I thought how much I'd have loved seeing someone like us streaming by.

This ending captures the essential power of image and gets at what literature does best: It places a maximal distance between the specific and the universal. A tiny moment – "he grinned and started to wave" – explodes the present moment into one of timelessness: "when I stood almost outside of time." It is indeed beautiful when something so small can stand for everything else. There is a kind of yin-and-yang quality to an effective image. As Robert Hass (1984) writes, "the stillness of the instant exists by virtue of its velocity. It is eternal because it is gone in a second" (p. 276). In the conjunction between what perishes and what lasts forever, there is a "feeling of release from the self" (p. 275).

This, too, captures the inductive structure that literature favors – a duality where narrative is "both linear and instantaneous" (White & Epstein, p. 3). This structure is a marked departure from the deductive structure favored by big data and analysis. Whereas deductive structures claim a fidelity to capital-T Truth, inductive structures make no such claim, instead appealing to emotional and subjective truths. While all works of literature achieve emotional truths across all genres, image does this best and at its most subjective level. Hence, why image is the closest thing we have to "pure story."

Denis Johnson is another writer adept at stringing together powerful images. In his book of linked short stories, *Jesus' Son*, he captures the following:

This boat was pulling behind itself a tremendous triangular kite on a rope. From the kite, up in the air a hundred feet or so, a woman was suspended, belted in somehow, I would have guessed. She had long red hair. She was delicate and white, and naked except for her beautiful hair. I don't know what she was thinking as she floated past these ruins.

Unlike metaphors or symbols, images resist interpretation, and they resist turning to stock symbols (birds, roses, seasons). Sure, a reader can make an interpretation as to what the naked parasailing woman means. But it will be an interpretation more supported by one's personal experience than by what the data of the story can provide. This is not a short story for lawyers seeking to trade in evidence. To quote J. Bruner (1986), "It is the 'relative indeterminacy of a text' that 'allows a spectrum of actualizations.' And so, 'literary texts initiate performances of meaning rather than actually formulating meaning themselves" (White & Epstein, 1990, p. 13). Images allow for a more intimate performance. To better understand this, it's worth understanding the difference between metaphor and image.

Metaphors often have an exact one-to-one meaning. Our most basic metaphors – primary metaphors – are embodied and even lived out. When you're feeling happy, you're up. When you're feeling depressed, you're down. Warmth is associated with closeness and coldness with distance. In that the physical body is a discrete entity with clear boundaries, metaphors serve to contain and package the abstractness of emotion into something that can be physically understood and embodied. To *fall* in love is to capture that intangible feeling of eros – impetuous, spiraling, all-consuming – and transfer it into the very tangible feeling of falling down (perhaps also comically capturing the inevitable pratfall once the honeymoon phase abruptly ends). While metaphors can corporally contain and give shape to the complexity

48 Aesthetic Ethics

of a life, they can also do the opposite: add layers of complexity and abstraction to what was formerly concrete.

Metaphors, ironically, often better capture the truth than the truth itself. Those in the practice of creative writing know that the more you try to go directly to the source of the truth, the further you get from it. Think of a dartboard whose bulls-eye is magnetized, repelling all incoming darts from hitting its center. The more you try to strike the heart of the truth, the less you capture its essential truth. The irony, then, is that in employing a metaphor – in telling it slant – you get closer to the truth. The dart player must throw the dart from the side to get the bullseye. So too must the writer craft a secondary means of conveying the truth of the source material. "Tell all the truth but tell it slant," wrote Emily Dickinson. In the short story "Chicxulub," T. C. Boyle (2004) braids the story of a meteor striking the earth with the grueling account of learning his daughter was hit by a car on the way back from the mall. "The rock is coming, the new Chicxulub, hurtling through the dark and the cold to remake our fate," he writes at the end, capturing the cruel randomness undergirding the potential tragedies hidden behind each day. This metaphor achieves what writers call the "punch of exactitude," the satisfaction of so accurately capturing a thing that you almost seem to be free of it. Images offer not a punch of exactitude but its opposite: something that seeks to ask questions and

Figure 3.1 Marriage a-la-mode: The marriage settlement.

highlight complexities rather than answer them. According to Hass (1984), "they do not say this is that, they say this is" (p. 275).

I've elaborated on image within literature, but it's worth considering image within visual domains. Building from the Enlightenment-era emphasis on rationality and empiricism, Victorian art was often so suffused with narrative so as to blunt you over the head with meaning. Take, for example, William Hogarth's work "Marriage A-la-Mode" (n.d.), which functions more like a comic strip or Victorian soap opera, capturing in six frames the ruinous results of marrying for social status over love.

To approach this painting is to first don your Sherlock Holmes cap and light up your pipe. Like a puzzle, you must scan it for visual cues that speak to the larger narrative (i.e., we see through the window that construction on the mansion has stopped; the father of the groom-to-be is bankrupt, necessitating a marriage arranged for money. The groom is eager for the financial boon – he's looking at himself in the mirror. Although Hogarth's efforts in satire are a worthy pursuit, to our modern sensibilities, we might say such paintings are too on the nose. Beyond the fun of piecing together little clues (favoring a deductive structure), they leave little room for subjective interpretation.

Compare Hogarth's work to that of Henri Cartier-Bresson, operating two hundred years later, whose style famously emphasized the capture of the decisive moment. Take, for example, his photograph taken in Brie, France, in 1968 of a perfectly symmetrical row of trees framing a desolate road in an otherwise sparse, expansive field. Down the road, the road and trees bend leftward, angling into the distance, introducing a gentle asymmetrical tension into the composition. Put down your pipe and deerstalker hat, we see here a shift from *telling* to *seeing*. Victor Shklovsky (1917) captured this transition well: "The technique of art is to make objects unfamiliar," to make forms difficult, to increase the difficulty and length of perception because the process of perception is an aesthetic end in itself and must be prolonged." Note here the shift in the balance of power: Hogarth is telling me what to think while Bresson is asking me to see. With the former, I become a passive subject. With the latter, I become an active participant. "Art is a way of experiencing the artfulness of an object: the object is not important," writes Shklovsky. Much like Marshall McLuhan's argument that the medium is more important than the message, we see a de-emphasis on content and an emphasis on process and positionality. The content of image-driven art is merely a means of awakening the sense perception of the person, making them autonomous subjects capable of experiencing the work on their own terms. Though the medium is ostensibly the same – visual representation – Hogarth's work is rooted in empiricism and rationalism, wrapped up in a neat narrative bow. Bresson's, by contrast, stems from image and invites the autonomous perception of the person invited to perceive.

There is an irony that while Hogarth's message is noble and politically disobedient, in that it was conveyed via narrative, it set its own agenda for power by making the consumer a passive subject (though we certainly don't feel passive with all the clues to piece together). Compared to image, narrative is pliant, flexible, and capable of being used for ideological ends. Image is more like an atom, resistant to the powers of political persuasion and therefore benign. That is, in part, because images, as Shklovsky (1917) writes, "change little; from century to century, from nation to nation, from poet to poet, they flow on without changing. Images belong to no one." This fact makes images a potent force in art and society.

According to Terry Eagleton (2016), "Power . . . works by fiction and charade, cloaking itself in ceremony in order to soften its rigour" (p. 67). Hegemony has an interest in shaping the narratives around us. Power, too, "must be similarly aestheticized, made gratifying and pleasurable, if it is to engage the loyalties of the common people" (p. 66). This aestheticized power is closer to ideology than culture. According to Eagleton, "ideology denotes those values and symbolic practices which at any given time are caught up in the businesses of maintaining political power." Given ideologies' creeping influence over aesthetics and narrative, it's easy to see how our commonly traded symbols and metaphors can be flecked with ideology, weighted with pre-packaged meaning. To quote Eagleton, "culture has shed itself of its innocence." Compare too how narrative, culture, and technology build off one another. Today, Hogarth and other creators with less noble intentions can forgo paint and canvas and opt for video and sound. By virtue of its powers to command so many of our sense perceptions, video makes us more susceptible to narrative's influence than ever before.

Drawing from Foucault's idea of power-knowledge, narrative is a means of knowledge that also frames a person's relationships with himself and others. For Foucault, narrative doesn't merely reflect power relations but actively constitutes them. And when narrative can be invented, coerced, or molded, we see its potential for both good and bad. Much like beauty replicates itself again and again, so too does power, making the alliance of beauty and power especially dangerous. If narrative is invented, then images are only ever found. As Shklovsky (1917) writes, "poets are much more concerned with arranging images than with creating them. Images are given to poets; the ability to remember them is far more important than the ability to create them." Images, therefore, have the potential to disrupt systems of knowledge-power.

Three: Imagine a deer grazing in a forest in spring. Sunlight filters through the trees. Bright patches cast against the ground quake with each passing breeze, as do the white chrysanthemum angling over the shin-high grass. Our inclination is to capture this deer in some measure. The hunter will kill it, taxidermy it, and place it on his wall. The photographer will similarly "shoot it" and may also put the print on their wall. Even the writer will perceive it and then express it, reducing the deer to words on a page. In this sense, the deer is hardly perceived in its original form but instead captured, expressed, and labeled. Why must we kill everything that is beautiful in our world?

We are prone to a similar process when consuming art and literature. I recall a meme in which a student and an English teacher were tasked with analyzing the sentence "the curtains were blue." The English teacher waxes poetic, claiming the color blue symbolizes the immense depression of the character, perhaps as blue and boundless as the vast ocean. What does the student opine? "The curtains were fucking blue." My point: we can never just leave a thing to be a thing; our powers of attention are always analyzing, churning meaning out of an always-running meat grinder. Remember, the best way to kill a joke is to analyze it.

The author Donald Barthelme (1978) makes this critique in his short story "The Glass Castle," where the literal and figurative worlds become flipped. It opens with a homeless man using two plumber's friend plungers as suction cups to climb to the top of a skyscraper: "Touching the side of the mountain, one feels coolness. Peering into the mountain, one sees sparkling blue-white depths. The mountain towers over that part of Eighth Avenue like some splendid, immense office building." Here, we are already in the metaphorical world. The metaphorical jump, "like some" instead, flips us into the literal world. "Like" is used not as a figurative launching point but as an absurdist reveal of reality. The story also seeks to conflate what is useful in semiotics with what is figurative. As the man climbs the mountain, Barthelme writes: "'The conventional symbol (such as the nightingale, often associated with melancholy), even though it is recognized only through agreement, is not a sign (like the traffic light) because, again, it presumably arouses deep feelings and is regarded as possessing properties beyond what the eye alone sees.' (A Dictionary of Literary Terms) . . . A number of nightingales with traffic lights tied to their legs flew past me." Here, we have a kind of cross-wiring of symbolism and meaning, deliberately inviting us into utter confusion where useful, straightforward semiotics (a traffic light) are conflated with the nightingale, a literary symbol weighted with pre-packaged but varied meaning. There is a challenge in the absurdity of interpreting it. Is the nightingale just a nightingale, or does the traffic light suddenly hold immense metaphorical meaning beyond its usual meaning of stop, yield, go? *Why bother interpreting at all*, Barthelme seems to suggest.

The driving plot of the short story is what sits at the top of the skyscraper: "At the top of the mountain there is a castle of pure gold, and in a room in the castle tower sits." The author abruptly cuts off the sentence for an aside. We naturally fill in the blank; a princess sits at the top of the mountain. But Barthelme (1978), aware of our proclivity to analyze stories to death, makes the princess not a tangible thing but "a beautiful enchanted symbol." When the homeless man finally reaches the top of the skyscraper, he narrates, "I approached the symbol, with its layers of meaning, but when I touched it, it changed into only a beautiful princess." Bathos, for sure. I wanted a literary idea, not a flesh-and-blood human. Shame on the writer who writes a character who is merely meant to be just a character. The result is that characters will be so flat as to become not characters but devices. Or perhaps the author *does* construct a rounded, authentic character. Are we so prone to analysis that we bulldoze over this effort by slapping on a simple meaning? That inclination to assign pre-packaged meaning and label a thing certainly calms an existential panic around uncertainty. But the inclination also wrests us away from the perceptual stage of experience.

Heidegger concerned himself with this phenomenon when he spoke of the German word Gelassenheit – a term elaborated by Pezze (2006) that means a tranquil submission, a "releasement." In defining Gelassenheit, Pezze draws a distinction between meditative thinking – an active and open awakening to what is actually happening around us – and calculative thinking, which is the thinking associated with science and economics in which we plan, investigate, set goals and wants and timelines. While calculative thinking is productive and yields material rewards, it also, according to Heidegger (1966, as cited in Dalle Pezze, 2006), leads to a "growing thoughtlessness" in which "we take in everything in the quickest and cheapest way, only to forget it just as quickly, instantly" (p. 45). It is a logic that never slows down, never pauses to reflect on itself. Meditative thinking, on the other hand, is a kind of quality of attention that slows us down and grounds us in the immediate reality. The cost for not developing the ability to think meditatively is to become a "defenseless and perplexed victim at the mercy of the irresistible superior power of technology" (pp. 52–53). As calculative thinking and technology ally themselves, we become estranged from our own reality, alien beings even in our own homes. It is a world in which "all that with which modern techniques of communication stimulate, assail, and drive man – all that is already much closer to man today than his fields around his farmstead, closer than the sky over the earth, closer than the change from night to day" (p. 48).

In writing about how media and narrative can discombobulate rather than clarify, Megan Garber, writing for the *Atlantic* (2023), notes that when something now happens in the real world, it is immediately picked and pulled apart by our media industry. Elizabeth Holmes's downfall actually happened, of course. Then that reality gave way to a *Wall Street Journal* article, a book, a true-crime podcast, a Hulu drama, a documentary, and possibly even an Adam McKay–produced feature film. Documentary inevitably elides details; fiction films must inevitably invent details to structure out a fictional plot. The result is that I often find myself googling "Did _____ actually happen?" Or I read articles about what was actually true in a movie that is reported to be based on real events and real people.

This phenomenon captures the present powers of interpellation. Interpellation, per Marxist theory, is the process by which apparatuses such as family, mass media, schools, churches, police, and government "hail" us (French: *interpeller*) with labels from an early age, constituting us as subjects who come to live voluntarily within societal norms. When a policeman shouts, "Hey, you!" to a Black teenage male, the policeman (by powers of his institutional backing and all the meaning behind its symbols and narrative) is constituting the boy as a subject who must behave and respond in a certain way. Now with the ubiquity of media technologies, that "Hey, you!" comes from our smartphones, comes from our apps.

The historian Warren Sussman argued that whereas Americans used to value "character" in individuals, we now value "personality." This marks a shift from an emphasis on honesty, diligence, and duty to one's charm and likability. "The social role demanded of all in the new Culture of Personality was that of a performer," Susman wrote (Garber, 2023). "Every American was to become a performing self." If, under Heidegger's view (as discussed by Pezze, 2006), we are made strangers in our own lands, we are also made to be strangers from ourselves, "constructing" ourselves under the watch of a hyperconnected and omnipresent media ecosystem. Note, again, that "performing" and "constructing" are active words that fool the person into believing we are the active authors in our lives. Rather, we are given our identity, our self, and then made to perform it – and the performance elides that it was ever imposed on us in the first place.

I acknowledge the comical transition to haiku, as if to suggest it as a wholesale antidote to the Orwellian state of our media ecosystem, but that is where we will start: small and unassuming haiku. If image, per Robert Hass (1984), can be considered "pure story," then haiku is the smallest discernible extension of that pure story. Haikus do not offer meaning or symbolage but resonance. They do not tell so much as evoke. In reading the haiku "snowflakes – / dust on the toes / of my boots," Higginson and Harter (authors of *The Haiku Handbook*) warn the reader "do not read this as a metaphor! The 'dust' is really dust" (p. 118) – a refreshing reminder that begins to salvage the perceptual stage lost through the expression stage. Indeed, with a good image, the perceptual and expressive stages ideally occur as one. Haiku is most famous for this collapsing, as it tries to best retain and convey the perceptual essence of the experience. From Basho: "the stillness – / soaking into stones / cicada's cry." In this way, according to Higginson and Harter, "both the language of the poem and the mind of the poet should be transparent to the reader" (p. 10).

I always appreciated the conciseness of the haiku form. It's as if the form is apologizing for itself, trying to convey as much of an aesthetic experience in as few words as possible: *Sorry for this brief intrusion of words, but I had to write something!* There is again the pleasure of the inductive structure, a tension between the singularity of the moment and the universality of the aesthetic experience – three lines of words evoking a sense of timelessness. This dialectic relates to Shklovsky's (1917) argument that the purpose of art is to "make forms difficult, to increase the difficulty and length of perception."

Four: In his book *Culture*, Terry Eagleton (2016) argues that our current economic system and culture have collapsed entirely into one another; we now have "capitalism with a cultural face" (p. 152). It is perhaps the natural end of neoliberalism where everything has a price and every interaction can be monetized. Indeed, we have all become our own brands. We speak not of personal morals or values but of reputation management. And we treat others the same way; the logic of consumerism has become the modus operandi of dating culture where we try to consume more and more of the other as another transaction in the marketplace. In short, capitalism has become aestheticized.

Art for art's sake has always been a relatively rare if not precious phenomenon, but it is increasingly in peril. Art is, more than ever, composed and created under the strictures of capitalist logic. The explosion of Hollywood sequels and its superhero universes – Marvel and DC – in recent years is not a product of good storytelling but rather of stable, predictable investment. The markets and clever data analysis now dictate what stories get told (and, to a degree, always did). Many famous art pieces are purchased and immediately stored in secure facilities to allow them to increase in value. If they are placed on walls, they are often exact replicas of the real thing. Where a work's meaning, its ability to be analyzed, almost becomes moot so long as it holds financial worth.

This is all to say, there is a futility when all art and all media must have, in some way, utility. It must be useful, if not just profitable. Again, it is a pleasure to return to the uselessness of the dada poets, or the uselessness of Herzog dragging a boat over a mountain. In an interview with Ezra Klein, the academic D. Graham Burnett (2024) eulogizes that "spaces of religion and institutions of education, study, teaching, and learning, and then museums and spaces of artistic production, symphonies, music, each of those institutions has meaningful traditions of non-instrumentalizable attention." Of course, non-instrumentalizable attention is not profitable, and that's precisely why it's under threat.

Of course, images *are* useful. But not in the way capitalism would prefer. It's worth returning to Heidegger's term, Gelassenheit, as discussed by Pezze (2006). That distinction between meditative and calculative thinking is ultimately what quality of attention we bring to bear on a thing. I doubt Heidegger could have predicted the extent to which our attention would be plundered by for-profit companies, but that is our present reality. Attention is a multibillion-dollar industry. And because interpretation and meaning are a product of attention, so has our world of meaning come under the logic of markets. If we are a storytelling species, then our pool of stories to introject into our own identity is increasingly spun from the weave of this aestheticized capitalism we now live in.

In our country, obsessed with rugged individualism, we consider identity development and self-expression to be the coup de grace of self-actualization. The philosopher Charles Taylor posits that Western societies orient toward "a generalized culture of 'authenticity,' or expressive individualism, in which people are encouraged to find their own way, discover their own fulfillment, 'do their own thing'" (Harper, 2024). However, "their own thing" often amounts to a soft rebellion. The irony is that in "doing our own thing," we are doing what everyone else is doing. We are performing faux-authenticity, perhaps original in its content but not its form. In this way, we herald identity as an active, not passive, accomplishment. However, interpellation (French: *interpeller*, to hail) posits that such identities are instead impressed upon us. Foucault's idea of the panopticon expands upon this; we are not responding to an external, objective form of hard power but instead responding to an internalized, subjective form of soft power. Power is decentralized, diffused. We enforce it in ourselves and others. And we are under it even as we are pretending to be rebelling from it (what has been referred to as therapeutic libertarianism). It is a smart trick of deceit for something coercive – social media, the culture industry – to appear as noncoercive.

It's worth bringing up Gayatri Spivak's definition of education as the "noncoercive rearranging of desire" (Klein, 2024). This definition aligns with what I see as the potential power of poetic image. To review:

> Effective poetic images are resistant to interpretation. Certainly, an individual may attempt to interpret an image, but images resist stereotypes or easily assembled metaphors. They are not puzzles to solve. They don't answer questions so much as raise them. Herzog takes delight in the fact that he still doesn't know what the image of a ship being hauled over a mountain means.

Effective images encourage subjective interpretation, insofar as they can be interpreted at all. In that they resist easily made interpretations, individuals are further pressed to form their own idiosyncratic meaning. That meaning is often at an unconscious level rather than a conscious one. For reasons unknown to me, I'm comforted by the image of a woman – "She was delicate and white, and naked except for her beautiful hair," to quote Denis Johnson – floating in the air on a kite. The Anabaptist tradition speaks of Gelassenheit as a "humble yieldedness." Image provides one the opportunity to give up their constantly churning proclivity for analysis. Image allows one to humble oneself, accept what one cannot understand, and nevertheless appreciate its beauty. I think of the often misattributed Thoreau quote (whose original penning belongs to a social worker in the 1970s): "Happiness is like a butterfly: the more you chase it, the more it will elude you, but if you turn your attention to other things, it comes and sits softly on your shoulder."

Effective images often utilize the inductive structure, whereas capitalism and its analytical imperatives rely on deductive reasoning. Inductive structures are rare these days, though their implicit claim on subjective truth is refreshing. To again cite O'Brien (1990): "Story-truth is truer sometimes than happening-truth" (p. 171). A sometimes unfortunate consequence of analysis and deductive reasoning is that its very process of logic legitimates it as the ultimate arbiter of truth. To borrow from Marshall McLuhan's theory that the medium is the message, the medium conveying the content is more important than the content itself; deductive reasoning and data are their own technology, just as image is. Whereas an image makes no claim to convey objective truth, deductive reasoning does, at its own folly.

In all these ways, images offer us a noncoercive rearranging of our attention. I see each image as a small tear in the fabric of an aestheticized capitalism; a chip off its foundational structure. Our brains are prediction-making machines. As Shklovsky (1917) argues, we over-automate the objects around us to permit "the greatest economy of perceptive effort." Amid the flurry of basketballs, we miss the great ape walking before us. Shklovsky's word choice spares little sympathy for this process: "Habitualization devours work, clothes, furniture, one's wife, and the fear of war." Images seem to disrupt that process. Sure, we can gloss right over an image and not let its powers move us; such is its noncoercive power. But each image gives a person another chance to humbly yield themselves to the power of its aesthetic force. In this way, images *are* useful, just not in the way capitalism would want or allow. Images, then, are tiny rebellions with implications larger than their tiny size would suggest. "Art exists that one may recover the sensation of life; it exists to make one feel things, to make the stone stony," as Shklovsky writes.

Effective images also have the power to dilute the stranglehold our present media ecosystem has over individuals. Images promote a quality of attention that is not useful and therefore outside of the realm of capitalist logic. Powerful images promote an attention that is closer to pure being, a moment suspended from markers of identity and free from consumerist labels. Image promotes the sense that *I am simply because I am*. To quote Walt Whitman, "Do I contradict myself? / Very well then, I contradict myself. / (I am large, I contain multitudes.)"

Reference

Barthelme, D. (1978). Glass mountain. In *City life*. Pocket Books. https://www.jessamyn.com/barth/glassmountain.html

Boyle, T. C. (2004, March 1). Chicxulub. *The New Yorker*. https://www.newyorker.com/magazine/2004/03/01/chicxulub

Bruner, J. (1986). *Actual minds, possible worlds*. Harvard University Press.

Burnett, D. G. (2024, May 31). Ezra Klein Podcast [Audio podcast]. *The New York Times*. https://www.nytimes.com/2024/05/31/opinion/ezra-klein-podcast-d-graham-burnett.html

Eagleton, T. (2016). *Culture*. Yale University Press.

Garber, M. (2023, March). TV politics, entertainment, and the metaverse. *The Atlantic*. https://www.theatlantic.com/magazine/archive/2023/03/tv-politics-entertainment-metaverse/672773/

Harper, T. A. (2024, February). Polyamory ruling class fad and monogamy. *The Atlantic*. https://www.theatlantic.com/ideas/archive/2024/02/polyamory-ruling-class-fad-monogamy/677312/

Hass, R. (1984). *Twentieth-century pleasures: Prose on poetry*. Ecco Press.

Herzog, W. (n.d.). *Werner Herzog [Interview with Charlie Rose]*. Charlie Rose. https://charlierose.com/videos/15920

Higginson, W. J., & Harter, P. (1985). *The haiku handbook: How to write, share, and teach haiku*. Kodansha International.

Lepore, J. (2023, April 3). The data delusion. *The New Yorker*. https://www.newyorker.com/magazine/2023/04/03/the-data-delusion

Marth, J., & Byrne, D. (2020, November 29). The familiar delight of David Byrne's American Utopia. *Scene & Heard*. https://www.sceneandheardnu.com/content/2020/11/29/the-familiar-delight-of-david-byrnes-american-utopia

O'Brien, T. (1990). *The things they carried*. Houghton Mifflin Harcourt.

Pezze, B. D. (2006). Heidegger on Gelassenheit. *Minerva: An Internet Journal of Philosophy*, 10, 94–122.

Shklovsky, V. (1917). *Art as technique*. https://warwick.ac.uk/fac/arts/english/currentstudents/undergraduate/modules/fulllist/first/en122/lecturelist-2015-16-2/shklovsky.pdf

Snyder, M. (2002). *Our "other history": Poetry as a meta-metaphor for narrative therapy*. Association for Family Therapy & Systemic Practice.

Trachtman, P. (2006). Dada: The movement that shocked the world. *Smithsonian Magazine*. https://www.smithsonianmag.com/arts-culture/dada-115169154/

White, M., & Epstein, D. (1990). *Narrative means to therapeutic ends*. Norton.
Wong, M. (2024, February). Bryan Johnson's "don't die" event. *The Atlantic*. https://www.theatlantic.com/technology/archive/2024/02/bryan-johnson-dont-die-event/677535/

Images

Hogarth, W. (n.d.). Marriage A-la-mode: The marriage settlement [Painting]. *Wikipedia*. https://en.wikipedia.org/wiki/Marriage_A-la-Mode_(Hogarth)#/media/File:Marriage_A-la-Mode_1,The_Marriage_Settlement-_William_Hogarth.jpg

Chapter 4

Meaning and Morality
Shaping How the Light Shines In

Marilyn Charles

Psychoanalysis teaches us that mind, memory, and meaning are inextricably connected to one another and that time affects meaning in ways that may not be easily perceptible. Knowing that meanings have unconscious underpinnings also informs our relationship to ethics, demanding that we consider motives we may not be aware of. Enigmatic, primal messages operate below conscious awareness, shaping meaning, experience, and also our values, beyond or even counter to our conscious intentions or motivations. Although we often think of time as linear, Bachelard (1971) offers an aesthetic rending of time, highlighting ways in which the duration of time is broken into and reconfigured by what he terms the *epiphanic instants* of *vertical or poetic time*. In this chapter, I will use two clinical examples to illustrate ways in which vertical time emerges, after considering links between primary process, the aesthetic vertex, and the call towards authenticity that is potentiated in an encounter with self through other.

Primary Process and the Aesthetic Vertex

In contrast to the current trend towards *objective* knowledge as the marker of truth, psychoanalysis has been built on an appreciation of the *subjective* as the realm in which human meanings and motivations can be found. Bion (1977) invites us to consider the *aesthetic* as a legitimate lens that privileges primary process, in line with our recognition of ways in which rhythmic patterns underlie the symbolic forms that configure psychic reality (Charles, 2002; Stern, 1985). Recognizing affect as a potentiating force, Bion marks *passion* as an embodied experience that orients towards potential meanings. Although we can always be wrong, orienting towards internal truths affords grounding in lived experience, including the affective signals so crucial to finding our way in the world, leading to an ethics that is both reflective and internally grounded. From this perspective, for Ricoeur (1970), "art, morality, and religion are analogous figures or variants of the oneiric mask. The entire drama of dreams is thus found to be generalized to the dimensions of a universal poetics" (p. 162). That poetics, for Bachelard (1971), occurs within the gap, as Lacan (1964/1977) frames it, a pause through which a new truth might emerge, unconstrained by memory, hope or desire, and grounded in "the categorical imperative of morality [that] has nothing to do with time as duration" but rather "seeks the moment" (Bachelard, p. 178).

In primary process, meanings are affectively driven, anchored in the positioning of subjects and objects in relation to one another. Feelings are both ephemeral and timeless. They become attached to images that come to represent the feeling as an instance of something universal that ties us to one another. Grounded in affect, "the expressive meaning attaches to the perception itself, in which it is apprehended and immediately experienced" (Cassirer, 1957, p. 68). This is the realm of myth, in which universal truths are located in relation to an ethos framed by culture, "grounded in experiences of pure expression rather than in representative or significative acts" (p. 68), providing "a kind of spiritual focus" (p. 108).

For Ricoeur (1984), time is a "transcultural form of necessity" that *"becomes human to the extent that it is articulated through a narrative mode"* (p. 52; italics in original unless otherwise noted). Although narrative provides a structure that helps us track transformations of expressive meanings across time (Charles, 2010), it is an imposed structure that must be flexible enough to recognize both universality and particularity, so that new meanings might emerge, coloured by lived experience and one's historical antecedents (Apprey, 2024; Charles, 2003). Narratives structure meanings through the relationships between the elements, "lending a peculiar mythical accent to each 'region' in space, to the 'here' and 'there,' ... the 'above' and 'below'" (Cassirer, 1957, p. 150). In this way, "totally different, spatially and temporally separate, phenomena can be understood as manifestations of one and the same subject" (Cassirer, p. 108), to be rediscovered and reflected on.

For Bion (1977), myth holds a privileged position as a model that helps anchor and give form to subtleties of experience, in relation to the 'facts' that are artifacts of the particular cultural and personal lenses through which they are viewed. Bion's (1977) use of Poincare's idea of the *selected fact*, to reference the powerful effects of perspective on how we organize information, is in line with Lacan's (1962–1963/2014) ideas of ways in which meanings become framed. Coherence is always in relation to the selected facts organizing the frame, and a focus on content can obstruct our ability to take note of the underlying factors at play. Whereas the scientific vertex pulls toward rational thought, the aesthetic pulls towards primary process, the affectively driven underbelly of human experience. Culture and experience come to define selected facts, and our stories provide containing structures through which latent meanings might be revealed through the use of symbols in relation to one another.

In the realm of primary process, meanings emerge through our ability to detect patterns – or, as Bion (1977) calls them, *constant conjunctions* – and to build narratives that make sense. The challenge is to recognize the pattern sufficiently to think about it reflectively. When deeply embedded in a culture, the road signs are implicit and not easily noted, and other perspectives may seem alien and incomprehensible. For those between cultures, there may be collisions between meanings and values that are not easily parsed. Psychic reality is such that our conceptions of self, other, and universe are informed by the conceptions of those around us, even when not consciously known. These ideas will be important as we consider the case material, including ways in which collisions between present and past create not only distress but also the *turbulence* through which unmetabolized meanings might be revealed (Bion, 1987).

Turbulence

During times of strain, it is easy to be reactive to distress rather than reflecting on its sources, creating further distress that spreads to those around us. The current level of tensions in the world leaves us all not at our best, inviting divisiveness and polarization even in our efforts to find safety and solace. Turbulent times not only pull towards regressive reactivity but also towards alignment with bureaucratic dogma, as we look to an external authority, rather than our own internal compass, to guide us. To oppose such compelling forces, psychoanalysis offers guideposts that might help us recognize when our rationalized ethics are inconsistent with basic principles of human decency or our own internal sense of what might be just or good. Lacan's (1964/1977) warning against becoming lost in an *external* Authority invites us to learn to locate ourselves, our desire, and our own moral authority, Bion's (1977) *internal truth* that provides a star we might steer by when chaos reigns.

Philosophy also offers useful insights. Arendt (2003) warns that hiding behind an external Authority cannot absolve us from our responsibility to one another, and Lévinas (1998) invites us to ground our ethics in the call from the suffering of the human face. Heidegger (1962) positions the call of conscience as coming "*from* me and yet *from beyond me*" (p. 320), a call that at times may seem uncanny, but is also an appeal "to one's ownmost potentiality-for-being . . . because the call comes from that entity which in each case I myself am" (p. 323). Apprey (2024) suggests that this call is fundamental to our humanity, bringing one back to oneself.

The paranoid slant currently guiding human relationships is one marker of the alienation from one another that can leave us strangers to ourselves. Learning to live in this world becomes ever more challenging as our sources of information become increasingly suspect. Inundated by more data than we can possibly manage, much less integrate, we need, even more, to build our reflective capacities, grounded in our own sense of ethics. From that place, we might better heed the call of conscience, Lévinas's call of suffering, that at times reveals itself in an alien voice (Apprey, 2024; Heidegger, 1962).

Even the call of suffering, however, becomes complicated when justice is valued in principle but not in practice. Oppressive social structures of power and privilege are inherently divisive, leaving some groups carrying their traumatic legacy as not only an important source of group identity but also a rallying cry (LaCapra, 1999). At the extreme, suffering can be used as a justification for mindless and even violent action, demanding mindful reflection on our own reactive stances.

In these turbulent times, when suffering seems endemic, we need to recognize ways in which threats to our economies, institutions, and even our planet lead towards ideological rigidity at the expense of the reflective thought and cooperation essential to our collective well-being (Jusup et al., 2014). The failure to consider the extreme suffering of those who are marginalized or excluded fuels a great deal of the violence threatening our ability to come together over issues of collective importance where even our survival as a species is at stake (Prefus et al., 2018).

And yet, in these current times, ideological shifts challenge psychoanalytic theory's presumption of an unconscious reason driving behaviour beyond our ability to 'know what we do'. Has a shift happened that requires a new envisioning of morality? The ethical underpinnings of psychoanalysis have been predicated on the value of recognizing and coming to grips with the truths underlying embodied experience, including "the *alienation* we experience when we know that the life we are living is a lie" (Thompson, 2005, p. 150). If we cannot trust the human face, where would morality be lodged? Aesthetics is a human, embodied value. What is the place of an embodied, aesthetic morality in current times? Can we look to those who are educating our young to build the type of reflective capacity on which empathy depends?

Žižek (1989) positions this sleight of hand in the realm of ideology, which rests on our not-knowing that there is an enjoyment hidden in the not-looking. Failing to recognize ourselves turns representation on its head. Rather than a means for recognizing oneself within the larger field of individual beings, "representation is resuscitated at the very moment it is called into question: we may not be able to trust what people say, but we can learn to trust the traces that indicate whether or not they are sincere" (Andrejevic, 2010, p. 50). As we learn to rely on external dictates to judge these traces, it is easy to lose touch with our internal indicators.

The ideological turn too easily inserts a false reassurance that opposes Heidegger's (1962) *call of conscience*, the morality Lévinas (1969/1991) locates precisely in the call received from the suffering of the other, leaving us searching, rather, for a truth beyond the human being. Questioning the legitimacy of that call alienates us from an essential aspect of morality and humanity, free to perpetrate harm under the banner of a 'greater good'.

Complicating our dilemma is the active promotion of uncertainty as a means for controlling people's ideas and opinions:

> Just when the prospect of an informed populace with access to technology for deliberation on an unprecedented scale appears on the horizon, the rules change: deliberation comes to be understood as a process of fragmentation and polarization, information proliferates without converging toward a shared understanding of reality.
>
> (Andrejevic, 2010, p. 57)

This uncertainty opposes our grounding in the truths that register over time in evolving interchanges between persons. Experiences of recognition, and of rupture and repair, build our capacity to learn (as an integrative process) through encounters with others. With no reliable anchors for such embodied truths, there is a generalized uncertainty that seeks relief through experts, knowledge, or the institutions we cannot entirely believe in. Countering the idea that truth could be found through successive iterations that build on one another, reflexivity has become a marker for disenfranchised meanings that reproduce themselves (Gibson, 2018). The proliferation of information and the recognition of the impact of cultural values and ideology on meaning have led not to greater respect for difference but to a greater uncertainty regarding meaning as such, Žižek's (1989) *demise of symbolic efficiency*.

Social Injustice and Marginalization

Bion's (1961) work on groups reminds us that as anxiety increases, dependency needs can obscure the task at hand. Under such circumstances, difference easily becomes divisive, and even well-intentioned efforts can falter or become misguided. Suspicion of difference results in the systematic delegitimization of marginalized voices and even their status as legitimate carriers of knowledge (Fricker, 2007). Failure to recognize the value of differing vantage points not only obstructs minority opinions, leaving the disenfranchised isolated behind a wall of imposed meanings (Stauffer, 2015), but also opposes attention to the new ideas and vantage points, so essential to growth, that our institutions and social systems both need and resist (Bion, 1977).

As social injustice impedes the ability of marginalized individuals to speak to and validate their own experience (Fricker, 2007), failures to redeem oneself – or be redeemed by one's sociocultural systems – accrue across the generations. Structural oppression results in feelings of abjection at the social level that are experienced as a shame-inducing inferiority by the individual (Kristeva, 1982), obstructing the person's ability to work through the problem. Fricker (2007) terms this dilemma *epistemic injustice*, marking how profoundly one's very ability to *know* can be subverted. Such delegitimization is toxic and profoundly isolating, resulting in the *ethical loneliness* that occurs in relation to unacknowledged systemic suffering (Stauffer, 2015).

Shame turns our glance downwards, our inability to face the oppressor becoming a source of further shame. At the extreme, abjection invites a masochistic surrender to a debased, devalued identity, obstructing the anger through which we might reclaim our own voice (LaCapra, 1999). Paradoxically, legitimizing our position often depends on receiving recognition from the very social structures in which we have been devalued (Stauffer, 2015), structures that persist because of socially sanctioned splitting that invites the majority to not-see how they are implicated in these ongoing abjecting processes. Valorizing the oppressed position tends to feed the polarization in ways that fuel divisiveness and invite resolution through further oppression – turning the tables rather than imagining how we might all sit at a table in which there might be mutual respect for difference.

Recognizing the social construction of shame and marginalization helps us imagine how we might move beyond our polarized positions, as we recognize the price we pay for turning defensively on those who are lost and vulnerable as a way of distancing ourselves from their distress. In turning a blind eye to the legitimate call of suffering, our dishonesty obstructs our ability to learn and to grow beyond our own narcissistic self-interest, thereby also threatening the strength and vitality of the social fabric.

In contrast, efforts to establish and speak to common human truths, grounded in self-experience, offer the possibility of an ethics based on personal responsibility in relation to common principles and to the call from the other that makes a legitimate demand on us. From such a perspective, ethics requires a willingness to find our common core. Opposing such a stance, however, is the socially constructed tendency for pervasive disrespect for certain persons and groups to become embedded into the social fabric in ways that make their perspective seem illegitimate or even invisible.

How we meet one another respectfully across these divides of difference is particularly compelling in this age of increased migration and social unrest, perhaps one reason why the avoidance of *inconvenient truths* has become so massive. As people flee homelands that have become oppressive and deadly, traumatic disruption and the fact of limit affect us all. Attempts to dehumanize those who have been so traumatized that they have left everything behind in search of safety or sanctuary further ripple already muddy waters. And yet, if we truly believe in a common thread linking all of humanity, we need to be able to find the link to the human suffering that can invite even the most desperate actions (Bosley, 2019). Of particular concern are the ways that devaluation can move underground and become embedded in our social systems in insidious, often invisible ways, as we will see in the clinical examples to follow. We cannot find the story underneath the story unless we are willing to look backward and trace the development, over time, of the problem at hand and allow even painful insights to emerge.

Recognizing how insidious our presumptions can be, Lévinas (1999) reminds us that all of our knowledge structures exist within an ethical frame that requires facing ways in which our encounters *have already been structured by the society in which violence has been done*. This perspective invites us to consider how our organizational and language structures perpetuate harm, including the paradox that the very diagnoses derived to provide better care can become reified burdens that are destructive and dehumanizing. The risks are not trivial, creating an important challenge for teachers and clinicians to actively consider whose needs are being served in our interactions (Dykeman, 1993).

Klein's (1946/1975) ideas regarding splitting and projective identification remind us of the all-too-human tendency to split off good from bad and project what we cannot manage into others. It is easier to see this in others than ourselves, and yet Bion's (1961) recognition of how these primitive anxieties play out in groups helps us recognize how profoundly meanings can become skewed in group experience. Further, the focus on the individual can blind us to the cultural forces at play through which social forces become personalized in ways that can be invisible and almost impossible to overcome, as affirmations by those who agree with us further blind us to our own prejudice.

Growth can be painful. Marginalizing certain groups helps us avoid recognition of how we might be implicated in their suffering. Trauma results in gaps in the story, such that it is in those very gaps that the story is told; the place where we hide from ourselves is also the site of our power (Lacan, 1964/1977). Psychoanalysis invites the possibility of a backward glance through which we might look at the forces that oppress us, to stand tall even in our vulnerability and demand respect for our *being*, not our *doing*, because an ethical humanism requires respect for all.

Marginalization and internalized disdain know no ethnic nor colour boundaries in terms of the damage done. Considering these issues helps lighten the sense of truth that goes along with the shame of recognition, providing, perhaps, a space for meeting. In the intense hatred playing out across the globe, we can see the price of isolating oneself behind the particularity of one's own ancestral haunting, as though people were not, at essence, more alike than different. And yet, there is something about our allegiance to what Volkan (2001) calls our *chosen trauma* that can keep us further isolated and marginalized behind these arbitrary dividing lines. To move beyond such a position, there must be a way of particularizing the loss sufficiently to mourn while also bridging the gap between self and other. In the cases that follow, self-marginalization is at the core of the dilemma, but initially, this core problem is obscured by the ways in which the sequalae of the traumatic ruptures are being read.

To contextualize these cases, it is important to consider how identity develops within the context of meanings passed between parent and child that become the background melodies through which we develop our own life story. What is known and valued can be passed along directly, whereas whatever has been hidden or repressed returns to haunt us. At the core of some of these developmental dilemmas is the *enigmatic signifier* that both calls to us and subverts itself (Laplanche, 1997). Such a message, says Laplanche, both "fails and succeeds at the same time" (1995, p. 665) because the unconscious of the parent speaks to the child in ways that compromise the message. The knowledge of the adult is inaccessible to the child who cannot yet formulate meanings from that world, making the transmission "opaque to its recipient and its transmitter alike" (p. 665). The nuances of such meanings are transmitted nonverbally, remaining unconscious and yet profoundly impactful, in part because they cannot be recognized, softened, or attenuated. Such messages are carried at such a deep level that recognition and repair are impeded, including encounters with an other that might move beyond the familiar impasses towards a true reckoning with the differences that can divide but also hold hope for a better future. Although such a confrontation can be terrifying to consider, it also offers the possibility of growth.

Laplanche (1999) invites us to notice the "fundamental inversion" (p. 257), in which the person positions themselves as though their origins are formulated through otherness, through whatever is implanted into us. Although there is truth to this fundamental sense of otherness that shapes us, an overemphasis on external oppression can become a shell game, in which we experience as an external threat something inherent in our own subjectivity – our relationship with ourselves – as we see in the case of John that follows. From that perspective, psychoanalysis requires

> a going back over which dissolves, which resolves, and not a going back to the so-called ultimate formula of my being. Beyond translations and past constructions, beyond the weaving it undoes, analysis goes back along the threads of the 'other': the other thing of our unconscious, the other person who has implanted his messages, with, as horizon, the other thing in the other person, that is, the unconscious of the other, which makes those messages enigmatic.
> (Laplanche, p. 258)

Psychoanalysis invites us to look backward and begin to recognize the threads of unelaborated meanings that compel us towards actions that do not serve us. We recognize the importance of enactments through which we replay meanings that have not been sufficiently encoded into conscious awareness to learn the lessons that might inhere, to push up against the Real that has become obscured by layers of time, avoidance, and false attributions. This would seem to be the territory of the après coup, the afterwardness through which unconscious, unelaborated meanings might be recognized, deciphered, and integrated into awareness. In this regard, Laplanche's metaphor turns us back to the unconscious that is inevitably represented in our language, in our symptoms, and in the discourse and the face of the other. To the extent that we allow ourselves to be othered, we lose ourselves, and to the extent that we allow ourselves to other, we lose the social link. We cannot afford to do either without paying too high a price, as we see playing out all around us.

Nachträglichkeit: The Backward Glance

Nachträglichkeit refers to events whose meanings are deferred to a point in time that renders them meaningful, that makes possible, in Freud's words, "a different understanding of what was remembered" (1895/1950, p. 356). As we have discussed, meanings accrue over time, formulated through the experiences that shape us, coloured by sociocultural, historical context and the stories that course across the generations. Lacan (1964/1977) highlights Freud's conceptualization of psychic temporality and causality in the case of the Wolf Man, inviting us to consider the particular intersections of the Real, the Symbolic, and the Imaginary, as they can be recognized through the retrospective lens of psychoanalysis. The power of this backward glance that shapes meanings, the *après-coup*, makes it an important mechanism, a constructive process through which to locate and integrate unformulated meanings into what is consciously known (Laplanche & Pontalis, 1964).

Laplanche (1995, 1997) and Aulagnier (2001) explicate this idea by pointing to how meanings become formulated in the unconscious, beyond our ability to *know*, in a secondary process sense, what has happened. As psychoanalysis teaches us, experiences carried in the unconscious are, to some extent, discernable if we can learn their language. Beyond what is inaccessible through trauma or repression, there are layers of meaning that have their antecedents in very early experiences that register but cannot be parsed. This is the realm of relational space, in which meanings are built and negotiated. In this realm, messages that come to us from the unconscious of the other can be experienced as truth without necessarily being conscious of them, Laplanche's *enigmatic signifiers*.

Aulagnier (2001) takes Laplanche's idea further, positing a *primal* level of experience, formed in the very first moments of life, that conditions all later experience, from embodied moments of seeking warmth and nourishment infused by the affective charge of the mother's relational stance towards the child. Together, Aulagnier and Laplanche help us recognize the importance of looking for the unaspirated meanings that cannot be parsed because they register affectively without the words through which they might be contextualized. That vantage point is also important in considering some of the sequelae of small-t trauma, appreciating how putting the story together can help alleviate the impact, as the meaning of the event changes in retrospect.

In his later writings, Lacan (1975–1976/2016) stresses that meanings are always conditional, compromises between the Imaginary and the Symbolic in their confrontations with the Real. Alongside the reality of the other person as *other*, Laplanche (1997) highlights "the reality of the object through the vicissitudes of my libidinal relation to it . . . *my* subjective representation of raw reality" (p. 659). He stresses the importance of respecting the inevitable alienness of the other in relation to whatever is real. In this way, he makes space for the unconscious of each of us, such that "the adult transmits a message . . . he 'makes a sign' from his own unconscious" (p. 660). For Laplanche, beyond our theoretical or personal constructions, "The analytic situation . . . bears witness to the upheaval caused . . . by a renewed confrontation with the enigma of the other" (p. 663). From this perspective, the message from the other is always there, however we may read it. Our *ideas* about those messages may be projections, coming from our own imaginaries, but their *origins* are not in us. There is a Real we are responding to.

Much as marked in Winnicott's (1971) pivotal *use of the object*, there is a transition that occurs in the recognition of our essential separateness from one another and, thereby, the limits of what can be known about or by the other. That separateness makes possible a creative engagement with the unknown, shifting away from the tyranny of the Master discourse towards one based on an experienced knowledge that is open to further discourse (Lacan, 1975–1976/2016). Laplanche (1997) describes creativity as an opening out set in motion by the *call* from the other. He writes: "Cultural activity is an opening out on to the other, an address to the other . . . related to that opening caused *by* the other" (p. 664). If we can find our position in relation to the very *alienness* of the address by the other, he suggests, we may have a different relation to inspiration and, with it, to our own creative capacities. Such a position, reminiscent of Winnicott's arena of creative possibility, allows us to be *informed by* the other rather than *defined in relation to* a projected Other.

Moving from the constrained space of defensive negation – Klein's (1946/1975) paranoid-schizoid position – to one in which we can affirm our own subjectivity *in relation to* others enables a backward glance that can enlighten, as we move from the *subjugation* of the *symptom* to the *possibility* of the *sinthome* (Lacan, 1975–1976/2016).

Intergenerational Transmission of Trauma

Complicating the call of conscience are what Apprey calls the *toxic errands* informed by unmetabolized intergenerational trauma. For Apprey, we are both destabilized and held in place by a call that precedes us, a claim we receive and endure as *already given*. Further destabilization must occur in order to *"overturn preexisting possibilities* so that we can *reconfigure the world anew"* (Apprey, p. 155). The timelessness inherent in trauma, and in unconscious processes more generally, affords the possibility of creating new possibilities by reconfiguring the world.

> By not being inscribed in time, the subject of the evential can exercise a structural delay, thereby making it accessible from its own posteriority from an-archaic welling up from nothing, whereas in Green (2004), the timelessness . . . reshapes what the event . . . means.
>
> (Apprey, p. 86)

We can recognize a new slant on ideas of *Nachträglichkeit,* through which meanings might be reconfigured in ways that liberate us from a traumatic dispossession so that the person might return to themselves: "after a structural delay, we have *a motivated and turbulent pluperfect errand*' that works itself through in a *"future anterior"* (p. 157). "I am pre-dated in ways where *I cannot take over my past. Now, active and passive alternate. Henceforth, I am stuck with a pluperfect sense of always coming after"* (p. 158).

Apprey prefers Lacan's translation of *Nachträglichkeit* as après coup because it "refers to *the circularity of deferrals* in the enactment" (p. 68). Apprey's *"spiral causality"* (p. 69), phenomenologically, marks the toxic errand that might, if it can be sufficiently recognized and metabolized, be transformed in psychoanalysis, "as we *dramatize and transform the events of history into a represented sense of history"* (pp. 69–70). For Apprey, the return to the past suggests a circularity that does not move in a circle but rather, in learning more about how that place – the past and our history and relationships to it – is constituted, we "know the place for the first time and in a newly configured way" (p. 159), affording a way out of the repetition. In psychoanalytic therapy, the person, in being witnessed within this history, is afforded a means for recognizing their place in the story and coming to a different understanding from a new perspective, which may take the form of Bachelard's (1971) epiphanic moment that arises in a *phoenix-flash*, from the ashes.

Apprey reminds us that we are all, to some extent, held captive by aspects of our history that hold us in their thrall, haunting us to the extent that we cannot receive the intergenerational messages that remain to be deciphered. "Historical grievances that are sedimented are embedded in contemporary politics as though an archive exists to conceal both past and present unconscious mental content" (p. 161). Unrecognized, these grievances become activated in ways that can preclude the type of reflective space required to move beyond the binaries through which the traumatic past is experienced, to transform our entrenchment into a sense of history that might move forward towards transformation.

Case Illustration

Embracing one's own particularity in relation to others allows a backward glance that can repair rather than retraumatize. Psychoanalysis, much like art, offers the possibility of seeing anew, as we reconfigure events in relation to what Bion (1977) terms the *selected fact* that organizes the whole. This terrain seems similar to Lacan's considerations of the quilting point that both hides and reveals the master signifier that organizes and obscures meanings. "Everything radiates out from and is organized around this signifier. . . . It's the point of convergence that enables everything that happens in this discourse to be situated retroactively and prospectively" (1975–1976/2016, p. 268). In clinical work, we are in search of the meanings that bind the person's narrative in ways that foreclose growth. Loosening those bonds so the person might find their own way through the tangle is the art in the work.

To enter this territory together, let's begin with a brief vignette from the case of a woman whose trauma occurred later in life, who had been afforded sufficient grounding in her early years to regain her bearings and achieve insight into troubles that were only revealed in retrospect. What could not be seen was further obscured by encounters with a mental health system that believed it could know answers without inquiring into the particulars of her being. Psychoanalysis is at its best when it moves aside from the master discourse, where all might be known, and also the university discourse, where scientific 'evidence' supersedes what one might know for oneself (Zwart, 2022). Finding the threads that inform the problems, as they present themselves, is the real work of psychoanalysis.

This woman, I will call her Cassandra, came to treatment frightened by a two-year descent into a suicidal depression so compelling that, in spite of her devotion to her family, she tried to kill herself three times. Having finally found, through medications, some relief from the darkness that enveloped her, she is terrified of having it return. In the brief time of our work together, I think Cassandra found sufficient containment to find *herself within* the traumatic narrative rather than merely being lost in it.

At one point, she tells me she has been listening to podcasts by Tara Brach. A particular line remains with her, "Through the wound is the place where the light enters," which Brach links to a quote from Leonard Cohen, which Cassandra misquotes as "In the broken pieces, light shines through." "I like that", she says.

I recognize this line as coming from the song "Anthem", a reminder of how memory shapes experience and also how that experience can be reconfigured by new insights.

The next day, she says, "Throughout my time here, I really feel my self-love is back. I feel it strongly. I'm more thinking about me. How being alive is a miracle, and spending the rest of my life in a meaningful way, and the quote I made you: 'That's how the light gets in'."

An Aside

Along with the hardships, COVID brought with it an insurgence of study groups. One that has persisted has been a Lacan group. Struggling together through *The Four Fundamentals,* we were rewarded, at times, by shining lights of illumination. One night, we went back to Lacan's (1964/1977) diagram of how we bend backwards towards ourselves, our fear preventing an actual encounter. He is talking about perversion, about a satisfaction achieved through a somewhat autistic use of the other that denies them any real presence, so that we encounter only the shadows of others. In Lacan's (1975–1976/2016) later language, we are each a *sinthome*, a system of meanings drawn from our own particular nexus in the contexts that shape us. Our being, as it evolves, *shows* us. We are revealed through the living of our lives.

As Kafka (1971) puts it in "The Penal Colony", the prisoner does not know his crimes but will learn them from his body, will decipher them from his wounds. In psychoanalysis, meaning reveals itself in retrospect, and the symptom marks the meaning in coded form. To read the meaning, we must come to know the person. We can recognize the presence – or absence – of meaning, but it is up to each person to fully grasp their own.

Lacan (1959–1960/1992) suggests that ideas about progressive development may obscure what is really at stake. Even imagining the development that might take place through psychoanalysis, does that come as a transition from the Imaginary to the Symbolic? Would that be a cure, in Lacan's terms? A colleague says that, for Lacan, the cure "comes as a bonus". I think of Bion's O, that we can touch it but can never stay there, the psychoanalytic notion of becoming that does not offer a resting place. I think of another line from Leonard Cohen, something about "comes as a refugee" that I think relates to love. Checking back, I find that this, too, comes from the song "Anthem": "Every heart, to love will come, but like a refugee". There is something in this that seems right to me.

I think of Cassandra, a foreigner in this land, who I think was mistreated *because* she was a refugee, and now, I encounter her as a refugee from our health care system that saw her as so hopeless and dangerous that their only offer of "cure" was to shock her brain for a year even though no benefit was derived. The fact that she came to me with any hope left was, indeed, both a miracle and a tribute to her capacity for love that affords her some faith in a humanity that has in so many ways failed her.

She muses on her mother but might be speaking about herself: "She had a tough life. And yet she's so strong, objective, loving – it's amazing."

Leonard Cohen comes back to me, echoing this issue of ways in which the light does seep in, enabling a different vantage point on what had been remembered.

My patient thinks lovingly of these cracks that allow the light in, which brings to my mind Kintsugi, which means "golden joinery," coming from the art of repairing broken pottery with lacquer and gold, suggesting that even something damaged may still be valuable and have meaning.

Going back to Lacan, there is the idea that we avoid recognizing our damage, our lack, which is also our particularity. If we can accept it, we might find a way to live in the world *as ourselves*. But we tend to stumble over the fact of limit, either looking for a way past it or to avoid being faced with it. The former is the neurotic solution, the latter the perverse. Lacan (1964/1977) locates the unconscious as a structural process – like a language, particular in its manifestations but universal in its rules. Like the prions, the organizations that replicate themselves, the body creates a template that organizes us, and *then* we create a story about it. From this perspective, psychoanalysis is a process whereby the story is deconstructed sufficiently that the light might show through the cracks, as we learn to accept the Real as we encounter it and move from symptom to sinthome.

People are often *most* distressed about the *cracks*, hoping to more effectively seal them up rather than being interested in what they expose. Shifting from shoring to opening up can be a painful process. Working with a man in middle age who blew up his life in a manic frenzy, I counter John's questions about what disaster we should be focusing on to wonder about the thread linking them. What preceded them, what was driving him so hard that left him unavailable to more effectively engage with problems as they arose? I told him that often, what we are running away from is something that we believe about ourselves. His focus on how others see him suggests that he cannot bear how he sees himself. John begins to recognize that underneath each separate disaster, we can find the child whose family broke apart and whose father left. More importantly, the father was never truly available, and his death killed John's dream of repairing his image of himself in his father's eyes.

Nachträglichkeit. The backward glance. John is beginning to find the story underneath the story. "My analyst told me that I had a rescue fantasy. But you have a different logic", he says. John is able to think about his own story in a different way because of *his* logic rather than applying his analyst's secondary-process formulation to his life. As he finds himself reflecting on his life in a new way, he finds *himself*. No longer so profoundly depressed at having lost his life but rather *in the depressive position*, he can imagine finding a way of truly living. That path, however, is predicated on reckoning with the profound shame at the core of his manic defenses, ways in which turning his own blind eye on his needs for love, affection, and nurturance have left him running in circles, tightening the knots of his own despair.

Psychoanalysis provides the opportunity for the backward glance that might disrupt the story as it has been told and leave room for insight, a real-ization of what has been left out. This is the process pointed to by Winnicott (1964) in his fear of breakdown paper and by Lacan (1964/1977) in his diagrams of the reversion around the point of exigency back towards the reassurance achieved precisely because of what continues to be excluded from the story. Laplanche (1997), then, in the enigmatic message that can only be recognized in retrospect, illuminates how unintegrated aspects of experience drive development.

Highlighting the subversive element in Freud's views of Nachträglichkeit, Faimberg (2007) shifts our views of meaning-making from the linear to one that is more respectful of the creative potential. She stresses the constructive aspect of Nachträglichkeit that occurs as meanings shift and are re-interpreted through the analytic process. In this regard, she sees Winnicott's (1964) ideas of *the fear of the breakdown that has already happened* as "paradigmatic of the broader concept of Nachträglichkeit" (Faimberg, 2007, p. 1222), the opening out that can occur when we open our eyes to what we fear to see and what might lie beyond the familiar view.

This is the territory I found myself in with Cassandra, recreating a story from the shards left when her self-construction collapsed. Our challenge was to reconstruct her life story in ways that did not do further violence to her feelings of vulnerability *or* to the truth of her experience. To enter this territory, we needed to respect the truths of her embodied experiences and move beyond even primary process, to Aulagnier's (2001) realm of the primal.

Psychoanalysts have positioned the body at the core of meaning (Bion, 1990; Ferrari, 2004), mental functions emerging from sensory and emotional experience (Carignani, 2012), but we are often disrespectful of this essential underbelly. Being aware of ways in which meanings are constructed invisibly helps us invite the other person to make meaning from whatever it is possible to know as they look inward and backward, through their own lens, from another angle. What psychoanalysis teaches us, at best, is to trust in our own internal experience sufficiently to help others attend respectfully to theirs, to learn to read their *own* signals and symptoms in ways that afford sufficient ground to more fully inhabit their own being and recognize, retrospectively, from this current moment, who they are, who they have been, and what they might become.

In these efforts, as Freud found, our essence can always be found in our dreams. Says Aulagnier, "If I can perceive the intelligibility of the image of a dream, a fantasy, a daydream, even if it is to criticize it for being senseless, it is because I may discover in it the work of a reason that, while not its own, nevertheless obeys a certain logic" (2001, p. 62). Recognition of our own particular logic brings us to the realm of what Lacan (1955–1956/1988) calls the master signifier, the meaning both integral and elusive to unraveling the knots in which we become mired.

In living our lives, we retell the story as best we can, and the ethics of psychoanalysis demand that the analyst recognize their own investments in the process sufficiently to stand back and allow each person to do the work that only they can do. From such a respectful position, psychoanalysis affords a backward glance, through which we can recognize the knots and untangle them, discovering, from a place of insight, the places that had been too painful or too enigmatic to make sense of, Bachelard's (1971) phoenix-moment. These epiphanic instants are experienced in vertical time, through which the threads of meaning and being are revealed in ways that mark an aesthetic of morality linked to our authentic relation to that inner sense of truth. Such moments of revelation are the prize of psychoanalysis, as we discover our *own* language as both familiar and remarkable and, through this, discover more profoundly the source and wellspring of our life.

References

Andrejevic, M. (2010). Thin-sliced thoughts and theory's ends. *Media Tropes*, 2(2), 45–64.
Apprey, M. (2024). *Transgenerational haunting in psychoanalysis: Toxic errands*. London & New York: Routledge.
Aulagnier, P. (2001). *The violence of interpretation: From pictogram to statement*. East Sussex, UK: Brunner-Routledge.
Arendt, H. (2003). *Responsibility and judgment* (J. Kohn, Ed.). New York: Schocken Books.
Bachelard, G. (1971). *The right to dream* (J. A. Underwood, Trans.). New York: Orion Press.
Bion, W. R. (1961). *Experiences in groups, and other papers*. London: Tavistock Publications.
Bion, W. R. (1977). *Seven servants*. New York: Jason Aronson.
Bion, W. R. (1987). *Clinical seminars and other works* (F. Bion, Ed.). London & New York: Karnac.
Bion, W. R. (1990). *Brazilian lectures*. London & New York: Karnac.
Bosley, C. (2019). Injecting humanity: Community-focused responses for people exiting violent extremist conflict. *US Institute of Peace*. http://www.jstor.org/stable/resrep20231
Carignani, P. (2012). I. The body in psychoanalysis. *British Journal of Psychotherapy*, 28(3), 288–318.
Cassirer, E. (1957). *The philosophy of symbolic forms: Volume three: The phenomenology of knowledge*. London: Oxford University Press.
Charles, M. (2002). *Patterns: Building blocks of experience*. Hillsdale, NJ: The Analytic Press.
Charles, M. (2003). Dreamscapes: Portrayals of rectangular space in Doris Lessing's *Memoirs of a Survivor* and in dreams. *Psychoanalytic Review*, 90, 1–22.
Charles, M. (2010). When cultures collide: Myth, meaning, and configural space. *Modern Psychoanalysis*, 34, 26–47.
Dykeman, C. (1993). Encountering the face of the other: The implications of the work of Emmanuel Levinas for research in education. *Journal of Thought*, 28(3/4), 5–15.
Faimberg, H. (2007). A plea for a broader concept of Nachträglichkeit. *Psychoanalytic Quarterly*, 76, 1221–1240.
Ferrari, A. B. (2004). *From the eclipse of the body to the dawn of thought*. London, UK: Free Associations Press.
Freud, S. (1895/1950). Project for a scientific psychology. In *Standard Edition* (Vol. 1, pp. 283–343). Hogarth Press and the Institute of Psycho-Analysis.
Fricker, M. (2007). *Epistemic injustice: Power and the ethics of knowing*. Oxford: Oxford University Press.
Gibson, T. A. (2018). The post-truth double helix: Reflexivity and mistrust in local politics. *International Journal of Communication*, 12, 3167–3185.
Green, A. (2004). Thirdness and psychoanalytic concepts. *The Psychoanalytic Quarterly*, 73(1), 99–135.
Heidegger, M. (1962). *Being and time* (J. Maquarrie, & E. Robinson, Trans.). New York: Harper & Rowe.

Jusup, M., Matsuo, T., & Iwasa, Y. (2014). Barriers to cooperation aid ideological rigidity and threaten societal collapse. *PLoS Computational Biology*, 10(5), 1–8.
Kafka, F. (1971). In the penal colony. In N. N. Glatzer (Ed.), *The complete stories*. New York: Schocken Books.
Klein, M. (1946/1975). Notes on some schizoid mechanisms. In *Envy and gratitude and other works, 1946–196* (pp. 1–24). London: Hogarth Press.
Kristeva, J. (1982). *Powers of horror: An essay on abjection* (L. S. Roudiez, Trans.). New York: Columbia University Press.
LaCapra, D. (1999). Trauma, absence, loss. *Critical Inquiry*, 25, 696–727.
Lacan, J. (1955–1956/1988). *The seminar of Jacques Lacan: Book III. The psychoses* (J.-A. Miller, Ed., and S. Tomaselli, Trans.). Cambridge: Cambridge University Press.
Lacan, J. (1959–1960/1992). *The seminar of Jacques Lacan: Book VII. The ethics of psychoanalysis* (D. Porter, Trans.). Norton: New York.
Lacan, J. (1962–1963/2014). *The seminar of Jacques Lacan: Book X: Anxiety, 1962–1963* (J.-A. Miller, Ed., and A. R. Price, Trans.). Cambridge, UK: Polity Press.
Lacan, J. (1964/1977). *The four fundamental concepts of psychoanalysis* (A. Sheridan, Trans.). New York: Norton.
Lacan, J. (1975–1976/2016). *The seminar of Jacques Lacan XXIII: The sinthome* (A. R. Price, Trans.). Cambridge, UK & Malden, MA: Polity Press.
Laplanche, D. (1995). Seduction, persecution, revelation. *International Journal of Psycho-Analysis*, 76, 663–682.
Laplanche, D. (1997). The theory of seduction and the problem of the other. *International Journal of Psycho-Analysis*, 78, 653–666.
Laplanche, J. (1999). Time and the other. In L. Thurston (Trans.), *Essays on otherness* (pp. 234–259). London & New York: Routledge.
Laplanche, J., & Pontalis, J.-B. (1964). Fantasy and the origins of sexuality. *International Journal of Psychoanalysis*, 49, 1–18.
Lévinas, E. (1969/1991). *Totality and infinity: An essay on exteriority* (A. Lingis, Trans.). Dordrecht: Kluwer.
Lévinas, E. (1998). *Otherwise than being: Or beyond essence* (A. Lingus, Trans.). Pittsburgh: Duquesne University Press.
Lévinas, E. (1999). Philosophy and transcendence. In M. B. Smith (Trans.), *Alterity and transcendence* (pp. 3–38). New York: Columbia University Press.
Prefus, C., Hamid, N., Sheikh, H., Ginges, J., Tobeña, A., Davis, R., Vilarroya, O., & Atran, S. (2018). Neural and behavioral correlates of sacred values and vulnerability to violent extremism. *Frontiers in Psychology*, 9, 2462. https://doi.org/10.3389/fpsyg.2018.02462
Ricoeur, P. (1970). *Freud and philosophy: An essay on interpretation*. Chicago & London: The University of Chicago Press.
Ricoeur, P. (1984). *Time and narrative: Volume I*. Chicago & London: The University of Chicago Press.
Stauffer, J. (2015). *Ethical loneliness: The injustice of not being heard*. New York: Columbia University Press.
Stern, D. (1985). *The interpersonal world of the infant: A view from psychoanalysis and developmental psychology*. New York: Basic Books.
Thompson, M. G. (2005). The way of authenticity and the quest for personal integrity. *European Journal of Psychotherapy, Counselling and Health*, 7(3), 143–157.
Volkan, V. D. (2001). Transgenerational transmissions and chosen traumas: An aspect of large-group identity. *Group Analysis*, 34, 79–97.
Winnicott, D. W. (1964). Fear of breakdown. *International Review of Psychoanalysis*, 1, 103–107.
Winnicott, D. W. (1971). *Playing and reality*. New York: Routledge.

Žižek, S. (1989). *The sublime object of ideology*. London & New York: Verso.

Zwart, H. (2022). Lacan's dialectics of knowledge production: The four discourses as a detour to Hegel. *Foundations of Science*, 27, 1347–1370. http://doi.org/10.1007/s10699-022-09832-6

Marilyn Charles, PhD, ABPP, is a psychologist and psychoanalyst at the Austen Riggs Center; Co-Chair, Association for the Psychoanalysis of Culture and Society (APCS); and Scholar of the British Psychoanalytic Council. Affiliations include Chicago Center for Psychoanalysis; Universidad de Monterrey; Harvard Medical School. An artist, poet, writer, and mentor, her research interests include creativity, reflective function, and the intergenerational transmission of trauma. Books include: *Working with Trauma: Lessons from Bion and Lacan*; *Psychoanalysis and Literature: The Stories We Live*; *Introduction to Contemporary Psychoanalysis*; and *Echoes of Trauma: Meaning and Identity in Psychoanalysis*.

Chapter 5

The Power of Art to Shape Our Ability to See

A Phenomenological Reflection on Rembrandt's *Aristotle With a Bust of Homer*

Karen E. Bohlin

This chapter is an invitation. It is not a philosophical treatise on aesthetics, nor a formal art historical analysis. Rather, it is a phenomenological reflection, an extended engagement with a single painting that has accompanied me for three decades, a painting that continues to instruct me and, I hope, will engage you in new ways.

I first encountered *Aristotle with a Bust of Homer* (1653) when a dear friend and mentor, Steve Tigner, gifted me a reproduction of it. Since then, I have carried this painting with me – from my office at Boston University, where I trained teachers and school leaders, to my office as Head of School at Montrose, where it became a touchstone piece in my new faculty induction. Now it hangs above my desk at the Practical Wisdom Project in Cambridge, still prompting reflection and offering me insights. This chapter is dedicated to Steve, who passed away on October 8, 2024, and whose introduction of this painting in his legendary course at Boston University, Cultural Foundations for Educators, continues to shape my own aesthetic and moral imagination.

I approach this painting as an educator, drawing from years of engaging with it in dialogue with students, faculty, and community members in Boston, Phoenix, Miami, Los Angeles, San Francisco, Dublin, Amsterdam, Rome, Toronto, and Bratislava. My aim is not to present a fixed interpretation but to guide you through an aesthetic experience, one that mirrors the kind of shared inquiry and community engagement with art I have facilitated in classrooms, workshops, and public lectures.

Learning to See

In his essay "Learning How to See Again," Josef Pieper laments that "man's ability to see is in decline," referring not to physical sight but to "the spiritual capacity to perceive the visible reality as it truly is" (Pieper, 1988/1990, p. 31). This decline, he suggests, stems from modern life's restlessness and overstimulation, which hinder genuine perception. Pieper advocates for a contemplative approach to art, urging us to engage deeply and attentively with what we observe. In a world that favors speed and superficial consumption, even of art, we need to be intentional if we want to learn to see again. Art educator Shari Tishman (2018) promotes "slow looking," a practice that encourages careful and prolonged observation, so we learn to notice the nuances and details that we might otherwise miss. Tishman formalizes slow looking as an approach to learning through sustained visual attention, reinforcing the idea that perception itself is an evolving process. This practice has roots in earlier museum education research, including Philip Yenawine and Abigail Housen's work on Visual Thinking Strategies (VTS), which emphasizes the role of careful observation and interpretive dialogue in meaning-making (Yenawine, 2013; Hailey et al., 2015). The slow art movement, which encourages prolonged engagement with a single work of art rather than hurriedly moving from one piece to the next (Tishman, 2018), and museum education initiatives, such as the National Gallery's Take One Picture program, reinforce the idea that sustained engagement fosters deep learning and greater aesthetic appreciation (National Gallery, n.d.).

Can art teach us to see and help us to perceive more deeply? In this chapter, we will use Rembrandt's *Aristotle with a Bust of Homer* as a case study to explore this question. I will be your Virgil, walking alongside you, not to prescribe an interpretation but to help you practice seeing.

The Schooling of Desire

In many respects, the beauty of art both captures our attention and directs our aim, and in doing so, engages our desires, our desires to know and understand what is happening, to be delighted and to be stirred emotionally. The idea that our desires are directed by aim has deep philosophical roots. Socrates in the *Republic* (trans. Grube) compares the capacity to learn to the eye's capacity to see and tells us that education is not about implanting sight into blind eyes but rather redirecting the learner's gaze toward what is worth seeing (Plato, 1992). Socrates argues that our desires are awakened by something external – an image, an experience, an encounter with beauty. Whether we are drawn to something on a screen or stand in awe of a sunset, what captures our attention shapes what we pursue. Thus, I argue that aesthetic experience directs our aim and schools our desires. As we stand before a painting, for example, we are confronted with choices, not only the artist's choices in composition, light, and subject, which direct our gaze, but also our own: What am I drawn to and why? How does this work of art reveal to me what I desire?

In my teaching and writing, I have explored how novels and poetry have the potential to prompt ethical reflection and inquiry, as they provide a window to the "schooling of desire" in the characters and speakers that animate them (Bohlin, 2005, 2023). Visual art functions similarly. A great painting does not merely illustrate an idea; it holds our gaze, stirs our emotions, and invites us to linger, unsettling us with new questions. A painting can also reveal, for example, the universal human experience of conflicting desires, how desires might be held in tension, or, without being didactic, even suggest the possibility of their reconciliation.

Aristotle with a Bust of Homer directs our aim, bringing salience to the nature of our desires as human beings and the tensions between conflicting desires, desires for power, fame, and enduring legacy. It does not merely highlight that these desires exist; it illuminates why reckoning with them is a powerful and fundamentally human endeavor. It is a reckoning we are all called to and one that, if undertaken thoughtfully, is deeply salutary. Throughout this chapter, we will come to see how Rembrandt's *Aristotle with a Bust of Homer* invites us to confront our own competing desires and aspirations and, in doing so, evoke a *catharsis* by which we can process the complex emotions that often accompany the conflicting desires within us (Aristotle, 2020, p. 23).

In this way, *Aristotle with a Bust of Homer* urges us to reflect on our humanity. Both the details of the painting as a whole provoke an encounter, prompting us to reflect not only on the subjects' desires but also the artist's and our own.

A Phenomenological Approach to Art

Philosophers and educators have long recognized the importance of art in human flourishing and its potential to shape our moral development (Bohlin, 2005, 2023; D'Olimpio, 2022; Schinkel et al., 2023). Art provides salience, drawing into vivid relief what is important: the beauty that arrests our attention, evokes catharsis, and literally directs our aim. Rembrandt does this masterfully in *Aristotle with a Bust of Homer* with light, fluid lines, and the curiously clad figure in the center of the composition. This is precisely what makes this painting a wonderful catalyst for moral and existential inquiry. It engages our whole person, stirring our emotions, inviting us to attend to the details, while simultaneously making us wonder about the big picture: What is really going on here and why?

Taking a phenomenological approach to art trains us to direct our gaze toward what the artist illuminates and leaves in the shadows. It hones our powers of perception, sharpens our attention, and increases our "ability to see." And because the experience of great art is never exhausted in a single encounter, it compels us to return. For a book-length phenomenological reflection on a work of art, see Henri Nouwen's (1992) *The Return of the Prodigal Son: A Story of Homecoming*. In his meditation on Rembrandt's masterpiece, which hangs in the State Hermitage Museum in St. Petersburg, Nouwen weaves together a deeply personal account of his encounter with the painting, reflections on Rembrandt's life, and an exploration of the themes in Luke's parable. The result is a narrative that exemplifies how an aesthetic experience can be spiritually and morally transformative.

Why does *Aristotle with a Bust of Homer* stay with me, even after I step away from it? Why has it continued to speak to me for three decades? Let's turn to the painting.

What Do First Impressions Reveal?

To make the most of this experience, call up Rembrandt's *Aristotle with a Bust of Homer* from the Metropolitan Museum of Art (The Met) in New York and keep it as a companion alongside this text. Once you have the Met's high-resolution image in front of you, set a timer for thirty seconds and simply sit with the painting. Do not read the description or any other interpretation. Just look at the painting itself. After thirty seconds, ask yourself: How does it make you feel? Why? What do you see? What are you wondering right now? Jot down your responses.

When I teach this painting, I begin by asking my audience these very same questions. In fact, do not even reveal the title of the painting until we have sufficiently wondered about the figures and the clues that Rembrandt gives us to understand who they might be. Allow me to share some first impressions of others:

"I feel peace."
"There's a sadness – he looks weary."
"Calm."
"Melancholy."
"Yearning."
"He looks contemplative, but also sad, like he's looking down at the bust of the man."
"Indebtedness."
"It feels like a conversation. Like he's about to say something or has just spoken."
"His expression is hard to pin down. He's thinking about something, but what?"

These first impressions are essential. Art arrests our attention by evoking a feeling, an aesthetic experience that awakens our moral imagination and curiosity. In what follows, we will practice being phenomenologically present, attending to the painting as a whole and then to its parts through three modes of inquiry:

1. Engaging Our Senses. What do you see? How does it make you feel? What details evoke that feeling for you?
2. Awakening the Moral Imagination. Who are these figures? Why has Rembrandt arranged them in this way? What story does this painting tell?
3. Arousing Curiosity. What does the painting make you wonder about? What details are most curious to you and why?

Now, let's return to the painting. The scene is dark – muted, almost austere. A central figure stands in a dimly lit space. He wears a large-brimmed black hat that casts a shadow over his brow, and he dons a heavy black tunic, fastened at each shoulder with pewter-like military clasps. Our eye is drawn to the billowing sleeves of the ivory gown that emerges from underneath his tunic. The flowing sleeves embroidered with gold thread and delicate beads frame the composition, adding grandeur and even flamboyance to this mysterious character.

Light falls upon the central figure's face, hands, and sleeves. His right hand rests on the bust of a classical figure, Greek or Roman, whose raised brow is expressive, almost animated. The room is simple, and the walls recede into darkness, creating an almost monastic stillness.

The central figure wears an honorific chain draped across his black tunic. It stretches from his right shoulder to his left hand, which rests comfortably on his left hip and holds the chain between two fingers. A simple table sits in the foreground on the left. In the shadows behind it, we see what appears to be a small hand mirror, face down, and barely visible in the background a stack of books, peeking out from behind a painter's cloth draped on the wall. The light, streaming from an unseen window or another source on the left, moves across the scene, illuminating and obscuring in equal measure.

This striking figure and bust are curiously staged. A mysterious bearded man, clad in black with grandiose bright sleeves, is adorned with a golden chain, and he wears a pensive gaze. The bust, frozen in time, is seemingly engaged. A silent room, yet full of questions. Who are these figures? What brings them together? And, more importantly – what is really happening here?

Who Are These Figures, and How Do We Know?

When I present this painting to audiences, their guesses reveal much about how aesthetic engagement shapes perception. And how that aesthetic experience becomes a catalyst of moral inquiry. Some immediately recognize the bust as a classical figure, noting the laurel crown and the deeply expressive, furrowed brow. "It must be a philosopher." The central figure is more enigmatic. "He looks like a wealthy merchant," someone ventures. Others note his posture, as proud yet contemplative, admiring the bust while holding a melancholy expression. "His gaze is solemn."

The title of the painting, *Aristotle with a Bust of Homer*, certainly holds the names of the key figures curators have agreed upon, but there is another presence in this scene. Can you find it? Return to the painting. Trace the chain Aristotle wears to its dip and notice the medallion that hangs there half hidden by his voluminous sleeve. If you look closely, you will notice a small, barely perceptible helmeted head. "That looks like a soldier," someone exclaims when I introduce this painting. And there is good reason to believe that this soldier is Alexander the Great.

How do we know these figures are Aristotle, Homer, and Alexander? Two pieces of evidence confirm their identities. First, there is artistic precedence. We know of an earlier Flemish rendering of the philosopher, entitled *Aristotle* (1476, Musée du Louvre) by Joos van Wassenhove, depicting him as an older, bearded man in contemporary Dutch dress. We also know Homer is traditionally depicted as a blind poet crowned with laurels. Second, the patron, Antonio Ruffo of Sicily, who "originally purchased (and possibly commissioned)" *Aristotle with a Bust of Homer*, later purchased two more paintings from Rembrandt (Beranek, 2022). The other two were *The Man in Armor* (1661, now lost), believed to be Alexander the Great, and *Homer Dictating His Verses* (1663, now housed in the Mauritshuis, The Hague). We also know that Rembrandt chose the thematic composition and explicitly requested that all three be hung together (*Encyclopedia of Art Education*, n.d.).

Ruffo's correspondence reveals that he only fully understood the subject of *Aristotle with a Bust of Homer* after seeing the other works, underscoring Rembrandt's deliberate choice of themes and their pairing (Seidenstein, 2016).

The Legacy of Influence: Aristotle, Alexander, and Homer

Rembrandt was classically educated. Bright and well tutored, he would have been well acquainted with these three giants of the Western intellectual tradition and their contributions. He entered university at the age of 14 and withdrew within a year to study art under masters, one of the most famous being Peter Lastman, and by the age of 23, he had already established himself as an independent master (Benezit Dictionary of Artists, 2011; van de Wetering, 2025). Rembrandt would have known that Aristotle, the great philosopher, tutored Alexander the Great from age 13 into young adulthood ("Timeline: 4th Century BCE", 2012). He would have also known that Alexander's education was not confined to philosophy and natural science. Aristotle introduced him to Homer, and historical accounts reveal that Alexander drew inspiration from Homer's *Iliad* for military strategy and courage in leadership, and it is believed he carried annotated scrolls of the text with him into battle and slept with them under his pillow ("Timeline: 4th Century BCE", 2012; Plutarch, 1919).

And this makes sense as Alexander's military prowess remains unparalleled. Historians regard him as one of the greatest commanders of all time, remembered for his ability to inspire his men, lead attacks in person, and endure the same hardships as his soldiers.

The influence of Homer on Aristotle and Alexander is documented not only in history. For a fulsome account of Homer's educational influence on Aristotle and Alexander – after all, those scrolls Alexander carried with him are said to have been annotated with notes from his tutor Aristotle – I highly recommend Steve Tigner's article, "Homer: Teacher of Teachers" (Tigner, 1993). Rembrandt captures more than three historical figures in this painting and his companion paintings. Tigner provides an intellectual and pedagogical lineage, a continuum of wisdom, heroism, and art, which would have been familiar to Rembrandt.

The Painting as an Inquiry: How Does Rembrandt Direct Our Aim?

Let's look at the choices Rembrandt makes in the way he juxtaposes these three figures. Aristotle's hand rests on the bust of Homer. He wears the medallion with the face of his most famous pupil, the conqueror of the known world. We cannot help but wonder: Why is Aristotle the only living figure here? What do his gestures and expression suggest?

These questions and others will guide our sustained phenomenological engagement with the painting. Let's look at how Rembrandt directs our gaze. The light draws our attention to three focal points: Aristotle's elaborate dress, his hands, and the expressions of both Aristotle and Homer. Return to the high-resolution image of the painting from the Met and take each of these focal points one at a time. Now, take a moment to zoom in on the details of dress first: What stands out for you? What draws your attention? Jot down your impressions before reading further.

Attire: Anachronistic and Enigmatic

Aristotle's sleeves trimmed in gold threads and beads frame his figure and evoke wealth and status, even flamboyance. His heavy black tunic bears down like a weighted garment restraining his voluminous gown and is fastened with Viking-like clasps at the shoulders. The chain bearing the image of Alexander the Great glistens strikingly across the tunic, bestowing a regal gravitas. On the one hand, we see in Aristotle what appears to be a celebrated figure wearing flowing sleeves and donning a wide-brimmed hat. On the other hand, we find a somber figure clad in a disciplined dark tunic of restraint.

Rembrandt was a collector of costumes and artifacts, and he often dressed and accessorized his subjects idiosyncratically (National Gallery of Art, 2007, p. 114). Here, he has chosen to depict Aristotle, who would have worn a simple Greek himation, in what appears to be aristocratic and even showy attire. Aristotle's dress is neither historically accurate nor contemporary to Rembrandt's own. Why does he dress the philosopher this way?

A further curiosity: Aristotle wears a pinky ring on his left hand, a subtle yet deliberate detail, the gold ring is positioned precariously at the tip of his pinky, as if about to slip off. Why?

Pliny the Elder documents that it was the fashion for men to wear rings on the third joint in ancient Greece and Rome (Hawley, 2007, p. 103). Moreover, when a man wore a simple ring without a signet, it implied greater wealth, suggesting that its owner had a private treasure locked away with a far more precious ring (Pliny, 1938). So, what might this pinky ring tell us about Aristotle as Rembrandt portrays him here?

This seemingly insignificant detail invites us to wonder. Rembrandt, who was classically educated, would have known exactly what a pinky ring like this would symbolize to the Greeks – a signal of fortune, a secret kept. He would also have known that Aristotle would have dressed in a traditional himation, not in these billowing, showy sleeves. Is Rembrandt playing with us just to ignite our curiosity? Is he inviting us to look beyond appearances, to imagine the hidden treasure this ring implies? Does Aristotle's grand attire suggest that Rembrandt wants us to question our traditional understanding of the great philosopher, or is he bestowing him with honor?

Hands: A Study in Contrast

Now I invite you to zoom in on Aristotle's hands. His right hand rests gently, almost reverently, on the bust of Homer, while the left hand at his hip holds the honorific chain in place between his index and pointer fingers. Rembrandt catches our attention with the pinky ring, and when he has it, we zoom in and notice that the left hand wearing it is raw and almost arthritic. The fingers are larger than the right hand, and the nails are noticeably blackened, perhaps with dye. A stark contrast to the fairer, less worn hand resting on Homer. The left hand appears to belong to a different person altogether; it is neither the hand of an aristocrat nor a philosopher but rather the hand of an aged artist.

Aristotle's hands tell two stories, one of an aristocratic philosopher and one of an artisan. His seemingly more youthful right hand reaches for the poet. His left hand lingers on the chain that holds an emblem of pride and legacy. And on this larger rough hand, we find the gold pinky ring. This little ring, almost hidden in plain sight, carries weight. Does it speak to Aristotle's inner world, to the wisdom and wealth that are not immediately visible? In this subtle detail, Rembrandt not only signals that there is more to Aristotle in his depiction than we might suspect based on our conventional understanding of the philosopher. He also leaves us wondering about the irony of the elderly hand that wears the ring and what it might signal about treasures unseen or what it might signal about the desires and aspirations that shape him and perhaps shape us.

The Countenances: What Do They Express?

Take a moment to study the faces. The light falls deliberately on the countenances of Aristotle and Homer, and we are invited to attend carefully to their expressions. We see in Aristotle a man mature in years, deep in contemplation. His dark, enigmatic eyes invite speculation. They are full, reflective, and searching. Some see sorrow; others see deep thought or preoccupation. His brow raised and forehead furrowed, his expression is pensive yet active, as if he has just realized something.

What is he gazing at? Aristotle's solemn and introspective eyes do not meet Homer's. Instead, they gaze beyond him. Homer's sculpted face, although frozen, also remains expressive. His raised brow and open mouth suggest movement, as if mid-speech. Though merely a bust, he appears almost animate, as if caught in a moment of recognition.

And what of Alexander the Great? His barely perceptible profile on the medallion is purposefully poised, almost as if Aristotle has intentionally positioned himself to present Alexander to Homer.

The question remains, what is going on here? Is Aristotle seeking wisdom from Homer? Is he offering tribute? Or is he reckoning with something else, perhaps his own place in the lineage of thinkers, poets, and rulers?

A Meditation on Fame or Wisdom?

New York's Metropolitan Museum of Art (The Met) describes *Aristotle with a Bust of Homer* as a "meditation on the meaning of fame." Their wall label offers a brief yet compelling account:

> *Among the most celebrated works of art at The Met, this painting conveys Rembrandt's meditation on the meaning of fame. The richly clad Greek philosopher*

Aristotle (384–322 BCE) rests his hand pensively on a bust of Homer, the epic poet who had attained literary immortality with his Iliad *and* Odyssey *centuries before. Aristotle wears a gold medallion with a portrait of his powerful pupil, Alexander the Great – perhaps the philosopher is weighing his own worldly success against Homer's timeless achievement.*

In this painting, Rembrandt presents Aristotle as the living bridge between two monumental legacies – Homer's enduring poetry and Alexander's military triumphs. The three figures are inseparably linked by inspiration, teaching, and history. If this is a meditation on fame, does Rembrandt suggest whose legacy is most privileged?

An Iconic Account: Three Types of Wisdom

A second, equally compelling interpretation comes from Steve Tigner (1999), who provides an iconic account of this painting as representative of the three types of wisdom described in Book Six of Aristotle's *Nicomachean Ethics*. Tigner believed that Rembrandt intended to reflect these wisdoms, what Aristotle describes as three aims of knowing. Aristotle, the great philosopher and natural scientist, embodies *sophia* (philosophic wisdom) aimed at understanding. Homer, as the poet and artist, embodies *techne* (creative wisdom) aimed at making. Alexander, as the military strategist and ruler, embodies *phronesis* (practical wisdom), aimed at taking wise practical action in the right moment. According to Tigner, "Aristotle, Alexander, and Homer are western antiquity's greatest example of excellence in each of these three areas." He argued that Rembrandt artfully arranged these figures to represent this triad of wisdoms, even signing his name at the base of Homer's bust, firmly identifying himself within this lineage of intellectual and creative pursuit (Tigner, 1999, p. 15). This iconic account is both fitting and profound, and Rembrandt, deeply familiar with the intellectual traditions that animate them, would have understood the weight of these figures and appreciated their embodied wisdom, whether he was deliberate about this or not. According to Aristotle, all three wisdoms or aims of knowing – understanding, taking practical wise action, and creation – require excellent activity or virtue, the highest of which is contemplation, evidenced in Aristotle. Yet, Rembrandt discreetly inserts his signature on the bust of Homer. Is he aligning himself with the artist or inviting us to debate which type of wisdom is the highest?

My goal is not to refute these two accounts but to extend them, to see beyond what is initially offered. In the sections that follow, I invite you to linger with the painting, to zoom out and be present to what you see and experience before *Aristotle with a Bust of Homer*. Is this painting a meditation on fame or an iconic account of wisdom? Is it an exploration of how our aims ultimately shape our desires and our wisdom? Rembrandt does not provide answers, but he invites us to continue being present to the scene and wondering. This phenomenological engagement ignites our aesthetic experience and prompts further inquiry.

When we stand before *Aristotle with a Bust of Homer*, we do not simply process an argument or decode a set of symbols. Homer, Aristotle, and Alexander the Great are not merely historical figures or iconic representations of different kinds of wisdom; they are present to us and to each other, connected by light, by touch, by gesture. Rembrandt does not merely juxtapose these figures; he binds them together in a shared legacy of wisdom, influence, and human endeavor. Rembrandt invites us to understand wisdom, then, not as an abstract idea but as something embodied, cultivated within relationships, and actively worked out in life. How does he do that?

Zooming Out: Arcs, Lines, and Fluid Motion

As we sit with this painting, whether in person or through a digital window, let's zoom out again to take in the whole. Notice the arcs and fluid lines Rembrandt masterfully uses to create sweeping motion: the flowing sleeves, the gentle dip of the chain, the incline of the heads that create a dynamic relationship among the three figures. This is not a static composition; it is alive with movement.

Rembrandt directs our gaze, inviting us to trace these arcs from Aristotle's hand on Homer's head, along the flowing right sleeve, up to Aristotle's countenance, down the chain to the medallion of Alexander and then across the chain to Aristotle's prominent left hand. The fluid movement draws our eye along a path that continuously ties these three figures together. Even the gentle tautness of Aristotle's sweeping chain suggests movement – almost as if he is bringing Alexander back to Homer, acknowledging the epic verse and wisdom that inspired both teacher and student.

The Light Invites Us to Linger

The more I spend time with this painting, the more I see this light as a fourth presence that transcends the historical connections among Homer, Aristotle, and Alexander and invites us to linger on the role of relationships in the pursuit of wisdom. Rembrandt's use of chiaroscuro is both precise and purposeful. The light, coming from an unseen source to the left, falls deliberately on Aristotle's face, his right hand resting on Homer's bust, and his left hand holding the honorific chain with the medallion of Alexander the Great, partially obscured by the folds of his sleeve. This is not merely a technical artistic feat; the light acts as a guide, drawing our attention to key relationships while leaving other areas in shadow.

Returning to the details of attire, hands, and expressions, we see that Rembrandt visually links the inanimate to the animate: Aristotle's living hand rests on Homer's sculpted form; the folds of his sleeve subtly frame the poet's face. These connections are not incidental. They underscore the interplay of wisdom across generations, binding poetic insight, philosophical reflection, and political ambition in visual and thematic relationship. It is precisely this interdependence that the light reveals.

Perhaps it is the arrival of the light that accounts for both Aristotle's and Homer's enigmatic expressions, serious yet vibrant, alive to something unseen. They reveal not only thought but also recognition. Rembrandt wants us to acknowledge the power of this interdependence. The figures are distinct yet linked, static yet dynamic, independent yet relational. If we create art without reflection, we produce works devoid of meaning. Their ultimate value is realized in their relationship. The medallion of Alexander, small and seemingly insignificant, without the wisdom of Homer and the guidance of Aristotle, is merely an object. Its value emerges only through the relationships that shaped it.

Rembrandt reinforces this theme beyond the canvas. He insisted that his later companion pieces *Homer Dictating His Verses* and *The Man in Armor* be hung alongside *Aristotle with a Bust of Homer*, emphasizing their thematic unity and shared legacy. The light gestures toward something ineffable, drawing us in, holding our gaze. The way Rembrandt manipulates light and shadow compels us to ask why – why these figures, why these relationships, why this dramatic moment?

Returning to Rembrandt: The Impact of Lived Experience

To fully appreciate *Aristotle with a Bust of Homer* (1653), we must also return to Rembrandt himself and the life experiences that had shaped him at the time he painted it. Classically educated and well tutored, Rembrandt left the university to study under the great art masters. He achieved extraordinary fame at a young age, setting himself up as an independent master by 23. He married Saskia van Uylenburgh, the niece of a prominent figure in the art world. Their relationship was not one of utility, though. They loved each other, and together, they enjoyed enormous success and the comforts of high-society living.

By 1653, When Rembrandt painted *Aristotle with the Bust of Homer*, Rembrandt had endured profound loss. Once celebrated as a prodigy in his twenties (1626–1634), he buried three of his children in quick succession: his first son died after one year (1635–1636), his daughter lived only two weeks (1638), and his third child, Cornelia, also died young (1640). Only his son Titus, born in 1641, survived. And in 1642, he lost his beloved wife, Saskia.

At the peak of this grief, Rembrandt painted *The Night Watch* (1642), his monumental masterpiece now housed in the Rijksmuseum in Amsterdam. Yet this masterpiece marked the decline of his public acclaim. By 1645, he had sold only three paintings. His personal life was marred by scandal when he moved in with his former servant, Hendrickje Stoffels, who became his partner. It was in this chapter of his life that Rembrandt painted *Aristotle with a Bust of Homer*.

I believe this painting reflects Rembrandt's own confrontation with loss, ambition, and the fleeting nature of fame. *Aristotle with a Bust of Homer* is not merely a meditation but an existential reckoning – a visual exploration of conflicting desires, of legacy and loss, shaped by Rembrandt's own lived experience. Rembrandt, having lost so many connections in his own life, returns to this theme, poignantly connecting the giants that shaped his intellectual and moral imagination, Homer, Aristotle and Alexander.

Perhaps Rembrandt is not asking us to measure their legacies against one another. Instead, he draws our attention to how they are bound together as part of a greater whole. The light invites us to attend to both the figure of Aristotle the philosopher and Rembrandt the artist. We see both the young artist in the grand embroidered sleeves and the seasoned, mature Rembrandt in the black disciplined tunic. We see Rembrandt in the gaze of Aristotle, looking just beyond the bust yet deeply grounded and connected to it. We see the youthful right hand drawing inspiration from Homer and the mature left hand bearing the marks of labor and of loss while paradoxically wearing a pinky ring that indicates his possession of a treasure beyond. Whether it is the students he taught, the legacy of his art, or the quiet satisfaction of giving himself fully to his work, his identity as an artist emerges.

Perhaps Rembrandt etches his signature on the base of the bust because at the end of the day, he is an artist, and his art is what he is called to create. And it is precisely the power of his art that evokes catharsis in us, that prompts our own reflection on lived experience and the meaning of our lives.

Art as a Catalyst for Moral and Existential Inquiry

This painting does not provide easy answers. Instead, it confronts us, not only with the figures it portrays but with ourselves. It compels us to grapple with the nature of wisdom, with the tensions between ambition and humility, and with the competing desires that shape our lives.

Steve Tigner provided a foundational account of this painting as an iconic representation of Aristotle's three types of wisdom from *Nicomachean Ethics* – philosophic wisdom (*sophia*) embodied in Aristotle the philosopher and scientist, practical wisdom (*phronesis*) embodied in Alexander the Great, and artistic wisdom (*techne*) embodied in Homer. This reading has served as a valuable touchstone, particularly for my work with faculty, reminding us that it is essential to cultivate all three types of wisdom when we teach.

The Metropolitan Museum of Art offers another lens, framing the painting as a meditation on the meaning of fame. The figures before us – Homer, Aristotle, and Alexander – represent three different forms of enduring greatness. Is Rembrandt asking us to consider whose legacy will last the longest? The poet, whose verses shaped civilization? The philosopher, whose ideas shaped knowledge? The conqueror, whose empire reshaped the world?

Both of these accounts provide insight. But the more time I spend with this painting, the more I see it asking something deeper, something more personally urgent. The details of the painting refuse a simple, iconic reading. The chain bearing Alexander's medallion is prominent, but Aristotle does not flaunt it. His left hand ensures it is taut just enough to be seen. His right hand rests on the head of Homer. His expression is not one of triumph but of contemplation. And the light, a fourth presence in the scene, does not simply highlight individual figures. It illuminates the connections among them.

Aristotle with a Bust of Homer does not merely depict three types of wisdom; it reveals their interdependence. The wisdom of the scientist and philosopher is incomplete without the wisdom of action. The wisdom of action is unmoored without the wisdom of artistic inspiration. The wisdom of artistic creation is limited without the pursuit of truth. If we isolate any one of these forms of knowledge from the others, it loses its power. Aristotle alone, without Homer or Alexander, becomes a solitary thinker. Alexander alone, without Homer or Aristotle, becomes a conqueror without a vision. Homer alone, without Aristotle or Alexander, becomes a voice unheard and unshared. Rembrandt is not just showing us these figures, he is showing us their relationship, their interdependence, and the vitality of their communion.

And yet our inquiry into the painting does not stop there. What is Aristotle thinking as he gazes beyond Homer's bust? Is he reflecting on his own legacy? Is he measuring his own achievements against those of Homer and Alexander? Or is he wondering about something more fundamental, something that moves beyond the tension between fame and obscurity?

Returning to Rembrandt's Gaze

To understand this painting fully, we must consider not only its subject but its creator. By the time Rembrandt painted *Aristotle with a Bust of Homer*, he was no longer the young, celebrated artist. He had lost three children and his beloved wife, Saskia. He had fallen from public favor, declared bankruptcy, and watched as his paintings and personal effects were sold at auction. Once sought after by the most prominent patrons, he was now criticized for scandal and reduced circumstances.

Yet here he was, painting Aristotle, not as a triumphant intellectual, but as a man marked by wisdom and loss. The elaborate dress evokes Rembrandt's own past, the days of youthful success and opulence. The pinky ring worn on the third joint, a subtle reference to Greek and Roman men's fashion, suggests a treasure hidden, something yet to be revealed. His hands tell their own story: the right hand, resting gently on Homer's bust, conveys gratitude and perhaps reverence. The fingers of his left hand, raw and worn, with blackened nails, hold Alexander's chain. This is the hand not of an aristocrat but of an artist who has labored and been shaped by struggle.

Rembrandt, in his later years, was no longer painting for status or acclaim. He was painting from lived experience. And in Aristotle's dark, searching eyes, I see the artist himself reflecting on his lived experience, his shifting desires, and his evolving understanding of what truly matters.

What does wisdom look like in the face of suffering? What remains when fame, wealth, and certainty are stripped away? This, I believe, is where the painting's true inquiry lies. The three types of wisdom are present, but there is also something beyond them, something the light itself seems to signify. A greater wisdom that

88 Aesthetic Ethics

Figure 5.1 Aristotle with a Bust of Homer

invites us to reconcile competing aims, to hold ambition and humility, loss and legacy, in tension and to find our peace within them.

And this is where Rembrandt leaves us, not with a conclusion but with an invitation, not just to see but to wonder. He asks us not just to contemplate these figures but to reflect on our own lives. What are we aiming at? What conflicting desires are present in our own lives? What wisdom do we need to reconcile them?

This is the power of great art. It calls us back – again and again – across time, across experience, across our own evolving understanding. Rembrandt painted *Aristotle with a Bust of Homer* not to resolve these tensions but to invite us into them. And if we are willing to stand before this painting, to return to it, to let it ask its questions of us, then we may find ourselves, like Aristotle, like Rembrandt, looking beyond what we first thought we were seeing – toward something more.

What still speaks to you in this painting?

The author would like to gratefully acknowledge Ashleigh Reen, who served as an invaluable interlocutor in this chapter's development and provided research and editorial assistance.

Works Cited

Aristotle. (2020). *Poetics* (S. H. Butcher, Trans.). Cosimo Classics.
Benezit Dictionary of Artists. (2011, October 31). *Rembrandt (real name Rembrandt Harmensz. van Rijn or Van Rynfree)*. Oxford University Press. https://doi.org/10.1093/benz/9780199773787.article.B00150778
Beranek, S. (2022). Rembrandt, Aristotle with a bust of Homer. *The Center for Public Art History*. https://smarthistory.org/rembrandt-aristotle-homer/
Bohlin, K. E. (2005). *Teaching character education through literature: Awakening the moral imagination in secondary classrooms*. Routledge.
Bohlin, K. E. (2023). Educating the heart: Why poetry matters. In L. D'Olimpio, P. Paris, & A. Peterson (Eds.), *Educating character through the arts*. Oxford University Press.
D'Olimpio, L. (2022). Aesthetica and eudaimonia: Education for flourishing must include aesthetic education. *Journal of Philosophy of Education* 56(2), 238–250. https://doi.org/10.1111/1467-9752.12661
Encyclopedia of Art Education. (n.d.). *Aristotle contemplating the bust of Homer by Rembrandt*. Retrieved March 11, 2022, from http://www.visual-arts-cork.com/famous-paintings/aristotle-contemplating-the-bust-of-homer.htm
Hailey, D., Miller, A., & Yenawine, P. (2015). Understanding visual literacy: The visual thinking strategies approach. In D. Baylen, & A. D'Alba (Eds.), *Essentials of teaching and integrating visual and media literacy*. Springer, Cham. https://doi.org/10.1007/978-3-319-05837-5_3
Hawley, R. (2007). Lords of the rings: Ring-wearing, statue, and identity in the age of pliny the elder. *Bulletin of the Institute of Classical Studies. Supplement*, 100, 103–111. http://www.jstor.org/stable/43767663
Introduction to Alexander the Great. (2011). *Pothos.org*. Retrieved September 1, 2024, from https://www.pothos.org/content/index5902.html?page=introduction-to-alexander
National Gallery. (n.d.). Take one picture. *National Gallery, London*. Accessed September 1, 2024, from https://www.nationalgallery.org.uk/take-one-picture
National Gallery of Art. (2007). *Painting in the Dutch golden age*. National Gallery of Art, Washington. https://www.nga.gov/content/dam/ngaweb/Education/learning-resources/teaching-packets/pdfs/dutch_painting.pdf
Nouwen, H. J. M. (1992). *The return of the prodigal son: A story of homecoming*. Image Books.
Pieper, J. (1988/1990). *Only the lover sings: Art and contemplation* (L. Krauth, Trans.). Ignatius Press.
Plato. (1992). *Republic* (G. M. A. Grube, Trans.). Hackett Publishing.
Pliny the Elder. (1938). *Natural history* (H. Rackham, Trans.). Harvard University Press.
Plutarch, A. (1919). *Plutarch's lives* (Vol. 7, pp. 226–227, B. Perrin, Trans.). Cambridge, MA: Harvard University Press.
Schinkel, A., Lynne W., Pedersen, J. B. W., & de Ruyter, D. J. (2023). Human flourishing, wonder, and education. *Studies in Philosophy and Education*, 42(2), 143–162. https://doi.org/10.1007/s11217-022-09851-7
Seidenstein, J. (2016). Grace, genius, and the Longinian sublime in Rembrandt's Aristotle with a Bust of Homer. *Journal of Historians of Netherlandish Art*, 8(2). https://doi.org/10.5092/jhna.2016.8.2.5
Tigner, S. S. (1993). Homer: Teacher of teachers. *Journal of Education*, 175(3), 43–64.

Tigner, S. S. (1999). *Nicomachean ethics books VI & VII: CLA/CC101Z1 + SED/CT500J6: Cultural foundations for educators I*. Teaching Handout, Boston University.

Timeline: 4th Century BCE. (2012). *Oxford reference*. Retrieved September 1, 2024, from https://www.oxfordreference.com/display/10.1093/acref/9780191735400.timeline.0001

Tishman, S. (2018). *Slow looking: The art and practice of learning through observation*. Routledge.

van de Wetering, E. (2025, February 21). *Rembrandt: Encyclopedia Britannica*. https://www.britannica.com/biography/Rembrandt-van-Rijn/Fourth-Amsterdam-period-1658-69

Yenawine, P. (2013). *Visual thinking strategies: Using art to deepen learning across school disciplines*. Harvard Education Press.

Part 2

Aesthetic Ethics as "Responsibility and Attentive Witnessing"

Chapter 6

Mourning the Dying of the Unharmed Self

Sandra Buechler

She came to treatment years after the assaults were over, but she was still haunted by dreams of her father forcing her to engage in sexual acts. But that wasn't her only nighttime intruder. She was also haunted by an image of who she, herself, might have been had the abuse not occurred. How might her life have been different? Mourning this woman who would never get a chance to live was even harder than mourning a death. There were no funeral rites, no other mourners. No way to pay respect. Like any mourning process, this grieving can't be hurried. But, unlike some, it had no discernible beginning, no clear process, no comparison points with the bearing of other losses.

The unharmed self is a vivid presence in Mary's psychic life. This parallel self has a healthy, womanly body, wears bright colors, dreams of her future, sleeps uninterrupted by terror. She embraces life and feels embraced by it. She is not afraid of being embraced. She is not repelled by sexual feelings in herself and others. She doesn't shake uncontrollably. She is not afraid of having children or of what would befall them. She is not afraid of life. She is everything Mary is not and feels entitled to the life Mary is sure she will never have.

Severe traumas sometimes leave their marks by altering or interrupting the narrative of one's life. Continuity of self-experience is lost. The tell-tale "footprint" of this process is dissociation (Bromberg, 2006). In an astonishing poem, "Pantoum for the Broken," Toi Derricotte (2021) gives us an unforgettable picture of a mind/heart/soul forever reeling in the wake of assault. The poem's form replicates the process of moving toward and away from traumatic memories. Remembering brings painful reflections in its wake. How many times did it happen? Who, or what, was I in the eyes of the assailant? Who, or what, is the assailant in my eyes? Will remembering heal or only replicate the pain? How does my body mindlessly, compulsively relive the trauma? Will it ever end? Should I try to silence it? When will I stop yearning for it never to have happened? Who might I have been?

In reading Derricotte's poem, our own minds keep driving forward and being pulled backward. Human bodies remember when minds won't or can't. Remembering while wanting to forget pulls us apart. We lose cohesion. The center cannot hold. Being broken into has some predictable consequences and some that are shaped by individual experience. When a person's body has been violently penetrated, their mind may try to resist entry, but where does that lead? If both body and mind try escaping, as from a burning building, where do they go? Mourning their lost unity can be a significant step toward recognizing the sufferer and helping her heal. But Mary couldn't even imagine a unified self. Unity of mind and body was as threatening as unity of self and unharmed self, but, perhaps, for somewhat different reasons. A unified mind and body might remember atrocities with fully sensing skin, pounding heart, unbelieving mind, shaking legs. A unified self and unharmed self might threaten the existence, the "realness" of the unharmed self, which, I came to believe, was an outcome I might desire more easily than Mary could. That fully alive imaginary twin made some nights excruciating. How was she also necessary?

Complicated Mourning: When Shame Accompanies Sorrow

My own clinical and theoretical work (Buechler, 2008) has suggested that sorrow accompanied by shame is an especially difficult combination of emotions. Ever since I began studying emotional experience, I have held that certain combinations of emotions are inherently acutely painful and debilitating. For example, shame can rob us of the very strengths that bearing sorrow requires. In effect, shame interferes with access to the compassion for ourselves that potentially leavens sorrow. Additionally, while for most people, coping with grief is facilitated by community participation in rituals, like funerals and mourning rites, as already mentioned, there are no memorials for fantasied unharmed selves. More broadly, shame impacted every aspect of my work with Mary. Put simply, Mary was ashamed of what had been done to her, of what she could not overcome, of the more and more frequent periods of depression she underwent as our work progressed and she remembered more. Like many who have been sexually abused, she felt defined by how she was treated. I was extremely worried that Mary would commit suicide and profoundly ambivalent about continuing to uncover her unbearable memories. But Mary's dreams and even her waking thoughts made retreat seem just as impossible as continuing forward. So we continued.

What, exactly, is shame, and how did it complicate Mary's treatment? Shame is a broad term, including many permutations and complex combinations with other feelings. Elsewhere (Buechler, 2008), I have suggested that shame's companions (such as anxiety, sorrow, or rage) greatly affect its impact. Just as our perception of a color changes depending on its background (Albers, 1963), shame is a different experience depending on its emotional context. One context, in particular, accompanies severe trauma most often. I have (2008) called it the "impossible/necessary."

Acute Shame and Anxiety: The "Impossible Necessary"

One understanding of shame that I think is especially suited to our most acutely traumatic experiences is the concept of shame as a sense of profound insufficiency.

In our worst moments of shame, we feel we are simply "not enough" to cope adequately with life. What is challenged is our most fundamental sense of ourselves as "going concerns." Buechler (2008, p. 57), I have described the dilemma of anxious shame as a feeling that something is absolutely necessary for survival but, at the same time, impossible to achieve. I highlighted the potent combination of annihilating shame and anxiety that can accompany trauma and remain its legacy for the rest of the survivor's life. Freud (1926/1959) understood trauma as a reaction when the ego is overwhelmed, but he emphasized only the element of anxiety in the emotional experience of the sufferer. However, I believe it is the combination of profound shame and overwhelming anxiety that can have the most deleterious effect. In my own language, after we have lived through trauma, we will always know how bad life can get. Like Winnicott's fear of breakdown (Winnicott, 1972, p. 6), the experience of extreme helplessness in shame/anxiety is etched into the survivor's consciousness.

What is the opposite of shame? And, perhaps more importantly, how can we help people achieve it in treatment? Since I focus on the combination of shame and anxiety, I would suggest confidence as a polar opposite of our worst moments of shame. In my own clinical work, I might find myself pointing out the patient's capacity to look in the mirror as they comment on what they see about themselves. Sometimes, it is a matter of shoring up the patient's sense of confidence in their interpersonal skills, as well as their self-approval, as our own compassionate voice becomes internalized. The battle for a sense of sufficiency takes place internally, so the clinician must become internalized, to a substantial degree, in order to effectively counter shaming voices. My own view is that treatment, especially with someone severely traumatized, has to go on 24/7 for the rest of their lives. A few hours a week, over however many years, is not enough. The only way for treatment to have that degree of constancy and longevity is for us to be securely internalized. Making that happen is the art of treatment. I have long thought about how we get internalized and have written about it frequently (2008, 2012, 2017, 2019). In a way, I was introduced to this idea by my first outpatient, a young man who had been severely neglected as a child and presented in treatment with absolutely no discernible affect. Without benefit of much training, experience, or knowledge of theory, I instinctively supplied words for emotions when he recounted his experiences. After two years of work, he came in one day, told me a story, and said something like "You would say I felt angry." While I still had no way to describe this theoretically, I knew it to be progress. Now, I would say that my voice had a place inside him and helped him connect lived experiences and emotions. It is many years since this treatment ended, but I can only hope that "You would say I felt angry" gradually became "I would say I felt angry."

I would like to pay tribute to a poet who has written about her father's sexual abuse of her as a child and its legacy. Lucille Clifton (1936–2010) was an award-winning poet, fiction writer, and author of books for children. She faced and outfaced enormous personal and professional obstacles. Self-taught, up against society's racial prejudices, Clifton raised six children, taught at Columbia

University, and was twice nominated for the Pulitzer Prize. A fellow author, Kamilah Aisha Moon, wrote about what Clifton's work offers her: "Permission to be and keep it real. To be shameless, unabashed. To be vulnerable as a show of strength. To wonder and be amazed. To decipher dreams. To rage eloquently and elegantly. To claim and proclaim" (Clifton, 2020, p. 247).

Clifton wrote a series of poems about her father's sexual abuse of her when she was very young. She (Clifton, 2020, pp. 106–108) called them "shapeshifter" poems, explaining that her father seemed like a different person when he abused her during the night. It was as though his shape shifted, from the man she knew as her father to a cold, cruel stranger with whom she was totally helpless. In the second poem of the series, Clifton speaks in her own voice as a child and plaintively asks who is there to protect her from her predatory father. Repetitively, the answer comes back that no one will help – not the observant windows, nor the watchful moon, nor the lamenting owl, nor the scarred woman she would later become. I picture an isolated child, spotlit, appealing to inanimate objects for compassion they cannot provide.

For me, the poem gains some of its evocative power from the repetition of the simple question, "who." Each object around the child witnesses but does not protect. Unavoidably, I begin to wonder who else, besides the window, moon, future self, and owl, didn't protect her. Then I come upon Clifton's poem, entitled "fury" and dedicated to her mother (Clifton, 2020, p. 151). The backstory to this poem is that Clifton's mother wrote poetry, but her father forbade the publication of any of his wife's work. So Clifton saw her mother burn all her poetry, and she wrote a poem in order to remember. In this poem, the child Clifton watches the flames consume her mother's poems. Along with the poems, her mother's well-being and her own remaining shreds of innocence seem to go up in flames. At the end of the poem, Clifton pledges always to remember and to bear anything for her mother's sake. I imagine that, from that point on, there are two Lucille Clifton's – the one before the burning and the one who pledged her allegiance to a fellow sufferer. I wonder whether Clifton, like my patient Mary, needed to keep them both alive. But unlike most of us, Clifton's poetic gift gave her pre-traumatic self an artistically expressive voice. Clifton could not stop her father from changing his shape, her mother from devastation, or herself from being affected by these subjugations. But she was able to survive psychologically by shaping her memories into poems. The poet and critic Edward Hirsch has written that a poem can speak "to the age-old and ongoing catastrophe of dehumanizing people and turning them into the Other" (Hirsch, 2021, p. 307). In his essay about the Derricotte poem "Pantoum for the Broken" (discussed earlier), Hirsch imagines that the poet "is holding and consoling her younger self, the broken part of her. She is being transformed" (Hirsch, 2021, p. 470). The transformative power of poetry has been celebrated by Jill Bialosky, whose memoir is meaningfully titled "Poetry Will Save Your Life" (Bialosky, 2017). Her experience tells her (Bialosky, 2017, p. 200), "Perhaps this is finally the very heart of what poetry can do and be. It gives shape to those empty spaces within us that we have no words for until we find them in a poem." I would like to imagine that for Clifton, finding poetic expression mitigated the shame and sorrow of remembering when she was at the mercy of a merciless shapeshifter.

Wild With All Regret

The phrase "wild with all regret" comes from a poem of love and loss (Tennyson, 1942), but I use it here to express how intense regret can feel as though it may drive us to unbridled extremes. The unharmed self continues to haunt the sufferer, making it impossible to conclusively mourn. As ghosts go, this one is particularly resilient. She may begin to fade, but then something serves as a reminder of what might have been. A potential partner invites intimacy, sexual longings are stirred, and the all-too-familiar pit-in-the stomach anxiety revs up. What might unharmed life have been like? Excitement without anxiety, passion without trepidation, without guilt? Wanting more without fearing that the response will be overwhelming?

Regret is a complicated feeling, generally thought to include both sorrow and some form of responsibility (Buechler, 2008). We feel sorrow for a loss but regret the opportunities we have squandered. Regret usually implies a greater sense of agency than sorrow. I suggest that regret can spur both mourning and a need to atone. Regret can play a huge part in the process of mourning the dying unharmed self. Just by its presence, the ghost makes manifest what might have been had Mary protected herself from harm. If only.

Of course, as a child in her father's house, Mary couldn't protect herself, and she knows that, but that doesn't seem to matter. It also doesn't seem to matter that she was trying to protect her siblings from being abused or that her mother was complicit, relieved of her husband's attention.

In my opinion, regret is conspicuously absent from most psychoanalytic literature and conspicuously present in most of our lives. In a previous publication (Buechler, 2008), I devoted a chapter to regret and described some clinical experiences with patients who fantasized what might have been:

Knowing that you could have been freer, happier, loved and trusted more easily aches the heart. To see, in your mind's eye, the person who would have been more at ease in the world, yet feel you will never be that person, brings exquisite pain. How can we help someone bear this? What does it mean to mourn the self that could have taken some things for granted? Do we aim to bury it, so that someone else might be born? Or, do we try to bring it back and resurrect innocence?

(Buechler, 2008, p. 98)

I generally favor keeping an open mind about burial vs. resurrection. One patient I described in the 2008 book (Buechler, 2008, pp. 99–102) seemed to benefit from my presence as she gave voice to the cost of maintaining the double identity of the harmed and unharmed selves. It seems to me very significant to appreciate how lonely life can be, shadowed by our unrealized potential.

I think of regrets as generally falling into one of two categories: regrets for acts of commission and regrets for acts of omission. It seems to me that the ghostly presence of an unharmed self would most likely trigger regrets for acts of omission.

Before her appearance, our inklings of missed opportunities may lack shape. But once she has materialized, her liveliness points up our spiritless, half-hearted existence.

W.S. Merwin gives omissions palpable shapes in his poignant poem "Something I've Not Done" (Merwin, 1973). The poet complains that something he has not done is following him, coming ever closer, perching on his shoulders, drinking up his breath, preceding him everywhere he goes. But the speaker is determined to lay hands on that interloper! Who will be eclipsed?

The idea of an unnerving, somehow superior double has played a leading role in much of our fiction, poetry, and philosophy. One example is the great short story by Dostoevsky, "The Double" (1923). As was true for some of my painfully haunted patients, the main character in this short story is haunted by a more capable facsimile of himself. Commenting on the story, Harden (1985, p. xix) suggests that it is really about the total disintegration of the speaker's self-esteem. Otto Rank's (1925/1971) study of this subject remains a valuable contribution. The existence of any double, but, perhaps, especially an unharmed self, guarantees that a person will always see themselves in contrast to someone else. One is never just simply oneself. Perhaps it is similar to having an unusually accomplished twin or other sibling. Whether or not it is made explicit, the contrast is always there.

Trauma transforms us, creating contrasts between before and after. At the furthest extremes, we can become unrecognizable, even to ourselves. I am reminded of the grief-stricken Ophelia, in *Hamlet* (Shakespeare, 2016, Act IV, Scene 5, lines 42–44), warning Claudius that "They say the owl was a baker's daughter. Lord, we know what we are but know not what we may be."

The distance between the grievously harmed and the fantasied unharmed self may widen or narrow over time. A widening gap can create unbearable regret for the life almost lived, for the joys only glimpsed. But is it even worse for the unharmed self to become unimaginable? However painful she is as a companion, is it better to keep her in sight? Better to hold onto her insight into who we might have been? Or might the pain become so intense that suicide seems preferable to enduring it? This was one of my fears for my patient, Mary. As her "unharmed self" became more vividly real, she seemed to me to be lost to depression. Sometimes, I found myself in the unaccustomed position of wishing my patient would stop remembering her past. But, at the same time, I felt I had no choice but to help her recover it. As a vast literature (Bromberg, 1998) on the treatment of trauma attests, the poet Maxime Kumin (1974) tells us that in order to become free of our ghosts, we must return to them.

Tolstoy etched a portrait of regret in his character Ivan Ilych. In his great short story, "The Death of Ivan Ilych" (Tolstoy, 1886/1982) Tolstoy recounts the thoughts of an inexplicably dying small town magistrate. As Ivan reviews his life, he comes to the unavoidable conclusion that he failed to really live it. He drifted from one superficial bureaucratic episode to another, showing the "proper" behavior to secure his post. Despite his great reluctance, his unlived life became clearer and clearer, until he had to admit that he had wasted his allotted time on earth. But

Ivan, though suffused with regret for his unlived potential, nevertheless came to a healing insight into the sacrifice that could give his death purpose. He would make his death into an expression of genuine caring about the quality of his family's lives. Fully embracing his regrets allowed Ivan to fashion a meaningful death. In what, for me, is one of the most moving passages in literature, Ivan finds that by truthfully facing his regrets, he became able to confront death without fear:

> . . . he must act so as not to hurt them; release them and free himself from these sufferings. "How good and simple!" he thought. "And the pain?" he asked himself. "What has become of it?" "Where are you, pain?" He turned his attention to it. "Yes, here it is. Well, what of it? Let the pain be. And death . . . where is it? He sought his former accustomed fear of death and did not find it. "Where is it? What death?" There was no fear because there was no death. In place of death there was light.
>
> (p. 279)

My patient Mary and I faced the question of whether recognizing her losses could help her finally heal. Eventually, Mary did forge a new purpose for her life. Though still struggling mightily with sorrow, by the end of the treatment, she was no longer in danger of taking her life.

If we think of regret as sorrow laced with a sense of responsibility, the clinical task often becomes finding ways to atone. It may not be possible, or, in some senses, even preferable to diminish the sorrow. The poet Rilke advises us: "Our instinct should not be to desire consolation over a loss but rather to develop a deep and painful curiosity to explore the loss completely, to experience the peculiarity, the singularity, and the effects of *this* loss in our life!" (Baer, 2005, p. 109, italics in original).

Atonement, on the other hand, may be both possible and helpful. Atonement has been understood (Bokser, 1978) as an intrapsychic process of becoming more "at one" within oneself and as an interpersonal process in which individuals join in community. My clinical and personal experience suggests that finding a way to atone can sometimes meaningfully counter regrets. Instead of only unmet goals, there are now some still unmet and some on a path toward fulfillment. Seizing opportunities can feel like atoning for missed chances at life.

In that spirit, I hope to become more respectful when I encounter fantasied unharmed selves. Maybe their dying will take a long time. Perhaps they will never die. They are painful companions to have but, sometimes, even more painful to lose. Reminders of what might have been, they may also point the way toward a more meaningful future.

References

Albers, J. (1963). *Interaction of color*. New Haven: Yale University Press.
Baer, U. (2005). *The poet's guide to life: The wisdom of Rilke*. New York: Modern Library.

Bialosky, J. (2017). *Poetry will save your life: A memoir*. New York: Atria Books.
Bokser, B. B. (1978). *Abraham Isaac Kook*. Mahwah, NJ: Paulist Press.
Bromberg, P. M. (1998). *Standing in the spaces: Essays on clinical process, trauma, and dissociation*. Hillsdale, NJ: The Analytic Press.
Bromberg, P. M. (2006). *Awakening the dreamer: Clinical journeys*. Mahwah, NJ: The Analytic Press.
Buechler, S. (2008). *Making a difference in patients' lives: Emotional experience in the therapeutic setting*. New York: Routledge.
Buechler, S. (2012). *Still practicing: The heartaches and joys of a clinical career*. New York: Routledge.
Buechler, S. (2017). *Psychoanalytic reflections: Training and practice*. New York: IPBooks.
Buechler, S. (2019). *Psychoanalytic approaches to problems in living: Addressing life's challenges in clinical practice*. New York: Routledge.
Clifton, L. (2020). *How to carry water: Selected poems*. New York: BOA Editions.
Derricotte, T. (2021). Pantuum for the broken. In E. Hirsch (Ed.), *100 poems to break your heart*. New York: Houghton Mifflin Harcourt.
Dostoevsky, F. (1923). The double. In C. Garnett (Ed.), *The eternal husband and other stories*. New York: The Macmillan Company.
Freud, S. (1926/1959). Inhibitions, symptoms, and anxiety. In *Standard edition* (Vol. 20, pp. 87–175). London: Hogarth Press.
Harden, E. (1985). *Fyodor Dostoevsky: The double-two versions*. Ann Arbor, MI: Ardis Publishers.
Hirsch, E. (2021). *100 poems to break your heart*. New York: Houghton Mifflin Harcourt.
Kumin, M. (1974). *Our ground time here will be brief*. New York: Viking Penguin.
Merwin, W. S. (1973). *Writings to an unfinished accompaniment*. New York: Athenium.
Rank, O. (1925/1971). *The double*. Chapel Hill: University of North Carolina Press.
Shakespeare, W. (2016). *Hamlet* (A. Thompson, & N. Taylor, Eds.). The Arden Shakespeare. London: Bloomsbury.
Tennyson, A. (1942). Tears, idle tears. In L. Untermeyer (Ed.), *A great treasury of poems* (Vol. 2). New York: Simon and Schuster.
Tolstoy, L. (1886/1982). The death of Ivan Ilych. In A. Maude, & L. Maude (Trans.), *The raid and other stories*. New York: Oxford University Press.
Winnicott, D. W. (1972). *Holding and interpretation*. New York: Grove.

Chapter 7

To Speak of Suffering
Art's Ethical Obligation

Hannah Lyn Venable

When faced with tragedy, human language often fails, forcing us to admit that there are some experiences that words cannot explain. No words can justify the death of a loved one to the bereaved. No precise description fully captures the experience of walking through a season of despair. No explanations are satisfying for the absurdity of feeling disconnected and isolated from others and from the world. No conversation rationalizes away the sorrow felt from broken relationships. Silence follows an experience of tragedy because words lack the power to express the depth of the pain. Not only does suffering bring silence to our spoken language, it can also quiet the inaudible language in our minds. In Emmanuel Falque's recent book *Hors-Phénomène*, he argues that in certain times of intense suffering, we may lose the ability to speak or even think about the suffering. He calls these experiences the Extra-Phenomenal or Outside the Phenomena (*Hors phénomène*), because they are circumstances that appear to be external to any meaning that can normally be found in the phenomena of life. We are sometimes prevented from even practicing the discipline of phenomenology, because in such tragic moments, we cannot study the phenomena to make sense of them and they appear to be bankrupt of all meaning. Falque writes:

> Out of time, even out of space and out of the subject, the 'Extra-Phenomenal' leaves one speechless [*bouche-bée*], and in this stupefaction there is no longer even an unthought, but only the unthinkable remains – namely the annihilation, at least initially, of the capacity to think.[1]

Descriptions of the event and the facts surrounding it speak *about* it, but they cannot speak *to* the event directly in a meaningful way, leaving us speechless or mute (*bouche-bée*).

If suffering is found then in the silent, unspoken places of our lives, is it impossible to express? Can we ever speak about it all? In his book, *Suffering and the Remedy of Art*, Harold Schweizer begins with a similar question: "But if suffering is in the unbearable, silent body rather than in the sharable, disembodied language of its narratives, how then can suffering speak? How can one hear the unspeakable?"[2] Søren Kierkegaard gives us a poignant example of the inability to speak about a

DOI: 10.4324/9781003598107-10

tragic event in his *Fear and Trembling* when he writes of the necessary silence of Abraham after God has asked him to sacrifice his son, Isaac.[3] Kierkegaard argues that it is not that Abraham chooses not to speak but that he *cannot* speak; he is unable to put together any words or phrases that would be intelligible to anyone. Kierkegaard writes, "Speak he cannot; he speaks no human language. Even if he understood all the languages of the world, even if those loved ones also understood them, he still cannot speak – he speaks in a divine language, he speaks in tongues."[4] Perhaps there would be a divine language, a language of the angels, that could tell of his task, but in terms of human language, the decision to kill his son for God cannot be explained with any words known to humans.

In these silent spaces of deep suffering, I believe that art has the power to speak to us, giving a voice to our lived pain. Art does not use a normal human language, but, like the divine language that Kierkegaard mentions, it speaks the unspeakable according to a different mode of expression. Drawing on Maurice Merleau-Ponty's idea that art arises out of silence and Friedrich Nietzsche's famous claim that art justifies existence, I will first offer further proof for why it is that art must speak of suffering. Because no human language – not even the language of phenomenology – can offer us satisfying explanations for tragedy, I will argue that art has an ethical obligation to speak to us in the midst of personal and communal suffering. Next, I will describe *how* art fulfills this obligation due to its facility with the vocabulary surrounding suffering including death, despair, absurdity and brokenness as seen in illustrations from the art of the French existentialists, Simone de Beauvoir, Gabriel Marcel, Jean-Paul Sartre and Albert Camus. Lastly, I will present *what* art says to us in suffering to demonstrate its indispensability; for the uncompromising message of aesthetic expression reveals to us the fullness of reality, the hard and the good, unlike anything else.

Although I believe that art can be broader than this, for the sake of this chapter, I am referring to art as a creative mode of expression, that includes beauty, meaning or craftsmanship, as seen in artworks such as paintings, novels, plays, sculptures and music. Furthermore, when I say that art has the ability to do something, I do not mean that every single piece of art does this but rather that art, as a practice, has this capacity. The characteristics discussed in this chapter are not necessarily found (nor should they be found) in each individual work of art.

A. The Obligation of Art

Maurice Merleau-Ponty describes the way that art speaks to us out of silence, and while he is not specifically thinking here of tragedy, his articulation of art as a voice of silence can be expanded to include the silence found in suffering. His essay "Indirect Language and the Voices of Silence," helps us see the ability and even the necessity of art to speak particularly during times of suffering.[5] He writes first of the way that all meaning comes out of silence, because meaning can never be fully attached to a "point for point correspondence" to words; he argues,

> Now if we rid our minds of the idea that our language is the translation or cipher of an *original text*, we shall see that the idea of *complete* expression is

nonsensical, and that all language is indirect or allusive – that it is, if you wish, silence.⁶

It is impossible to defend the idea that meaning can be completely located in a series of words or categories because true meaning evades all constraints and goes beyond mere words. Yes, there *is* meaning in the words themselves, but the full meaning must include the silence that rests between the words. This general sense of silence, which grounds all meaning, is not a lack of something, as Glen Johnson comments: "Silence is not a negative phenomenon for Merleau-Ponty, the sheer absence of thought or meaning."⁷ Instead, silence is the spirit of meaning that cannot be reduced to the words that have been said. This means that silence and language cannot be separated from each other as each contributes to one another, intertwining with one another to express sense. To illustrate this, Glen Mazis states that we must see "Merleau-Ponty's treatment of silence as being not the mere absence of sound or simply the opposite of language, but as being its other side."⁸ This idea of silence, or deep silence as Mazis writes, is the other side to language and signifies a general openness to encountering the world.⁹

While meaning is present in all forms of silence found in human experiences, meaning in silence is often best illustrated in a work of art, because in art, we no longer have the expectation that its meaning will be contained in the words used to describe it. In this way, art often gives us a way to think and to reflect on things that words on their own, even words found in a philosophical analysis, cannot accomplish. To demonstrate this, Merleau-Ponty writes that the problem with formalism, as a method of art criticism, is not that it tries to categorize art according to a "form," but rather because "it detaches [the form] from meaning."¹⁰ Instead, we must see that it is the form of the work of art that gives us access to a world beyond the form:

> What is irreplaceable in the work of art, what makes it, far more than a means of pleasure, a spiritual organ [*un organe de l'esprit*] whose analogue is found in all productive philosophical or political thought, is the fact that it contains, better than ideas, *matrices of ideas* [*matrices d'idées*] – providing us with emblems whose meaning we never stop developing [*dont nous n'avons jamais fini de développer le sens*]. Precisely because it dwells and makes us dwell in a world [*parce qu'elle s'installe et nous installe dans un monde*] we do not have the key to, the work of art teaches us to see and ultimately gives us something to think about as no analytical work can; for when we analyze an object, we find only what we have put into it.¹¹

Nothing can replace the power of art to speak to us, to teach us to see and to give us fresh thoughts. It cannot just be for entertainment, a way to feel pleasure, because it is like an organ of the mind or spirit (*l'esprit*) which unlocks the door to a world and places us (*nous installe*) in that world. We can try to push the door open on our own, through logical analysis for example, but it will not budge, because we need a matrix, a grid or an opening to the world (*matrices d'idées*) beyond the categories themselves. It is not that art is the only discourse that can open the world to us; philosophical and political discourses can mirror this type of access if they leave behind a reliance on formal analysis. But art cannot be substituted with anything else because we need it to instruct us that analysis cannot provide the full picture. To conclude his essay, Merleau-Ponty writes, "In short, language speaks [*dit*], and the voices of painting are the voices of silence."[12] Both language and art tell (*dire*) something, but in spoken language, we falsely assume that the meaning is expressed only in the words. It is the mute or "silent forms of expression" (*formes muettes de l'expression*) found in painting that remind us that silence is essential to accessing true meaning.[13]

Art is irreplaceable because it helps us navigate the world; it is no longer a side benefit or a nice hobby but is actually necessary in order to make sense of the world. Applying this particularly to tragedy, we find that our usual narratives cannot contain the silent and unbearable weight of suffering, and so we need a new language that can actually speak to us. In response to the questions posed at the beginning of this chapter of "How then can suffering speak? How can one hear the unspeakable?" Schweizer writes, "Perhaps the very language of the aesthetic, a language without any meaning other than its own occurrence, might echo the mysterious occurrence of suffering."[14] The language of art does not contain meaning like other human languages, because its occurrence, its mode of expression, is its meaning. Drawing from different illustrations than what will be offered in this chapter, Schweizer applies literature and poetry to studies in medicine and argues that there is an analogous nature between suffering and art, and this is exactly why art must be the voice of suffering. Thinking of the analogy in terms of silence, it is precisely because tragic silence is always bound up with suffering that art, the expert at expressing something out of silence as Merleau-Ponty demonstrates, is able to give us a message.[15]

Unfortunately, we do not always recognize the duty that art has to speak to us in suffering, because we become too obsessed with the ideal, what is given in the "phenomenologies of good health," as Falque puts it, and, as a result, we ignore experiences of suffering, death, chaos and solitude.[16] Phenomenologists, for example, focus on a 'general silence' as a way of putting the world back together, a way of giving unity to the world, but can forget about the importance of the 'tragic silence' as a way of experiencing the world as falling apart, a sense of it being broken into pieces.[17] Merleau-Ponty, himself, leaves space for the tragic element of existence, but does not fully explore it and thus needs to be supplemented with others who are willing to engage the darker sides to existence. We might consider Martin Heidegger, for example, as someone who is sensitive both to the tragic found in life (with his idea of 'being toward death') and to the importance of art, but he actually does not explicitly bring these together. Working outside phenomenology, Theodor Adorno can offer a corrective to this as he does see the important relation between art and suffering. Discussing political movements rather than personal suffering, he writes that art's reason for existing is that there is "something in reality" which "objectively *demands* art and it *demands* an art that *speaks* for what the veil hides."[18] The veil of rational knowledge hides suffering, "the incomprehensible horror" of this world, for "suffering remains foreign to knowledge . . . suffering conceptualized remains mute and inconsequential."[19] Making truth concrete, then, can only be done by art, for the "darkening of the world makes the irrationality of art rational."[20] Adorno writes that suffering demands that art must speak of it – it dictates that art must express it – because rational discourse cannot give it a proper voice.

Applying Adorno's ideas to all contexts of suffering, we would do well to pay closer attention to Nietzsche's famous repeated claims in *The Birth of Tragedy* on the obligatory role of art in the face of the suffering of existence: "For only as an *aesthetic phenomenon* is existence and the world eternally *justified*."[21] To exist in the world without the mediation of art is not possible according to Nietzsche. On its own, raw existence is unpalatable; its weight will crush us. With the advent of the modern age and the death of myth, all past comforts have failed, as he laments, "now, no solace has any effect" as man can only see "what is terrible or absurd in existence wherever he looks."[22] Nietzsche sees art as a justification for horrors of existence not in spite of suffering but in freely embracing the suffering. Through the miraculous unity between the aesthetic drives of the Apolline, which represents the calm, dreamy, individual and truthful drive, and the Dionysiac, which represents the intoxicated, musical, communal and surreal drive, a true work of art allows us to embrace the absurdity of reality while finding joy in this acceptance.

Even during his so-called positivist period in *The Gay Science*, Nietzsche never loses sight of our desperate need for art due to the suffering of existence. Honesty, on its own, he writes, would only "lead to nausea and suicide," and so we must turn to art.[23] He then repeats a slightly-altered version of the statement from *The Birth of Tragedy*: "As an aesthetic phenomenon existence is still *bearable* to us."[24] Again, this is not to fix the suffering but to choose to find beauty in the suffering as seen in his famous *Amor Fati* (love of fate): "I want to learn more and more how to see what is necessary in things as what is beautiful in them – thus I will be one of those who make things beautiful."[25] Suffering is a determined part of existence, as Nietzsche learned from Schopenhauer, but art is not a way to escape existence, because art creates a space of freedom where I can make things beautiful even in the suffering. Kathleen Higgins and Robert Solomon capture this well: "To see the world as beautiful, in spite of suffering – even because of suffering – remains one of the explicit aspirations throughout [Nietzsche's] philosophy."[26]

What makes art's obligation *ethical* is that without art, we have nowhere else to turn. It is up to art to speak to us of suffering, help us find meaning in it and carry us through our sorrows, or we will be left with nothing. Art has the ability to provide meaning to us, unlike anything else, and thus, it must act on our behalf so that we can accept our existence. For the way in which art allows us to accept and even enjoy reality is how it justifies existence to us. Certainly, this is not 'justification' in the manner that we normally think; art does not offer a rational proof that the good of existence somehow outweighs the bad.[27] This is why art is so critical in moments of tragedy when rational justification is impossible: we need a nonrational justification which gives us a love for life when life doesn't make sense. The gift that art gives us is something outside of ourselves; as Daniel Came writes, "it is clear that the value of art for Nietzsche is extrinsic."[28] Through art, we *feel* that existence is worth it and *feel* that life has something of merit, because we are drawn out of the individual self and caught up in an aesthetic experience. It is simply the moment of the occurrence, the moment of the aesthetic experience, as Schweizer writes, that offers meaning to the experience of suffering.

B. The Language of Art

To fulfill its obligation, art is able to draw on an unspoken vocabulary which includes themes of death, despair, absurdity and brokenness in order to speak to us *honestly* and *deeply* during experiences of suffering. Although many illustrations are possible to demonstrate art's facility with this vocabulary, I believe that the practices in "existentialist aesthetics" are especially helpful to us for two reasons: first, these French 20th-century philosophers are also artists themselves such that the making of art is intimately connected to their practice of philosophy, and second, they are particularly sensitive to the personal and global experiences of suffering after the events of World War II.[29]

1. Death

Because death serves as a crude reminder that there is something not quite right in this world, any effort to explain death will always fall short, creating a kind of silence around it. For the existential philosopher and artist, art's ability to speak into the silence of death begins surprisingly not in any experience of human death, but rather it first faces a metaphysical death: the death of God.[30] Following Nietzsche's observation that "God is dead! God remains dead! And we have killed him!" in *The Gay Science*, existentialist aesthetics argues that art must be created without any recourse to divine answers or spiritual illusions.[31] Art must begin with the acceptance of the death of God; for even if God exists, God cannot be a metaphysical placeholder used to fit reality together and could only be experienced after an acceptance of God's death.

Simone de Beauvoir reflects on her experience of encountering the absence of God as a young girl of 15 years old, gazing out at a cherry tree outside her window:

> 'I no longer believe in God,' I told myself, with no great surprise ... For a long time now the concept I had had of Him had been purified and refined, sublimated to the point where He no longer had any countenance divine, any concrete link with the earth or therefore any being. His perfection cancelled out His reality. That is why I felt so little surprise when I became aware of His absence in heaven and in my heart ... Until then ... all things murmured softly of His glory. Suddenly everything fell silent. And what a silence! ... Alone: for the first time I understood the terrible significance of that word.[32]

The more God becomes for her an abstract entity, too perfect and distinct from this world, the more Beauvoir realizes that this God could not possibly exist. Out of the silence that arises with the death of God, art provides a way for Beauvoir to express herself; it gives her the freedom to fight against the loneliness and emptiness. This fight is vividly illustrated in the life of her character, Françoise, in her first novel, *She Came to Stay*. The story revolves around the challenges that come when Françoise and her partner, Pierre, invite a young woman, Xavière, into their relationship. With God absent from the narrative, Françoise must learn not to rely on anybody else but herself to arrange her life, as she instructs Xavière, "I think you make yourself what you are of your own free will."[33] This making of yourself, for Beauvoir, is the artistic expression, as seen in writing novels and more broadly, living life, which combats the suffering felt at God's death.

In a similar way, Gabriel Marcel writes of accepting the absence of God early in his own life; looking back at his childhood, he feels that he was raised under the assumption that God is dead. He writes, "It was only much later that I would become acquainted with Nietzsche's 'God is dead'; but in a way everything during my childhood, and even at the beginning of my adolescence, happened as though in fact God were dead."[34] As a playwright, Marcel attempts to describe the helplessness experienced in life when there is "no faith to guide it."[35] In his play *Ariadne* (*Le Chemin de crête*), Violetta, a poor, single mother who is having an affair with a married man, laments the deception of her life: "more lies – *more* lies coiled in the very heart of our life."[36] Surrounded by her own lies and the lies of others, she feels as though she is being swallowed up by a false world and wonders if there is any escape from the darkness. Although Marcel comes to believe that there is hope in an experience of God, he argues that art must express all experiences of death; it must even speak of the darkness at the loss of God without providing "some kind of ready made truth [to] absorb like a calming drug or tranquilizer."[37]

Just as art responds to the silence at the death of God, it can also speak to the death of self. Art expresses the deep angst that comes with suicidal thoughts, as Jean-Paul Sartre poignantly displays in his character, Roquentin, in his famous novel, *Nausea*:

> I . . . was *In the way* [*Moi aussi j'étais de trop*] . . . I dreamed vaguely of killing myself to wipe out at least one of these superfluous lives. But even my death would have been *In the way* [*de trop*]. *In the way* [*De trop*], my corpse, my blood on these stones, between these plants, at the back of this smiling garden. And the decomposed flesh would have been *In the way* [*de trop*] in the earth which would receive my bones, at last, cleaned, stripped, peeled, proper and clean as teeth, it would have been *In the way* [*de trop*]: I was *In the way* [*de trop*] for eternity.[38]

In life and in death – in fact, for all eternity – Roquentin feels like he is too much (*de trop*); that he is in the way of everything, alone and without purpose. Sartre describes this so well perhaps by drawing on his own feeling of superfluousness when he was a young boy. He writes in his autobiography:

> I did continue to feel that one is born superfluous unless one is brought into the world with the special purpose of fulfilling an expectation. My pride and

forlornness were such at the time that I wished I were dead or that I were needed by the whole world.[39]

Art has a way of speaking to the feeling of being unneeded, superfluous and excessive and, ultimately, to the desire to be rid of the self.

Thinking about the possibility of suicide, Marcel describes how life can feel like being "imprisoned in a cell the walls of which draw imperceptibly closer together at every minute."[40] He displays this feeling of helplessness in his main character, Claude, in his most popular play, *A Man of God* (*Un homme de Dieu*). Throughout the play, Claude wrestles with his own existence due to the unwinding of his marriage, his family and his faith.[41] Plagued by despair, he contemplates suicide by the end of the play, and the spectator is left wondering whether he will actually kill himself or if his forgotten faith will yet save him.

Art also has the language to speak of the death of a loved one. Music, for example, is often known for expressing the fullness of grief with us. As a pianist, Marcel reflects on the way that music invites us into a deeper sense of reality than can be spoken.[42] He writes: "It is music almost exclusively . . . which has been for me an unshakable testimony of a deeper reality."[43] This is why one of Marcel's characters, Doris, asks in the play, *Quartet in F sharp*: "Isn't music like the immortality of everything we think is dead but in fact lives on?"[44] Because music is never fixed in a time or place, it testifies to the deeper reality that the presence of our loved one retains an eternal significance.

Sculptures also have a way of presenting something timeless which Sartre calls the "unreal" or "irreal" (*irréel*). In "The Quest for the Absolute," Sartre writes that when speaking of the full meaning of a sculpture, "there is no real distance between us" and the sculpture, because it also dwells beyond the real, material world.[45] The transcendence of time and space reflected in a sculpture also can speak to death of a loved one. In Michelangelo's *Pietà* statue, we find Mary forever holding the dead body of her child (see Image 7.1). Here, the pain of losing a child never ends but is continually expressed in the facial expression and posture of Mary.[46]

From these illustrations, it becomes clear that it is the language of art that is able to speak of the experience of death. No other language can capture something like the intense helplessness experienced without the aid of God, as seen in Beauvoir's Françoise and Marcel's Violetta. It is only an aesthetic expression of angst, as seen in the stories of Sartre's Roquentin and Marcel's Claude, that can match the feeling of purposelessness behind the desire for one's own death. Nothing communicates the endless grief of losing a loved one like a work of art, as seen in the timeless power of piece of music or the fixed expression of a sculpture, such as that of Mary in the *Pietà*.

2. Despair

Despair at one's existence is another experience of suffering of which art can speak. Sartre writes of his despair as a young boy in his autobiography: "*I was*

Image 7.1 *Pietà*
Michelangelo, 1499

not substantial or permanent ... In short, I had no soul" and later, "I was *nothing*: an ineffaceable transparency."[47] Like the silence of suffering, the nothingness of existence is empty, without sound or substance. Such emptiness due to the loss of identity brings on an overwhelming sense of despair. Art can speak into this empty silent space of despair as seen in Sartre's play *The Flies*. In the play, the character Zeus tries to persuade Orestes to keep the people under the false pretense that there is hope in religion and a purpose in life; otherwise, they may see their lives as repugnant and pointless:

Zeus: You will tear from their eyes the veils I had laid on them, and they will see their lives as they are, foul and futile, a barren boon ... what will they make of it?

Orestes: What they choose. They're free; and human life begins on the far side of despair [*désespoir*].[48]

To take on this necessary despair and to get rid of any false hope (*espoir*), Orestes must pay a high price: he murders the queen and king, who are his own mother and step-father. Through this homicide, he allows the people of his kingdom to be free, no longer held captive by their oppressive regime, and encounter the despair found in facing true reality. And yet the despair here is not entirely without hope; somehow in just the dialogue of the play, there is a kind of meaning experienced by the spectator, a hope that honesty will prevail over falsehood.

In a similar way, we can consider again Marcel's character Violetta in his *Ariadne* as another example of a meaningful expression of despair. In the play, Violetta has a conversation with Jerome, a married man whom she loves, asking, "since we're condemned to live in the dark and to wander without hope, oughtn't we to – oh, how can I put it? – oughtn't we to draw the power to help others from the very darkness of our own despair [*désespoir*]?"[49] The darkness and the hopelessness are felt here in this story, and yet, at the same time, there is a sense of the deep desire to commune with others for solace.

Despair, in existentialist art, is often seen as provoking a response of nausea. Sartre's description of nausea in his novel shows the strong link between the emotional feeling of despair and the bodily reaction of nausea to it; aesthetic expression, here, has a way of capturing the way suffering is experienced in the whole person, body and mind. At first, the nausea for Roquentin seems to come from the objects around him:

Now I see: I recall better what I felt the other day at the seashore when I held the pebble. It was a sort of sweetish sickness. How unpleasant it was! It came from the stone. I'm sure of it, it passed from the stone to my hand. Yes, that's it, that's just it – a sort of nausea in the hands.[50]

In a feeling of despair, even the smallest objects bother him and bring him a feeling of sickness. Selected quotes from the novel cannot do justice to reading it as it gradually and slowly presents the nausea to the readers. And although Roquentin tries hard to avoid these bouts of nausea, it often sneaks up on him when he is unprepared. Later, he wonders if this nausea is not due to objects but due to himself: "The Nausea has not left me and I don't believe it will leave me so soon; but I no longer have to bear it, it is no longer an illness or a passing fit: it is I."[51] Facing the truth, Roquentin realizes that his nausea comes from himself, his own lack of identity.

Through these illustrations, we see the power of art to speak of a profound experience of despair, the kind of despair that comes when our worst fears have been realized. Art encapsulates what it is like when we are forced to face the harsh truth – the tearing away of the veils from the citizens' eyes as seen in Sartre's *The Flies* or the exposure of the lies at the heart of life as seen in Marcel's *Ariadne* – in a way that nothing else can quite capture. Furthermore, it is aesthetic expression that clearly exhibits the way suffering can be felt in our bodies, like the visceral response of nausea to the feeling of despair as seen in Sartre's Roquentin.

3. Absurdity

An encounter with the 'absurdity' of suffering is perhaps not referred to as often as death and despair. But drawing on Albert Camus's definition of absurdity, we will recognize how it pervades human life and is another element of human suffering aptly shown by art. In *The Myth of Sisyphus*, Camus writes: "Absurd is not in man . . . nor in the world, but in their presence together. For the moment it is the only bond uniting them."[52] For Camus, absurdity is found at the most basic level in the unexplainable connection between humans and the world. We are dependent on our bond with the world for existence, but to attempt to say why it is there based on our lived experience is impossible. In fact, any explanations for our absurd existence are what Camus calls a "leap" or an "appeal" because we have to go beyond existential reality in order to try and make sense of things. Camus argues, "The leap in all its forms, rushing into the divine or the eternal, surrendering to the illusions of the everyday or of the idea – all these screens hide the absurd."[53] Genuine art, then, will not offer us any illusions, from the divine or the eternal, that will hide away the absurd foundation for reality. Camus writes how a person walking in this absurdity "wants to find out if it is possible to live *without appeal*" and then realizes that life "will be lived all the better if it has no meaning."[54] Perhaps lived experience eventually reveals the divine, but before taking this leap, we must first start by facing the absurdity of reality, and it is to art that we must turn to make sense of it.

Camus presents the Greek mythological figure Sisyphus as an example of person willing to embrace an absurd existence. Sisyphus is condemned by the gods to roll a heavy stone up a mountain in Hades; every time he makes it to the top, the stone rolls back down only for him to repeat the process again and again. For all eternity, he rolls the stone up the mountain, watches the stone roll back down, and starts all over again. In the deep moments of suffering, we sometimes feel that our lives are like the fate of Sisyphus. Devoid of meaning, we may continue to work on a project or pursue a relationship, even while knowing that our efforts are in vain, just like rolling a stone up a mountain, knowing it will come back down. Camus's expression of Sisyphus as the "absurd hero" profoundly relates to this feeling of meaninglessness.[55]

Absurdity is one of the primary manifestations of meaningless suffering, as Emmanuel Levinas notes in his short essay, "Useless Suffering." Speaking against any kind of explanation or 'use' of suffering, he states: "All evil refers to suffering . . . The evil of pain, the harm itself, is the explosion and most profound articulation of absurdity."[56] Levinas remains skeptical whether art can display suffering, because it may just distract us and make us feel "indifferent to the world's suffering."[57] But if art is done in a certain way, Levinas reflects, perhaps there is a way to make visible some of the absurdity of suffering. In an interview on the works of Sacha Sosno, Levinas comments that there is an ethical dimension to the "art of obliteration" done by Sosno which "exposes the ease and lighthearted casualness of the beautiful, and recalls the wear and tear of being, the 'repairs' which art covers over . . . to appear and show itself."[58] In other words, art has the ability to profoundly display the beauty of being, but at the same time illustrate the rough or hidden parts of being. Sosno does this in his *Vénus oblitérée*, which is a beautifully crafted torso of a Venus sculpture with a rectangle cut out from its center; such strangeness forces us to imagine what is missing (see Image 7.2).

As even Levinas admits, art has a way of communicating something that can't be communicated: the irrational and absurd experiences of our lives. Art expresses the suffering that comes from monotonous and pointless work, as seen in Camus's retelling of Sisyphus, or the frustration from the absurd gaps in our existence, as seen in Sosno's sculptures, and it is art's honesty about this feeling of meaninglessness that intensely resonates with us.

Image 7.2 *Vénus oblitérée*
Sacha Sosno, 1980
Photo by André Villers © 2025 Artists Rights Society (ARS), New York / ADAGP, Paris

4. Brokenness

Broken objects, broken bodies and broken relationships are all ways that we encounter the suffering of brokenness in our personal lives. Although sometimes these things can be fixed – objects glued back together, broken bones healed and relationships reconciled – there are other times that we know that there is no way to repair the fragmented pieces. When no solution presents itself, we feel stuck, unable to act or speak, living in a space of passivity and silence. Here, art speaks to us, conveying the depth of personal suffering, but also signaling to us the brokenness of the larger world around us.

In the play *The Broken World* (*Le monde cassé*), Marcel portrays a young, accomplished woman, Christiane, who loved a man who ended up choosing the monastic life; through this choice, he severed his connection with everyone and unknowingly broke her heart. To escape her grief, Christiane enters into marriage with a man she does not love. She confides in her friend, Denise:

Christiane: Don't you feel sometimes that we are living . . . if you can call it living . . . in a broken world [*un monde cassé*]? Yes, broken like a broken watch. The mainspring has stopped working. Just look at it, nothing has changed. Everything is in place. But put the watch to your ear, and you don't hear any ticking. You know what I'm talking about, the world . . . it seems to me it must have had a heart at one time, but today you would say the heart had stopped beating.[59]

The world, like a broken watch, looks fine on the outside, but suffering makes us recognize that none of the hands ever move and no sound is ever made. In this broken world, due to her lost love, Christiane feels that she has personally lost her own identity: "Since then I have been beside myself . . . I no longer know who I am."[60] The people around her also seem empty, without care for others or for the world: "Each one wrapped up in himself, his own little thing, his own little interests. They meet, clash, with a rattling noise."[61] To try and cope with it all, she surrounds herself with a group of male flatterers, and since her husband no longer shows her love, she has an affair with another man that she does not love. The despair in all areas of life leads her to despise religious ideas and anything that tries to make sense of reality.[62] Christiane's personal brokenness taps her into the general brokenness she feels all around her.[63]

Art also expresses brokenness on larger scales as seen in Camus's *The Plague*. Here Camus describes a small town in Algeria, Oran, that is struck with an awful plague and is closed off from the rest of the world as hundreds and hundreds die from the untreatable disease. The brokenness becomes palpable for the reader when the narrator writes:

Without memory and without hope, they settled into the present. In truth, everything became present for them. It must be said that the plague had taken away from everyone the possibility of love and even the possibility of friendship. For love requires a little bit of future, and we had only a few moments left.[64]

At the end of the novel, the plague has finally subsided, and the doctor makes his routine visit to an asthmatic who comments on those who want to be honored for their work during the plague: "They might as well be asking for a medal. But what does it mean, the plague? It's life, that's all."[65] The story of a plague is simply an honest story about life; by alluding to plagues that took place in Algeria in the past and to the Nazi occupation of France and to many other crises, Camus's art exposes us to our harsh reality, but in the creative telling of it, he gives us an awareness of the world that pulls us outside of ourselves.

It is only through an experience of art that our personal brokenness is opened up to global brokenness; in short, art has a way of telling me, 'It's not just me, it's the whole world that feels off.' Nothing can describe so honestly the way brokenness invades all aspects of our lives like a work of art, as seen in Christiane's acute disillusion with life, others and God in Marcel's play. Art pulls us out to face the greater brokenness of the world, as seen in Camus's depiction of the town of Oran; no longer is a world crisis just an abstract problem, because art calls on our hearts to recognize brokenness beyond our individual lives.

C. The Message of Art

Through the glimpses provided by existential art, we can start to see how art speaks to us with authenticity and profundity in the silent moments of suffering. But the power of aesthetic expression is found not only in *how* it is being said but also in *what* is being said. Art offers us an uncompromising message for two reasons: because of its refusal to soften or diminish reality and because of its intolerance for passivity.

Beginning with the first, art refuses to make light of the pain of suffering because it presents it in the fullness of its reality. The message of art is not didactic nor prescriptive, at least at first, but is rather just one of understanding. In a lecture, Camus states, "The aim of art . . . is not to legislate or to reign supreme, but rather to understand first of all."[66] Art's ability to understand is due to the way it captures all of reality, the hard and the good, the rational and the irrational. Considering first the way art conveys the weight of the suffering, we can think of how art faithfully depicts something that we have personally experienced. Thinking again of Michelangelo's *Pietà*, if parents who have lost a child encounter this work of art, they will resonate with it in a distinct way, knowing that they too have felt that kind of suffering (see again Image 7.1). The unspoken pain of losing a child is not diminished but is revealed in its gravity.

Furthermore, the unexplained and irrational aspects of suffering can be said by art because it can communicate, unlike a rational discourse, things outside of reason.[67] This is why the 'meaning' that is expressed through art is not a rationalization of the suffering, for the suffering itself will still feel unjustifiable; rather, it is the creation of something out of the suffering that provides a new kind of meaning to it. As David M. Goodman and M. Mookie C. Manalili write in their preface to an edited volume on political and cultural suffering, we, as humans, must create meaning out of what feels meaningless: "meaning-making is part of human life . . . meaning here also captures the enactment of values, rather than the explanatory set to reduce suffering's implications."[68] The full disclosure of suffering offered by art is part of the new creation of meaning, which portrays lived values rather than analysis. In her chapter on bereavement, Kathleen Higgins beautifully describes how our experience of time and space changes during times of suffering and how desperate we are for something that will make sense of this. She writes, "Artistic modes of communication can help convey features of experiences when direct verbal statement seems to fail."[69] Spoken sentences fall short in describing our instability, but art helps us feel understood by conveying irrational aspects of our experience.

Turning now to the second reason for art's uncompromising message, we also see that art cannot fully accept the reality of suffering, because it cannot tolerate passivity. Art will not allow complacency in suffering but instead awakens us and calls us to respond. Although sometimes hidden or implicit in the work, the message of art contains in itself a call to action, a silent rebellious cry against injustice. Camus explains:

> Art is neither complete rejection nor complete acceptance of what is. It is simultaneously rejection and acceptance . . . The artist constantly lives in such a state of ambiguity, incapable of denying reality and yet eternally bound to question it in its eternally unfinished aspects. In order to paint a still life, there must be a confrontation and mutual adjustment between a painter and an apple.[70]

Art cannot totally refuse reality, nor can it consent completely to it; in this ambiguity, the artist must present what is real but, at the same, time put out a call for action to change what is wrong in this world. Just like in a still life, an artist works to display the reality of an apple but, at the same time, confronts it and adjusts it in order to tell us something about that reality. For, as Camus adds later, "art disputes reality, but does not hide from it."[71] It does not hide the truth of suffering but, at the same time, pushes back against it. In a painting about death, the painter walks in the ambiguity between depicting the reality of death and expressing a new perspective on it. Paul Cézanne's *La maison du pendu* (*The hanged man's house*) presents a scene of stillness and silence that might reflect the loss of death through its muted and gray colors (see Image 7.3). At the same time, though, it invites us to actively participate in the solitude and perhaps ponder the reason for the man's death, whether by suicide or punishment.[72]

This call to the action found in the message of art is what both Marcel and Merleau-Ponty describe as art's power to awaken us. In Marcel's autobiography, he explains his thought process behind his art:

> I don't think that a playwright . . . should have to worry about reassuring anyone. Of course, this doesn't mean that . . . the writer has to ignore what the

Image 7.3 *La maison du pendu*

Paul Cézanne, 1873

spectator could think or experience. But . . . the writer has to treat the spectator *as an awareness to be awakened* . . . There could be no question of providing him with some kind of ready made truth that he would have to absorb like a calming drug or tranquilizer . . . the theater should help renew him interiorly.[73]

Marcel desires his art to awaken people and make them aware of what is going on around them and in themselves. It may not be a comfortable feeling; we recall the angst that we feel at the end of many of his plays, but this angst is an active angst that drives us to action while at the same time it inwardly transforms us.

In his article "Cézanne's Doubt," Merleau-Ponty writes also of the need for art to wake us up: "It is not enough for a painter like Cézanne, an artist, or a philosopher, to create and express an idea; they must also *awaken* the experiences which will make their idea take root in the consciousness of others."[74] Yes, artists must genuinely express reality, but not only that, they must do it in such a way as to awaken in us a response. Cézanne's *La maison du pendu* can call us to reflect on the silence of death while at the same time rousing in us a longing for peace, solitude and justice (see again Image 7.3).

D. Conclusion

Rational explanations, and even phenomenological descriptions, are not sufficient when we encounter suffering and tragedy. It is the voice of art that must pierce the silence of these moments, because it alone has a language that can be heard. I am certainly giving a tall order to art in this chapter: it must speak of suffering, it must not let us sit in utter silence, it must tell us honestly of reality and it must provoke us to fight. I will even add to this list: Art must speak of all tragedies. There is no tragedy that art cannot face. Because art's goal is never to justify or rationalize suffering, art can face all suffering and, as a result, it has the responsibility to voice the things that nothing else can articulate. Now, this is certainly not the only goal for art as art also can communicate experiences of unspeakable joy and delight. Thus, as mentioned in the opening, every artwork does not need to convey suffering, but art, as a discipline, must. To fully accomplish this task, our definition of art will need to be expanded. In this chapter, I have focused on the narrow view of art, but the role that the traditional forms of art play in our lives actually points us to how the broader forms of art are necessary as well, such as creating one's life as a work of art and creating relationships with others and the divine in a dynamic and aesthetic way.

Limiting ourselves to the confines of this chapter, however, we can conclude that because art can speak to a general silence, as Merleau-Ponty argued, and because art offers a justification for existence, as Nietzsche claims, all the more it can and must speak into tragic silence. As seen in the examples from literature, plays, music, statues and paintings, aesthetic expression utilizes a vocabulary that surrounds suffering, including themes of death, despair, absurdity and brokenness, to communicate to us in a genuine and deep way. The content of art's message is simple and uncompromising: It tells us the whole truth and tells us not to stand still. It's an unspoken message that somehow still speaks; through the power of its voice, it provides us the first step in accepting suffering, the first step in fighting against what's wrong, the first step in creating our new identity and the first step in finding new hope.

Notes

1 Emmanuel Falque, *Hors phénomène: Essai aux confins de la phénoménalité* (Paris: Hermann, 2021), 181, my translation: "Hors temps, voire Hors espace et Hors sujet, le << Hors phénomène >> laisse bouche-bée, dans cette sidération il n'y a même plus d'impensé, mais seul demeure l'impensable – à savoir l'annihilation, au moins dans un premier temps, des capacités de penser."
2 Harold Schweizer, *Suffering and the Remedy of Art* (New York: State University of New York Press, 1997), 12–13.
3 Kierkegaard is drawing on the Biblical story found in Genesis 22. The verses of Genesis 22 do not explicitly say that Abraham did not tell others what God asked him to do, but his two recorded responses to his servants ("Stay here with the donkey while I and the boy go over there. We will worship and then we will come back to you.") and to Isaac ("God himself will provide the lamb for the burnt offering.") seem to imply that he does not reveal the full truth of his errand to others (Genesis 22:5, 8).
4 Søren Kierkegaard, *Fear and Trembling*, trans. C. Stephen Evans (Cambridge: Cambridge University Press, 2006), 101.
5 Published in July 1952, this was Merleau-Ponty's final essay in *Les Temps Modernes*, the journal that he founded with Jean-Paul Sartre and Simone de Beauvoir. The essay is a response to Andre Malraux's *The Voices of Silence* and Jean-Paul Sartre's *What is Literature?* He is both affirming and criticizing Malraux and Sartre here in this essay.

For further information on this, see Galen A. Johnson's introduction: "Structures and Painting: 'Indirect Language and the Voices of Silence'" in Maurice Merleau-Ponty, *The Merleau-Ponty Aesthetics Reader: Philosophy and Painting*, ed. Galen A. Johnson (Evanston, IL: Northwestern University Press, 1993), 14–34.
6 Maurice Merleau-Ponty, "Indirect Language and the Voices of Silence," in *The Merleau-Ponty Aesthetics Reader: Philosophy and Painting*, 80, italics his.
7 Johnson, "Structures and Painting," 33.
8 Glen A. Mazis, *Merleau-Ponty and the Face of the World: Silence, Ethics, Imagination and Poetic Ontology* (New York: SUNY, 2016), xiii.
9 Mazis, *Merleau-Ponty and the Face of the World*, 11–12. Mazis is using the category of "deep silence" from Bernard Dauenhauer's *Silence, The Phenomenon and Its Ontological Significance*.
10 Merleau-Ponty, "Indirect Language and the Voices of Silence," 114.
11 Merleau-Ponty, "Indirect Language and the Voices of Silence," 114, italics his. French: Maurice Merleau-Ponty, "Le langage indirect et les voix du silence," in *Signes* (Paris: Gallimard, 1960), 96–97, italics his.
12 Merleau-Ponty, "Indirect Language and the Voices of Silence," 117. French: Merleau-Ponty, "Le langage indirect et les voix du silence," 101.
13 Merleau-Ponty, "Indirect Language and the Voices of Silence," 118. French: Merleau-Ponty, "Le langage indirect et les voix du silence," 101.
14 Schweizer, *Suffering and the Remedy of Art*, 13.
15 To illustrate this ability of art to speak of suffering from a historical perspective, please see the volume edited by Celinscak and Hutt on artworks over history which have displayed suffering. In the opening to the volume, they write: "Some artists attempt to heal themselves and the world through exposing and reconciling us to past and present horrors. Indeed, art offers a way to approach the unspeakable" (Mark Celinscak and Curtis Hutt, "Preface: Art and Suffering," in *Artistic Representations of Suffering: Rights, Resistance, and Remembrance*, ed. Mark Celinscak and Curtis Hutt (Lanham, MD: Roman & Littlefield, 2021), xvi).
16 Falque, *Hors phénomène: Essai aux confins de la phénoménalité*, 8: "phénoménologies de la bonne santé." Falque's book on the extra-phenomenal (*hors phénomène*) is written as a corrective to the over-emphasis on the ideal found in phenomenology.
17 Mazis's work provides an excellent reflection on Merleau-Ponty's ideas of silence, ethics and poetry, but he highlights mostly a positive silence which is ultimately the "source for ethics" (Mazis, *Merleau-Ponty and the Face of the World*, 8). Steven Bindeman's *Silence in Philosophy, Literature and Art* also tends to focus on the positive side to silence by defining silence as an indirect discourse which "reflects what surrounds it" (Steven Bindeman, *Silence in Philosophy, Literature and Art* (Leiden, The Netherlands: Brill, 2017), 3). He does, however, argue for two interconnected types of silence, disruptive silence and healing silence (Bindeman, *Silence in Philosophy, Literature and Art*, 3). His disruptive silence is more of an overall disconnection with self in linear time, but I think we could expand it to include tragic silence as seen in his discussion of silence and the Holocaust (Bindeman, *Silence in Philosophy, Literature and Art*, 129–134).
18 Theodor Adorno, *Aesthetic Theory*, trans. Robert Hullot-Kentor (Minnesota: University of Minnesota Press, 1998), 18, italics mine.
19 Adorno, *Aesthetic Theory*, 18.
20 Adorno, *Aesthetic Theory*, 19.
21 Friedrich Nietzsche, *The Birth of Tragedy*, trans. Raymond Geuss and Ronald Speirs (Cambridge: Cambridge University Press, 1999), Section 5, p. 33, italics his. The second quotation reads: "I repeat my earlier sentence that only as an aesthetic phenomenon do existence and the world appear justified" (Section 24, p. 113).
22 Nietzsche, *The Birth of Tragedy*, Section 7, p. 40.

23 Friedrich Nietzsche, *The Gay Science*, ed. Bernard Williams, trans. Josefine Nackhoff (Cambridge: Cambridge University Press, 2001), Book 2, Section 108, p. 104.
24 Nietzsche, *The Gay Science*, Book 2, Section 107, p. 104, italics his. To see comments on how this statement might differ from the earlier one in *The Birth of Tragedy*, see Daniel Came, "The Aesthetic Justification of Existence," in *A Companion to Nietzsche*, ed. Keith Ansell Pearson (Malden, MA: Blackwell Publishing, 2006), 39–57.
25 Nietzsche, *The Gay Science*, Book 4, Section 276, p. 157.
26 Robert Solomon and Kathleen Higgins, *What Nietzsche Really Said* (New York: Schocken Books, 2000), 182.
27 See Daniel Came: "When Nietzsche speaks of the aesthetic justifying life, he does not mean that it shows us that life is *actually* justified but rather that it educes an affectively positive attitude towards life that is *epistemically neutral*" (Came, "The Aesthetic Justification of Existence," 42). In other words, art does not give us more positive knowledge to counter the epistemically negative aspects of life, but it does produce in us an attitude that positively accepts existence.
28 Came, "The Aesthetic Justification of Existence," 47.
29 Almost all the examples of art in this chapter are from the actual works of art created by the existentialists, which means there will be a privileging of prose, theatre and music, but to diversify, I have added a couple of additional examples from other forms of art and have then included commentary from one of the thinkers. Also, for further confirmation on the pivotal role of art in existentialism, see the research presented here: Jean-Philippe Deranty, "Existentialist Aesthetics," in *The Stanford Encyclopedia of Philosophy* (Spring 2019 Edition), ed. Edward N. Zalta. URL = <https://plato.stanford.edu/archives/spr2019/entries/aesthetics-existentialist/>.
30 See Philip Pacey, *A Sense of What Is Real: The Arts and Existential Man* (London: Bentham Press, 1977), 5: "Existentialism begins here – with the despair of man without proof of God."
31 Nietzsche, *The Gay Science*, Book 3, Section 125, p. 120.
32 Simone de Beauvoir, *Memoirs of a Dutiful Daughter*, trans. James Kirkup (New York: Harper Collins, 2005), 137–138.
33 Simone de Beauvoir, *She Came to Stay* (New York: Norton & Company, 1999), 245.
34 Gabriel Marcel, Music in My Life and Works, in *Music and Philosophy* (Milwaukee: Marquette University Press, 2005), 45.
35 Gabriel Marcel, *The Existential Background of Human Dignity* (Cambridge, MA: Harvard University Press, 1963), 113: Here, Marcel is commenting that his play *Ariadne* (*Le Chemin de crête*) ends similarly to his play *A Man of God* (*Un homme de Dieu*), as there is an "inarticulate cry for help," but, for the character of Ariadne, there is "no faith to guide it."
36 Gabriel Marcel, Ariadne, in *Three Plays with a Preface on the Drama of the Soul in Exile*, trans. Rosalind Heywood (London: Secker & Warburg, 1952), 201.
37 Gabriel Marcel, *Awakenings*, trans. Peter S. Rogers (Milwaukee, WI: Marquette University Press, 2002), 147.
38 Jean-Paul Sartre, *Nausea*, trans. Lloyd Alexander (New York: New Directions Publishing Corporation, 2007), 128–129, italics his. French: Jean-Paul Sartre, *La nausée* (Paris: Gallimard, 1938), 183.
39 Jean-Paul Sartre, *The Words*, trans. Bernard Frechtman (New York: Braziller, 1964), 165–166.
40 Gabriel Marcel, *Creative Fidelity*, trans. Robert Rosthal (New York: Fordham University Press, 2002), 141.
41 Gabriel Marcel, A Man of God, in *Three Plays with a Preface on the Drama of the Soul in Exile*, 35–114.
42 While none of his compositions are well known, Marcel wrote over thirty pieces for the piano and often improvised on the piano. See Marcel, *Awakenings*, 175–177.

43 Gabriel Marcel, *The Existential Background of Human Dignity* (Cambridge, MA: Harvard University Press, 1963), 21.
44 Marcel, *Quartet in F Sharp*, as quoted in Music in My Life and Works, 55.
45 Jean-Paul Sartre, The Quest of the Absolute, in *Essays in Aesthetics*, ed. Wade Baskin (New York: The Citadel Press, 1963), 86, italics his. (He is referring to a sculpture of Ganymede in this quote).
46 For two additional examples on art speaking of the death of a loved one, see Kofod's chapter on the expression of poetry after losing a child (Ester Holte Kofod, Poetic Representations of Parental Grief, in *Cultural, Existential and Phenomenological Dimensions of Grief Experience*, ed. Allan Køster and Ester Holte Kofod (London: Routledge, 2021, 119–136) and see Cumming's preface on the power of Velasquez's painting, *Las Meninas*, on speaking to her after the death of her father (Laura Cumming, *The Vanishing Velázquez: A nineteenth Century Bookseller's Obsession with a Lost Masterpiece* (New York: Scribner, 2016), 4).
47 Sartre, *The Words*, 88, 90, italics his.
48 Jean-Paul Sartre, The Flies, in *No Exit and Three Other Plays*, trans. Stuart Gilbert (New York: Vintage Books, 1976), 119. French: Jean-Paul Sartre, Les mouches, in *Huis clos suivi de Les mouches* (Paris: Gallimard, 1947), 238.
49 Marcel, Ariadne, 184. French: Gabriel Marcel, *Le chemin de crête*, in *Cinq Pièces Majeures* (Paris: Plon, 1973), 304.
50 Sartre, *Nausea*, 11.
51 Sartre, *Nausea*, 126.
52 Albert Camus, *The Myth of Sisyphus and Other Essays*, trans. Justin O'Brien (New York: Vintage Books, 1991), 30.
53 Camus, *The Myth of Sisyphus*, 91.
54 Camus, *The Myth of Sisyphus*, 53, italics his.
55 Camus, The Myth of Sisyphus, 120.
56 Emmanuel Levinas, "Useless Suffering," in *The Provocation of Levinas: Rethinking the Other*, ed. Robert Bernasconi and David Wood (New York: Routledge, 1988), 157.
57 Emmanuel Levinas, *On Obliteration: An Interview with Françoise Armengaud Concerning the Work of Sacha Sosno*, trans. Richard Cohen (Zurich: Diaphanes, 2019), 29. Please see Leanor Reis's helpful dissertation on Levinas's view on art: Leonor Neves da Costa Luis dos Reis, "Art in Spite of Itself: The Ambiguity of Art in the Work of Emmanuel Levinas" (Unpublished Dissertation, 2023), especially 145–147 on art and suffering.
58 Levinas, *On Obliteration*, 31.
59 Gabriel Marcel, The Broken World, in *The Existentialist Drama of Gabriel Marcel, I: The Broken World and the Rebellious Heart*, ed. Francis J. Lescoe (West Hartford, CT: McAuley Institute of Religious Studies, 1974), 36. French: Gabriel Marcel, "*Le monde cassé*," in *Cinq Pièces Majeures* (Paris: Plon, 1973), 121. "Le monde cassé" (The Broken World) is a key phrase that Marcel uses to describe suffering.
60 Marcel, *The Broken World*, 137.
61 Marcel, *The Broken World*, 36, translation slightly modified.
62 Marcel, *The Broken World*, 138.
63 Robert Wood helpfully characterizes these three aspects of brokenness as brokenness with self, others and God. See Robert E. Wood, "Introduction," in *Music and Philosophy* (Milwaukee: Marquette University Press, 2005), 15.
64 Albert Camus, *The Plague*, trans. Laura Marris (New York: Vintage Books, 2022), 194.
65 Camus, *The Plague*, 330.
66 Albert Camus, "Create Dangerously," in *Resistance, Rebellion and Death*, trans. Justin O'Brien (New York: Vintage Books, 1961), 266. This is a lecture given at the University of Uppsala in 1957.

67 See again Adorno, *Aesthetic Theory*, 19: "darkening of the world makes the irrationality of art rational."
68 David M. Goodman and M. Mookie C. Manalili, "Introduction: Problematizing Meaningful Suffering," in *Meaningless Suffering: Traumatic Marginalization and Ethical Responsibility*, ed. David M. Goodman and M. Mookie C. Manalili (New York: Routledge, 2024), 203.
69 Kathleen Higgins, "Distorted Space, Unmoving Time – Aesthetic Practices in Bereavement," in *Cultural, Existential and Phenomenological Dimensions of Grief Experience*, ed. Allan Køster and Ester Holte Kofod (London: Routledge, 2021), 62.
70 Camus, "Create Dangerously," 264.
71 Camus, "Create Dangerously," 224.
72 Although the viewer may naturally think of death from the title of the painting, it's possible that it was not Cézanne's intention and that the name reflected a person or poem.
73 Marcel, *Awakenings*, 147, italics mine.
74 Maurice Merleau-Ponty, "Cézanne's Doubt," in *The Merleau-Ponty Aesthetics Reader: Philosophy and Painting*, ed. Galen A. Johnson (Evanston, IL: Northwestern University Press, 1993), 70.

Bibliography

Adorno, T. (1998). *Aesthetic theory* (R. Hullot-Kentor, Trans.). Minnesota: University of Minnesota Press.
Beauvoir, S. de. (1999). *She came to stay*. New York: Norton & Company.
Beauvoir, S. de. (2005). *Memoirs of a dutiful daughter* (J. Kirkup, Trans.). New York: Harper Collins.
Bindeman, S. (2017). *Silence in philosophy, literature and art*. Leiden, The Netherlands: Brill.
Came, D. (2006). The aesthetic justification of existence. In K. Ansell-Pearson (Ed.), *A companion to Nietzsche* (pp. 39–57). Malden, MA: Blackwell Publishing.
Camus, A. (1961). Create dangerously. In J. O'Brien (Trans.), *Resistance, rebellion and death* (pp. 249–272). New York: Vintage Books.
Camus, A. (1991). *The myth of Sisyphus and other essays* (J. O'Brien, Trans.). New York: Vintage Books.
Camus, A. (2022). *The plague* (L. Marris, Trans.). New York: Vintage Books.
Celinscak, M., & Hutt, C. (2021). Preface: Art and suffering. In M. Celinscak, & C. Hutt (Eds.), *Artistic representations of suffering: Rights, resistance, and remembrance* (pp. xiii–xxvi). Lanham, MD: Roman & Littlefield.
Cumming, L. (2016). *The vanishing Velázquez: A nineteenth century bookseller's obsession with a lost masterpiece*. New York: Scribner.
Deranty, J.-P. (2019). Existentialist aesthetics. In E. N. Zalta (Ed.), *The Stanford encyclopedia of philosophy* (Spring ed.). Stanford University.
Falque, E. (2021). *Hors phénomène: Essai aux confins de la phénoménalité*. Paris: Hermann.
Goodman, D. M., & Manalili, M. M. C. (2024). Introduction: Problematizing meaningful suffering. In D. M. Goodman, & M. M. C. Manalili (Eds.), *Meaningless suffering: Traumatic marginalization and ethical responsibility* (pp. 1–3). New York: Routledge.
Higgins, K. (2021). Distorted space, unmoving time – aesthetic practices in bereavement. In A. Køster, & E. H. Kofod's (Eds.), *Cultural, existential and phenomenological dimensions of grief experience* (pp. 54–68). London: Routledge.
Johnson, G. A. (1993). Structures and painting: "Indirect language and the voices of silence". In M. Merleau-Ponty (Ed.), *The Merleau-Ponty aesthetics reader: Philosophy and painting* (pp. 14–34). Evanston, IL: Northwestern University Press.

Kierkegaard, S. (2006). *Fear and trembling* (C. S. Evans, Trans.). Cambridge: Cambridge University Press.

Kofod, E. H. (2021). Poetic representations of parental grief. In A. Køster, & E. H. Kofod's (Eds.), *Cultural, existential and phenomenological dimensions of grief experience* (pp. 119–136). London: Routledge.

Køster, A., & Kofod, E. H. (Eds.). (2021). *Cultural, existential and phenomenological dimensions of grief experience*. London: Routledge.

Levinas, E. (1988). Useless suffering. In R. Bernasconi, & D. Wood (Eds.), *The provocation of Levinas: Rethinking the other* (pp. 156–167). New York: Routledge.

Levinas, E. (2019). *On obliteration: An interview with Françoise Armengaud concerning the work of Sacha Sosno* (R. Cohen, Trans.). Zurich: Diaphanes.

Marcel, G. (1952a). Ariadne. In G. Marcel (Ed.), *Three plays with a preface on the drama of the soul in exile* (pp. 115–224). London: Secker & Warburg.

Marcel, G. (1952b). *Three plays with a preface on the drama of the soul in exile* (R. Heywood, Trans.). London: Secker & Warburg.

Marcel, G. (1963). *The existential background of human dignity*. Cambridge, MA: Harvard University Press.

Marcel, G. (1973a). *Cinq Pièces Majeures*. Paris: Plon.

Marcel, G. (1973b). Le chemin de crête. In G. Marcel (Ed.), *Cinq Pièces Majeures* (pp. 217–355). Paris: Plon.

Marcel, G. (1973c). Le monde cassé. In G. Marcel (Ed.), *Cinq Pièces Majeures* (pp. 105–216). Paris: Plon.

Marcel, G. (1974). The broken world. In F. J. Leslie (Ed.), and Sister J. M. P. Colla, & Rev. F. C. O'Hara (Trans.), *The existentialist background of Gabriel Marcel: The broken world and the rebellious heart* (pp. 19–144). West Hartford, CT: McAuley Institute of Religious Studies.

Marcel, G. (2002a). *Awakenings* (P. S. Rogers, Trans.). Milwaukee, WI: Marquette University Press.

Marcel, G. (2002b). *Creative fidelity* (R. Rosthal, Trans.). New York: Fordham University Press.

Marcel, G. (2005a). *Music and philosophy* (S. Maddox, & R. E. Wood, Trans.). Milwaukee, WI: Marquette University Press.

Marcel, G. (2005b). Music in my life and works. In G. Marcel (Ed.), *Music and philosophy* (pp. 41–70). Milwaukee: Marquette University Press.

Marcel, G. (1952c). A man of God. In G. Marcel (Ed.), *Three plays with a preface on the drama of the soul in exile* (pp. 35–114). London: Secker & Warburg.

Mazis, G. A. (2016). *Merleau-Ponty and the face of the world: Silence, ethics, imagination and poetic ontology*. New York: SUNY.

Merleau-Ponty, M. (1960). Le langage indirect et les voix du silence. In *Signes* (pp. 49–104). Paris: Gallimard.

Merleau-Ponty, M. (1993a). Cézanne's doubt. In M. Merleau-Ponty (Ed.), *The Merleau-Ponty aesthetics reader: Philosophy and painting* (pp. 59–75). Evanston, IL: Northwestern University Press.

Merleau-Ponty, M. (1993b). *The Merleau-Ponty aesthetics reader: Philosophy and painting* (G. A. Johnson, Ed.). Evanston, IL: Northwestern University Press.

Merleau-Ponty, M. (1993c). Indirect language and the voices of silence. In M. Merleau-Ponty (Ed.), *The Merleau-Ponty aesthetics reader: Philosophy and painting* (pp. 76–120). Evanston, IL: Northwestern University Press.

Nietzsche, F. (1999). *The birth of tragedy* (R. Geuss, & R. Speirs, Trans.). Cambridge: Cambridge University Press.

Nietzsche, F. (2001). *The gay science* (B. Williams, Ed., and J. Nackhoff, Trans.). Cambridge: Cambridge University Press.

Pacey, P. (1977). *A sense of what is real: The arts and existential man*. London: Bentham Press.

Reis, L. N. da C. L. dos. (2023). *Art in spite of itself: The ambiguity of art in the work of Emmanuel Levinas* (Unpublished Dissertation).
Sartre, J.-P. (1938). *La nausée*. Paris: Gallimard.
Sartre, J.-P. (1947). *Les mouches*. In *Huis clos suivi de Les mouches* (pp. 97–247). Paris: Gallimard.
Sartre, J.-P. (1963). The quest of the absolute. In W. Baskin (Trans.), *Essays in aesthetics* (pp. 82–92). New York: The Citadel Press.
Sartre, J.-P. (1964). *The words* (B. Frechtman, Trans.). New York: Braziller.
Sartre, J.-P. (1976). *The flies*. In S. Gilbert (Trans.), *No exit and three other plays* (pp. 45–124). New York: Vintage Books.
Sartre, J.-P. (2007). *Nausea* (L. Alexander, Trans.). New York: New Directions Publishing Corporation.
Schweizer, H. (1997). *Suffering and the remedy of art*. New York: State University of New York Press.
Solomon, R., & Higgins, K. (2000). *What Nietzsche really said*. New York: Schocken Books.
Wood, R. E. (2005). Introduction. In G. Marcel (Ed.), *Music and philosophy* (pp. 11–40). Milwaukee: Marquette University Press.

Chapter 8

Psychoanalysis, Art, and the Vale of Soul-Making[1]

Michael Parsons

Psychoanalysis has both a curative and a developmental aspect.

Freud was a doctor, and the new therapeutic method he created was a medical treatment for an illness – hysteria – that did not respond well to current treatments. Doctors aim to cure, or at least alleviate, pathology; and medically trained or not, analysts seek to help patients resolve their emotional disturbances. Questions about the effectiveness of psychoanalysis as a treatment rest on the assumption that this is its purpose.

Freud indicated another kind of function for analysis when he wrote about training:

> We hope and believe that the stimuli received in the candidate's own analysis will not cease to act upon him when that analysis ends, that the processes of ego-transformation will go on of their own accord and that he will bring his new insight to bear upon all his subsequent experience.
>
> (Freud, 1937, p. 402)[2]

This shows psychoanalysis – and not only in the training situation, of course – aiming to initiate a process of internal transformation that will have a continuing effect on the rest of a person's life. There is no end point to such a transformation, and it has no goal that can be known in advance. From this perspective, the function of analysis is simply to facilitate the evolution of the process.

This is the developmental aspect of psychoanalysis. It implies the idea of an interior life as something with its own movement and sense of direction; significant in its own right, not an adjunct to the rest of a person's existence. The *internal world* is a familiar concept to analysts, but an *interior life* is different. The internal world is a metaphorical landscape where relationships play out between different aspects of the psyche and where various processes operate at conscious and unconscious levels. Analysts work to understand how the dynamics of a person's internal world affect their emotional and intellectual functioning, their personal relationships, and the way they live in the world around them. The aim of resolving difficulties in these areas belongs to the curative function of psychoanalysis.

The idea of an interior life is not articulated as a concept in analytic theory. It reveals itself, however, in the developmental aspect of clinical work. When analysts aim not only to resolve difficulties but also to foster the process of transformation Freud refers to, helping patients to develop themselves as fully and creatively as possible, this indicates a concern with their interior lives in the sense I mean.

The curative and developmental aspects of psychoanalysis are intertwined. The same analytic process is at work in both. It may be impossible for someone's interior life to develop without problems in their internal world being resolved, while the resolution of such problems may actively promote the development of an interior life. Clinical emphasis can shift from one facet of analysis to the other. At the same time, though, there is a tension between them.

Freud saw himself as an empirical scientist, rigorously observing the workings of the psyche and drawing general conclusions about it, as his scientific education had trained him to. His observations and inferences gave a theoretical underpinning to his clinical technique, which allowed Freud to interpret patients' symptoms and dreams in a way that fell comfortably within this empiricist paradigm.

However, 'There is at least one spot in every dream at which it is unplumbable – a navel, as it were, that is its point of contact with the unknown' (Freud, 1900, p. 111, n. 1). As Freud explained at greater length:

> There is often a passage in even the most thoroughly interpreted dream which has to be left obscure; this is because we become aware during the work of interpretation that at that point there is a tangle of dream-thoughts which cannot be unravelled and which moreover adds nothing to our knowledge of the content of the dream. This is the dream's navel, the spot where it reaches down into the unknown.
>
> (Freud, 1900, p. 525)

At this point of encounter with the unknown, the technique of interpretation, with its curative aim of uncovering and resolving unconscious psychic conflicts, has no more to offer. Such moments are not confined to dreams. Freud stressed more than once that patients' dreams, their symptoms, and their free associations are all structured by the same psychic mechanisms. This implies that not only in dream-interpretation, but in other areas of the analysis also, an analyst will arrive at tangles that cannot be unravelled and spots that reach down into the unknown.

These are moments of potential. When ordinary interpretations have run their course, a space appears for the active expression of the poetic and imaginative functions of the psyche. Here is the creative core of the interior life. If the work is to progress forward from such a point, it must be by faith in analysis as a process of psychic development that is worth pursuing on its own account, aside from therapeutic objectives. This is how psychoanalysis values the interior life.

In March 1900, Freud described to Wilhelm Fliess the depression he felt after a setback in his work:

> I really believed I would have to give up on the spot. I found a way out by renouncing all conscious mental activity so as to grope blindly among my riddles. Since then I am working perhaps more skilfully than ever before, but I do not really know what I am doing.
>
> (Masson, 1985, p. 404)

There are two different ways in which analysts do not really know what they are doing. Their free-floating attention needs to be aimless, just as a patient's free association does, so that unconscious processes can reveal themselves. Freud made this advance in 1900 by 'renouncing all conscious mental activity', and in 1912, he wrote that the analyst 'should withhold all conscious influences from his capacity to attend' (Freud, 1912, p. 112). The other way follows from the second of the two functions of analysis that I described. In facilitating the development of a person's interior life, analysts do not know what they are doing because there is no way of knowing where the process may lead or how this individual's interior life will turn out to evolve. Analysts cannot second-guess the growing personhood of their patients.

The aimless listening of free-floating attention requires faith in the theory of the unconscious and in the clinical technique of analysis. Not knowing what one is doing in the second sense calls for a different kind of faith: a faith that fostering the evolution of a person's interior life is something intrinsically good, to be valued for its own sake.

Two views of the psyche are in play here. The curative function of psychoanalysis implies that the psyche has something the matter with it, from which analysis may help it to recover. The developmental function does not carry any suggestion of pathology. It implies rather that the psyche is engaged in a process of growth, which analysis may be able to assist.

There is an interesting parallel between these two views of the psyche and different views of the human soul. Does psychoanalytic thinking, however, have any room for the soul?

The German word '*Seele*' occurs frequently in Freud's writings. Its normal translation is 'soul', but all through the *Standard Edition* of Freud's works, '*Seele*' and its corresponding adjective '*seelisch*' are translated as 'mind' and 'mental'. There is a revealing footnote in the *Standard Edition* where Strachey explains that he has used the word 'mind' to translate Freud's '*Seele*', 'a word which is in fact nearer to the Greek "psyche" than is the English "mind"' (Strachey, 1953, p. 283fn). Strachey knows that 'mind' is a mistranslation, but the word 'soul' has to be avoided. Perhaps it conflicted with the image of psychoanalysis as an empirically based, scientific enterprise. In addition, Freud's (1927) attack on religion as a projection of the believer's inner world and a set of obsessional rituals made it something of a no-go area for psychoanalysts, and 'soul' might have seemed an uncomfortably religious sort of word.

Bruno Bettelheim pointed out, however, that German has exact equivalents for 'mind' and 'mental' in '*Geist*' and '*Geistig*', which Freud chose not to use. The German '*Seele*' does not have such religious overtones as 'soul' does in English. It connotes not so much a mental structure as a sense of interior depths not easily to be fathomed. On Freud's deliberate use of '*Seele*' instead of '*Geist*', Bettelheim writes:

> [Freud's] greatest concern was with man's innermost being, to which he most frequently referred through the use of a metaphor – man's soul – because the word 'soul' evokes so many emotional connotations. It is the greatest shortcoming of the current English versions of his works that they give no hint of this.
>
> By evoking the image of the soul and all its associations, Freud is emphasising our common humanity. Unfortunately, even in these crucial passages the translations make us believe he is talking about our mind, our intellect. This is particularly misleading because we often view our intellectual life as set apart from – and even opposed to – our emotional life . . . The goal of psychoanalysis, of course, is to integrate the emotional life into the intellectual life.
>
> (Bettelheim, 1983, pp. xi, 71)

Already in Freud's time, his friend the Lutheran pastor Oskar Pfister told him he had a restricted perception of religion (Pfister, 1993), and nowadays religion is not so routinely dismissed by analysts as it used to be. A broader view has opened it to more positive psychoanalytic discussion, and a considerable literature has grown up in this area (Rizzuto, 1979; Meissner, 1984; Spezzano & Gargiulo, 1997; Black, 1993, 2006; Starr, 2008; Sochaczewski, 2017). 'Soul' is no longer such a taboo word in psychoanalysis, and the parallel I mentioned between views of the psyche and views of the soul is worth exploring.

Writing in the 3rd century C.E., Plotinus viewed the soul as being by nature beautiful and perfect. It originated in a higher, non-material realm, but was imprisoned in the grossness of the body and physical world. The purpose of life was for the soul to undergo purification and growth so as to return to its proper home. This was possible through moral and intellectual training, and inward contemplation of the Divine Unity.

These neo-Platonist ideas influenced Christian theologians such as Origen, who emphasised a moral and spiritual discipline by which the soul could progress towards salvation. Augustine, on the other hand, about a hundred years later, believed that the human soul is necessarily corrupt and helpless to do anything by its own resources. It could only be healed by the redemptive action of Christ, and the purpose of life was for the soul to have its fault put right in this way.

Plotinus' picture of the soul corresponds to a developmental view of the psyche, while Augustine's account sees the soul as requiring an external curative intervention. These two narratives jostled each other in the early Christian church, until Augustine's won out and the doctrine of original sin was accepted. They have different implications about the kind of change that the soul needs to undergo, which correspond to the implications for psychic change of the developmental and curative approaches in psychoanalysis.

Despite their differences, Plotinus and Augustine both thought the soul needed to be freed from its involvement with the world of the senses. Psychoanalysts, on the other hand, have always known that the psyche is an embodied psyche. From the 'mysterious leap from the mind to the body' (Deutsch, 1959) in Freud's cases of conversion hysteria to his statement that the ego is a body-ego (Freud, 1923b, p. 27), from the analysis of psychosomatic states to Winnicott's (1975, pp. 243–254) concept of the 'psyche-soma', analysts have never doubted that the psyche is rooted in the sensory life of the body.

Sensory experience, residing as it does in the body, includes the body's sexuality. For Augustine, it was by sex that original sin was transmitted down the generations, and Christianity has always been ambivalent about the relation between the soul and the world of the senses. In general, it has preferred to keep them separate, existing in parallel and staying safely apart. This implies that soul and body are different entities, each with its distinct mode of existence: people exist as their physical selves, while they 'have' souls; at the same time, they are souls that 'have' bodies.

Dualism of this sort, between the body on the one hand and some thinking or feeling substance on the other that exists independently of the body, is problematic. In the philosophy of mind, it has been largely superseded by one version or another of a materialist view that sees mental and emotional states as expressions of neurological processes in the brain. Neuroscientific research appears to reinforce this. The soul has traditionally been regarded as the seat of belief and spiritual experience, of moral values and agency – acts of forgiveness, for example – and of emotions like compassion and empathy. However, brain imaging and other neuroscientific studies have shown specific neural correlates in the brain for moral judgments, emotion and its relation to reason, and the sense of personal agency (LeDoux, 1996; Greene et al., 2001; David et al., 2008; Simič et al., 2021).

Evolutionary biology and psychology pose problems as well. Theologically speaking, possession of a soul is unique to human beings; it is what distinguishes them from other creatures. The transition from animal to human, though, is an evolutionary continuum. Where in that continuum is the demarcation point at which certain bodies acquired souls and became separate from the rest of creation? Some theologians accept that the soul cannot be a distinguishing feature of humanity after all, and give up the concept altogether (Murphy, 2006). Others extend it beyond mankind, saying that 'everything alive must in some way be "ensouled"' (Haught, 2001, p. 27). Opposite solutions, both of them abandoning orthodox doctrine. It is also claimed that religious belief and care for one's fellow beings evolved as mechanisms for promoting group solidarity and survival. As with the neuroscientific research, if what belongs to the soul can apparently be explained without reference to it, defending its existence becomes challenging. It is understandable if the concept of the soul has caused some embarrassment to theologians.

Among psychoanalysts too, the change of climate about religion and the soul is only partial. William Meissner, a psychoanalyst and Jesuit priest who wrote extensively in both areas, asserted:

> The term *soul* has never been described, defined, or articulated in specifically psychoanalytic terms or recognized as a term with theoretical relevance within psychoanalysis. Its usage from Freud on seems to have been commonsensical, poetical, metaphorical, or relatively ambiguous and indeterminate. It is thus not an authentic or definitive psychoanalytic concept.
> (Meissner, 2008, pp. 337–378)

Meissner is concerned to keep the vocabularies of psychoanalysis and religion separate, but this makes for a restricted view of what sort of concept can be useful analytically. He writes:

> Were I to proclaim, 'My soul doth magnify the Lord,' I would be pronouncing a metaphor in the form of a personal synecdoche – use of a part to represent the whole: 'my soul' thus stands for myself as a personal agent, but it is only a constitutive part of my total self as a human person.
> (Meissner, 2008, pp. 328–329)

This does not seem right. If 'my soul' is no more than a reference to myself as a personal agent, Meissner is reducing Mary's 'My soul doth magnify the Lord' to 'I magnify the Lord'. Both may be true statements, but the gravity and impact of Mary's utterance is lost in the second. The words 'my soul' show that her declaration issues from a profound emotional depth; it is an expression of her whole self. Listening with an analytic ear, one would know that the two statements were coming from somewhere very different and that something different was happening in each case.

The Roman Catholic church did seem to let the idea of the soul slip out of sight, rather as Meissner wanted to banish it from psychoanalysis. More recently, it has come back into view. In 2012, the church revised its liturgy. Previously, before receiving Communion, worshippers would say "Lord, I am not worthy to receive you, but only say the word and I shall be healed". In the new version, this became "Lord, I am not worthy that you should enter under my roof, but only say the word and my soul shall be healed". This was a return to the language of an older rite from which the reference to the soul had tacitly been dropped. Now it was being revived, and with an implicit emphasis, in the words 'enter under my roof', on its relation to the body (Tyler, 2016, pp. 13–15). The Catholic Church also produced, for the first time in 400 years, a new version of the Catechism, its official statement of belief. This made a point of insisting that 'the human body . . . is a human body precisely because it is animated by a spiritual soul . . . Man, though made of body and soul, is a unity' (*Catechism of the Catholic Church*, 1994, p. 365; Tyler, 2016, pp. 13–15). The soul, after a conceptual eclipse, is reappearing in religious discourse, specifically with an affirmation of its relation to the body. Perhaps this indicates a realisation that like the psychoanalytic soul, the religious soul also grows through a poetic and imaginative creativity that is rooted in the body.

Around Easter 2015, My wife and I encountered this creativity, and also the anxiety it gives rise to, when we walked into the Jesuit church in Vienna. What appeared to be a huge rock was soaring above our heads (Figures 8.1a, 8.1b).

Its massive physicality and tactile roughness challenged the otherworldly religiosity of the church with the earthly world of the senses. In another way, though, this rock is anything but earthly. Floating in mid-air, it subverts our normal sensory assumptions.

It seemed that it might also subvert ideas about the soul. Commenting on the work, the priest in charge of the church asked 'Why was this particular place chosen for this mountain-moving installation?', and his answer was 'Because the Jesuits had the courage to go for it' (Schörghofer, 2014). Why the need for courage? The core belief of Christianity is that in the person of Jesus Christ, the creator became part of his own creation. The doctrine of the Incarnation embodies the idea that the divine and material worlds interpenetrate each other. It is built into Christianity that soul is not an adjunct to the sensory world but an intrinsic part of it. Such a close relation between soul and the senses is the very thing this rock in a church seems to underline. So how could it be subversive?

Figure 8.1a To Be in Limbo, Steinbrener/Dempf & Huber

Figure 8.1b To Be in Limbo (detail). Steinbrener/Dempf & Huber. Permission of the artists

Ever since Augustine, the Church has been uneasy about the link between the soul and sensory experience. To say that this installation required courage shows how hard that ambivalence has been to shake off. Soul and the senses may be meant to exist safely in parallel, but the rock in the church shows that parallel lines can meet after all.

Christianity struggles with the idea that soul and sexuality are inextricable. Not so Hinduism, whose erotic temple art celebrates this (Figure 8.2).

In Christianity, however, the prevailing impulse has been to sever the link. This can make a work like Bernini's *St. Teresa in ecstasy*, which refuses the separation of soul and sexuality, appear shocking (Figure 8.3).

The theologically dangerous thing that the Jesuits were doing, when they floated a rock in the sacred space of their church, was – like Bernini – to subvert this split between soul and the senses.

If body and soul are what go to make up an individual, it would seem they must both be there from the beginning. Christians are born with an immortal soul; *atman* is present throughout a Hindu's cycle of reincarnations; in the Torah, 'the Lord God formed man out of the dust of the ground, and breathed into his nostrils the breath of life; and man became a living soul' (Gen. 2:7).

What does it mean, then, to describe someone as 'soulless', or to say a person 'has no soul'? This reveals a different view of human nature, one in which the

132 Aesthetic Ethics

Figure 8.2 Khajuraho temple sculpture

existence of a soul cannot be taken for granted. There is a famous letter of the poet John Keats in which he writes of the world as 'the vale of soul-making'. For Keats, the soul does not exist automatically from the beginning; its creation and development are a central task in life. The common view, he writes, is that the natural tribulations of life cannot be much alleviated. They must simply be endured. The world is seen as:

> 'a vale of tears' from which we are to be redeemed by a certain arbitrary interposition of God and taken to Heaven – What a little circumscribed straitened notion! Call the world if you Please 'The vale of Soul-making' . . . Soul as distinguished from an Intelligence – There may be Intelligences or sparks of the divinity in millions – but they are not Souls till they acquire identities, till each one is personally itself.
>
> (Rollins, 1958, pp. 101–102)

Keats does not reject the idea of divinity, but he denies that human beings are fated only to suffer passively. Instead, he sees life as the occasion for what psychoanalysts might call a kind of psychic work, to which Keats, who in his short life knew a lot about suffering, gives the name of 'soul-making'.

Keats struggles to put this into words: 'I can scarcely express what I but dimly perceive'. He identifies three elements. There is intellectual functioning; there is

Psychoanalysis, Art, and the Vale of Soul-Making 133

Figure 8.3 Bernini, *St. Teresa in ecstasy*

what he calls 'the human heart (as distinguished from intelligence or Mind)'; and there is the world, in which mind and heart act on each other to form the soul.

> Do you not see how necessary a World of Pains and troubles is to school an intelligence and make it a Soul? A place where the heart must feel and suffer in a thousand diverse ways!

What was [a person's] soul before it came into the world and had These provings and alterings and perfectionings? – An Intelligence – without Identity – and how is this Identity to be made? Through the medium of the Heart? And how is the Heart to become this Medium but in a world of Circumstances?

(Rollins, 1958, pp. 102–104)

'Intelligence without Identity' implies a lack, but a lack that carries potential; and Keats insists that the actualisation of this potential – the formation of a soul – depends on sensory experience.

For Keats, soul-making involves the creation of an identity, and this takes place through the interaction of mind and heart. In psychoanalysis, the role of interpretation is also to bring mind and heart together (Parsons, 2014, pp. 176, 181). May psychoanalysis be a way of soul-making?

The concept of identity was introduced into psychoanalysis by Erik Erikson at a time when the metapsychological weather was changing (Erikson, 1956). The idea that development springs from the internal drives of a self-contained individual was no longer adequate. Instead, it was becoming understood that relationships are sought for their own sake from the beginning of life and that psychic development – the evolution of a person's identity – takes place only in that context (Parsons, 2014, p. 223ff, 2021, pp. 1184–1185). When Keats said that only 'in a world of Circumstances' could the Heart be the medium for this Identity to develop, he too understood that the identity which is the soul can only develop through the senses and in a context of relationships.

A striking expression, or exploration, of identity is for an artist to paint a self-portrait. Figure 8.4 shows a prodigiously talented 23-year-old capturing his own lively, but somewhat unformed curiosity about the world, tinged perhaps with anxiety about what life holds in store. Figure 8.5 shows the same man capturing himself again aged 55. He is not just thirty-two years older chronologically; his identity has grown. There is an ironic resignation in his gaze; beyond the melancholy, there is compassion and an acceptance of suffering. Rembrandt's extraordinary gift lets him show us that between these two paintings, a lot of Keats' soul-making has taken place.

Analysts talk about 'psychic change'. Do their various ways of describing it relate to Rembrandt's journey through the vale of soul-making? Paintings cannot be 'analysed' like a patient on the couch, and to say that these two show something unconscious becoming conscious, or reveal developments in the subject's ego, would have no meaning. Notice, though, how in the second of them, the figure engages the viewer with his gaze. We cannot escape a connection with this person. We feel that whatever has happened to him, and in him, since he was 23, comes not from having stood outside life but from engaging with it: from the relationships which, for better or worse, he has made with other people. This pair of self-portraits shows, in Keats' terms, the soul-making that depends on a world of circumstances; in psychoanalytic terms, an identity that grows only in a context of relatedness.

Analysts view identity as involving a complex integration of different aspects of the psyche. For sociologists too it is a multifaceted concept, including such things

Figure 8.4 Rembrandt, *Self-portrait*, 1629

Figure 8.5 Rembrandt, *Self-portrait as the Apostle Paul*, 1661

as a person's gender, social class, ethnicity, religion, and value systems. Complicated issues surround all of these, and Zygmunt Bauman's concept of 'liquid modernity' describes the fluidity of contemporary life which continually subverts the idea of stable moral and conceptual landmarks (Bauman, 2004).

To deal creatively with a complex and changing environment calls for an openness to what feels unfamiliar and even alien. Will the challenge be accepted or rejected? Externally, the unknown other may be dealt with by control and subjugation: the British in India, the French in Indonesia, apartheid South Africa. Or one can simply withdraw from contact with the other, as when countries retreat from inclusive internationalism to a xenophobic and isolationist stance. Internally also, we may be taken beyond our habitual boundaries into strange and uncomfortable areas of our psyches. It is disconcerting to encounter aspects of ourselves that feel alien. Can we be interested in these and want to get to know them? Or is their uncanny quality too frightening, so that we retreat into a simplistic, closed-minded identity?

If soul-making involves accepting complexity and engaging with what seems alien to us, this puts us squarely into psychoanalytic territory. Free association allows people to discover in themselves a growing proliferation of ideas and feelings. As well as providing the analyst with clues to the unconscious workings of a patient's mind, it reveals to patients how vastly more complex their internal worlds are than they suspected. Patients may be frightened of exploring unknown avenues in themselves or interested to take the risk. Impulses to retreat and to explore will appear in every analysis, and the analytic work is to help a patient shift from the former to the latter.

Free association both reveals and increases the mind's complexity, but by definition, it must not be consciously directed and there can be no expectations about its outcome. This might seem an irrational way of soul-making. The other side of the coin, however, is the analyst's attention. Freud described this as the counterpart to the demand made on patients to communicate freely whatever occurs to them (Freud, 1912, p. 112). Freud's phrase for what this demands of the analyst – *'gleichschwebende Aufmerksamkeit'* – is commonly translated as 'free-floating attention'. Insofar as it registers whatever comes its way, without discrimination or preconceptions, it is indeed the counterpart to the patient's free association. Free-floating attention, however, is not only free-floating but also attentive. While letting their minds float in parallel with the patient's associations, analysts need to find another position from which to observe the interaction between the patient's associative process and their own free-floating responses to it. For anything to float, there must be something for it to float on: water or air, perhaps, but it cannot float on nothing. The analyst's attention can float freely because it is supported by an area of attentive stillness in the analyst's mind. It is this stillness that comprehends the free mobility of the patient's and the analyst's minds together.

Another common translation of *'gleichschwebende Aufmerksamkeit'* is 'evenly suspended attention' (Freud, 1912, p. 111, 1923a, p. 239). The different metaphor raises the same question. If the attention is evenly suspended, what is it suspended from? Some point of constancy must be there to sustain the oscillations and excursions of the analyst's attention. In Bion's terms (1965/1977, pp. 89–92), what is the vertex from which the evenly suspended quality of the analyst's attention originates? The rock in the church floated freely in the air because somewhere there was a point from which it was suspended.

A goal of psychoanalysis is for patients to internalise the analytic function and become capable of self-analysis. This implies finding the same kind of position in themselves that underlies the analyst's free-floating attention. To help people discover a still point from which to comprehend the idiosyncratic complexity of their own minds seems like a step in the direction of what Keats described as 'soul-making'. If there is a point of open, constant, attentive stillness that is important for bringing a soul into being, both art and psychoanalysis may help us to catch sight of it.

Figure 8.6 shows another painting, Piero della Francesca's *Baptism of Christ*.

Figure 8.6 Piero della Francesca, *Baptism of Christ*

Its imagery is Christian, but the metaphor of baptism signifies universally the transition from one state of being to a new one. It is a watershed (apposite word) of internal growth. Such a moment of transition may imbue the figure undergoing it with a particular quality of 'presence'. Piero denotes this in several ways. A person has to open themselves to the possibility of this change of being, and there is a vulnerability about the figure of Christ. The figure behind John the Baptist prepares for baptism by divesting himself of his ordinary state, and we see that Christ must have done the same. He is then placed very much in his own space. The background landscape between Christ and John the Baptist separates their bodies; the stance and gesture of the Baptist show him keeping a distance from Christ, even in their proximity. The paleness of Christ's body also sets him apart from the rest of the painting. Most importantly, he is at the centre of an absolute stillness. Above him, the dove hovers motionless; the river beneath has come to a standstill. Christ's serious and contemplative gaze reflects the interior stillness in which a new identity is coming into being, and the quality of presence in his figure declares this with direct, unmistakable simplicity.

Art objects that have this quality are specially prized in the Japanese aesthetic for their understated naturalness and the absence of any straining for effect. Soetsu Yanagi, a Japanese pottery master, wrote that such an artefact 'may be defined as one that reposes peacefully where it aspires to be' (Yanagi, 1972, p. 129).

Figure 8.7 shows a brush-and-ink drawing made by the Zen monk Sengai in the early 19th century. Its apparent simplicity has not prevented all sorts of intellectual interpretations of it, but the image has an immediacy that is incontestable

Figure 8.7 Sengai, *Circle triangle square*

Figure 8.8 Retired townsman

and self-sufficient. The relation between the three forms, and their layering, gives a subtle sense of depth, movement, and transformation. The drawing is simple yet also evocative of something beyond itself that does not find a way into words.

Another Japanese piece that has this same quality is a late-17th-century wooden portrait carving (Figure 8.8). It is only 17 inches high, but for all its small size, the figure radiates stillness, along with a strong sense of inner aliveness. He seems very much to 'repose peacefully where he aspires to be'.

Such a work does not wear its heart on its sleeve. Its understatement runs counter to any demonstration of the artist's mastery. The Japanese word for this is *shibui*. Yanagi writes:

> It is this beauty with inner implications that is referred to as *shibui*. It is not a beauty displayed before the viewer by its creator; creation here means, rather, making a piece that will lead the viewer to draw beauty out of it himself. In this sense *shibui* beauty is beauty that makes an artist of the viewer.
>
> (Yanagi, 1972, p. 129)

140 Aesthetic Ethics

What brings about change in analysis is not an interpretation in itself but what a patient is able to do with it. The most useful interpretations are those which stimulate patients to do conscious and unconscious work of their own as a result of them. If *shibui* beauty makes an artist of the viewer, such interpretations make an analyst of the patient.

Presence works in the same way. Certain art objects have the capacity, by their clarity in simply being what they are, to arouse in us a greater awareness of what we ourselves are. In the *Baptism*, Piero's compositional expertise and technical skill give an immediacy and naturalness to the figure of Christ. He is a man fully present, poised on a new threshold in the discovery of who he is. As we allow the quality of his presence to make its impact on us, we are subtly drawn into becoming more present to ourselves.

Another painting (Figure 8.9), by the same artist as Figure 8.6, shows the same man at a later stage of his life.

Figure 8.9 Piero della Francesca, *Resurrection of Christ*

This is Piero's risen Christ, no longer poised on a threshold but having completed the discovery of who he is. What commands attention is again the sense of presence in the figure, but its quality has changed. All works of art which, like the *Baptism*, convey this sense of presence offer the viewer an implicit challenge. Piero's *Resurrection* makes it fiercely overt. As in the *Baptism*, Christ occupies a space of his own, highlighted by the paleness of his body. He is framed by the uprights of the trees and the horizontal top of the tomb, which separates him from the soldiers. Again he is motionless, having risen a moment ago from the tomb. In the *Resurrection*, the stillness is heightened by contrast with the explosive event that has just taken place, and set against the unconscious soldiers, the risen Christ is totally aware. If he seemed introspective at the threshold of baptism, now his uncompromising outward gaze challenges the viewer to meet him in the same state of awareness as Christ's own.

This is both an intellectual and a sensory awareness. Piero gives the risen Christ an extraordinary physicality: one evidently more powerful than that of the rock that sealed the tomb. *I am suggesting that, from infancy onwards, what we mean by 'soul' develops when we are as present to our experiencing selves as possible, with as full an awareness as possible of who we are, at all levels of our being: intellectual, emotional, and sensory.* This is not just an existential but a psychoanalytic statement. Bernard Leach, an English potter immersed in the same Japanese tradition as Yanagi, wrote:

A distinguished Japanese potter, Mr. Kawai of Kyoto, when asked how people are to recognise good work, replied simply: 'With their bodies'; by which he meant, with the mind acting directly through the senses, taking in form, texture, pattern and colour, and referring the sharp immediate impressions to personal experience of use and beauty combined.

(Leach, 1945, p. 17)

Such an awareness depends on viewers of an artwork, like analysts and their patients, being able to sustain in themselves the same poised attentiveness that I have been describing.

This kind of attention is, in fact, the only true way of responding to the 'presence' of a person or an object that is simply being, totally and completely, who or what they are. If we are offered something – a gift or a threat, for example – or shown a feeling, like sadness or joy, we may accept or refuse the gift, defend against the threat, empathise with the feeling or reject it. Faced, however, with the simplicity of bare 'presence', there is nothing for us to do. Indeed, there is nothing we *can* do with that except to meet it with the quality of attention that I am trying to indicate: an attention through which we ourselves become more fully and completely present.

Two philosopher-mystics who gave special emphasis to this kind of attention are Simone Weil and Martin Buber. Weil stresses that it is not a matter of willpower.

Attention consists of suspending our thought, leaving it detached, empty and ready to be penetrated by the object; it means holding in our minds, within reach of this thought but not in contact with it, the diverse knowledge we have acquired . . . Above all, our thought should be empty, waiting, not seeking anything, but ready to receive in its naked truth the object which is to penetrate it.

(Weil, 1951, p. 56)

When we stand in front of a work of art, not seeking to grasp it but waiting to see how the work may speak to us, we are giving it this quality of attention. Psychoanalysts will recognise in the clinical situation the same letting go of any focus, the same emptying of the mind and waiting. This is the receptivity of free-associative listening. Another famous idea of Keats, that of 'negative capability', has been much used in analytic writing to describe the inner patience that does not reach for premature understanding.

'Attention' means more than this, however. I said that when we encounter this quality of 'presence' in another, there is nothing for us to do with that presence except attend to it. Likewise, there is nothing to be asked of it except that it should continue. In his painting *The Milk Maid* (Figure 8.10), Vermeer pictures a woman who may happen right now to be pouring some milk, but who in doing that is totally present in herself, reposing peacefully where she aspires to be.

Figure 8.10 Vermeer, *The Milk Maid*

Her presence is understated compared to Piero's risen Christ, but its quality is unmistakable. What could one possibly ask of her, except to continue being who she is? And the presence of the other asks nothing of us, except our own presence: a presence which our attention to this other has made fuller than it was before. In both directions, it is the presence that matters: of the other to us and of us to the other. Simone Weil's attempt to capture this in words was to say: 'The name of this intense, pure, disinterested, gratuitous, generous attention is love' (Miles, 1986, p. 92; Parsons, 2024).

For Martin Buber, there exist two 'primary words', as he called them. One is the combination 'I-Thou', the other the combination 'I-It'. These are different existential stances towards the world. 'I-It' is an attitude that examines things and people and seeks to categorise them. 'I-Thou', by contrast, takes the world into a personal relationship.

Buber writes that the primary word 'I-It' can never be spoken with the whole being, while 'I-Thou' can be spoken only with the whole being. 'I become through my relation to the *Thou*; as I become *I*, I say *Thou*. All real living is meeting' (Buber, 1937, pp. 3, 11). The process is continuous. As I become able to say '*Thou*', I become more myself; as I become more myself, I become more capable of saying '*Thou*'. This is Buber's description of the process of soul-making. He makes clear the different quality of attention involved in his two primary words. 'I-It' implies a careful, focused attention that preserves a distance from the other. The attention of 'I-Thou' is an open, welcoming attention that discovers the other and greets its unknownness. 'When *Thou* is spoken, the speaker has no *thing* for his object; he has indeed nothing. But he takes his stand in relation' (Buber, 1937, p. 4). It is not that one stance is right and the other wrong, or one good and the other bad. They do different things. 'I-It', with its desire to understand the world by classifying it, is a binary mode of thinking: something or somebody does or does not belong in a certain category. This is how scientists approach the world, and Freud's need to see himself as an empirical scientist may have pushed psychoanalysis in this dualistic, categorising direction. A shift away from such thinking can be observed nowadays both in psychoanalysis and in social terms. The movement for a non-binary perspective on sexuality and the fresh scrutiny of conventional political dichotomies are examples. Psychoanalysis, for its part, has come to understand that judgments about the world always involve a complex mixture of reality-testing, identification, projection, and transference. In this sense, we 'take our stand in relation' all the time, whether we are conscious of it or not.

This emphasis on relation brings us back to Weil's use in the passage I quoted earlier of the verb 'penetrate': thought should be 'empty and ready to be penetrated by the object' and 'ready to receive in its naked truth the object which is to penetrate it'. The symbolism reflects the link between soul and sexuality and shows that soul-making – whether by an attention whose name is love or the primary word of 'I-Thou' or in psychoanalysis – involves a relationship with another that is generative, lifting human experience out of repetitive sterility.

Analysts know that developing this quality of attention is not easy. Its apparently passive receptivity is the fruit of long, hard psychic work. Where might we look for an artistic representation of such work?

There is a series of paintings that date originally from 11th-century China, known as the 'Ox-herding pictures'. They represent the progressive discovery and purifying of the self, showing stages on the road to enlightenment as understood in Taoism and Zen Buddhism: another version still of 'soul-making'. The illustrations show a Japanese version of the paintings dating to 1278 (Figures 8.11–8.18). They are accompanied by short poems written by Kuoan Shiyuan, a 12th-century Chinese monk. The series shows the quality of attention and the immediacy of relation to the world that are required. They also show that, like the analytic relationship, the attention and mode of relating are loving but can be confrontative when they need to be.

Figure 8.11 The search for the ox

> *In the pasture of the world,*
> *I push aside the tall grasses in search of the ox.*
> *Following unnamed rivers,*
> *lost upon the paths of distant mountains,*
> *I cannot find him.*
> *I only hear the crickets in the forest at night.*

Figure 8.12 Perceiving the ox

> I hear the song of the nightingale.
> The sun is warm, the wind is mild,
> willows are green along the shore.
> Here no ox can hide!
> What artist can draw that massive head,
> those majestic horns?

146 Aesthetic Ethics

Figure 8.13 Catching the ox

> *I seize him with a terrific struggle.*
> *His great will and power are inexhaustible.*
> *He charges to the high plateau*
> *far above the cloud-mists,*
> *or in an impenetrable ravine he stands.*

Figure 8.14 Taming the ox

*The whip and rope are necessary,
else he might stray off down some dusty road.
Being well-trained, he becomes naturally gentle.
Then, unfettered, he obeys his master.*

148 Aesthetic Ethics

Figure 8.15 Riding the ox home

> *Mounting the ox, slowly I return homeward.*
> *The voice of my flute intones through the evening.*
> *Whoever hears this melody will join me.*

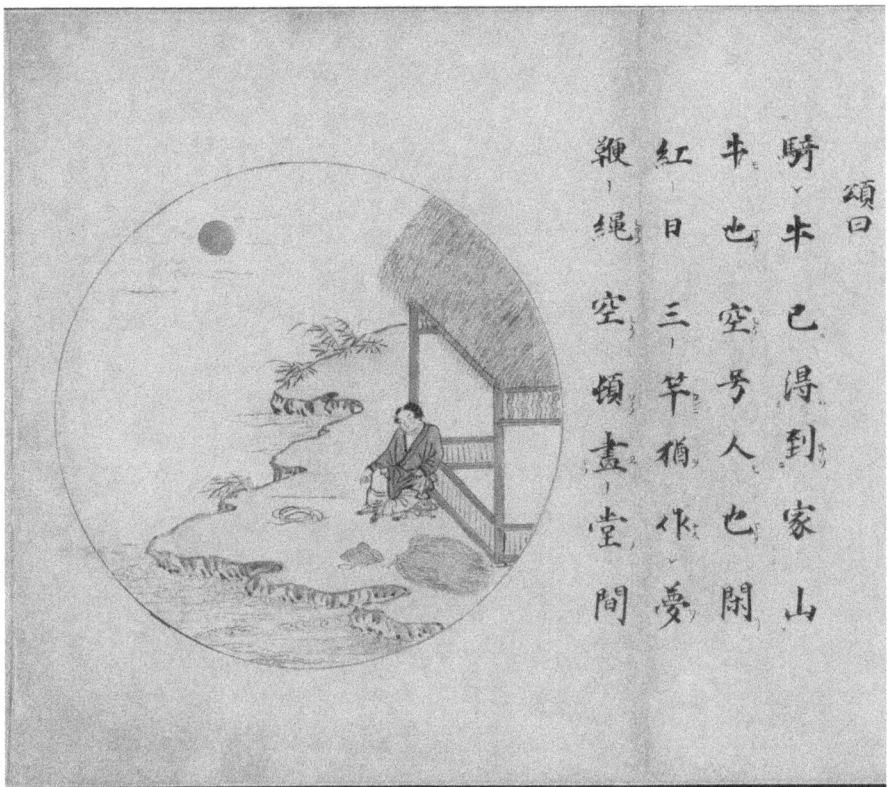

Figure 8.16 The ox transcended

Astride the ox, I reach home.
I am serene. The ox too can rest.
The dawn has come. In blissful repose
within my thatched dwelling,
I have abandoned the whip and ropes.

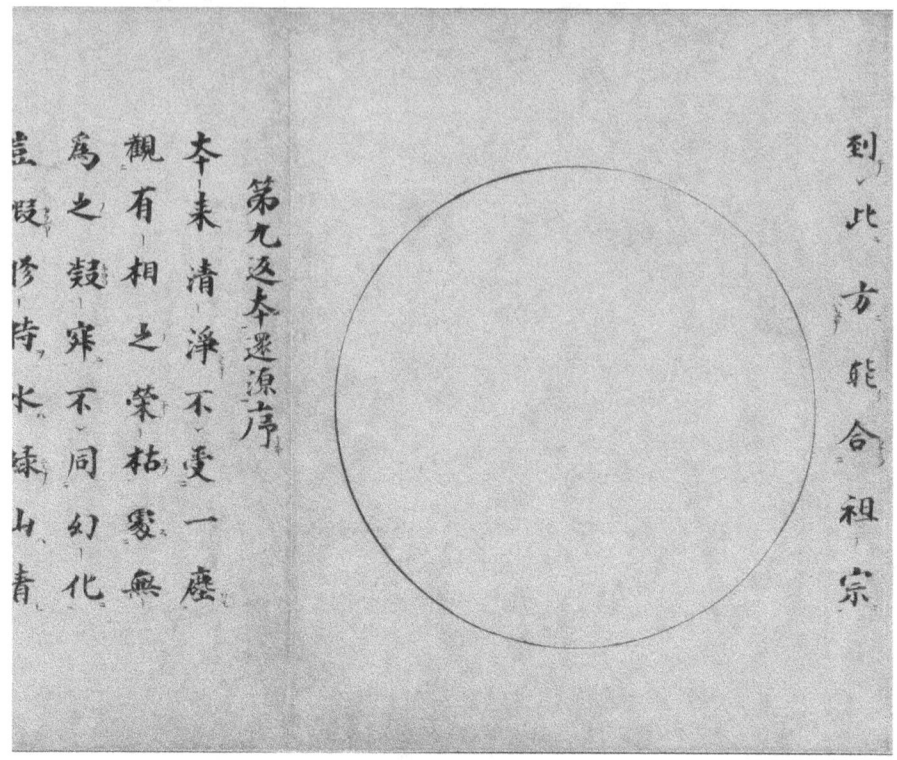

Figure 8.17 Both ox and self transcended

> *Whip, rope, person, and ox: all merge in No Thing.*
> *This heaven is so vast, no message can stain it.*
> *How may a snowflake exist in a raging fire?*
> *Here are the footprints of the Ancestors.*

And finally . . .

Figure 8.18 In the world

*Barefoot and naked of breast,
I mingle with the people of the world.
My clothes are ragged and dust-laden,
and I am ever blissful.
I use no magic to extend my life.
Now, before me, the dead trees become alive.*

It turns out that the true self is the ordinary self, doing ordinary things – like Vermeer's milkmaid – in a way that is not ordinary. The ox-herding pictures confirm that this calls for intense involvement, not to say struggle, in the physical world of the senses. It is by looking intensely at the ordinariness of the everyday world that artists discover something extraordinary within it. Psychoanalysts know well the struggle of patients to give up their idealisations and to see that they can only discover meaning in their lives as ordinary people living in an ordinary world.

The work of both artists and analysts is rooted in the relation between conscious and unconscious processes. Regarding artistic creativity, Stefan Zweig, a good friend of Sigmund Freud, wrote:

> To create is a constant struggle between the conscious and the unconscious. Without these two elements, the creative act cannot happen. They constitute the indispensable foundation; it is within the law of contrast, the final compromise between conscious and unconscious that the artist is imprisoned. Within the limits of this law he remains free.
>
> (Zweig, 2016, p. 153)

Zweig gives the analogy of chess, which allows a virtually limitless number of possible moves, within the limits of 64 black and white squares and thirty-two black and white pieces. The theatre director Peter Brook called his book on the theatre *The Empty Space* (Brook, 1968). Brook was famous for encouraging unconscious process to reveal itself in theatrical terms. This depends on that empty space being a precinct: a designated setting in which such freedom is possible.

I referred earlier to Keats' 'Intelligence without Identity' as a state of potentiality. The framed empty space, that is both outside and inside ourselves, is an arena of potential. Within the artist, and then shared between artist and viewer, it is an arena of aesthetic creativity. Within the analyst, and shared with the patient in the framework of the analytic setting, it is an arena of free-associative discovery. The potential function of this arena, wherever it may be found, is to be a meeting point for mind, heart, and the body with its sexuality. When that potential is realised, soul goes on coming into being.

Notes

1 An earlier version of this chapter was presented as the inaugural Anton O. Kris Lecture at the Boston Psychoanalytic Society and Institute on October 29, 2022.
2 I have quoted the translation published originally in the *International Journal of Psychoanalysis*, which captures better than the *Standard Edition* the meaning that I want to bring out.

References

Bauman, Z. (2004). *Identity*. Cambridge: Polity Press.
Bettelheim, B. (1983). *Freud and man's soul*. London: Chatto and Windus, Hogarth.
Bion, W. (1965/1977). *Transformations*. Reprinted in *Seven Servants*. New York: Aronson.
Black, D. (1993). What sort of thing is a religion? A view from object-relations theory. *The International Journal of Psychoanalysis*, 74, 613–625.
Black, D. (2006). *Psychoanalysis and religion in the 21st century: Competitors or collaborators?* London: Routledge.
Brook, P. (1968). *The empty space*. London: McGibbon & Kee.
Buber, M. (1937). *I and thou* (R. Gregor Smith, Trans.). Edinburgh: T. & T. Clark.
Catechism of the Catholic Church. (1994). London: Continuum.
David, N., Newen, A., & Vogeley, K. (2008). The "sense of agency" and its underlying cognitive and neural mechanisms. *Consciousness and Cognition*, 17L, 523–534.

Deutsch, F. (1959). *On the mysterious leap from the mind to the body: A workshop study on the theory of conversion*. New York: International Universities Press.
Erikson, E. (1956). The problem of ego identity. *Journal of the American Psychoanalytic Association*, 4, 56–121.
Freud, S. (1900). The interpretation of dreams. In *Standard edition of the complete psychological works of Sigmund Freud* (Vols. 4–5, pp. xxiii–621). London: Hogarth.
Freud, S. (1912). Recommendations to physicians practising psycho-analysis. In *Standard edition of the complete psychological works of Sigmund Freud* (Vol. 12, pp. 111–120). London: Hogarth.
Freud, S. (1923a). Two encyclopaedia articles. In *Standard edition of the complete psychological works of Sigmund Freud* (Vol. 18, pp. 235–259). London: Hogarth.
Freud, S. (1923b). The ego and the id. In *Standard edition of the complete psychological works of Sigmund Freud* (Vol. 19, pp. 12–59). London: Hogarth.
Freud, S. (1927). The future of an illusion. In *Standard edition of the complete psychological works of Sigmund Freud* (Vol. 21, pp. 5–56). London: Hogarth.
Freud, S. (1937). Analysis terminable and interminable. *International Journal of Psycho-Analysis*, 18, 373–405.
Greene, J. D., Sommerville, R. B., Nystrom, L. E., Darley, J. M., & Cohen, J. D. (2001). An fMRI investigation of emotional engagement in moral judgment. *Science*, 293(5537), 2105–2108.
Haught, J. R. (2001). *Responses to 101 questions on god and evolution*. Mahwah, NJ: Paulist Press.
Leach, B. (1945). *A potter's book* (2nd ed.). London: Faber & Faber.
Ledoux, J. E. (1996). *The emotional brain: The mysterious underpinnings of emotional life*. Simon & Schuster.
Masson, J. (1985). *The complete letters of Sigmund Freud to Wilhelm Fliess 1887–1904*. Cambridge: Harvard.
Meissner, W. W. (1984). *Psychoanalysis and religious experience*. Yale University Press.
Meissner, W. W. (2008). A note on the use of the concept of the soul in psychoanalytic discourse. *Psychoanalytic Quarterly*, 77, 327–340.
Miles, S. (Ed.). (1986). *Simone Weil: An anthology*. London: Virago.
Murphy, N. (2006). *Bodies and souls, or spirited bodies?* Cambridge University Press.
Parsons, M. (2014). *Living psychoanalysis: From theory to experience*. London: Routledge.
Parsons, M. (2021). Authority and Freedom. *Journal of the American Psychoanalytic Association*, 69, 1163–1190.
Parsons, M. (2024). Practice and praxis: Psychoanalysis as an act of love. *Psychoanalytic Quarterly*, 93, 219–248.
Pfister, O. (Ed.). (1993). The illusion of a future: A friendly disagreement with Professor Freud. *International Journal of Psychoanalysis*, 74, 557–579.
Rizzuto, A.-M. (1979). *The birth of the living god: A psychoanalytic study*. Chicago: University of Chicago Press.
Rollins, H. E. (1958). *The letters of John Keats 1814–1821* (Vol. 2). Cambridge University Press.
Schörghofer, G. (2014). *To be in Limbo*. Unpublished essay.
Simič, G., Mladenka, T., Vukič, V., Mulc, D., Španič, E., Šagud, M., Olucha-Bordonau, F., Vuksič, M., & Hof, P. (2021). Understanding emotions: Origins and roles of the amygdala. *Biomolecules*, 11, 823. https://doi.org/10.3390/biom11060823
Sochaczewski, J. (2017). Psychoanalysis and religion in the 21st century: Examining the possibility of integration. *Contemporary Psychoanalysis*, 53, 247–268.
Spezzano, C., & Gargiulo, G. (Eds.). (1997). *Soul on the couch: Spirituality, religion and morality in contemporary psychoanalysis*. Hillsdale: Analytic Press.
Starr, K. E. (2008). *Repair of the soul: Metaphors of transformation in Jewish Mysticism and psychoanalysis*. London: Routledge.
Strachey, J. (1953). Editorial note to "psychical (or mental) treatment". In *Standard edition of the complete psychological works of Sigmund Freud* (Vol. 7, p. 283). London: Hogarth.

Tyler, P. (2016). *The pursuit of the soul: Psychoanalysis, soul-making and the Christian tradition*. London: Bloomsbury.
Weil, S. (1951). *Waiting on god* (E. Craufurd, Trans.). London: Routledge.
Winnicott, D. W. (1975). *Through pediatrics to psychoanalysis*. London: Hogarth.
Yanagi, S. (1972). *The unknown craftsman: A Japanese insight into beauty*. Tokyo: Kodansha.
Zweig, S. (2016). *Messages from a lost world* (W. Stone, Trans.). London: Pushkin.

Chapter 9

How to Build the Other From Scratch After Its Destruction?

Françoise Davoine

I dedicate this talk to my dear friend, the late William Richardson, who invited Jean-Max Gaudillière and me to the Austen Riggs Center in 1979 to speak about Lacan's conception of the death drive. Our presentation was followed by a wide-ranging discussion, opening for us the field of psychodynamic psychoanalysis with persons who were reputedly unable to enter transference – precisely because there was no "Other" for their experience.

A Hermeneutic of Trust

I am also deeply honored by the presence of Donna Orange as a discussant. Her book, *The Suffering Stranger* (Orange, 2011),[1] presents psychoanalysts who affirm the possibility of transference even when it appears doomed to failure – despite orthodox critics who declare, "That is not psychoanalysis!" Donna Orange responds that these analysts follow a "hermeneutic of trust" rather than one of "suspicion."

Trust is also central to Lacan's definition of the unconscious as "the Discourse of the Other," the Symbolic Other, rooted in the given word. Yet truth and trust may be shattered by ruthless agencies in the lived experiences of psychosis and trauma. Lacan, however, did not fully address this issue in his *Preliminary Question for the Treatment of Psychosis*, arguing that doing so would imply going beyond Freud, while psychoanalysis has instead regressed to a previous stage (Lacan, 1977).[2]

And yet, during World War I, analysts who treated traumatized soldiers and civilians had already gone beyond Freud's Oedipus complex. They sought to reconstruct the Other from scratch when trust had been betrayed and the ghosts of lost comrades returned through the looking glass in a frozen temporality.

Time stops. Chronology is structured by symbols, and when the symbolic chain collapses, causality dissolves. Causality depends on the past of the cause for the future of its effect, yet when trauma disrupts this process, it becomes unavailable. If we say, "You are traumatized because in the past" patients respond, "I know, but nothing changes." In such cases, transference occurs not in the logic of past events but in the here and now of the session. It manifests as an interference with the analyst's background, as I will illustrate through a clinical story.

Another Paradigm of Psychoanalysis

That experience was familiar to pioneers in the psychoanalysis of psychosis, such as Frieda Fromm-Reichmann, Ferenczi, William Rivers, and later, Bion, who worked in military hospitals in Germany, Hungary, and England. In such circumstances, another paradigm of psychoanalysis emerges in the treatment of trauma, one that deals with an unconscious that is not *repressed* but *suppressed*, as neurologist and anthropologist William Rivers (1918) stated in his address to the Royal Society of Medicine regarding his treatment of traumatized officers at Craiglockhart War Hospital in Scotland.[3] In her *Regeneration Trilogy*,[4] written from his clinical notes, novelist Pat Barker (1992) portrays Rivers reading Freud and modifying his technique to access dissociated parts of the unconscious.

Freud himself had discovered this paradigm with Freud and Breuer (1896)[5] before he turned toward the Oedipus complex and abandoned his *Neurotica*, the psychoanalysis of trauma. In a famous letter to Fliess dated September 21, 1897, he argued that the prevalence of sexual abuse against children was too great and that he did not want to incriminate fathers, including his own (Freud, 1897a, 1897b). In a previous letter, dated February 8, he had confided to Fliess that his own father had sexually abused his younger siblings (Freud, 1985).[6] However, Freud would later return to this other paradigm, in which the unconscious is not repressed but suppressed.

As early as 1907, he wrote in his commentary on Wilhelm Jensen's *Gradiva* (Freud, 1907):[7] "Everything that is repressed is unconscious, but we cannot assert that everything unconscious is repressed." This is precisely the case in Jensen's short story, which depicts the healing of a young archaeologist's delusion at the actual site of Pompeii, frozen in the arrested time of the Vesuvius eruption in 79 AD. Freud also advises us to take "creative writers as valuable allies, for they are apt to know a whole host of things between heaven and earth of which our psychoanalytic wisdom has not yet let us dream."

Indeed, in cases of delusions and traumatic revivals, the unconscious is not articulated through repressed signifiers of the discourse of the Other. Instead, it is expressed through sensorial images, a phenomenon identified by art historian Aby Warburg as *nachleben* – "surviving images" – which are dissociated as a means of survival.

Aby Warburg may be counted among our "valuable allies," as he himself was healed from a delusion that emerged at the outset of World War I. After the war, he was hospitalized at Binswanger's clinic in Switzerland, where he repeatedly cried out that his Jewish family would be deported and exterminated. In 1924, he was discharged and resumed his research until his death in 1929. His recovery was made possible by his disciple, Fritz Saxl, who visited him regularly and persuaded Binswanger to release him – on the condition that Warburg could deliver a one-hour lecture before the hospital staff and patients. Thus, his famous *Lecture on the Snake Ritual among the Hopis* (Warburg, 1939)[8] was born. He delivered it without reading from his notes, placing his trust in Saxl, a genuine Other, who assured him that his research – whether scientific or delusional – stemmed from the same intelligence.

At the same time, after World War I, Freud found himself at a loss concerning the Other and became, in his own way, "a suffering stranger." In 1921, when young American psychiatrist Abram Kardiner asked him (Kardiner, 1997),[9] "What is it for you to be an analyst?" Freud responded, *"I am happy you ask me that question, since, to be honest, therapeutic problems don't interest me anymore. I am burdened by certain handicaps that prevent me from being a great analyst"* – likely referring to his worsening jaw cancer. He then added, *"And I am too much a father."* His daughter Sophie had just died from the Spanish flu. *"Besides,"* he continued, *"I am always writing theory. Too much theory."*

Later, his suffering deepened when his favorite grandchild, Heinele, Sophie's son, died of tuberculosis in 1923. According to his physician, Max Schur (1972),[10] Freud was devastated and had to endure the torture of numerous surgeries. When the Nazi persecutions began, his books were burned at the stake in Berlin in 1933. In response, Freud (1939) began writing *Moses and Monotheism*,[11] a work on the destruction of Pharaoh Akhenaten's civilization, which culminates in a chapter entitled *The Historical Truth*. Here, what is at stake is not simply the subject of repressed desires but rather *a political subject* (Gaudillière, 2021),[12] emerging from the erased parts of history.

Frozen Words

Another valuable ally on this issue is François Rabelais (1552), particularly his chapter "Frozen Words"[13] in *The Fourth Book*, written at the beginning of the religious wars in France. The story takes place during Pantagruel's voyage across the ocean with his companions. At one point, the giant hears voices. The ship's pilot explains that a bloody battle took place the previous winter on that very site of the frozen sea – what Pantagruel is hearing are words that have been frozen in the ice. At that moment, ice drops of various colors fall onto the deck, which Pantagruel picks up and warms in his hand: the red ones scream with the voices of soldiers dying from slit throats, while others, in different colors, echo the cries of women and children, the neighing of horses, and the blast of cannons.

The encounter with a reliable Other – one who, like Pantagruel, can warm frozen words rather than sending the hearer to electroconvulsive therapy (ECT) – occurs by chance, when causality is no longer available. *Chance plays an undeniable role*, as Freud (1909) wrote in a letter to Jung.[14] This is something I will now illustrate with a clinical story, in which the ghosts of a bloody civil war unexpectedly entered our sessions.

"The Unconscious or the Oblivion of History"

This is also the story of a suffering stranger who led me down a bloody, rough way, as Wittgenstein puts it, pushing me aside at every step until we reached a severed place and time in history. Still, I wonder whether my stubborn determination to remain by his side as an Other should be called empathy – or rather, a form of resistance that I learned in the cradle, having been born into a Resistance network during the last war, at the foot of a pass in the Alps.

This story took place when I began my private practice, after having worked as an analyst in public psychiatric hospitals for thirty years, where I saw patients once a week. There, my patients taught me that they were Principal Investigators, engaged in a relentless quest for an Other. I, in turn, became their co-researcher – a passionate witness to events without a witness, to borrow Dori Laub's expression. Laub, one of the founders of the Fortunoff Video Testimony of the Holocaust[15] at Yale, captured the essence of this work: bearing witness to histories that have been silenced (Laub, 1992).

At the time of this story, in 1977, I was training at Lacan's *École Freudienne*, where I never once heard the names of Frieda Fromm-Reichmann or Harry Stack Sullivan – until Jean Max and I visited the Austen Riggs Center in 1979. It is no surprise, then, that transference in cases of psychosis and trauma was not Lacan's primary concern. In his 1946[16] lecture on *Psychic Causality*, he managed to avoid mentioning the recent war, aside from a brief paragraph noting the interruption of his practice during that period (Lacan, 1967).

Recently, the young French historian Hervé Mazurel (2022) published a book entitled *The Unconscious or the Oblivion of History*.[17] In discussing his manuscript, I agreed with his critique of the psychoanalytic neglect of history. However, I also pointed out that he had overlooked those who worked according to Thomas Salmon's Principles[18] – psychoanalysts who treated trauma on the front lines and in military hospitals, dealing with an unconscious that was not *repressed* but rather one in which the *Other had been destroyed and had to be rebuilt from scratch* (Davoine & Gaudillière, 2004).

Ludwig Wittgenstein experienced a similar struggle in 1929 when he returned to Cambridge after spending ten years in Vienna following World War I, carrying the symptoms of PTSD. At that time, there was no Other for him. In his *Tractatus Logico-Philosophicus*, written on the front lines of the war, he had famously concluded: *"Whereof one cannot speak, thereof one must remain silent."* Yet ten years later, back in Cambridge, he revised this despairing assertion and opened the possibility of an Other, stating instead, *Whereof one cannot speak . . . one cannot help showing what cannot be said* (Wittgenstein, 2001; 1984).[19]

To whom? That is the question in the story I am about to tell.

At the Crossroad of a Singular Story and History

My clinical story dates back fifty years, so I feel permitted to tell it as it happened, following the advice of psychiatrist Maurice O'Drury (1973),[20] a disciple of Wittgenstein, who suggested sharing such stories after they have matured, like good old whisky – or good old wine, in my case.

At that time, as I mentioned, I intended to start a private practice. The French psychoanalyst François Roustang kindly referred one of my first patients to me. He had seen this patient for a while and labeled him as borderline. The young man had stopped studying medicine for two years and described himself as a voyeur, as his main activity involved watching women undressing through the windows of the building across from his.

This young man was very aggressive. To start with, he refused to pay me, citing the large sums he had already spent in vain with his previous analyst. Since I had a salary from the Institute of Social Sciences where I worked,[21] I agreed and told him, "Okay, you will pay me when you get better," following the custom of Chinese doctors.

For a long time, our sessions were spent under his relentless attacks against what he called *"the psychoanalytical octopus"* – a stance reminiscent of Donna Orange's *hermeneutic of suspicion*. He would recite, almost ritualistically, the theories of his previous analyst, invoking concepts such as *jouissance*, the phallic mother, his denial of castration, and other Lacanian terms, all converging into the supposed proof that I was *the worst analyst in the world*, incapable even of writing books like Roustang.

Still today, as I reflect, I wonder what made me persist. Perhaps it was the small victories over his relentless negativism – like the day when he once again declared that his analysis was a failure, and I countered that his greatest success was in ensuring that his analysis failed. Yet this statement, reminiscent of the Zen dialogues I was reading at the time, led nowhere. I was *no Other* for him, neither big nor small. All possible interpretations had already been spoken – before I could even open my mouth – ranging from the Oedipus complex to the foreclosure of the name of the father.

The issue came by chance, through a blunder so significant that it filled me with shame. To make a long story short: My front door had been left open, and one day, he arrived unusually early for his session and sat silently in the waiting room. Unaware of his presence, I had left my office door slightly ajar while speaking on the phone with a friend, announcing to her my second pregnancy. This must have been in early 1977. So there I was, casually chatting about the changes in my body – a real *striptease* for his voyeuristic ears.

When he coughed, I thought it was the end of his analysis – and I was right. Entering the room, he exploded in anger at my lack of professionalism. With nothing more to say, he stormed toward the door, threatening to kill himself, just as a friend of his had done after a session with his own analyst. Without thinking, I heard myself mumble that if there was nothing left to say, he could *draw* something instead.

Soon after, he called to tell me that he was still alive. I felt relieved – but not for long.

At our next session, he brought a crumpled piece of paper with a drawing that resembled a grid, like a chessboard. When I asked him what it was, he shouted that I should train with Françoise Dolto. A French child analyst, Dolto would have immediately recognized, he claimed, that the drawing depicted the building across from his window, the one where he watched women undress. Looking closer, I saw that some of the squares were filled with scribbles. I made a second blunder: *"They do not look very sexy."* Furious, he slammed the door again, shouting, *"Throw it in the garbage!"*

Instead, without thinking, I counted the number of scribbled squares. When he returned, I simply said: *"There are seven cases."* Instantly, for the first time, he calmed down. *"Seven Cases,* Siete Casas"* – that was the name of the Spanish village on the French border that my grandmother had fled during the Civil War, leaving behind her dead baby daughter and her deceased husband. She later remarried in France and gave birth to my mother, but she never spoke about that time – except in Spanish, so that I would not understand.

Roustang was almost right with his diagnosis of *"borderline,"* except that he had pointed in the wrong direction – toward a psychological structure rather than a *martyr* borderline village.

So, I said to him, *"The women you keep watching are tortured women."* I was speaking from my own background. My mother had been imprisoned by the Nazis while pregnant with me, and among the few words she ever spoke about that experience, she mentioned the torture chamber next to the overcrowded cell she shared with other women. She also said, *"Had I been Jewish, I would not be here."* Nor would I.

The murderous agency had finally entered our transference, interfering with my own story. From that moment on, he cried often. *"It is mourning,"* he said. He resumed his studies, working night shifts to pay me. He had been keeping track of the number of our sessions – I had not. One day, he simply said goodbye. Much later, I learned from one of his colleagues that he was married, had children, and was now the head of a palliative care ward. He later sent me a card with just two words: *thank you.*

Years later, I recounted this story at a conference in Spain, modifying it for the sake of confidentiality – changing, for instance, *Seven Cases* to *Nine Cases*. After my talk, the young woman responsible for videotaping the session approached me. *"Are you sure you're not mistaken? I'm quite certain that the name of the village where women were raped and tortured is Seven Cases."* That first, slightly altered version of the story is recounted in my book, *La Folie Wittgenstein* (Davoine, 2023), recently published by Routledge.[22]

This story illustrates what I mean by my title: how to build another from scratch when it has disappeared. In conclusion, I will turn to Homer as an ally, for in the *Iliad*, he offers us a word that encapsulates the two functions of the analyst when tasked with rebuilding another from nothing. The Homeric word is Therapôn, which Gregory Nagy (1996), a Hellenist at Harvard, translates as "the second in combat" – Patroclus for Achilles, Sancho Panza for Don Quixote, Corporal Trim for Captain Toby in Tristram Shandy, to name a few of my favorite allies. It also carries the meaning of "the ritual double", the one entrusted with funeral rites – a role ultimately fulfilled by the young man at the end of our chance encounter . . .

Abstract

Madness and trauma, experienced as violent ruptures of the social link, challenge mainstream psychoanalysis in its neglect of history. Historical catastrophes, such as recent pandemics and wars, create zones of loneliness and silence that are transmitted across generations. These suppressed histories resurface uncannily through unconscious revivals. I argue that the unconscious at stake here is not the repressed unconscious structured by the symbolic chain. Instead, in these cases, mirrors explode, and surviving sensorial images of disaster emerge through the looking glass.

People with extreme lived experiences are intimately familiar with a dissociated unconscious, which they use not only as a tool for survival but also as a method of research – to fight ruthless agencies for whom the Other does not exist. I will present critical moments from my practice, in which an embryonic Other emerges from analogous zones in my own background. In these instances, transference manifests as an interference that occurs by coincidence, in a rupture of time. At such moments, I become a Therapôn, a term attested in the *Iliad*, where it means both "the second in combat" and "the ritual double" – the one entrusted with funeral duties. The rhythm of the epic reanimates the breath of life, just as ritual theater has done for centuries across cultures. By drawing on literary works, I will demonstrate that madness and trauma demand a different paradigm of psychoanalysis – one that accounts for the way plagues and wars have always shaped the human psyche.

Notes

1 D. Orange, *The Suffering Stranger* (Routledge, 2011).
2 J. Lacan, *Écrits: A selection: On the Possible Treatment of Psychosis*, trans. A. Sheridan (W. W. Norton & Company, 1977).
3 W. H. R. Rivers, "The repression of war experience," *The Lancet*, 191(4920) (1918), 173–177.
4 P. Barker, *The Regeneration Trilogy* (Penguin, 1992).
5 S. Freud and J. Breuer, "Studies on Hysteria," in *Standard Edition of the Complete Psychological Works of Sigmund Freud*, trans. J. Strachey (The Hogarth Press, 1896).
6 S. Freud, *The Complete Letters of Sigmund Freud to Wilhelm Fliess, 1887–1904*, trans. J. M. Masson (Harvard University Press, 1985).
7 S. Freud, "Delusions and Dreams in Jensen's Gradiva," in *Standard Edition of the Complete Psychological Works of Sigmund Freud*, trans. J. Strachey, Vol. 9 (The Hogarth Press, 1907), 1–95.
8 A. Warburg, "A Lecture on Serpent Ritual," *Journal of the Warburg Institute*, 4 (1939), 277–292.
9 A. Kardiner, *My Analysis with Freud* (W. W. Norton & Company, 1977). [My translation from the French].
10 M. Schur, *Freud: Living and Dying* (International Universities Press, 1972).
11 S. Freud, *Moses and Monotheism* (Vintage Books, 1939).
12 J. M. Gaudillière, *The Birth of a Political Subject*, Vol. 2. Seminars at the EHESS transcribed by F. Davoine (Routledge, 2021).
13 F. Rabelais, "The Fourth Book (Chapter 55)," in *Gargantua and Pantagruel* (Penguin Classics, 2006).
14 Freud, S., & Jung, C. G. (1994). *The Freud-Jung Letters: The Correspondence Between Sigmund Freud and CG Jung*. Princeton University Press.
15 D. Laub and S. Felman, *Testimony* (Routledge, 1992).
16 J. Lacan, *Écrits: Propos sur la causalité psychique* (Paris: Seuil, 1967).

17 H. Mazurel, *L'inconscient ou l'oubli de l'histoire* (La Découverte, 2021).
18 F. Davoine and J. M. Gaudillière *History beyond Trauma* (The Other Press, 2004).
19 L. Wittgenstein, *Tractatus Logico-Philosophicus* (Routledge, 2001). L. Wittgenstein, *Philosophical Investigations* (Basil Blackwell, 1984).
20 M. O'Drury, *The Danger of Words* (Routledge, 1973).
21 École des Hautes Études en Sciences Sociales (EHESS). Paris, France.
22 F. Davoine, *Wittgenstein's Folly*, trans. W. Hurst (Routledge, 2023).

References

Barker, P. (1992). *Regeneration trilogy*. Viking.
Davoine, F. (2023). *La Folie Wittgenstein*. Routledge.
Dolto, F. (1984). *The unconscious image of the body* (F. M. Cottrell, Trans.). Northwestern University Press.
Freud, S. (1897a). Letter to Fliess, February 8, 1897. In J. M. Masson (Ed.), *The complete letters of Sigmund Freud to Wilhelm Fliess, 1887–1904* (pp. 207–209). Harvard University Press.
Freud, S. (1897b). Letter to Fliess, September 21, 1897. In J. M. Masson (Ed.), *The complete letters of Sigmund Freud to Wilhelm Fliess, 1887–1904* (pp. 272–274). Harvard University Press.
Freud, S. (1907). Creative writers and day-dreaming. In *Standard edition of the complete psychological works of Sigmund Freud* (Vol. 9, pp. 141–153). The Hogarth Press.
Freud, S. (1939). *Moses and monotheism* (K. Jones, Trans.). Vintage Books.
Jensen, W. (1907). *Gradiva: A Pompeiian fancy* (H. W. Chase, Trans.). Moffat, Yard & Co.
Lacan, J. (1946). Psychic causality. In *Écrits: A selection* (A. Sheridan, Trans.). W. W. Norton & Company.
Laub, D. (1992). Bearing witness or the vicissitudes of listening. In S. Felman, & D. Laub (Eds.), *Testimony: Crises of witnessing in literature, psychoanalysis, and history* (pp. 57–74). Routledge.
Mazurel, H. (2022). *The unconscious or the oblivion of history*. Gallimard.
Orange, D. (2011). *The suffering stranger: Hermeneutics for everyday clinical practice*. Routledge.
Rivers, W. H. R. (1917). The repression of war experience. *The Lancet*, 189(4886), 173–177.
Schur, M. (1972). Freud's concept of the "death instinct". *Journal of the American Psychoanalytic Association*, 20(4), 793–816.
Warburg, A. (1939). A Lecture on Serpent Ritual. *Journal of the Warburg Institute*, 4, 277–292.
Wittgenstein, L. (2001). *Tractatus logico-philosophicus*. Routledge.
Wittgenstein, L. (1984). *Philosophical investigations*. Basil Blackwell.

Chapter 10

Levinas, Decreative Hermeneutics, and Holocaust Testimony

Robert C. Reed

To read Emmanuel Levinas as giving us a moral philosophy is invariably to find oneself faced with what appears to be an extreme and impractical "ethics," enjoining "substitution" for the other person and "responsibility for one's persecutor," for example. While Levinas's work cannot fail to have ethical implications, if only because it forces us to rethink some of our most basic assumptions about the sources of moral obligation, reading Levinas as a moral philosopher too easily overlooks his claim to being a phenomenologist. Levinas's principal aim is not to prescribe ethics but to "describe" the signification or sense of ethics in general,[1] a primordial sensibility to the Other as basic as sense perception, which Levinas, somewhat misleadingly, denotes by such ordinary terms as *the ethical relation*, *responsibility*, or simply *ethics*. In this chapter, the question that will arise is that of the *form* an application of Levinas's phenomenology would therefore need to take. How, for example, would we apply his idea of the phenomenological sense of ethics to the problem of interpreting the testimony of the Other's affliction, especially if their suffering is of a nature utterly foreign to one, a dehumanizing experience of extreme pain and violence?

In his major work, *Otherwise Than Being, or Beyond Essence*, Levinas formulates his idea of the phenomenological sense of ethics in terms of what he calls the *saying* and the *said*. The said embraces all forms of expression and conscious action – everything we do or say or think that involves any sort of mental representation of its object. Thus the said is *language* in the broadest sense of the word: anything whatever that is capable of conveying a *meaning*. The saying, by contrast, is the "non-conscious" or "preoriginal" ethical relation of responsibility to the Other which Levinas claims is the underlying signification of every said. All human relations, before so much as a word is spoken, involve one non-consciously in "saying" to the Other, and in turn "hearing" from them, the declaration "Here I am" – in French, *me voici*, literally translatable as "You see me here" – effectively placing oneself at the Other's service, if not for ethical action at the very least in the way of exposure to the Other's critique of one's understanding of her and of one's version of the world in which one has peremptorily situated her. What ultimately gives meaning to ethics is the fact that everything one says or does is a largely unconscious self-exposure in response to the Other's presence, structurally prior to all

DOI: 10.4324/9781003598107-13

conscious choice, action, and thought. We *cannot help but respond*, and solicit the other's response, with every person we meet, even when we seem to ignore them. As a result – and this will be crucial for all that follows – *every* encounter with the Other is a disruption, to some minimal degree, of one's going-on-in-the-same-way. Levinas describes this disruptive effect only in very general terms, using a variety of metaphors and images: it is a "transcendence in immanence," "a *difference* in relation to the 'remaining-the-same,'" a "tear[ing of] the I out of its coincidence with itself," "being turned inside out," an "awakening" (Levinas, 1998b, pp. 23, 27, 29). Being "awakened" to the Other is the preoriginal significance of ethics. Levinas's phenomenological reduction reduces the said to the saying, the saying "in" the said, by producing what he calls "traces" of this awakening. The reduction becomes "philosophy's task" (Levinas, 1981, p. 7), an *ethical* task in the preoriginal sense that Levinas gives the word. In light of skepticism over the viability of ethics "after Auschwitz," this task would seem to be especially relevant to the interpretation of Holocaust testimony.

Normally, the disruption Levinas calls the ethical relation goes unnoticed, but it can happen occasionally that something we do or say strikes us unexpectedly as a reaction, in spite of ourselves, to the Other's *otherness*. One can easily imagine that such an occurrence would have the potential to serve as a trace, in Levinas's sense, of the non-conscious ethical relation itself. Such a trace could take the form of an unpremeditated action, perhaps on the Other's behalf, so abruptly spontaneous that it defies description as an intentional act. The "otherness" of one's action, as compared to the things one normally does, would bring to mind the otherness of the other person and therefore the ethical relation that motivates our interactions. I give an example of such an unpremeditated and personally surprising action in the next section. I then propose a reinterpretation of Levinas's phenomenological reduction in which the reduction takes the form of one's consciousness of such an unexpected act, a refinement of Levinas's reduction based on a practice of attention developed by his contemporary, Simone Weil. Finally, in the second half of the chapter, I demonstrate the usefulness of the refined reduction by applying it as a hermeneutics to the reading of Paul Celan's poetry.

Simone Weil's Practice of Decreative Attention

Reality, as Weil conceives it, is whatever forces itself upon the mind against the resistance of one's self-oriented representations of the world. More often than not, we tend to "read" the world in a way that maintains its comfortable "sameness" and thus obscures the "otherness" of other persons and the ethical significance of the situations in which we happen to encounter them. Ethics for Weil is therefore not primarily a matter of deliberating on how one should act but of realizing in oneself a self-abdicating, reality- or Other-directed *orientation* she calls *attention* that delays self-interested "reading." What is essential to attention is not that one make an effort of concentration on a particular "object" but rather that one remove every distraction that would interfere with or conceal the reality that consciousness normally works hard to render inoffensive and harmless. In a sense, Weil's practice of attention has no object; it is utterly free and undiscriminating.[2] Expressed another way, its "object" is a *void* that one must work to leave empty so that the "real" can make an appearance or impact on its own (Weil, 1956, pp. 153, 198, 1970, p. 159). To leave the void empty, one must continually set aside or "bracket" every thought, every impulse to act, every hint of will, and do so relentlessly, since consciousness hates a void and continually tries to fill it. Aside from that, one simply *waits*, a waiting that, to borrow a phrase of Levinas's, is *an awaiting without an awaited* (Levinas, 2000, p. 115, 139). One does nothing but bracket and wait until literally *forced* into some other action, perhaps in response to or on behalf of the person who happens to have come into view as a result of one's attention.

Here is an example from ordinary life of the kind of action I mean. Suppose you are in the midst of an awkward dilemma involving another person where you cannot see any appropriate resolution. Out of desperation, you begin to doubt everything you thought you knew about the other person, perhaps even your working understanding of human relations in general. At that point, having temporarily emptied your mind of all your preconceptions, there might ensue an uncomfortable pause – and then, from out of nowhere, the appropriate action suddenly appears clear and obvious, perhaps as little as asking the other person "Are you in pain?" or Weil's favorite, "What are you going through?" You find yourself interrupted, as it were, by your own action, an action of which you might become conscious only in the doing or even some moments afterwards. More precisely, this *non-willed action* just *is* the "negative effort" of attention carried out until *not* acting is no longer possible (Weil, 1973, p. 111).

It should be evident that attention demands a self-deposing that allows the other person to acquire a significance in which one's self plays little or no role. Weil calls this uprooting or abdication of the self *decreation*. A decreated self loves reality and others "impersonally," without reference to its own "person" – "in the way that an emerald is green" (Weil, 1970, p. 129). The practice of attention is therefore decreative. It must be emphasized that decreation is an *ideal limit* of attention. Since consciousness continually works against the self-abdication of decreation, one is never, according to Weil, ever completely "decreated" in conscious life.

As an unanticipated interruption or discontinuity not just in one's personal history but in one's very sense of self, non-willed action is all the more likely to call to mind the *otherness* of the Other who seems to instigate it. For a moment, one experiences a displacement between one's conscious action and one's going-on-in-the-same-way, a temporary inability to connect the present with one's past. This makes non-willed action an obvious candidate for what Levinas calls a trace: any action or expression (a said) that reminds one of the ethical relation (the saying) which is its preoriginal signification. Given the non-conscious status of the ethical relation or saying, the trace is necessarily ambivalent, subverting its own reference in a perpetual ambiguity.[3] Thus Weil's attention can be practiced with the intention of making more likely a non-willed action that can then be interpreted ("reduced") to the saying – a variant or refinement of Levinas's phenomenological reduction. I now show how this *decreative reduction* can be employed as a hermeneutics.

Decreative Hermeneutics

It is typical of experiences that have a strong sensory content that their interpretation seems instantaneous and irrefutable, but the fact that we often "misread" the world – as when, to give the classic example, we mistake a tree alongside a lonely road at night to be a man – proves that the feeling of irrefutability is often, and perhaps to some extent always, a function of acquired interpretive habits (Weil, 2015, p. 24). Even when the reading we give to sense impressions is immediate, it is nonetheless a reading that reflects meanings we have adopted unquestioningly from other people apart from the evidence of the senses. To give an extreme example of Weil's: in wartime, enemy combatants and even civilians are often "read" immediately as "someone to kill," with predictable if at times unintentional and tragic results. Weil finds this somewhat paradoxical. "Meanings," she writes, "which if looked at abstractly would seem to be mere thoughts, arise from every corner around me, taking possession of my soul and shaping it from one moment to the next in such a way that, to borrow a familiar English phrase, 'my soul is no longer my own'" (Weil, 2015, p. 25). This in spite of the fact, as she claims elsewhere, that "the mind is not forced to believe in the existence of anything" (Weil, 1956, p. 308).

Given the power of meanings, holding back from interpreting a text by delaying one's habitual practice of "reading" the world so as to corroborate the meanings one already accepts would not be easy. The exercise of attention is essentially the discipline of this hesitation, a holding back that would allow the text, much like a person, to alter one's relation both to itself and to the Others for whom it might represent a voice. One leaves oneself vulnerable in the same way that is required, according to Levinas, simply in order to recognize the Other as *other*. Decreative attention is ethics; "facing" the text indeed involves a responsibility to the Other which Levinas often describes through the metaphor of *the face*. Thus one is not justified in saying that one is reading a text as a testimony of affliction simply because it is a transcript of an interview with a Holocaust survivor, for example. It would count as such only if one read it with attention – face-to-face with it, as it were, allowing the testimony to place one into question, as does the Other.

The main obstacle to learning the necessary optics for such a decreative reading is our tendency to read any text – and indeed, the world as a whole – in a way that keeps things safe and "same." As Weil puts it, we read in such a way that what we desire appears good rather than reading so that the truly good appears desirable (Weil, 1956, p. 36). We tend to assume, consciously or not, that the continuation of the life we already live is a good, and this assumption effectively obscures evidence otherwise. Thus most of us who live in comfort will, often unconsciously, read the testimony of the destitute so as to minimize if not nullify our responsibility for their condition. Our defenses go up immediately the moment we begin to read. Hence, what is called "reading for meaning" too easily takes the form of unconsciously deciding on the meaning that makes the things we desire appear good. We read in a way that validates what we think we already understand. If we aim for the second form – reading so that the good appears desirable – then fundamentally, we are no longer reading for the "meaning": reading becomes an expression of the desire for the good and not for understanding, except insofar as the latter comes about on its own. The real "meaning" or significance of a testimony of atrocity might then be the action it inspires in the reader. The apparently innocent desire to *understand* what we are reading is therefore the most common form of interference with the more difficult but ethically more essential practice of decreative reading. If the result is non-willed action on the Other's behalf, one acts not with explicit intention – an action which would still carry the marks of the self in its tendency to rely on *representations* of the Other – but as though directly inspired by the Other's demand for respect for their otherness. It follows that in order that one's action be dictated by the Other's claim on one's responsibility, it is necessary that the interfering self be temporarily deposed.[4]

As an application of decreative hermeneutics, I now take up the work of perhaps the most influential and at the same time enigmatic of post-Holocaust poets, Paul Celan. One might recall in this connection Theodor Adorno's famous claim that it is impossible to write poetry after Auschwitz without engaging in barbarism.[5] Adorno's work and that of Max Horkheimer following the war could be summarized as trying to find a way to philosophize, indeed to *live*, after the Shoah. What does it mean to live in solidarity with those who, in Horkheimer's words, suffered "horrors intended for us as for them" (Horkheimer, 1974, p. 122) – horrors one has been fortunate enough to avoid but which were inflicted on those others simply because they were human like oneself, and therefore essentially intended for oneself? It should at least mean that one brackets not only every thought that obscures the reality of those horrors but even the very *self* that interprets the world in ways that obscure not only the Other's suffering but the need to consider the relevance of their suffering to one's own idea and practice of who one is and how one relates to Others in general. This is the heart of a "decreative" approach to the problem of interpreting Holocaust literature, an approach that acquires, in Levinas's phenomenology of the Other, the phenomenological grounding that Weil was unable to give it.

Reading Paul Celan Decreatively

A Jewish Romanian poet of international renown who wrote in German, Paul Celan struggled to express through his poetry an experience of the Shoah marked by eighteen months in a forced labor camp and, most significantly for his poetic output, the deportation and subsequent deaths of both parents when he was in his early twenties. That loss haunted him for the remainder of his life, leading him to view the language in which he chose to write as doubly defiled – personally and historically – by the crimes of the perpetrators. In what follows, I argue that Celan's aim as a poet might well have been to show us, in effect, the way to a *decreative reading* not only of his own poetry but of Holocaust testimony in general, indeed any testimony to affliction. The need for such a reading is reflected in Celan's conviction that one must try to express what defies expression. This paradox sets up a tension between reader and poem in which the poem deliberately frustrates the reader's every attempt to reduce the text to her understanding of the world by interpreting it in terms of her subjective knowledge and action. For Celan, the poem's resistance amounts to an encounter with an Other. A decreative hermeneutics would aim to bring to mind Levinas's ethical relation in this very encounter.

But let us start with Philippe Lacoue-Labarthe, who early in his 1986 study of Celan, *Poetry as Experience*, claims that many of Celan's poems "*necessarily* escape interpretation; they forbid it. One could even say they are written to forbid it." Lacoue-Labarthe then adds: "That is why the sole question carrying them, as it carried all Celan's poetry, is that of meaning, the possibility of meaning" (Lacoue-Labarthe, 1986/1999, p. 13). The real "meaning" of Celan's poetry would be that it places in question the very possibility that a poem – indeed any human endeavor "after Auschwitz" – can have meaning. For a poet, according to Lacoue-Labarthe, this is a question of the "translation" (not representation or interpretation) of a unique experience, "a transcendental question . . . that inevitably takes away, as Heidegger found with both Hölderlin and Trakl, all forms of hermeneutic power, even at one remove: for example, envisioning a 'hermeneutics of hermeneutics.'" I would contend, however, that Celan's poetry nonetheless can – in fact, on Lacoue-Labarthe's own skeptical terms, *must* – lend itself to a *decreative* hermeneutics. Hardly characterizable as a form of "power," decreative hermeneutics is rather an abdication or *subversion* of one's interpretive capability, whether one interprets a work of art or the silence of the Other who suffers. A decreative hermeneutics "translates" the encounter with the Other directly into non-willed action that resists representation and thereby concedes the Other's primordial resistance.

Thinking of Celan's impossible task of expressing the inexpressible experience of the Holocaust, Lacoue-Labarthe goes on to question the very possibility of any "singular" or "silent experience" at all, insofar as experience might be meaningful only as mediated through language:

> Is there, can there be, a singular experience? A silent experience, absolutely untouched by language, unprompted by even the most articulated discourse? If, impossibly, we can say "yes," if singularity exists or subsists despite all odds (and beyond empirical considerations, the presence of a witness . . . or of someone else who knows), can language possibly take on its burden? . . . These questions pose neither the problem of solipsism nor that of autism, but very probably that of solitude, which Celan experienced to what we must justly call the utmost degree.
>
> (Lacoue-Labarthe, 1986/1999, p. 15)

The solitude referred to here is not just that of a poet confronted by the problem of conveying something of his private experience but also undoubtedly the loneliness of the Holocaust survivor who finds himself among those who either cannot or do not want to know what he has been through. But Celan is not simply alone; he is alone *with* that silent experience, which indeed is something like an Other. If the poem invites the reader into the relationship Celan has with this Other, how does one accept the invitation without betraying it?

The answer is that one cannot – at least, not without betrayal. A respectful reading of a poet who, fearing betrayal, intentionally resists being "understood," would deliberately *multiply* interpretations, precisely in order to bring out the betrayal they cannot avoid. To borrow an image Levinas uses for his phenomenological reduction (Levinas, 1981, p. 44), a subversive hermeneutics appropriate to this situation would be a spiraling process, repudiating each interpretation only to return to another, but on a different "level" of what might be called its evolving anti-interpretive history. Like Levinas's reduction, and in some ways resembling Midrash,[6] this self-subverting hermeneutics would continually defer to the reticence of which Lacoue-Labarthe writes, the poem's tendency to frustrate understanding by calling into question the reader herself, much as the reduction continually contests the interpretive said that would claim to express the inexpressible saying. In the final section of Chapter V of *Otherwise Than Being* ("Skepticism and Reason"), Levinas even follows an earlier reference to the reduction (Levinas, 1981, p. 165) with a rare mention of poetry, insisting that the preoriginal "language" of the saying remains irrevocably beyond the interpretive said, which, despite betraying it, must nevertheless untiringly gesture toward that saying:

> Language would exceed the limits of what is thought, by suggesting, letting be understood without ever making understandable, an implication of a meaning distinct from that which comes to signs from the simultaneity of systems or the logical definition of concepts. This possibility is laid bare in the poetic said, and the interpretation it calls for ad infinitum.
> (Levinas, 1981, pp. 169–170)

A decreative reading is still a reading, and as such, it cannot help but "interpret" and supply "meanings." It cannot help but betray the Other by "filling the void." What sets decreative hermeneutics apart with respect to the otherness of the neighbor, the "otherness" of their experience, or the "otherness" of a work of art that tries to represent otherness, is the subversive hermeneutical refusal to allow the void to *remain* filled. Filling the void means disengaging the process of constant re-interpretation that requires that one be skeptical of one's ability to com-prehend (grasp together), to make the "same." Emptying the void is a continual spiraling movement whose multiple interpretations are implicated in (or toward) a "meaning" that cannot be grasped, that in fact *negates* one's comprehension of self and other, but the awareness of which is nonetheless the whole point of the process.[7]

It is possible that Levinas's own interest in Celan may have been motivated by a belief that Celan's work was in effect – although probably not consciously[8] – an attempt to develop a poetry of the *ethical* in Levinas's sense of that word. More precisely, Celan's would be a poetic practice in which a poem is experienced as a unique invitation seeking an encounter with a reader who would be its unique responder, making the poem a "trace" of the ethical relation. To employ an image of Celan's, the poem would be a message in a bottle ("*Flaschenpost*") that, having survived a long journey over the impossibly rough seas of the Shoah, washed up on some other person's remote "heartland" and was picked up and not simply read but *encountered* (Celan, 2001, p. 396). The poem would be, again in Celan's words, but sounding yet more like Levinas, both a "going towards" and a "being for" the reader who is its Other.[9]

This possibility is reinforced when we find Levinas, at the beginning of his own essay on Celan,[10] quoting Celan's enigmatic assertion that there appeared to him to be no difference between a handshake and a poem.[11] One recalls Levinas's observation in a much earlier work, *Existence and Existents* (1947), that "to shake hands with a friend is to express one's friendship for him, but it is to convey that friendship as something inexpressible, and indeed as something unfulfilled, a permanent desire" (Levinas, 1978, p. 35). If equating a poem with a handshake suggests that a poem could aim to relate to its reader in a manner similar to that of a person, then we might surmise that the poet would hope for a reading that would respect what is, like a person, inexpressible in the poem, something the poem "desires" and which provokes in the reader a feeling of obligation or responsibility rather than soliciting her cognitive grasp. The goal would *not* be to "understand" the poem, to "solve" it like a riddle, thus revealing "what it means."[12] Such a grasping after a positive gain for oneself characterizes the for-itself of com-prehension, not the one-for-the-other of ethics. Rather than demanding something from the poem, the goal would be to experience the poem as requiring something specifically *from oneself* as its unique reader. In his Meridian speech on the occasion of his accepting the Büchner Prize in 1960, Celan's startling answer to the question of what the poem demands is to imply that it desires *company*: "The poem unmistakably shows a strong bent toward falling silent. . . . The poem is lonely [Das Gedicht ist einsam]" (Celan, 2001, p. 409). To the question, what right does a poem have to make a demand on its reader comparable to that of a person seeking company, one might answer that "after Auschwitz" poetry can do nothing else. For the post-Holocaust poet, it is enough simply to make some genuine connection with the reader.[13]

Levinas, as though echoing Lacoue-Labarthe, observes that the "loneliness" of the poem consists in its isolation from any unambiguous meaning. The poem does not straightforwardly refer; it cannot communicate in any meaning-full way with its reader, and therefore, to this extent, resembles Weil's void. For Celan, on Levinas's reading, a poem, like a person, has no reference other than itself: the poem is "*dire sans dit*," "a saying without a said." It is "a sign that is its own signified: the subject makes a sign of this sign-making to the point of making itself wholly sign."[14] When Celan describes it as "ambiguity without a mask,"[15] the poem likewise becomes a sign that signifies that it has no signified, "signifying" the "real" by its undisguised refusal to resolve or disguise reality's contradictions. For Weil, reality is not the way things truly are, their objective truth, but a relationship one has with the "otherness" of things, destabilizing one's "same": a relationship between oneself and the way things *seem* to be that calls for skepticism about one's ability to know, a willingness to remain open to what can only show itself on its own, and a tolerance for what appears to ordinary consciousness as illogical or even absurd. On her view, reality shows itself not as a revelation of coherence that converts the unfamiliar into the familiar but as paradox and personal disturbance.[16] In its ambiguity, the poem signifies not the real, representing it, but its inability to signify the real. The same paradox is the motivation for Weil's belief that self-abdication is a necessary condition even for simply *noticing* another person as not merely an entity in one's world. Others "appear" *as other*, as real, to the exact extent that one brackets one's representations of them. To be open to reality's contradictions – not only, but especially, when face-to-face with the Other – means giving up something of the familiar coherence of one's personal world, in which one almost always interprets things in a way consistent with one's capabilities and desires.

As a personal construct, the coherence of one's world is supremely vulnerable, a vulnerability to which Celan may have been referring when he remarked in an interview that reality must be sought and won ("Wirklichkeit will gesucht und gewonnen sein").[17] Thus the poet must be engaged in a struggle to maintain an orientation that largely goes against the grain of ordinary life, an *other*-orientation – particularly if he hopes to reference an experience which, as traumatic, itself goes against the grain of everyday experience. Quoting from Celan's Meridian speech, Levinas writes concerning this unnatural vocation that

> the poet does not retain . . . his proud sovereignty of creator. In Celan's terms: the poet speaks "from the angle of inclination [inclinaison] of his existence, and from the angle of inclination in which the creature declares itself. . . . He who writes it (who writes the poem) remains dedicated to it."

Levinas then comments: "Singular de-substantiation of the *I*! to make oneself wholly sign [*tout entier signe*], it [the poem] is perhaps just that."[18] To make oneself *nothing more than* a sign: this is reminiscent of a "de-substantiation" reflecting the extreme – a *necessary* extreme – of decreative attention. In a footnote, as though hinting this very idea, Levinas refers the reader to Weil's entreaty, "Father, tear from me this body and this soul in order to make them your things, and let nothing else subsist of me eternally but this tearing itself' (Levinas, 1996, p. 176n16, 1976, p. 189n15).[19] This prayer for self-negation is immediately followed in Levinas's main text by a passage worth quoting in full because it strikingly reveals further resonances with Weil's practice of attention. Writes Levinas:

> A gesture of recognition of the other, a handshake, a saying without a said – these things are important by their interpellation rather than by their message; important by their attention! "Attention, like a pure prayer of the soul," of which Malebranche speaks, in so many unexpected echoes from Walter Benjamin's pen:[20] extreme receptivity, but extreme donation; attention – a mode of consciousness [*de conscience*] without distraction, i.e. without the power to escape

through dark underground passages; full illumination, projected not in order to see ideas, but in order to prohibit evasion; the first meaning of that insomnia that is conscience [*la conscience*] – rectitude of responsibility before any appearance of forms, images, or things.

(Levinas, 1996, p. 43)

Attention, Levinas is saying, is an ethical act, a response to the Other which is itself the desire for a response, a passive reception accomplished in self-donation, a donation evidenced by an openness to the Other's reception. "Dark underground passages" may refer to psychoanalysis, reflecting Levinas's judgment of it as a fashionable obsession with the unconscious, really a fascination with the *self*, which can only distract one from one's ethical obligations.[21] Against this, what he calls "illumination" would be needed not to bring knowledge to light but to prevent one's "knowledge" from obscuring recognition of the Other. In short, attention is all about responsiveness – responsibility – to reality, and in particular, to the Other – just as Weil says. One cannot help wondering how much of Weil Levinas had in fact read when he wrote these lines.

Likewise in Levinas's version of Celan's remark from his Meridian speech, *inclinaison* is not something intentional but the preoriginal orientation (*pente* rather than *gout*) of the speaker simply as speaker – that is, the *saying* as opposed to the *said*, the responsibility behind the "logos of response," the subjectivity of the subject rather than a subject's conscious expression (Levinas, 1981, p. 102). The saying does not make clear either an object or a project but signifies one's *substitution* for the Other *tout entier*, by which extraordinary metaphor Levinas means to convey the idea that responsibility takes the form of acknowledging every Other's vulnerability as fundamentally one's own. Thus Levinas's notion of substitution signifies that there is no concern of the Other's which does not have the potential of becoming one's own concern. Physically as well, one occupies a space that could theoretically be the Other's. In effect, one has always already substituted for an Other who could be anyone and everyone, making one, in Dostoevsky's words as Levinas quotes them in *Otherwise Than Being*, responsible "before everyone for everyone, and I more than the others" (Levinas, 1981, p. 146). Indeed, what makes the Other *other* is precisely this tendency to be continually responsibility-inducing in that everything the Other says or does (the said) signifies this compulsion (the saying) to reveal oneself as, ultimately, nothing more than responsibility for others (Levinas, 1996, pp. 62–63). In much the same way, Weil claims that one is nothing more than love of neighbor, however little this love actually manifests itself in one's outward actions. All the rest that one identifies as one's *self* is the work of imagination.

Is it possible to read a text not for what is *said* but for the *saying* which is structurally prior to the said? *Can* the poem itself be, as we saw Levinas suggest earlier, the saying? Perhaps only its trace. Referring to the saying, Levinas writes: "The fact of speaking to the other – the poem – precedes all thematization." Then Levinas quotes Celan: "the poem 'lets otherness's ownmost also speak: the time of the other'" (Levinas, 1996, p. 44). Falling silent in the midst of its speaking, continually interrupting itself in a "strange coherence'" that defies logic (Levinas, 1996, p. 41), Celan's poetry might appear deliberately to prevent the reader from incorporating its said too quickly into the reader's "same" and thus further obscure the saying. Similarly, Holocaust survivors perversely refute an interviewer's attempts to rephrase their testimony in everyday terms the interviewer thinks listeners will find easier to comprehend – as though one could comprehend what defies comprehension! Alluding to the futility of trying to *grasp* the Other in his or her otherness, Levinas maintains that "coherence dissimulates a transcendence, a movement from the one to the other, a latent diachrony, uncertainty, and a fine risk" (Levinas, 1981, p. 170) – that is, logical coherence denies the ethical relation which, in Weil's terms, would signify contact with the real. Thus Levinas provides a phenomenological basis for Weil's claim that comprehension is the very opposite of the practice of attention, suggesting that her practice of attention is a way to Levinas's (and the poem's) incomprehensible saying – although only by way of the traces the saying leaves in the said.

Facing reality was the point of Celan's work if anything was, a reality filled with pain and loneliness, complicated by his decision to write in German, a language despoiled at the hands of the perpetrators of the disaster from which he suffered. Nonetheless, he says, the language survived:

> It, the language [*Sprache*], remained, not lost [literally, unlost, *unverloren*], yes in spite of everything. But it had to pass through its own answerlessness, pass through frightful muting, pass through the thousand darknesses of deathbringing speech [*Rede*]. It passed through and gave back no words for that which happened; yet it passed through this happening. Passed through and could come to light again, "enriched" by all this. In this language I have sought, during those years and the years since then, to write poems: so as to speak, to orient myself, to find out where I was and where I was meant to go, to sketch out reality for myself.[22]

As employed by Celan, language itself became a witness to the dark times it – and Celan – had "passed through." Thus the poetic medium in which Celan carried out his search for an orientation in that darkness often took the form of interruptions and silences, suggesting an attempt impossibly to "say" *other*. The orientation he sought, as I suggested earlier, was an Other-orientation. For a reader to suppress or "explain" these interruptions, giving the silences of Celan's poetry a "voice," would suppress the reader's own contact with the poem's otherness and the reality to which it gestures. To prevent this, the poem might attempt to express the Other's alterity negatively, in terms of a demand upon the reader. A decreative interpretation of such a poem would bring this demand to consciousness – and to conscience – against the totalizing tendency of consciousness to maintain the "same." Decreative hermeneutics respects the otherness of a poem which, like a person, refuses interpretation while continually demanding "rereading" and new failures of interpretation. The very failures would be one (but only one) measure of the poem's success.

To what end? That will depend on the reader. Decreative hermeneutics is nothing if not radically context-*dependent*. The process might end with the solicitation of a response from the reader in the form of political action on behalf of present-day sufferers of oppression. Or it might result in simply an awareness of the impossibility of mourning a past suffering which is incomprehensible, on the order of James Hatley's idea that one can mourn the loss of mourning (Hatley, 2000, pp. 75, 195, 246n38). Decreative hermeneutics could then itself become a form of mourning resembling so-called "postmemory," sometimes experienced by children of Holocaust survivors: one mourns the inability to relate to a significant Other's memory of traumatic violence.

Or perhaps decreative hermeneutics results in nothing more than an awareness of a "bad conscience" regarding one's own complicity with injustice in some present-day form. A critic familiar with the circumstances surrounding the deportation of Celan's parents might reasonably surmise that the "meaning" of much of his poetry is the expression of "survivor's guilt."[23] But for Levinas in the 1980s, "bad conscience" is the signification of the saying, signifying ethics as responsibility not simply for what one has done or omitted to do but for every Other's suffering and "unjust death."[24] The goal of interpretation would not be the "meaning" of the poem but "the meaning of [one's] survival" (Spargo, 2006, p. 116), if not literally survival of the Holocaust then of present-day "hatred of the other man," for which the Holocaust continues to serve as both metonymy and exemplar (Levinas, 1981, p. vii). This would be the meaning of survivor's guilt as it could apply to me, whether or not I am aware of the extraordinary proximity of this "could," which signifies my very subjectivity as responsibility for "the other man."

Celan's figuring of the poem as like a person, a human subject of suffering and responsibility, allows for this extra-ordinary reading based on Levinas's phenomenology of the Other, made practical as a hermeneutics through Weil's decreative attention. As Levinas expresses it, "The poem goes toward the other. It hopes to find him freed and vacant" (Levinas, 1996, p. 41) – that is, to find him having emptied, or in the process of emptying, a void which is the *awaiting without an awaited* that constitutes decreative hermeneutics.

Notes

1 The term *description* (and, for purists, the term *phenomenological reduction* used below) is somewhat problematic here, too, since Levinas's is a *quasi*-phenomenology, applying some of the ideas and techniques of phenomenology to what are not phenomena, hence not strictly speaking describable, namely the Other and the otherness of the Other.

2 "Our thought should be in relation to all particular and already formulated thoughts, as a man on a mountain who, as he looks forward, sees also below him, without actually looking at them, a great many forests and plains. Above all our thought should be empty,

waiting, not seeking anything, but ready to receive in its naked truth the object that is to penetrate it" (Weil, 1973, pp. 111–112).
3   Levinas compares the trace to the fingerprints inadvertently left behind by the burglar in trying to efface his fingerprints (Levinas, 1998a, p. 104).
4   Weil calls this a "beautiful action" because, like the appreciation of beauty, it allows reality to *be* – specifically the reality of the Other as *other*: "Action which springs from a situation, which expresses it. How to define it? Beautiful action. Action which concludes, suspends the indefinite dialogue between the unbalanced elements that respond to each other, and establishes the unique balance corresponding to the given situation. Action in which the person behind it does not appear" (Weil, 1956, p. 29). The "unbalanced elements" to which Weil refers here might well be the incongruity between one's comfortable existence and the suffering of Others. The "unique balance" is not a resolution of the incongruity but a concern that maintains the contraries in a tension that allows the Other to appear *as other*. Weil's notion that only beauty can save the afflicted from dehumanizing atrocity or exploitation is one of her most important themes. See Rozelle-Stone & Stone, 2013, Chapter 5.
5   A claim Adorno later retracted in his *Negative Dialectics*. See Felstiner, 1995, p. 232.
6   "In adopting a midrashic approach, in which one must continually move to other texts, to other citations, in order to make sense of what one has just read, the poem refuses any conception of organic unity or immediate presentation" (Hatley, 2000, p. 148; cf. 124–127). See also Derrida, 2005, p. 27.
7   In his essay on Celan, which I discuss next, Levinas similarly describes a "going out toward" the Other which returns to the Other's "non-place," not by an intentional act of "turning back" but by the "circularity" of a "perfect trajectory" (Celan's meridian) in which I seem, in following its circuit to the end, "as if in going toward the other I met myself and implanted myself in a land, henceforth native, and I were stripped of all the weight of my identity" (Levinas, 1996, p. 44). The "end" of the circuit, at the non-place of the Other, is thus the end, the deposing, of the self.
8   According to Felstiner (1995, p. 320n10), Celan read, at least, Levinas's essay on Franz Rosenzweig, "Between Two Worlds" (Levinas, 1990, pp. 181–201). Whatever Celan read of Levinas would have to be mediated by his close reading of several works by Heidegger, whom he met in 1967 – a meeting Levinas was told " 'changed [Heidegger] deeply' according to an unquestionable testimony I received in these very words" (Levinas, 1996, p. 174n1). Heidegger was allegedly relieved not to have been rejected or denounced, while Celan was deeply disappointed that there had not been the slightest hint of apology from Heidegger for his involvement in National Socialism. See Lyon, 2006.
9   Celan, 2001, pp. 408–409. On the meaning of "going toward" in Levinas, see Levinas, 1981, pp. 18, 84.
10 "De L'Être a L'Autre" (Levinas, 1976, pp. 59–66), translated as "Paul Celan: From Being to the Other" (Levinas, 1996, pp. 40–46).
11 "Craft – that is a matter of hands. And these hands belong in turn to *one* person only. . . . Only true hands write true poems. I see no basic distinction between a handshake and a poem" (Celan's letter to Hans Bender, May 1960, quoted in Felstiner, 1995, p. 155).
12 Writes J. M. Cameron: "It is not the job of the translator to make what is obscure clear but to give us an equivalent obscurity. I once heard a man say that a certain modern translation of Paul Celan's letters made them understandable for the first time. I thought this a dubious compliment and a misconception of what a good translation is for" ("Poet of the Great Massacre," *The New York Review of Books* (1990, January 18). Surely the same might be said about the "job" of commentary? The commentary Celan's poetry calls for would not aim for a single meaning but deliberately multiply them. As though to prove this point, Bianca Rosenthal has compiled the continually surprising *Pathways to Paul*

Celan: A History of Critical Responses as a Chorus of Discordant Voices (New York: P. Lang, 1995). See also Derrida, 2005, p. 26. All of this is not to deny the value, in its place, of an exegesis of Celan's poetry.
13 "[Celan's] deepest impulse as a writer – the need to be heard, to reach another person" (Felstiner, 1995, p. 6).
14 Levinas, 1996, p. 40, translation modified: "signe qui est son propre signifié: le sujet donne signe de cette donation de signe au point de se faire tout entier signe" (Levinas, 1976, p. 59).
15 Quoted in Samuels, 1993, p. 31.
16 Does this contradict Weil's belief that poetry should point us toward the beautiful? But while beauty is related to perfection and hence coherence, it is never unambiguous, since it arouses a desire for the good and perfect, a desire that cannot be satisfied by any work of art. See Rozelle-Stone & Stone, 2013, Chapter 5, pp. 135–141.
17 Quoted in Samuels, 1993, p. 31. See also Felstiner, 1995, p. 112.
18 Levinas, 1996, p. 43, translation modified. Levinas's French (which italicizes the translation of Celan he is quoting) reads: "le poète parle *dans l'angle d'inclinaison de son existence, dans l'angle d'inclinaison où créature s'énonce . . . qui le trace (qui trace le poème) se révèle à lui dédié*. Singulière dé-substantiation du Moi! Se faire tout entier signe, c'est peut-être cela" (Levinas, 1976, p. 62). In John Felstiner's translation, the passage in Celan's speech from which Levinas quotes runs: "he speaks from the angle of inclination of his very being, his creatureliness. . . . Whoever writes one [a poem] stays mated with it" (Celan, 2001, p. 409, my brackets).
19 "May I disappear in order that those things that I see may become perfect in their beauty from the very fact that they are no longer things that I see. . . . I do not in the least desire that I should no longer be able to feel this created world, but that it should not be to me personally that it is made sensible. To me it cannot confide its secret, which is too lofty. But if only I go away, then creation and Creator will be able to exchange their secrets" (Weil, 1956, pp. 383, 422). Weil's prayer evidently made an impression on Levinas, who quotes it on two separate occasions (the second in Levinas, 1981, p. 198n3). Elsewhere, however, he is highly critical of certain tendencies in Weil's thought: see his "Simone Weil Against the Bible" (1952), in Levinas, 1990, pp. 133–141.
20 Levinas had mentioned earlier in the essay Celan's "daring [in the Meridian speech] to cite Malebranche from a text of Walter Benjamin's on Kafka and Pascal, according to Leon Chestov" (Levinas, 1996, p. 41).
21 Of course this is not entirely fair. On Levinas's uneasy relation with psychanalysis, see Bloechl, 2022, pp. 72–95.
22 Celan, 2001, pp. 395–96: Celan's speech on the occasion of accepting the Bremen prize (1958). See also Hatley, 2000, pp. 153–155.
23 By accident, Celan, living with his parents at the time, happened not to be at home when they were picked up to be deported. For the remainder of his life, Celan reproached himself for not having done more to save them, as others he knew had done, following their loved ones to whatever fate was in store for them (Felstiner, 1995, p. 14).
24 See, for example, "The Bad Conscience and the Inexorable" (1981), Levinas, 1998b, pp. 172–177.

Bibliography

Bloechl, J. (2022). *Levinas on the primacy of the ethical: Philosophy as prophecy*. Chicago: Northwestern University Press.
Celan, P. (2001). *Selected poems and prose of Paul Celan* (J. Felstiner, Trans.). New York: Norton.

Derrida, J. (2005). *Sovereignties in question: The poetics of Paul Celan*. New York: Fordham University Press.
Felstiner, J. (1995). *Paul Celan: Poet, survivor, Jew*. New Haven: Yale University Press.
Hatley, J. (2000). *Suffering witness: The quandary of responsibility after the irreparable*. Albany, NY: State University of New York Press.
Horkheimer, M. (1974). *Critique of instrumental reason* (M. J. O'Connell, Trans.). New York: Continuum International.
Lacoue-Labarthe, P. (1986/1999). *Poetry as experience* (A. Tarnowski, Trans.). Stanford, CA: Stanford University Press.
Levinas, E. (1976). *Noms propres*. Montpellier: Fata Morgana.
Levinas, E. (1978). *Existence and existents* (A. Lingis, Trans.). Pittsburgh: Duquesne University Press.
Levinas, E. (1981). *Otherwise than being, or beyond essence* (A. Lingis, Trans.). Pittsburgh, PA: Duquesne University Press.
Levinas, E. (1990). *Difficult freedom: Essays on Judaism* (S. Hand, Trans.). Baltimore: Johns Hopkins University Press.
Levinas, E. (1996). *Proper names* (M. B. Smith, Trans.). London: Athlone Press.
Levinas, E. (1998a). *Collected philosophical papers* (A. Lingis, Trans.). Pittsburgh: Duquesne University Press.
Levinas, E. (1998b). *Of god who comes to mind* (B. Bergo, Trans.). Stanford, CA: Stanford University Press.
Levinas, E. (2000). *God, death, and time* (B. Bergo, Trans.). Stanford, CA: Stanford University Press.
Lyon, J. K. (2006). *Paul Celan and Martin Heidegger: An unresolved conversation, 1951–1970*. Baltimore: Johns Hopkins University Press.
Rozelle-Stone, A. R., & Stone, L. (2013). *Simone Weil and theology*. London: Bloomsbury T&T Clark.
Samuels, C. (1993). *Holocaust visions: Surrealism and existentialism in the poetry of Paul Celan*. Columbia, SC: Camden House.
Spargo, R. C. (2006). *Vigilant memory: Emmanuel Levinas, the Holocaust, and the unjust death*. Baltimore: Johns Hopkins University Press.
Weil, S. (1956). *The notebooks of Simone Weil* (A. Wills, Trans., Vols. 2). London: Routledge and Kegan Paul.
Weil, S. (1970). *First and last notebooks* (R. Rees, Trans.). London: Oxford University Press.
Weil, S. (1973). *Waiting for god* (E. Craufurd, Trans.). New York: Harper.
Weil, S. (2015). *Late philosophical writings* (E. O. Springsted, Ed., and E. O. Springsted, & L. E. Schmidt, Trans.). Notre Dame, IN: University of Notre Dame Press.

Part 3

Aesthetic Ethics as "Political and Prophetic Action"

Chapter 11

Whom Shall I Walk With? Reflections of a Black(ish) South African Scholar in the North American Academy

Leswin Laubscher

The philosopher Jacques Derrida alerts us to "the circular complicity of the metaphors of the eye and the ear" (Derrida, 1982, p. xiii); to the ways the eye, relying as it does on sight and consciousness, differs from the ear, which engages with the world and the other through sound and the unconscious. Elsewhere, in a text titled *The Ear of the Other* (Derrida, 1985), he goes even further, by linking the notion of autobiography and the presentation of a self to the "ear of the other that signs" and from whom "my signature will have taken place" (Derrida, 1985, p. 51).

This difference (one might also say "tension") is a particularly acute concern for this chapter, which represents a translation from its original form as an address, a talk, at a scholarly conference to an inscription, now, in written form, for the eyes and apostrophizing engagement with an imagined and distant audience. Intuitively, and without much of an intellectual demand, it is abundantly clear that there is a difference in the "sensual perception" (*aisthetikos*) of the oral form and hearing reception (its *aisthanesthai* and *aisthanomai*), and its written translation, as an inscription that both flees and fixes memory. Moreover, inasmuch as my argument privileges my appearance for the resonance of its message, the seeing audience of my talk had a ready-to-hand corporeal impression to yoke my blackish-brownish confessional to. What figural, imagined impression does the reading audience, who cannot see me, conjure from an impression of ink and text? How thick are my lips, how black is my brown, or how might I sound as you behold me, *ecce homo*, the man who writes here? "Where am I to be classified? Or, if you prefer, tucked away?" (Fanon, 1952/1967, p. 113). When he writes as Black, how will the written word hide him? Or better still, if his confession calls him out, how does the seeing word reckon with his appearance, different from the hearing syllable? Especially, as well, if he writes and speaks in a language that isn't his.[1]

I still don't know how to do this. How to revise and re-present an aural moment in written form[2] – how to write such that the eye can hear and the ear can see. An impossibility, of course, but also the only one worth striving for.

***

I'd like to start by describing a scene from Safaa Fathy's documentary film, *Derrida's Elsewhere* (Fathy, 1999). She takes us into Jacques Derrida's lecture hall at the Sorbonne. It is packed; every available seat is taken, people are sitting on the stairs and standing all along the walls. We see Derrida walking in through a side door up front; he glances around briefly, seemingly unruffled by the throng of people who have come to see him. After rummaging through a weathered briefcase for his lecture notes, he sits down and announces that the lecture will be on pardon. He invites the audience as witnesses to this scene, the scene of pardon. "Act I, Scene I," he says: "four characters are waiting to appear on stage – Hegel, Mandela, Clinton, Tutu. They all know a thing or two about pardon, about amnesty, perjury, repentance, reconciliation, forgiveness." Let us listen to their testimony, he says.

Something peculiar is afoot: the audience has come to see Derrida, to listen to him, but now he is telling them he would much rather they listen to these others whom he will invite to speak. These others who aren't there, or here, as we might say. One wonders how he will give them speech. Maybe he will ventriloquize them; will he "channel" them, whatever that might mean? Maybe he will script for them what to say, or maybe his talk will be written, will be given, by them, these specters he will be conjuring for us. Would we know the difference? Would we know who is speaking? The scene has the makings of a séance.

It has been quite a few months now since I was invited to speak here, and shortly after accepting that invitation, I was asked, "What will your talk be about?" Or maybe it was "What would you like to talk about?" On the spot, I ventured to say something about Fanon, Levinas, and Freud; as a scholar, I've written about them most, and as a clinician, they've visited as frequently – sometimes as supervisor, sometimes as analyst, even as analysand. At the time, I had little idea about just what I would say about them. At a flagship scholarly conference, and as a plenary speaker no less. But I did realize a certain arrogance in the presumption to speak about all three – one needs a lifetime of speech for any one of them. So I said to myself – You need to narrow it down, find a phenomenal hook, a more circumscribed question to depose them with. Thus it was that I offered something about the ways I've kept company with these three for over thirty years now, something about the way they have kept company with me.

Of course, there are many companions to a life, many whom we break bread with (from the Latin, *com-* [with] and *-panis* [bread]). In life and in the everyday. But what is it to break bread with the dead – to commune, to have communion with ghosts, with absence? With absence, which is not the opposite of presence. In life and in the everyday. For myself, for example, there is the regularity of an intimacy with such phantoms; the likes of Gustav Mahler and Gustave Caillebotte, for example. Or John Coltrane, Abdullah Ibrahim, N. P. van wyk Louw, Arthur Nortje, Edith Piaf, Nina Simone, Steve Biko and Robert Sobukwe, Emmett Till and Antwon Rose, my father, my friend Selwyn, killed in a motorcycle accident, or an unknown, nameless young woman who – every other day – smiles sorrowfully and accusingly from within me, as she does joyfully from a photo at the Auschwitz

Birkenau death camp. Every two years or so, for the past decade, I have gone to see her there, pinned on a display of photos gathered from the luggage of those who were marched to the gas chambers immediately upon arrival at Birkenau and who, more than seventy years later, have not been identified yet – one of the nameless about whom Levinas asks, "Who will say the loneliness of those who thought themselves dying at the same time as Justice?" (Levinas, 1996b, p. 119). If now, as Derrida urges us, "intellectuals of the future," to learn how to talk to the ghost, to "learn how to let them speak or how to give them back speech," how might such specters cause us "to rethink the 'there' as soon as we open our mouths, even at a colloquium and especially when one speaks there in a foreign language" (Derrida, 1994, p. 176). What does fidelity to spectral companions demand, here below, where they are not as we are? Here, where their only response is with us, within us, by us, and by ours.

Maybe I digress. *When will his talk begin?*

All these companions, these revenants,[3] notwithstanding, this is a learned conference; perhaps I should confine myself to scholarly ghosts, to some of the ways in which those few I am most familiar with – Freud, Levinas, and Fanon – keep me company as I walk in this world and this academy, with this black and brown skin, with this skin which becomes body, this body which becomes specimen, this specimen which becomes specie. I'd not only conjure them. I'd issue a subpoena, a summons to testify, to them and myself, to them in me. I'd charge their counsel as I appear before you at this scholarly court. As a plenary witness. Dare I say an expert witness? I'd testify about lived experience. By calling on ghosts.

Now, as I promised the truth of the *proprius*, of the signature and proper name that is uniquely my own, even where it isn't, I keep coming back to that scene of Derrida's – the scene of the film and the scene of pardon. I cannot shake it. It haunts me. Like some traumatic delay, some *nachtrachtlikheit*, some afterwardness, some après coup, some laplanchian enigmatic signifier, some uncanny *unheimliche* familiarity, some message from a fecund Jungian archetypal prospectus, or some fetid Freudian fixation – I don't quite know which it is or will be. A wounded delay or a fermenting one, maybe a fomenting one? Langston Hughes also knew this feeling – something about raisins in the sun (Hughes, 2002). Maybe I'll work it out, as in good therapy; maybe *we* will work it out, as in better therapy. But for all I did not know about this dis-eased feeling, I did know it kept coming back to trouble things, to make trouble, to cause trouble. Exactly what kind of trouble – that I also don't know. John Lewis's good trouble, his necessary trouble, part of me hopes (Lewis, 2013). We shall see. Perhaps.

The scene of Pardon. Let us remind ourselves of the word's unconscious – from *perdonare* – which is "to give completely". Other than death, what is it to give completely? Is it not an impossibility, really, for those of us who aren't martyrs or saints? Is not the best we can hope for to make a withdrawal from the impossible desire, the aporetic condition for what we name as such? Have I not betrayed the promise already, in the inability, if not the reluctance, to give completely? Truth be told, what is it I promised to give, with this body, with this speech, with my truth, even if not completely? And at what point and when does giving for become forgiving, which is *also* perdonare's meaning?⁴ Who gives, who forgives? What is to be given or forgiven at a talk like this? Which is also to ask about the economy of the gift and giving: what is it I imagine, if not want, my story, a story of lived experience, to do? What might I dream you do with it, outside of my control, as you co-sign my promise and cash my truth, from an account which is an accounting? And what about accountability?

Shall we leave these questions in suspension? Are they mere digressions? He hasn't even started his speech yet, you may say. He is just feigning a step, pretending to walk, pretending to talk; this is all a marching in place, a preparing to step, or a threatening to. Or better yet, all of this – these last 10 minutes or so – was nothing more than a stepping sideways, from digression to digression. A journey by detour, if one were generous. But then, in some ways, this whole talk is about detour and digression, from the Latin to walk beside, to walk aside (*di* plus *gradi*). Whom shall I walk with? Let us not forget that a bas relief of Gradiva – she who walks – hung at the foot end of Freud's famous couch; between delusion and dream, Freud tells us, Gradiva effects a "cure by love" (Freud, 1907/1959).⁵ There is a couch in my office as well. Three posters keep watch over this couch. In the middle, there hangs a reproduction of Freud's famous early drawing of the psyche (which I bought at his home in Vienna, right where he drew it). Flanking Freud, at the head end of the couch, there is a beautiful election poster of Nelson Mandela. At the foot end of my couch is an even bigger poster – a street painting of Frantz Fanon. Whom shall I walk with? Whose love can cure? Go ahead: Take pause, a moment to think, to analyze even. There is, after all, no question without a delay, without an interval, without address; without a groping that marks the beginning of thought, even as it does not mark its origin. Levinas tells us a traumatism does that (Levinas, 1985).

Maybe that is what this body promises: a traumatism groping around for thought, for Gradiva's step, which is to say her cure.

So let us begin; let us pretend we have not already. Let us begin like Derrida did. Let us say "Act 1, scene 1," like he did. We will pretend Fanon and Levinas, and Freud have not appeared yet. But then, another stumble in stepping. I realize I cannot really begin like Derrida does. Whether he directs the action, whether he presides over it, whether he narrates it, it doesn't quite matter; he can do something I cannot. He can move in and out of the scene as he wishes and at his will. When he is not a Jew, he is white. And when he is white, he can direct his dis/appearance. I cannot. With this body and this accent, the action starts when I appear, when I walk onto the stage under the weight of my melanin (Fanon, 1952/2008, p. 128). In fact, even before, when my photo was published in the conference program and on the publication poster, my body already spoke. I am implicated by my appearance; incriminated by it.

Thus, we challenge Levinas, Fanon, and I: we tell him not for us the exorbitant human of the instant, outside of time or place. The Black and Brown is already there, having appeared before they do, woven as they are from myth, story, history, and of fantasy become structure; of structured, sociogenic fantasy (Fanon,

1952/2008). Not for them the face of infinity as much as the totality of the Black body too late on the scene[6]; "I cannot go to a film without seeing myself. I wait for me . . . The people in the theater are watching me, examining me, waiting for me. A Negro groom is going to appear. My heart makes my head swim" (Fanon, 1952/1967, p. 140).

Pre-reflective and pre-linguistic, even "children know that innocence is not black" (Sexton, 2015, p. 161); even children, Black and Brown children, can tell the learned philosopher theirs is not to confuse the ontological with the metaphysical.[7] It is an always belated striving for a freedom that the "existentialists" presume an existential given, and the early, phenomenological Levinas for the hypostatic existent who assumes the burden of consciousness (Levinas, 1987, 1947/2001). But even for the later Levinas of *Totality and Infinity* (1961/2013), upon the intimate meeting of the two, when it involves the black and the white, is that not "just an occasion for the reproduction of a relational mode whose forms are already fixed, under conditions that traditional ontology is uncapable of accounting for" (Macherey, 2012, p. 17)? The ethical command issues from a face, we tell Levinas, and if one appears as an object, faceless . . . well, an object cannot order or ordain; "The Black man has no ontological resistance in the eyes of the white man" (Fanon, 1952/1967).

But if that is the case, if the lived experience of the Black is unintelligible within the field of ontology, what is the possibility of my talking here, today, precisely about lived experience? Gayatri Spivak still asks, Can the Subaltern speak (Spivak, 1988)? What is there to hear? Does it even matter that you show up to this talk, as opposed to the other six or so this weekend where people of color spoke, several about such lived experience precisely? What is the possibility of our speaking if you could show up to any other of our speeches to listen to the Black experience, to consume it? A repetition compulsion? Or are we simply imagining Sisyphus happy? What, still, is there to learn about race and racism, after all, after so long, still? What is supposed to happen upon giving such papers at a conference like this?

The possibility of speaking must also consider the conditions for hearing.

We moved to Pittsburgh in 2000, my wife and I. We had just bought a house, our first, and I had just started my job at Duquesne University. Julie was carrying our first child (I could have said *we* were pregnant, certainly more fashionable if not sensitively "woke"; but saying it thus flattens the way in which we are pregnant so differently, my wife and I, in the experience of pregnancy, and in our bodies, does it not?). So, Julie was pregnant in a way I could not be – she was carrying our child. I was trying my damndest to kick a smoking habit. Occasionally, though, I would falter, believing I had some time still to fail, at least until she would give birth, until we would bear its birth, until we would provide it a welcoming berth.[8] Again, I digress – back to the story: I sneak out of the house, lean against the corner of a wall in our backyard, and light up a Newport – or maybe it was a Salem. It seems always one or the other of those, for those of us like me, does it not. Another mystery, that – another sideways step. In any event, our backyard looks out onto another, and whereas I saw the rustling of curtains in the adjacent house, I paid little heed to it. I had just about snuffed out the cigarette, washed my hands, and stuck three wads of spearmint gum in my mouth to hide the smell from Julie when there was a knock on the door. Two burly policemen who, truth be told, were quite civil and polite, even friendly – but then, we bought a house in a neighborhood where the streets and the gardens are all civil and polite; "a good neighborhood, with good and friendly people," our realtor told us. A white neighborhood. We had a report of a suspicious person loitering around, the policeperson said, and we are just following up. I told them I think they are looking at the suspicious person. I think they knew that already. The next day, I recounted the story to my colleagues at a faculty meeting, presuming a certain hearing of my story, of my experience, of my body. Upon doing so, a colleague remarked – a good and well-meaning, smart, warm, and progressive colleague; she said: "Isn't it nice that there are still communities where people look out for each other, for their neighbors". I felt like an idiot for telling the story. For sharing the experience of my brown and sometimes black body. Maybe it is a feeling I'll revisit again, today. The odds are good. Well bad. The point is that one calculates this burden of speaking, of the Black body that speaks. One calculates an incalculable because it is also this very burden that gives speech, that actually compels it. As much as one, anyone, sometimes says about an experience that it "just cannot be put into words", it is precisely because we cannot that we try, that we stammer and grope and attempt the impossible. It is, after all, Levinas whispers, not by knowledge, but by sensibility, that we stutter.

But if good people put paid to the notion of racism as a problem of knowledge, and Fanon says that there is an aberration of affect that only psychoanalysis can lay bare, maybe we need to call on the good doctor Freud to help us out. My kids have, on occasion, asked me what I teach, what I write about, and of course names get thrown around or become present in the demand for some explanation – Freud especially. Hence, what did Freud say about this or that, or what do you teach students about Freud? I admit on more than one occasion I responded to that question of Freud's lesson, of what he teaches us: quite simply, "That people suck." Behold – the psychologist for whom hell is other people (apologies to philosophers who must groan at my perpetuation of such an erroneous rendering of Sartre's quote). I jest of course. Mostly. Maybe. Seriously, though, the point is that there is an irrationality to racism, to shooting Ralph Yarl through a closed door, after he simply rang a doorbell; or Yoshihiro Hattori, or Renisha McBride, or Payton Washington or Heather Roth or . . . good lord, a list so long it spills out of memory, remembrance, or notice. It is an irrationality that lays bare the error of the contact hypothesis and the reductionism of racism to stereotype and prejudice as the variables of cognition and affect, and by which the behavior of discrimination is fueled. As such, it is an irrationality that Freud and Fanon remind us we cannot respond to simply with diversity training, laudable and necessary as those may also be. My good friends and colleagues Derek Hook and Sheldon George (George & Hook, 2021; Hook, 2018) argue this point in much finer detail, as does Ilhan Kapoor (Kapoor, 2020). Only thus can we begin to make sense of how the negro becomes a phobogenic object, or how the fetish of his castrated penis (BBC[9] is consistently one of the most searched for terms on pornography websites) acts as proof of his beastly nature. Or why I am no longer followed in stores anymore, as I was when I was in my twenties – I must be less threatening now, I've become more brown than black. Heck, these days I could even be a doctor or a shopkeeper – not quite a taxi driver, though (we are in Pittsburgh, after all, not New York). And we are not in Phoenix or Dallas, where I am Mexican. Or Detroit, where I am amorphously Middle Eastern and unambiguously Muslim. Even so, even as an Indian and a Paki and a Mexican or some Racial Oreo (at a bus stop on the South Side of Chicago, I was asked by a kindly African American woman – "so which one of your parents were Black"); for all those black and brown ascriptions, for all these complications, it also does not quite matter all that much when the empty seat next to me on the bus is still the last to be filled. Three days a week, I place bets on the white folk who walk into the door at the front of the bus at Homewood station, where, invariably, there are only three or so open seats left. I've crafted it into a fine science, from the Latin "to know" – even an *oiconomia*, an economy, the law of the house. I am entertaining pitching my experience as a new betting category for FanDuel® or DraftKings®. You hold up your phone, with the camera on, and you bet on who will sit next to me. Or someone like Clarence Thomas – who might well be outraged at the odds of the bet against him. But then, maybe he read Fanon as well: "I sit down next to the fire and discover my livery for the first time. It is indeed ugly" (Fanon, 1952/2008, p. 94).

Upon Fanon turning to Freud, however, it is not enough to acknowledge the spectacle of the Black's appearance in terms of unconscious fantasy, nor only to think it as Lacanian jouissance, as the libidinal enjoyment, the titter and titillation of racism, or the spectacle of blackness as the main event of a plenary. It is also to chart how libidinal enjoyment is sedimented in social and intersubjective relations. By which *social* fantasy does masochistic or narcissistic enjoyment demand a parade of blackness, and by which sociogenic *structurality* is such an exhibit consumed and "enjoyed"? A question with particular relevance for us at the ground zero of conferences such as these, where the siren of jouissance prompts, all too often, an intellectual masturbation disguised as activism. Or for myself, of the libidinal affectation of righteous castigation. Or guilt and shame, as heightened affect, which may serve not only (or even primarily) to "beat up" but also to libidinally "lift up" when, faced with the racism of my fellows and the life of the black, my guilt serves precisely as evidence of my goodness, of my difference from them. A dollar in the panhandler's cup, a Bernie Sanders sticker on my car, a Black Lives Matter poster on my lawn – a small price of admission, this; a libidinal bargain, really. A fire sale, even, the bargain-basement purchase of goods damaged by fire, sold by a distressed seller, a seller in distress.

And yet. We still speak. We must.

On the plane, travelling here, I scrolled through the list of presenters for the conference – for most of us, there is a presenter's photo on the conference app, and from there one can link to an abstract of the person's talk. I devised a new betting game: among the few persons of color on the program, and for whom there was a photo, I wondered what their presentations would be about. What are the odds? Let's bet. Christin F. – click; Lauren B. – click; Alvalyn D-G.B – click . . . I would have made a lot of imaginary money, had the bookie not been me, giving myself negative odds to begin with. What else would they talk about but race, racism, its experience, and its reach? Implicated by the material of their appearance, they become the matter of their speech, of what matters.

I sometimes say that everything I've ever written, or every talk I've ever given, bears the mark of Apartheid. It's scars. It feels I can only appear to show off a wound and to expose and trace a scar; whether I teach or preach, whether I scream in rage or weep tears of frustrated impotence, I always feel naked, undressed for such speech, such speaking. Even when I speak of hope, it is Emily Dickinson's hope, that thing with feathers that sings, but sings its tune without words precisely in a gale, in a soul that knows despair. This is not Tennyson's skylark, or Shelley's, and if it is a meadowlark, it is Paul Laurence Dunbar's, that sings its happy song in the slaving cotton fields of Kentucky, at the end of a grieving day, in a mantle gray, under dank winds and gray skies.[10]

I thought to myself, the other night: what would it be for me to speak at some learned conference about something, something completely unrelated to race, but something creative still, something scholarly still, something I might have something to say about as well, maybe even something interesting. Give it thought, give it a title: How about this – "An Existential-Phenomenological Analysis of Gustav Mahler's Ninth Symphony". How would you start, I asked myself? What about a quote from Mahler's – about his music and his world, no least given his insistence that music must contain the world? Well, I continued, we have to start with homelessness then, with exile, "as a native of Bohemia in Austria, as an Austrian among Germans, and as a Jew throughout the world – always an intruder, never welcomed" (Mahler, 1969, p. 109). And then Fanon whispers in my ear, advises me to prick up my ears and pay attention, they are also talking about you – "an anti-Semite is inevitably anti-Negro" (Fanon, 1952/1967, p. 122). Even when I want to be a human being, just a human being, even if it is in secret, even if it is to be in secret, disembodied and immaterial, the truth of its lie, its dissimulation, is that there is no secret. Derrida reminds us, in a text rather appropriately titled "How to avoid speaking" (Derrida, 1989), that in the secret of denial and the denial of the secret lies its unpossessability; lies the impossibility of Theseus's pledge to Oedipus, as it is for Oedipus's desire to die forgotten and unknown so that others may live free from the curse of his existence.

So I must speak. Even if, or especially when, the burden of such speech involves betrayal and a retraumatizing dehiscence.

Well into his sixties, I accompanied my father on a road trip of sorts. This was not too long after apartheid's fall, in the late nineties. We went to the little farmhouse where he was born, and some of the places of his childhood. But then we ventured further, about a three-hour drive inland, to a two-room rural farm school, his first appointment as a school teacher. One room was the classroom, the other where he lived. In South Africa, the scene would be familiar, but I will have to live with the betrayal of cultural and geographical translation. Try to imagine a white farm, as vast as the eyes would have it – in fact, my father would say, turn around 360 degrees and everything that the eye can see is the farm. Which concedes that the word "farm" is a misnomer; it has always been land. Often, churches would come to some agreement with the farmer to build a small school on the farm, which they would run and pay the teachers' salaries for. In that way, at least the farmworkers' children would get some education; they certainly could not rely on the apartheid state to provide it. Such was the school my father went to and the little backroom he slept in. So we crossed time, to ask if anyone was still alive, was still around from his time there. It turns out almost everyone had died or moved. Except for one: *Oom Klasie* – Uncle Klasie. "He must be in his eighties now", my father said. Yes, they said, "he now does odd jobs up at the farmer's home . . . pulls out weeds and waters the lawn and such". So we drove up to the farmer's home, about a kilometer or two away, completely separated from sight of the farmworkers' homes. As we got out of the car, *Oom Klasie* spotted us, and upon seeing my father immediately recognized him. He respectfully took off the tattered hat he was wearing, clutched it to his chest, and with a smile that collapsed time, he said "*my hene meester*" (my goodness, teacher/master). Just about then, into this Levinasian scene, a voice boomed from somewhere to our right: "*Wat maak julle hier?*" (what are you doing here?). The white farmer. Or rather his son, my age. The father, the farmer of my father's time, had died long ago. But to my father, this white son *was* the father, the white father. In front of my eyes, he became a twenty-year-old black man again. This big man, a legendary lock forward, for those of you who know rugby, one who could play for the national team but for the color of his skin – this big man, this man I love . . . before my eyes, he became smaller, his legs became bent, his shoulders slumped, his eyes downcast, a shuffle settled in his feet, about to stammer some explanation. But before he could, my legs grew tall, taller than the land, my land, and I rose to meet the white father's son, and my chest puffed out, and I stepped out from Fanon's anger to speak. I said, "This is my father, he was a teacher on this farm forty years ago." He came to say hello to Oom Klasie ("Kiss the handsome Negro's ass, madame!" (Fanon, 1952/1967, p. 114)). And as I said it, and for the challenging way I said it, there was a moment of time's freezing – maybe even a diachrony of time, the meanings of which we will leave Levinas and Freud to fight over. In that moment, the glorious anger and accusation of my eyes met the *schuld* (in both senses of the word's German meaning – guilt *and* debt; one which English readers of Heidegger easily miss). He said, "*nee maar dis goed so*" (ok, that is fine then), and turned around, somehow less upright, less assured, maybe even burdened, too. The Laws of the Father and the *schuld* of the sons is also why we speak, why we both must speak, trapped as we are, Fanon reminds us, Black and White both, within a Manichean tragicomedy ("Estragon: 'Let's go'. Vladimir: 'We can't'. Estragon: 'Why not?'. Vladimir: 'We're waiting for Godot'. (Beckett, 1952/1994, p. 31)).

It is a violent demand, this kind of speech, this kind of talk about lived experience. I resent presenting my father to you as some bumbling Uncle Tom; resent having to do so, as if you made me do so, which in a sense you did, too. The truth is, there were many moments where the heroic moment of my rage was also my father's, and the unconscious of subservience also in the silences of my speech. And sometimes, rather simply, silence is much less collusion or cowardice than fatigue, of just being so damn worn down; an existential phenomenology of racism remains to take fatigue seriously, a lassitude that saps the soul and the will. It is tiring, this speech, this speaking, this nakedness, this vulnerability, this demand, this "weight of blackness" one feels when one meets "the white man's eyes" (Fanon, 1952/1967, p. xi). Would I could just walk out of this hall right now – down the lane right there, outside these hallowed windows; just leave, just walk, just leave to be alone and pretend I can still hear that thing with feathers in the soul.[11]

We arrive back where we started, and where we've been all along. At the invitation to witness and the demands of testimony. At the recognition that this does not want, simply, to be a talk about some or other Blackness, about some or other Brown lived experience, or even about racism. It is not – at least not primarily – to learn about steps and methods with which to combat racism; those are important, to be sure, but for it to be more than a workplace requirement or feelgood homily, must come after, after the exposure of witness, after the exposure to exposure, to the nakedness of the other. A testimony of exposure asks not to grasp anything about my lived experience, asks not for your understanding as much as it does for a sensibility which is before the touching back of a prodding, poking ego. It is about an inspiration, that is, a "breathing into" (inspire, from the Latin *inspirare* – "to breathe into") the ego such that it can catch its own breath, animated now to the vulnerable offering of itself by which it comes to itself as a learning to love, a learning to live. *Lieben und Arbeiten*, finally.

Citing his friend Maurice Blanchot, Emmanuel Levinas buries in an endnote to his essay "Useless Suffering" (Levinas, 1988), the observation that the notes discovered in the crematoria of Auschwitz simultaneously say "Know what has happened,' 'Do not forget,'" and also, at the same time, "you will never know?" (p. 167). What is one to say between "'You won't understand, ever' and 'you must understand, always?'" What is one to say when one must, nonetheless, speak?

But perhaps that is not the only question to ask. Much rather also, "How have you been addressed by those who suffer?" (Hatley, 2000, p. 2) such that your "first duty is not to classify and compare but . . . to respond" (p. 2). It is then for the response to be one that exceeds epistemological determination to become ethical involvement – to bear witness to the impossible, and to suffer the testimony of a haunting. Maybe that is what this is all about, ultimately. If it does not expect or demand any closure, resolution, acceptance, empathy, comparison, or redemptive virtue, this story, this life, this speech wishes for a response to remain in front of an "accusation without foundation . . . prior to any movement of the will" (Levinas, 1974/2004, p. 110); for the exorbitant ethics of a "*here I am*, answering for everything and everyone" (p. 114, emphasis in original). That, Levinas tells us, is what the word "I" means, after all (Levinas, 1974/2004).

To bear witness is to carry a singular and irreplaceable responsibility. It is to be marked, and to bear the mark of the other as a haunted subject; for speech to testify is not for it to be a bringing back in the sense of a copy as much as it is to allow for a recuperation, a reiteration, a bringing back, as if for the first time – a seeing again, a seeing differently, which is also to say an unseeing and an unhearing. It is to solicit a response not from knowledge but from a command to responsibility, to response, where my response is my responsibility; my responsibility my response. I have been called out, apostrophized such that I can be: "To be an I then signifies not to be able to escape responsibility" (Levinas, 1996a, p. 55).

Inasmuch as it is clear that the model of the witness and testimony is not quite the one we are most familiar with, as in the juridical and the court of law, there is nonetheless a ritual from that model which affords us to think about speech with ghosts and about response and responsibility. Remember, firstly, the threat of the subpoena, the "under penalty", should one violate the summons to truth in perjury by lying. We are asked to swear an oath, to answer the summons on pain of an oath, as in "I swear to tell the truth, the whole truth, and nothing but the truth". An oath is always to an other, always to promise before an other, a witness, mortal or divine,[12] to my testimony. The "so help me God" always concedes that whereas there may be no consequences to my perjurious and lying testimony, if I lie in secret, here below, the fact *that* no one knows is only true in the world of the living and the material empirical. The divine witness to whom one promises nonetheless sees and commands, nonetheless "orders and ordains" from a no-place wholly elsewhere and exterior, which is also to say wholly interior by the other in me.

My speech, now, is also a pledge to the dead and the not yet. Truth be told, often even more so. Sometimes I believe everything I say here addresses my father, or Adri Faas, Antwon Rose, Mahsa Amini. But also the children of my children, who are not yet, of a still to come. They all demand a response, these ghosts and specters. The scholar of absence and ghosts is in a relationship that is not so much about us seeing them as them seeing us. They look at us in the persecuted and haunting injunction of a response, such that the speechless and the without response make us respond, make us speak. Having witnessed, compelled to speak, agency has, in a sense, passed to the dead and the not yet, by a testimony "where the one who speaks bears the impossibility of speaking in his own speech" (Agamben, 1999, p. 120).

For speech to pledge, is for speech to promise, to say yes, to say yes-yes. To be sure, the very nature of the promise is the possibility of its betrayal. If I promise to give you $50 tomorrow or to deliver a speech on lived experience, it is only a promise because I may not give you that $50 or deliver that speech. If you knew for a fact I'd give you $50, either you are a prescient god or it isn't a promise but a fact. But to say yes, I promise, to say yes, I've seen and heard, I've been exposed to exposure, is not enough. I have to say, yes-yes. A singular yes will not suffice. After saying to my children or my wife – after saying to them I promise to love you for as long as I live, I would have to say it again, over and over, throughout all the days of my life. There would not come a time when I would say to my son or my daughter, "I now no longer have to love you". When you say yes, you always have to say yes again. A promise is not a promise unless it is repeated, again and again. What the originary yes inaugurates is a future that remains to come – and every reiteration, every yes, continues to honour the memory of the first yes. The double affirmation, therefore, depends upon the promise to remember, and the memory of the promise. To paraphrase Levinas, it is not the last judgment that is decisive but the judgment of all the instants in time (Levinas, 1961/2013).

I've promised to speak, and now I have. You've committed to listening, and now you have. I can only hope that you've heard and seen even just a glimpse of my said's saying,[13] as it is from there that one can promise outside of economic exchange . . . from ethical exposure.

I feel, whenever I end a talk like this, as I am about to now, that it is the morning of Feb. 27, 1973, at Wounded Knee, or 16 June 1976 as the sun rises over Soweto, or March 7, 1965, on the Edmund Pettus bridge. I look around at who will link arms with me. I wonder – whom shall I walk with?

Notes

1 The astute reader will register the allusion to Derrida's *Monolingualism of the Other* (1998); the issues of language, identity, translation, cultural relationships, and politics Derrida addresses there are also all at play here.
2 The sentence betrays its rehearsal, well before opening night: to revise is to see again (*re*-again + *visere/videre*-to see) and re-present is to show again, to bring before an audience (*re*-again + *praesentare* – to place before).
3 Quite literally, that which comes back, those who hauntingly return and re-turn.
4 Through old English, *for*- (completely) plus *giefan* (to give), from the Saxon/German (*fargeban/vergeben*) loan-translation of *perdonare*.
5 In fact, not only with respect to Jensen's Gradiva, but "Every psycho-analytic treatment is an attempt at liberating repressed love which has found a meagre outlet in the compromise of a symptom" (Freud, 1907/1959, p. 90).
6 The sentence plays with the title (and philosophy) of Levinas's seminal book, *Totality and Infinity* (1961/2013).
7 For a more detailed examination of this claim and challenge, staged as conversational difference between Levinas and Fanon, see Laubscher (2022).
8 Between the aural and written forms, there is a nice example here of Derridean supplementarity and differánce (Derrida, 1973): the listening audience would not be able to hear the difference between "birth" and "berth", and the reader will not be prompted to think the meaning of "welcoming birth".
9 On pornography sites, BBC is an abbreviation for "Big Black Cock".
10 Each of the referenced poems are easily accessible online, for example, "Hope" by Emily Dickinson at https://www.poetryfoundation.org/poems/42889/hope-is-the-thing-with-feathers-314; "The Skylark" by Frederick Tennyson at https://allpoetry.com/poem/8572697-The-Skylark-by-Frederick-Tennyson; "To a Skylark" by Percy Bysshe Shelley at https://www.poetryfoundation.org/poems/45146/to-a-skylark; "The Meadowlark" by Paul Laurence Dunbar at https://www.paullaurencedunbar.org/2022/p246.
11 The allusion is to Emily Dickinson's poem, *Hope*, that ". . . thing with feathers – / That perches in the soul – / And sings the tune without the words – / And never stops – at all–". See Footnote 10.

12 Indeed, by Derrida's reframing ". . . God, as the wholly other, is to be found everywhere there is something of the wholly other", so that what can be said about the relation to God, ". . . can be said about my relation to *every other (one) as every (bit) other [tout autre come tout autre]*, in particular my relation to my neighbor or my loved ones who are as inaccessible to me, as secret and transcendent as Jahweh" (Derrida, 1996, p. 78, emphasis in original).

13 The reference is to Levinas's later distinction, in *Otherwise than Being* (1974/2004), between content (the "Said") and the ethical Saying, prior to language, but also the "condition for all communication, as exposure" (p. 48).

References

Agamben, G. (1999). *Remnants of Auschwitz: The witness and the archive* (D. Heller-Rozen, Trans.). Zone Books.

Beckett, S. (1952/1994). *Waiting for Godot*. Grove Press.

Derrida, J. (1973). *Speech and phenomena* (D. B. Allison, Trans.). Northwestern University Press.

Derrida, J. (1982). *Margins of philosophy* (A. Bass, Trans.). University of Chicago Press.

Derrida, J. (1985). *The ear of the other* (P. Kamuf, Trans., and C. V. McDonald, Ed.). Schocken Books.

Derrida, J. (1989). How to avoid speaking: Denials. In H. Coward, & T. Foshay (Eds.), *Derrida and negative theology* (pp. 73–136). SUNY Press.

Derrida, J. (1994). *Specters of Marx: The state of the debt, the work of mourning, and the new international* (P. Kamuf, Trans.). Routledge.

Derrida, J. (1996). *The gift of death* (D. Willis, Trans.). University of Chicago Press.

Derrida, J. (1998). *Monolingualism of the other, or, the prosthesis of origin* (P. Mensah, Trans.). Stanford University Press.

Fanon, F. (1952/1967). *Black skin white masks* (C. L. Markmann, Trans.). Grove Press.

Fanon, F. (1952/2008). *Black skin, white masks* (R. Philcox, Trans.). Grove Press.

Freud, S. (1907/1959). Delusions and dreams in Jensen's Gradiva. In J. Strachey (Ed. and Trans.), *The standard edition of the complete psychological works of Sigmund Freud* (Vol. 9, pp. 7–95). The Hogarth Press.

Fathy, S. (1999). *Derrida's elsewhere*. L. S. A. G. Films; First Run/Icarus Films.

George, S., & Hook, D. (Eds.). (2021). *Lacan and race: Racism, identity, and psychoanalytic theory*. Routledge.

Hatley, J. (2000). *Suffering witness: The quandary of responsibility after the irreparable*. State University of New York Press.

Hook, D. (2018). Racism and jouissance: Evaluating the "racism as (the theft of) enjoyment" hypothesis. *Psychoanalysis, Culture and Society*, 23(3), 244–266.

Hughes, L. (2002). Harlem. In *The collected poems of Langston Hughes*. Vintage.

Kapoor, I. (2020). *Confronting desire: Psychoanalysis and international development*. Cornell University Press.

Laubscher, L. (2022). When "there is" a Black: Levinas and Fanon on ethics, politics, and responsibility. *Middle Voices*, 2(1), 1–18.

Levinas, E. (1947/2001). *Existence and existents*. Duquesne University Press.

Levinas, E. (1961/2013). *Totality and infinity: An essay on exteriority* (A. Lingis, Trans.). Duquesne University Press.

Levinas, E. (1974/2004). *Otherwise than being, or beyond essence* (A. Lingis, Trans.). Duquesne University Press.

Levinas, E. (1985). *Ethics and infinity* (R. Cohen, Trans.). Duquesne University Press.

Levinas, E. (1987). *Time and the other* (R. Cohen, Trans.). Duquesne University press.

Levinas, E. (1988). Useless suffering (R. Cohen, Trans.). In R. Bernasconi, & D. Wood (Eds.), *The provocation of Levinas: Rethinking the other* (pp. 156–167). Routledge.

Levinas, E. (1996a). *Emmanuel Levinas: Basic philosophical writings* (A. T. Peperzak, Ed.). Indiana University Press.

Levinas, E. (1996b). *Proper names*. Stanford University Press.

Lewis, J. (2013). John Lewis talks about getting into "good trouble". *Speech at the National Constitution Center* [Video]. YouTube. https://www.youtube.com/watch?v=e-8DThtP36Q&t=146s

Macherey, P. (2012). Figures of interpellation in Althusser and Fanon. *Radical Philosophy*, 173(May/June).

Mahler, A. (1969). *Gustav Mahler: Memories and letters* (D. Mitchell, Ed.). Viking.

Sexton, J. (2015). Unbearable blackness. *Cultural Critique*, 90, 159–178.

Spivak, G. C. (1988). Can the subaltern speak? In C. Nelson, & L. Grossberg (Eds.), *Marxism and the interpretation of culture* (pp. 271–313). Macmillan Education.

Chapter 12

Spoken Futurities
Poetry, Prophecy, and Psychology

Manòn Voice

The disciplines of poetry, prophecy, and psychology have the potential to meet at creative intersections, bringing forth futures that would otherwise have been unimaginable.

Akin to psychological practice, in poetry, we learn to inhabit a safe space where we interrogate the wild and unknown layers of our consciousness. Identity, then, is a salient theme threading through the fields of psychology and poetry as individuals enter and engage in a healing journey, striving to wrest from the cruel conditioning of society and personal origin story an authentic voice and expression that offers their genuine self back to them. Poetry and psychology allow us to give voice to a fragmented self-concept and bravely integrate the exiled pieces of ourselves. James Baldwin (1962), who transgressed the delineations of poet, writer, and prophet, wrote,

He (the artist) is also enjoined to conquer the great wilderness of himself. The precise role of the artist, then, is to illuminate that darkness, and blaze roads through that vast forest, so that we will not, in all our doing, lose sight of its purpose, which is, after all, to make the world a more human dwelling place.

Indeed, narrative theory points to this, as we constitute identity not merely through experience, yet through the exploration and arrangement of lived experiences through a temporal narrative.

The known and unknown layers of our consciousness bear the stories, myths, hopes, and dreams given within by the world around us. While conquering the great wilderness of oneself can be claimed as an interior function of poetry, there is also an exterior function of poetry, where poets have been brave enough to see the world for what it is, call it out, and then call it in into its best version, reflective of prophetic work. The poet's calling to the world often springs from the convictions and callings that are urgently imposed upon them from within. Baldwin further writes,

And we are frightened, all of us, of these forces within us that perpetually menace our precarious security. Yet the forces are there: we cannot will them away. All we can do is learn to live with them. And we cannot learn this unless we are willing, to tell the truth about ourselves, and the truth about us is always at variance with what we wish to be.

DOI: 10.4324/9781003598107-16

The human effort is to bring these two realities into a relationship resembling reconciliation. The poet, by engaging in a deeply psychological work to mend and make peace with their inward vulnerabilities, tensions, and paradoxes and then to turn outward and practice this same mending in the lived world, is prophetic practice. Lastly, Baldwin writes,

> Societies never know it, but the war of an artist with his society is a lover's war, and he does, at his best, what lovers do, which is to reveal the beloved to himself and, with that revelation, to make freedom real.

Indeed, prophecy serves a function of drawing forth a call to action. Rather than predicting a future (as is colloquially believed), prophecy brings to mind possible futures. The realm of aesthetics, even beyond logic and ethics, invites folks to the realm of imagination. Is this not what good poetry, therapy, and prophecy allow for . . . Futures beyond oneself?

My First Love: The Transformative Power of Poetry

When I visit inner-city elementary and middle schools as a teaching artist or introduce myself to my collegiate students on the first day of class, I always share a story to establish my roots as a lifelong creative and my deep love for writing and lyricism. I recount how I first fell in love with poetry around age seven or eight.

I vividly remember the bookmobile – a magical, mobile library – that would roll into the parking lot of my elementary school, just a block from my home. It was stocked with free books, meant to inspire a love for reading in public school kids like me. Stepping into that decked-out van, the coolest thing I'd ever seen, I was drawn to a book with a vibrant, kaleidoscopic cover. Like any second grader, I was captivated by the colors, not knowing that the contents of that book would change my life forever.

When I got home and opened its cover, I was transported to an artistic and linguistic cosmos – a universe brimming with sentience and sacredness. That book lifted me out of my small, prepubescent body and placed me in a realm of imagination and wonder, where the boundaries between the inner and outer worlds blurred. At that moment, I was transfigured – claimed by the power of poetry.

Even at such a young age, I couldn't fully articulate what I felt, but I knew it was profound. Poetry had opened a door to a sacred correspondence between who I was and the world beyond me. And from that day on, I knew I was forever changed.

Poetry, Trauma, and Healing: The Legacy of Maya Angelou

What I often omit from this love story are the intimate, delicate, and mystical threads woven through it – the ones that speak to despair, trauma, a prolonged journey of healing, and how poetry became a revelatory, redemptive, and salvific force throughout my life. You see, at the same time I was falling in love with poetry, I was a young girl whose outward appearance – ruffle socks, church dresses, patent leather shoes polished to a shine, and neatly tied hair bows – stood in stark contrast to my inner world. Beneath that polished exterior was a child prematurely initiated into woundedness, a girl who had already lost the innocence of giggles and girlish naivete.

I often view my early connection to poetry as Divine, Otherworldly, and even prophetic. When I entered the world of poetry, I was met by a cloud of witnesses – a chorus of voices that walked with me through the medium of the written word. Among those voices was the oracular Maya Angelou: author, poet, and activist. Her poem "Phenomenal Woman" became an anthem for my young soul, infusing it with strength and a profound sense of worth.

In my small earthly purview, Maya Angelou was larger than life – an oak of a woman whose branches spread wide and roots ran deep. She was a valiant Black woman who, having waded through the depths of herself, elegantly carried the weight of a charged history and exuded self-confidence and charisma forged in the crucible of life's troubles. The deep timbre of her voice, spoken slowly and deliberately, was a balm to my timidity – a warmth reminiscent of any Black grandmother of the South, tried and true through life's storms. Only later did I learn that her inimitable voice had come at an unimaginable cost.

In her earliest years, Maya endured the unspeakable trauma of rape at the hands of her mother's boyfriend. After his brief imprisonment, he was killed upon release. Believing her confession of the abuse had caused his death, young Maya retreated into silence for six years. "I thought, my voice killed him," she wrote in her first autobiography, *I Know Why the Caged Bird Sings* (Angelou, 1969). "I killed that man, because I told his name. And then I thought I would never speak again, because my voice would kill anyone." The unspeakable cruelty inflicted on her young body and soul had threatened to silence her forever.

It was a local teacher, Bertha Flowers, who helped Maya find her voice again. In her autobiography, Angelou vividly recalls Flowers's words: "Your grandmother says you read a lot. Every chance you get," she told the young girl. "That's good, but not good enough. Words mean more than what is set down on paper. It takes the human voice to infuse them with shades of deeper meaning." Flowers challenged Maya's relationship with poetry, insisting, "You do not love poetry, not until you speak it."

At first, Maya rejected her teacher's assertion, but eventually, she found herself compelled to utter the words from a book of poetry. When she spoke the verses aloud, she felt them come alive in her own voice. Gradually, at the age of 13, she began to speak again.

Maya Angelou's complex narrative of speech, trauma, betrayal, and silence mirrored my own and provided me with a living example of someone who understood this peculiar kind of suffering. Yet she had also transmuted her tragedy into a healing force for others – a testament to resilience and transformation.

The Psychological Depths of Poetry and the Call to Truthtelling

My struggles with using my voice were both psychological and physiological. On one hand, I was a terrible stutterer, and forming words often felt like a daunting, humiliating ordeal. The experience left me vulnerable to ridicule from my peers, which only deepened my insecurity. In third grade, a speech pathologist offered me a lifeline by teaching me to sing the words I wanted to say. This became my first creative method of bypassing my fears and stuntedness – a way of reclaiming my voice through melody and rhythm.

On the other hand, I was mentally afraid of speaking because I believed my voice could disrupt the status quo by revealing uncomfortable truths. I feared the power my words could wield. So I turned to writing instead. I poured my thoughts into poetry and journals, imitating the forms of poets I admired. Through writing, I found a way to say the unsayable, and over time, I began to speak aloud the words I had written. Writing became both sanctuary and practice – a way to rediscover my voice on my terms.

Tawhida Akhter, in her article "Relation between Poetry and Psychology with Special Reference to the Poetry of Kamala Das," highlights this connection between creativity and the unconscious:

> According to modern psychologists, the unconscious processes are more important than the conscious ones. It is these unconscious impulses that lead the poet or any artist to produce a poetical work or any other work of art. What poetry may refer to as the abyss, or wilderness, or wild, psychology more likely refers to as the unconscious. Poetry offers psychology its own perspective on the reaches of the realm, a unique repository not only of energy but also of imagery, metaphor, paradox, inversion, contradiction, and often enough, beauty. Poetry valorizes and embraces the resources of the unconscious. The poem invites our fascinated commerce with our deep world beneath the world; it invites us to linger in the sensory experience of its inhabiting. Stay awhile, it says.
>
> (Akhter, 2013, p. 14).

This interplay between poetry and the unconscious resonated deeply with me. Writing became my way of lingering in the sensory, exploring the depths of my inner world, and unearthing the beauty and contradictions within. Through poetry, I found a voice that had long been buried, and with it, a path toward liberation. I didn't know it then, but poetry held space for me. It provided a sanctuary for the exiled parts of my psyche, creating a safe container where I could slowly work my way back to them through writing and speaking. When I couldn't voice the unsayable, I leaned on metaphor, imagery, paradox, and contradiction – elements of verse that allowed me to explore my truth without fully confronting its weight. During those years, with my notebooks tucked beneath my bed, poetry became my private refuge, offering me a retreat in the room I shared with my sister. It permitted me to enter the world of the soul's imagination – a space where suffering could momentarily dissipate and realms of beauty and hope could unfold.

For a time, poetry offered hiddenness, a veiled comfort from the reality of my trauma. But, as with Maya Angelou's experience, the lineage of poetry soon demanded more of me. The poetic tradition called me toward truthtelling, urging me to engage with integrity in the rites of passage inherent in artistic struggle.

James Baldwin (1962) articulates this struggle with eloquence, stating, "The poets (by which I mean all artists) are finally the only people who know the truth about us. Soldiers don't. Statesmen don't. Priests don't. Union leaders don't. Only poets" (Baldwin, 1985, p. 316).

Psychiatrist and poet Richard Brostoff (2008) further illuminates poetry's power, writing:

> [P]oetry seeks to embody itself in the moment of its activation as it is read, to embody and unfold itself in voice, breath, and rhythm, and in the particularity of the world. Rather than beginning with an overarching interpretive frame as psychology does, poetry begins in specificity. It feeds the phenomenal world through the eye of its needle, takes up residence, and seeks to waken itself.
> (Brostoff, 2008, p. 15).

Through these revelations, I came to understand that poetry is more than a medium of solace; it is an invitation to engage deeply with truth, presence, and the full spectrum of human experience. In *Conflict Resolution for Holy Beings*, Poet Laureate, musician, and playwright Joy Harjo (2015) calls readers to "gather their spirit in pieces" as an act of return (p. 158).

Call your spirit back. It may be caught in corners and creases of shame, judgment, and human abuse.

You must call in a way that your spirit will want to return.

Speak to it as you would to a beloved child.

Welcome your spirit back from its wandering. It may return in pieces, in tatters. Gather them together. They will be happy to be found after being lost for so long (Harjo, 2015, p. 158, 1983).

The more I wrote, spoke, and performed poetry, the more the fragmented pieces of myself seemed to heed that call. Parts of me that had long been exiled from my awareness began to emerge, seeking recognition, seeking home. It felt as though, through the act of creation, I was issuing a prophetic summons to the dismembered parts of my psyche. Poetry became a sacred dialogue with the untamed wilderness of my own psychological terrain, illuminating the aspects of my being that were yearning to be reclaimed and known.

In time, my poetic journey also led me to confront deeper layers of pain – those tied to epigenetic and intergenerational trauma. My work began to delve into themes of ancestry, opening a discourse not only about who I was but about where I had come from – both geographically and in a psychospiritual sense. As a so-called African American and a descendant of those who were enslaved in North

America, my writing naturally turned toward the complex tensions woven into the Black experience in the United States.

Reclaiming My Ancestral Voice

Through poetry, I began awakening to the grief and bewilderment of an amputated, disconnected history. I felt the deep ache of cultural displacement, the despair of existing in a strange land that had once been alien to my ancestors, who were forcibly brought here. My work became a vessel for exploring these tensions, for interrogating questions of identity, belonging, and worth. Who was I, truly? Where did I belong? These were not only personal questions but ones intricately intertwined with the broader consciousness of Black identity, womanhood, and the struggle for self-definition in a world shaped by oppression.

In 2019, I had a dream in which my great-grandmother, Estella, visited me. She was a woman born in the 1890s in Greenwood, Mississippi, whose parents had likely been enslaved. In the dream, she urged me to delve deeper into the well of ancestral discovery and exploration. Yet what struck me most profoundly was that we were speaking in a language that was not English – a language I didn't consciously know but seemed to understand in the dream.

When I awoke, I felt compelled to write. My hand moved across the page as if guided, producing something that felt less like a poem and more like a transmission – a download from somewhere beyond myself. The words explored the profound irony of our relationship with language. My ancestors had a language that was violently taken from them through forced migration and the institution of slavery. Given new names and a new language upon arrival in America, they were simultaneously denied full access to that imposed language through systemic prohibitions on reading and education.

Four generations later, here I was – a descendant of those ancestors, a woman who had once struggled with a debilitating stutter, now wielding words as a vocation and a source of empowerment. In that moment of inspiration, I wrote a poem in honor of Estella and those who came before her. It was my attempt to carry forward the legacy of the spoken word as a vehicle for liberation, reclaiming the power of language that had once been stripped away.

Broken Language by Manòn Voice

I have been shaped
by the name I have been given
and the one I left in the soil,
sailing from my mother's land.

The tongues of her offspring were split,
broken into a new language –
like bread, they broke it again

to commune,
to keep the ferment of their spit
thick with flavor.

Their phonics folded into spirituals,
coded with shadowy railroad tracks,
deepening in the black,
a traveling train of whispering ghosts.

Soon and very soon,
exiled from the huddled miles of silence,
the crackling laughter spilling from their jowls
slipped into the weeping of work-weary blues,
banjo moans,
Saturday sippin' and Sunday shouts –
backs breaking over other tongues.

In their bones hid the speechless mourn,
the keening of jazz,
tempting them to remember
their ache to scratch.

And even in the beats and breaks of Hip Hop,
there –
a specter,
a haunt of stuttered pain.

These days,
my grandmother visits me in sleep,
cracked golden skin, a sheepish smile.
She will not show me her Mississippi hands,
bound behind her back,
but I can smell the cotton,
pasted with blood in the bed of her fingertips –
and know who laid her down.

I taste the crops she begged
not to blight for the bellies of her children,
fore' winter.
I know she bent her back beneath the sun
when they didn't call it praying,
but preying upon her –
they did.

And in all their taking,
her God from her song,
and making Him the color of the sheets
they wrapped around their envy –
the chiefest of sins.

She spoke then to the wind to carry her through,
and when it blew her
on the black-bound train,
stretching decades into the cities of North and new,
I imagine her cobbler and rice pudding satisfaction,
her voluptuous elbows swaying,
stirring in the kitchen on Baltimore Street,
where she belongs to a heat
that isn't the plantation.

I tell her,
"Don't be shy, Grandma,
your fingers still walk tall,
your rings – crowns.
You rise as good as that cobbler under fire."

And when she sits down,
elated with her golden sugary goodness,
we eat slowly,
like the last supper this dream will always be.

And I feed her truth from her own plate.
We eat, and see,
and eat, and see together.

Jaw ajar,
I speak in her new names –
as if my mouth could wash away
the words they tried to swallow her with.
As if my mouth could be a vault of new memory.
As if my mouth could be a sanctifying sea
of salt and spirit.
As if my mouth could be a prophet of her history,
calling her back.

As if my mouth could be a refining fire,
a wind, heaven, and earth,
where she is called good.

I once could not speak well at all.
My own speech splattered
on an English-chalked wall.
My tutors pulled from me my pain
when they made me say my name.

Sweet mother,
I am the muscle of your memory.
In my cells are your chains.
The freedom of my city feet
has gone no further
than your own imagination.

There are no more thorns in our flesh to enumerate,
no more crosses to carry
that you have not already.
It is only now about speaking it.
Saying it.

She is both embarrassed and enlightened
by this gospel I excavate,
these scrolls I pull from the cave in her cheeks.
And we eat, and see,
and eat, and see together.

And I speak in her new names.
I call them to her,
and hope that her mouth will be a catcher,
an open letter –
making of these words
what she will: her sword and shield.

Sweet mother,
for this, I have studied.
I have become a language.
These words, even if they are not mine,
ours.

They are the ferry,
the boat that carries
the luggage of our history –
for now.

These words will deliver us to new ones.
Though they hurt like stones,
stones they are not.
I promise.

These words, too,
will break open –
like they did our fleshly insides,
so tender.

I promise –
through this broken language,
we will come to know
what we need to remember.

The Poetry That Disrupts

Growing up in the 1990s, I discovered a transformative form of poetry that was neither insular nor strictly academic (though undeniably literary) or bound by rigid formalism. It was the loud, outspoken, and provocative lyrics of artists like Tupac Shakur, Ice Cube, Nas, and The Notorious B.I.G. These artists revolutionized the era with a different kind of poetry – one that spoke truth to power. This was poetry that defied conventions: raw, unfiltered, and multifaceted. It could be angry, offensive, dangerous, beautiful, didactic, inspiring, empowering, mournful, or even vile. It was poetry born of necessity. This is when I was introduced to the poetics of Hip-Hop as prophecy.

Today, Hip-Hop is a worldwide cultural force, deeply embedded in societies across the globe. It has influenced music, fashion, technology, art, entertainment, language, dance, education, politics, and media. As described by the Kennedy Center, Hip-Hop's global reach is evident:

> DJs spin turntables in São Paulo, Brazil. MCs rap in Arabic in the clubs of Qatar. B-boys and B-girls execute intricate freezes in Finland. Graffiti murals rise on the Great Wall of China. Young poets slam their truths on stages in Washington, D.C.
> (The John F. Kennedy Center for the Performing Arts, 2019)

Although Hip-Hop has grown into a multibillion-dollar industry, its origins remain humble – a testament to resilience and creativity born from hardship.

Hip-Hop emerged in the South Bronx during a time when the community bore the brunt of failed social and economic policies that disproportionately affected Black and Latino residents. Displacement, poverty, addiction, and crime plagued the area. Many African-American and Puerto Rican families were uprooted from

Manhattan's ghettos and relocated to public housing projects in the Bronx – a borough already reeling from the loss of 600,000 manufacturing jobs following the construction of the Cross Bronx Expressway. This highway, a controversial project spearheaded by urban planner Robert Moses, facilitated white flight from the Bronx and left marginalized communities behind in economic devastation (Chang, 2005; Rose, 1994).

By the mythological birthdate of Hip-Hop in 1973, much of the optimism from the 1960s Civil Rights Movement had dissipated. As Chang (2005) and Forman and Neal (2004) note, the Bronx had become a wasteland of abandoned and burned-out buildings. Landlords, incentivized by a black-market economy, often set fire to their own properties to collect insurance payouts. Amid this turmoil, Hip-Hop emerged as an art form of survival and self-expression, channeling the frustrations and aspirations of a community left to fend for itself (Chang, 2005; Forman & Neal, 2004).

Hip-Hop music, at its inception, served as both an outlet and a voice for disenfranchised youth from marginalized and low-income communities. It authentically reflected the social, economic, and political realities of their lives, offering a platform for those silenced by systemic neglect and abandonment by government and social services. Out of this suffering emerged a culture rooted in improvisation, imagination, resistance, and liberation. This culture represented a vibrant multicultural exchange between African Americans, Latino Americans, and children of Caribbean immigrants, particularly from Jamaica. This exchange gave rise to the core elements and pillars of Hip-Hop, which all have their own vibrant subcultures: DJing/turntablism, MCing/rapping, B-boying/breaking, and graffiti art (Pough, 2004; Rose, 1994).

Mari Evans (2006), a pioneering poet, writer, dramatist, and central figure of the Black Arts Movement, encapsulated the essence of this cultural response in her book *Clarity as Concept*. She writes:

> Conversely, we as the outsiders, the others, the classic 'them' of the society, have of necessity reacted to what is real, what is impending, not merely perceived, as part of our daily interaction with the society. Therefore, the creative spirits of our artists (and those of our intellectuals who carry the weight of our concerns upon their backs by resisting rather than acquiescing to this society's assault) produce a fruit that is interpretive, didactic, and pulsed by an urgency unlike any other. As a result, our literature has been, and hopefully will continue to be, a literature of issues, of complaints, of charges, and in a desperate and very necessary way, a literature of affirmation and solutions.
>
> (Evans, 2006, p. 47)

This "literature of issues, complaints, and charges . . . and of affirmations and solutions" – is embodied in Hip-Hop culture through rap. By the 1980s, rap had become the most visible and defining element of Hip-Hop. The role of the rapper, or emcee, was to craft intricate narratives in rhythm and rhyme, serving as both a truth-teller and a cultural reporter. These Hip-Hop poets captured the gritty realities of poverty, inner-city living, and systemic oppression, delivering their messages over rock-solid four-beat rhythms or meters (Chang, 2005; Forman & Neal, 2004).

Rap, as a vernacular art form, draws deep inspiration from the spoken-word tradition. Before the rise of Hip-Hop and rap in the United States, spoken-word poetry often found its place in jazz performances. Many historically minded rappers trace their craft back to groups like The Last Poets, a Harlem-based collective, and The Watts Prophets from Los Angeles. Emerging in the late 1960s, these groups fused political poetry with improvisational jazz, laying the groundwork for what would become rap. Gil Scott-Heron's iconic piece, "The Revolution Will Not Be Televised," stands as a clear precursor to rap, embodying its rhythmic and revolutionary spirit before it had a name (Scott-Heron, 1971).

Furthermore, Hip-Hop-influenced literary forms can be traced back to the politically charged Black Arts Movement of the 1960s. This movement, which inspired a generation of African American, Latino, and feminist writers, catalyzed voices such as Amiri Baraka, Maya Angelou, Nikki Giovanni, Sonia Sanchez, and the Last Poets. These writers sought to amplify stories and perspectives that were often overlooked or outright rejected by mainstream America. Their work provided a foundation for the social and political commentary that would later permeate Hip-Hop culture.

Along the way, spoken word, a forerunner to rap, brought new vibrancy to performance. It injected energy, urgency, and raw emotion into the art of delivering words, contributing to the rise of Hip-Hop as a powerful mode of expression and activism (Forman & Neal, 2004).

Inspired by the poetry and spoken word of the Black Arts Movement in the 1960s and 1970s, rap music brought dynamic energy to the genre, demonstrating its capacity for political activation, social commentary, and prophetic power.

In dialogue with Christa Buschendorf, Political activist and philosopher West (2014) frames the Black prophetic tradition as "the great moral and spiritual awakening of the modern world" (p. 10), situating figures such as Douglass, Du Bois, King, and Davis within a lineage of revolutionary love.

Black Prophetic Fire contends that the Black prophetic tradition – alongside similar traditions from other oppressed groups – offers a potent counterforce to the injustices of extractive capitalism, colonization, and imperialism. Political activist and philosopher Cornell West argues that this prophetic tradition involves bearing witness to suffering while also offering visions of justice, love, hope, and liberation (West & Buschendorf, 2014).

In the early days of Hip-Hop, many artists embodied the legacy of the Black Prophetic tradition, engaging in a form of cultural reporting that was insurrectionary in nature. These Hip-Hop poets bore witness to the suffering of their communities, challenged unjust systems, called for liberation, and provoked reflections on love. In doing so, they followed in the footsteps of the Hebrew prophet Isaiah, who declared in the Tanak, "Cry aloud, spare not" (Isaiah 58:1). These artists used their platforms to loudly proclaim the truths of their time, giving voice to marginalized communities and demanding change.

Songs like *"The Message,"* released in 1982 by Grandmaster Flash and the Furious Five, epitomized this prophetic tradition. It became the first rap song to be added to the National Recording Registry by the Library of Congress for its cultural, historical, and aesthetic significance. As Serrano (2015) observes in *The Rap Year Book*, *"The Message"* marked the moment rap became more than party music – it became social commentary. Its iconic lyric, *"Don't push me, 'cause I'm close to the edge, I'm tryin' not to lose my head,"* served as a stark representation of the psychological despair and turmoil that had long plagued marginalized communities of color. Similarly, Chang (2005) situates the song within a lineage of Hip-Hop's prophetic tradition, arguing that its raw realism and refusal to sanitize urban suffering transformed the cultural and political power of rap itself (Chang, 2005).

Another example is Queen Latifah's *"U.N.I.T.Y."* (1993), which confronted the pervasive disrespect toward women in both society and Hip-Hop itself. The song boldly addressed issues such as street harassment, domestic violence, and misogyny within the culture – well before the #MeToo movement brought these conversations into the national spotlight. As Pough (2004) argues, Latifah's work exemplifies how Black women in Hip-Hop have used lyricism as a form of rhetorical resistance, reclaiming space in a genre often shaped by patriarchal norms (Pough, 2004).

In more contemporary examples, Hip-Hop continues to bear prophetic witness to racial injustice and state-sanctioned violence. DaBaby's *"Rockstar (Black Lives Matter Remix)"* (2020) confronted police brutality and racial profiling in the wake of nationwide protests following the deaths of George Floyd, Breonna Taylor, and countless other African Americans. Similarly, Childish Gambino's *"This Is America"* (2018) offered a provocative commentary on Black life in the United States, exposing the dissonance between popular culture's commodification of Black expression and the persistent reality of racialized violence. Through its startling juxtapositions – joyful choruses interrupted by scenes of chaos and gunfire – Gambino's work expands the prophetic function of Hip-Hop into the realm of visual and sonic performance, forcing audiences to confront the contradictions of American identity (DaBaby, 2020; Childish Gambino, 2018; Glover, 2018).

Mari Evans further expounds on this underlying theme of *resistance language* in *Clarity as Concept*, writing,

> The unstructured language of resistance took many forms, particularly among the alienated young where it became a constantly revolving mélange of shapes and sounds: the heavy boom boxes of the eighties stumbling the streets; the bass turbos of the nineties cruising the early mornings and rattling house windows as they pass—all of this is a symbolic, but fierce, singing of a confrontational language: resistance to powerlessness and the seizing of control over something—your neighborhood, your home, your mind even if just for a moment.
> (Evans, 2006, p. 51)

To utilize the poetic art of rap music to gain power over one's own mind, amid powerlessness, is an earnest psychological endeavor to reclaim one's sense of self in a system where that self is continually assailed by systemic injustices. It is a courageous, renegade effort to rewrite the rules of the game by employing oneself as the narrator of one's own story and, thus, the shaper of one's own destiny. This speaks directly to the prophetic tradition, articulating possibilities for oneself, one's community, and one's nation that might otherwise seem unthinkable. This kind of linguistic fortitude has served as a tool for cultural preservation, spiritual intensity, and separation from colonial assimilation. It has created a forum for the delivery of resistance language, birthed out of necessity.

This same necessity – the conviction that language and art are tools for survival – is what poet and activist Audre Lorde articulated most powerfully in her 1985 essay *"Poetry Is Not a Luxury."* She writes:

> Poetry is not a luxury. It is a vital necessity of our existence. It forms the quality of the light within which we predicate our hopes and dreams toward survival and change, first made into language, then into idea, then into more tangible action. Poetry is the way we help give a name to the nameless so it can be thought of. The farthest horizons of our hopes and fears are cobbled by our poems, carved from the rock experiences of our daily lives. As they become known to and accepted by us, our feelings and the honest exploration of them become sanctuaries and spawning grounds for the most radical and daring of ideas. They become a safe house for that difference so necessary to change and the conceptualization of any meaningful action. . . . We can train ourselves to respect our feelings and to transpose them into a language so they can be shared. And where that language does not yet exist, it is our poetry which helps to fashion it. Poetry is not only dream and vision; it is the skeleton architecture of our lives. It lays the foundations for a future of change, a bridge across our fears of what has never been before.
>
> (Lorde, 1985, p. 37).

Lorde's insistence that poetry is "the skeleton architecture of our lives" mirrors the animating spirit of Hip-Hop – a form that constructs communal futures from fragments of pain, joy, and survival (Lorde, 1985).

Through the necessary poetry of Hip-Hop, artists have been able to name the nameless and, with the power of their imaginations, catalyze horizons of existence made possible through creative action. The prophetic potency lies in their artistic ability to shape that which seems abysmal or void, much like the early Hip-Hop breakdancers who invented power moves on sheets of cardboard laid atop ashes and rubble, thus shaping a future into being. Even in more commercial forms of Hip-Hop, where artists rap about and glorify lavish and hedonistic lifestyles, there remains evidence of resistance to poverty, invisibility, inferiority, and the absence of pleasure. These artists, though often seemingly depicting fantastical worlds, are still bearing witness to the human condition in graphic, uncompromising terms and are seeking ways to transcend the psychological and physical bondage that has historically constrained their communities.

In engaging the *language of resistance* by calling out systems of harm, cruelty, and injustice, Hip-Hop also embodies the power to *call in* – to welcome, to gather, and to hold communities accountable to higher standards of truth. This dual function has contributed to Hip-Hop's status as a global phenomenon. While rooted in the United States, Hip-Hop culture has invited reinterpretation by communities across the world. Although uniquely American in origin, it has spread internationally, offering a powerful tool for social change.

As Simeone (2023) reports in the NPR article *"The Sound of Global Hip Hop: Why the Genre Resonates Around the World,"* rappers in Tibet use Hip-Hop to preserve their traditional language, and in Tunisia, Hip-Hop helped catalyze the Arab Spring. These artists employ Hip-Hop as a prophetic tool – not merely foretelling but *forth-telling*, speaking with such clarity, truth, and passion that, in hindsight, we recognize their insights as prophetic. The original Hebrew word for *prophet* simply meant "one who sees." A prophet is a seer – one who perceives through the layers of reality (Simeone, 2023).

References

Akhter, T. (2013). Relation between poetry and psychology with special reference to the poetry of Kamala Das. *IOSR Journal of Humanities and Social Science*, 9(6), 13–16.
Angelou, M. (1969). *I know why the caged bird sings*. Random House.
Baldwin, J. (1962). *The creative process*. Ridge Press.
Brostoff, R. (2008). The psychological poetics of presence. *Journal of Poetry Therapy*, 21(1), 11–22.
Chang, J. (2005). *Can't stop won't stop: A history of the hip-hop generation*. St. Martin's Press.
DaBaby. (2020). *Black Lives Matter (Remix)* [Song]. On *Blame It on Baby (Deluxe)*. Interscope Records.
Evans, M. (2006). *Clarity as concept*. Black Classic Press.
Forman, M., & Neal, M. A. (Eds.). (2004). *That's the joint!: The hip-hop studies reader*. Routledge.
Glover, D. (as Childish Gambino). (2018). *This Is America* [Song]. RCA Records.
Harjo, J. (1983). *She had some horses*. Thunder's Mouth Press.
Harjo, J. (2015). *Conflict resolution for holy beings*. W. W. Norton & Company.
The Kennedy Center. (n.d.). *Hip hop culture: The John F. Kennedy center for the performing arts*. Retrieved September 18, 2023, from https://www.kennedy-center.org/education/resources-for-educators/classroom-resources/media-and-interactives/media/hip-hop/hip-hop-a-culture-of-vision-and-voice/
Latifah, Q. (1993). *U.N.I.T.Y.* [Song]. On *Black Reign*. Motown Records.
Lorde, A. (1985). Poetry is not a luxury. In *Sister outsider: Essays and speeches* (pp. 36–39). Crossing Press.
Pough, G. D. (2004). *Check it while I wreck it: Black womanhood, hip-hop culture, and the public sphere*. Northeastern University Press.
Rose, T. (1994). *Black noise: Rap music and black culture in contemporary America*. Wesleyan University Press.

Scott-Heron, G. (1971). *The revolution will not be televised* [Song]. Flying Dutchman.

Serrano, S. (2015). *The rap year book: The most important rap song from every year since 1979, discussed, debated, and deconstructed.* Abrams Image.

Simeone, N. (2023, September 12). The sound of global hip hop: Why the genre resonates around the world. *Texas Public Radio.* https://www.tpr.org/2023-09-12/the-sound-of-global-hip-hop-why-the-genre-resonates-around-the-world

West, C. (2014). *Black prophetic fire.* Beacon Press.

Chapter 13

Aesthetic Motivation in Religious Activism

Brandon Vaidyanathan

Introduction

This chapter explores the potential role of aesthetic experiences in religious activism. In doing so, it aims to bridge the fields of sociology of religion and the social-scientific study of social movements to address gaps shared by both fields. As detailed in what follows, early theorists in both disciplines entertained similar assumptions about their objects of inquiry as being motivated by forces that social scientists considered "irrational." On the heels of this current, dominated by psychopathology, followed an economic approach which assumed a conception of human action as the product of instrumentally-rational cost–benefit calculation. Empirical criticisms quickly arose in both sub-fields to challenge the rationalist claim to general theory. The advent of the cultural turn in the social sciences further challenged the prevailing behaviorist approaches in both disciplines, advocating the importance of cultures and interpretive meaning-systems. Pluralism and pragmatism have now become the norm, replacing attempts to form totalizing grand theories that explain all aspects of the phenomenon at hand. Studies in both subfields over the past decade or so have thus narrowed scope, seeking primarily to bring to bear insights from other theoretical approaches (e.g., organizational studies, feminist theory, social network theory, globalization theory, etc.). Interestingly, however, both subfields have come full circle in a renewed emphasis on the importance of emotions.

A consideration of the role of aesthetics in religious movements seems in continuation with this recent program. What it addresses is the neglected study of emotions beyond "moral shocks" (i.e., negative emotions which provoke outrage) and "positive" pleasures, most of which considered in the literature seem instrumental (e.g., Jasper, 1997, 2018). Aesthetic factors are overlooked in the study of social movement activism, and even research on the role of aesthetics in religion (e.g., Ezzy, 2016) neglects the relationship between aesthetic experience and activism.

Considering the role of aesthetics can help us better answer certain questions that have been of interest to these disciplines from their inceptions – namely, what attracts people to and sustains commitments to truth and justice. Sociologists tend to reduce aesthetic experiences to tastes, which are seen simply as a means to

DOI: 10.4324/9781003598107-17

reproducing class distinctions. But the fact that people have aesthetic experiences is not a function of social class any more than feeling moral outrage is. I want to draw attention not so much to the *content* of what people are shocked by (which is certainly shaped by class) but simply the fact *that* they are thus shocked, though I want to turn the focus away from negative emotions, such as "moral shocks" (Jasper, 1997, 2018), to something that might be considered perhaps "positive emotional shocks" – i.e., aesthetic experiences that can spur people into action. This category of experience has been neglected in scholarship and seems relevant to the study of both religion and social movements. In particular, to what extent might such aesthetic experiences contribute to religious activism?

Background

Irrationality

Early approaches to the sociological study of religion and social movements tended to assume both to be driven by forms of irrationality. The idea of religion as irrational was an assumption by no means original to sociologists. Hobbes, for example, dismissed religion as "ignorance" and "lies" – a phenomenon generated by people "stand[ing] in awe of their own imaginations," worshipping "creatures of their own fancy" (1956, 1, p. 8). Similarly for Feuerbach and Durkheim after him, gods were evidently human projections of self or society (Feuerbach, 1841/1957, pp. 29–31; Durkheim, 1912/1915, p. 206).

Another way to understand this irrational response was as driven by deprivation and suffering (Davis, 1949, p. 532; Simmel, 1905/1959, p. 32). Religion was seen as a result of the pervasive need (of the weak and susceptible) to resolve psychological disturbances, usually caused by external strains. Historical accounts of populist religiosity among the working classes, for example (Pope, 1942; Thompson, 1964) reveal this sedative function of religion, which scholars would denounce as illusory distractions from fighting the real (structural) causes of these problems.

Whether generated by psychological or sociological processes, the phenomenon of religion was essentially "an illusion" (Freud, 1927/1961) – "hallucinations produced by an intellectual activity at the mercy of the passions," as Comte put it (1896, 2, p. 554) – or the product of mental imbalance (Trenchard, 1709). For early anthropologists, as Evans-Pritchard notes, religion was simply an offshoot of primitive irrationality (see Evans-Pritchard's (1965, p. 15, assessment of this irrationalism account among early anthropologists). Religion, for many early social scientists, was a phenomenon doomed to decline, if not disappear altogether, with the progress of scientific modernity: "Belief in supernatural powers is doomed to die out, all over the world, as the result of the increasing adequacy and diffusion of scientific knowledge" (Wallace, 1966, p. 265).

Similar assumptions of irrationality and pathology pervaded early sociological accounts of social movements. The phenomenon of collective protest was clumped together with a host of phenomena such as mobs, panics, manias, stampedes, propaganda, fashions, and so on (e.g., Blumer, 1969). Crowds were propelled by unconscious motives and "very simple and very exaggerated" emotions, thus susceptible to ignite at any moment by orators spurring them on to violence (Le Bon, 1895/1960, pp. 51–52). Developments in the early half of the 20th century such as fascism and communism led scholars to assume peculiar kinds of people were more prone to be susceptible to such movements – people with violent temperaments (Allport, 1924); alienated, isolated individuals (Kornhauser, 1959); immature personalities (Lasswell, 1930), or fanatics desperate for something to believe in (Hoffer, 1951). Such assumptions shaped the sociological study of "collective behavior."

Like religions, such forms of collective behavior were considered essentially deviant: "Crowd behavior consists, in essence, of deviations from the traditional norms of society" (Turner & Killian, 1957, p. 143). Collective behavior, at its roots, was based on some form of "unrest or disturbance in the usual forms of living or routines of life" (Blumer, 1969, p. 71). So-called episodes of collective behavior required as a precursor some "impairment of the relations among and consequently inadequate functioning of the components of action" (Smelser, 1962, p. 47).

Several problems plague this irrationalist approach in both religion as well as social movements, many of which could not be supported by empirical data: the unfalsifiable assumption of religious or collective behavior as somehow abnormal or deviant; the assumption of people as passive and susceptible, with emotions being essentially thrust upon them by crowds or collective frenzies or fanatical demagogues; the assumption of weak, isolated, needy, flawed, disturbed, and immature people as being the only ones who would be susceptible to such phenomena; the assumption that the need for religion or social protests would disappear with psychological maturity, or civilizational maturity from primitive states of living, or with the resolution of social-structural problems (Goodwin & Jasper, 2006, p. 614; Stark, 2003, pp. 368–372). Precluded in most of these accounts was the possibility that either religious or social-political movements could offer people something intrinsically meaningful, fulfilling, or satisfying or generate positive emotions such as hope or love or even commitments to truth and justice. Yet, even critics of this approach at the time did little to advance such possibilities.

Rationalism

By the 1970s, the sociological perspective on social movements shifted from one based on irrationality to an assumption of "rational, purposive, organized action" (Tilly, 1978). One reason for this is likely that several scholars themselves had been participants in progressive movements. As Goodwin and Jasper note, the experiences and sympathies of these scholars were not represented by the prevailing view of the collective behavior tradition, in which protesters were "[d]riven by mysterious forces outside their control, whether subconscious motivations or the pull of the crowd" – they were clearly "not rational agents with purposes of their own" (Goodwin & Jasper, 2006, p. 614).

This emphasis on rationality is not merely a function of biographical resonance; rather, it is also shaped by the larger zeitgeist pervasive throughout the social sciences, which by this time had set aside the complexity of psychoanalysis, taking up instead the more parsimonious (read "scientific") approach of economic modeling. The sociological study of social movements as well as of religion are at least two areas in which new scholars began to emphasize the instrumental rationality of actors and saw social action as the consequence of interest-maximizing cost–benefit analyses of these actors.

A central postulate of the "religious economies" school that emerged in the sociology of religion was that "[i]ndividuals act rationally, weighing costs and benefits of potential actions, and choosing those actions that maximize their net benefits" (Iannaccone, 1997, p. 26). Or, stated with more of an attempt at specifying scope-conditions (but really providing little additional information as to what precisely such "rationality" means): "Within the limits of their information and understanding, restricted by available options, guided by their preferences and tastes, humans attempt to make rational choices" (Stark & Finke, 2000, p. 38).

Similarly, in the study of social movements, scholars began to make explicit a notion of protesters as rational (i.e., self-interested) actors seeking "selective incentives" and making cost–benefit calculations (Olson, 1965; Oberschall, 1973; McCarthy & Zald, 1977). Their overarching concern was to establish social movements as part of the ordinary political process rather than as an irrational exception. Especially important in such considerations was the availability of resources – material as well as non-material, internal as well as external – such as money, links to elite allies, employment, friendships, authority, and so on.

Critics, however, came to argue that this "resource mobilization" view in its focus on strategy and tactics neglected structural concerns (Melucci, 1982; Piven & Cloward, 1992). McAdam (1982, p. 26), among others, argued that resource mobilization was simply "inadequate as a general explanation of insurgency" for several reasons – for instance, it was inconsistent in its explanations of the relationships between elites and challengers; it assumed disadvantaged groups to be impotent and overlooked the importance of indigenous resources; its definition of resources was vague and all-inclusive; it did not distinguish objective social conditions from people's subjective perceptions of these conditions. Scholars focused on the "political opportunity structure" paid more serious attention to structural factors, such as electoral stability/instability, the availability of allies, the degree of openness of political access, and so on (Jenkins & Perrow, 1977; Piven & Cloward, 1977). Yet this approach too – even McAdam's (1982) attempt to get at subjective meanings through his notion of "cognitive liberation" – was essentially rationalistic.

A similar structuralist component is seen in the rationalist approach to the sociology of religion in the conceptualization of "religious economies" as markets (Stark & Finke, 2000, p. 35). Market competition then becomes the key explanatory factor for why religious involvement is high in certain times and places and low in others: Religious entrepreneurs are forced to offer better and improved "products" to gain a larger share of the religious market. A pluralistic religious market-structure, as a result of the market-mechanism, causes religious vitality. For both religious "firms" as well as social movement organizations, then, success is determined by strategic use of resources and structural opportunities. In both approaches, leadership and organizational strength are crucial determinants of strategy and success. Both approaches, thus, are highly instrumental. For scholars of religion as well as of social movements, the focus on irrational "passions" shifted to a concern with rational "interests," to use Hirschman's (1977) terms.

Also "in the air" was the concern with the free-rider problem, which scholars of religion as well as social movements found themselves preoccupied with (Iannaccone, 1994; Olson, 1965). In addition, it is interesting to note that the key concerns of the irrationalist perspective are bracketed in this approach: Both "grievances" – the psychological disturbances or strains that provoked protest movements – as well as "demand" for religion are assumed, with little supportive evidence, to be constant (Jenkins & Perrow, 1977, p. 250; McCarthy & Zald, 1977; Stark & Finke, 2000).

In both sub-fields, rationalism was a pendulum-shift away from prevailing approaches, and lost in the transition was the importance of emotions. Emotions were epiphenomenal, if not absent altogether, from actors' rational calculations of benefits and strategies – left out of the equation were "allegiances, jealousies, hatreds, demonizations, disappointments, hopes, and so on" (Goodwin & Jasper, 2006, p. 615) that characterize so much of social life in religious or social movement organizations. While the restrictions of newspaper and historic data may have driven some of this neglect of emotions, perhaps an important driver here was the implicit assumption of emotions as irrational.

The Return of the "Irrational": The Emotional Turn

The "cultural turn" in the social sciences which took place in the 1980s brought a new concern for subjective dimensions of human experience and action that were previously neglected. Particular attention was paid to interpretations and meaning-making processes, manifested in discourse, beliefs, values, symbols, and artifacts (e.g., Johnston & Klandermans, 1995; Wuthnow, 1987). While this approach did not preclude a consideration of emotions, as Goodwin and Jasper note, it had a strong cognitive bent (2006, p. 616). A clear manifestation of this is the development of studies on "framing." A concern for scholars of religion as well as social movements was how organizations recruited members. Snow and Benford (1988), for example, made distinctions between different kinds of rhetorical framing strategies that influenced the success of recruitment efforts. Yet, as Benford admitted, their approach simply neglected to take emotions into consideration (1997, p. 419). Studies of identity, similarly, focused on cognitive and interpretive elements.

It is only more recently, in the last decade or so, that an interest in the importance of emotions has surfaced – more, it seems, in the study of social movements than in the sociology of religion (where studies of emotion seem focused on "special" cases such as Black Protestants or Pentecostals). As Smith (2008) points out, sociologists of religion have only recently begun to pay serious attention to the importance of emotions. This development, too, seems to reflect a broader sociological interest in emotions (e.g., Collins, 2004; Turner & Stets, 2006).

In the study of religion, for instance, Smith (2007) argues for the role of emotions in why Christianity "works" for its adherents – namely, belief in its tenets and participation in its practices help generate feelings of security, belonging, and purpose in the cosmos; love – passionate love even; gratitude; "euphoric lightness" (174) upon the resolution of guilt, shame, and remorse; feelings of reverence and devotion; and a sense of moral bearings.

In the study of social movements, some of the most systematic theorizing on the topic has been done by James Jasper (1997, 2018; Goodwin & Jasper, 2004, 2006). One of the key contributions of Jasper's work on emotions is that he underscores how and why protest activity is pleasurable and satisfying. Participation in social movements, he argues, is able "to provide a moral voice . . . They give us an opportunity to plumb our moral sensibilities and convictions, and to articulate and elaborate them" (1997, p. 5). A similar case could be made for involvement in religious organizations and movements, since Jasper argues that "[p]rotest is like religious ritual: it embodies our moral judgments, so that we can express allegiance to moral visions through actions (1997, p. 14).

Secondly, unlike some of the earlier theoretical approaches we have seen, Jasper's account is multifaceted and multicausal. Even though his perspective emphasizes culture, he insists that

> culture isn't everything: it is not physical resources and the money to buy them, nor strategic interactions with other groups and individuals, nor the biographical idiosyncrasies of individuals. Culture helps define resources, strategies, and biographies, but it is not the same thing as they are.
>
> (1997, p. 12)

As a result, his account is distinct from stronger culturalist accounts such as that of Ann Swidler (2003), in that he allows a larger role for goals and values in shaping action. Innovation and artfulness are central in his conception of human agency.

Another contribution of Jasper's work is the notion of "moral shocks," which encapsulates how emotions, identity, and biography matter together in understanding the moral motivations for people to join social movements: "an unexpected event or piece of information raises such a sense of outrage in a person that she becomes inclined toward political action, with or without the network of political contacts emphasized in mobilization and process theories" (1997, p. 106). The "raw materials" for moral shocks are a combination of "[p]ositive feelings toward one's home and surroundings, coupled with strong negative affect toward a proposal that seems to threaten these" (p. 107). His approach also accounts for how collective rituals, particularly in activities such as singing and dancing, reinforce identities, beliefs, and moral commitments (pp. 192–194).

The key argument here is that protest activity is driven by pursuit of pleasurable satisfactions. Previous models ignored these pleasures: Crowd models "viewed participants as overwhelmed by anxieties and fears," while rationalist ones "reduce[d] protest to the pursuit of economic interests." Jasper does not want to deny such motivations but wants to highlight that they have missed out on "the pleasures along the way" (p. 217). Such pleasures include the excitement of crowds, possibilities of romance and sex, glimpses of a hopeful future, creativity and flow, empowerment, intellectual pleasure, and a shared sense of purpose (pp. 217–221; Jasper, 2018, pp. 30–31).

Despite these strengths, however, Jasper's account suffers from certain shortcomings. First, the pleasure-driven nature of his account at times seems indistinguishable from the cost–benefit model of rational choice theories. As with Jerolmack and Porpora's (2004) critique of rational choice approaches to the sociology of religion, there seems to be an inbuilt assumption here of psychological egoism, in the sense that people act primarily because of an awareness that they will receive certain rewards (here pleasures) – external or internal, they are conceptualized as benefits alike. Even his conceptualization of moral commitments and "affective loyalties" seems to hinge on the pleasure derived from following these or the pain derived from not following these (see Jasper, 1997, p. 221). A second weakness of relying on the importance of pleasure is that it seems susceptible to the same vagueness and generality that characterize notions such as "benefits," "resources," or "political opportunities."

Such an account is also unable to adequately answer some questions that remain unanswered in both the sociology of religion and the study of social and political movements, such as, why are some people drawn to certain beliefs or ideological commitments or frames to begin with? What circumstances incite or amplify the emotions that are relevant to religious/political commitments, and how are these emotions and commitments sustained (Walder, 2009, pp. 404, 406; Smith, 2008, pp. 1564–1566)?

One possibility I would like to suggest here is to return to certain elements of the classical "irrationalist" tradition that scholars may be reticent to reconsider. In particular, it might be worthwhile reconsidering whether we are, after all, susceptible to certain phenomena exerting overwhelming emotional pressures or forces on us in ways that dislodge, or reduce the scope of, our strategic calculations. However, while the focus of the "irrationalist" approach was on "negative" elements, such as brainwashing by demagogues, the sort of phenomenon I want to consider here is, at least *prima facie*, positive: aesthetic experience.

I do not mean to imply here that aesthetic experiences should be considered irrational. Doing so would simply perpetuate the mistake of reducing rationality to its instrumental variant. Beauty, for instance, might certainly be a reason for attending to an object, although perhaps not a sufficient reason – not in the way that the truth of a proposition is sufficient reason to believe in it (Scruton, 2009, pp. 2–3; Collier, 1994/1998, p. 448). My point here is to emphasize the way in which the experience of something we perceive to be beautiful, bracketing all considerations of whether or not anything can be "objectively" beautiful, is distinct from both our strategic, calculating mode of operation as well as ordinary emotions of fear, anger, and pleasure. To extend Jasper's terminology, I would call it a "positive emotional shock."

As an imprecise definition, beauty can be characterized as "aesthetic experience that emotionally moves a beholder, an affective response that takes us beyond ourselves into new (and often unexpected) positions of being and feeling" (Zuber, 2006, p. 296). Considering such a phenomenon allows us to appreciate the ways in which people are often moved to do things that did not involve strategic calculation or even perception of benefit (for example, falling in love, which can certainly be unexpected and inconvenient!). A key distinction here is that the experience is one that pulls us out of ourselves, in contrast to the experience of "rewards" or "pleasures" that have a self-focused character. Aesthetic experiences may also be self-transcendent.

We also need to consider the role of aesthetics beyond its confinement in sociology to topics such as studies of aesthetic consumption or taste more generally (see de la Fuente, 2000, for a review of the literature in the sociology of aesthetics). While this research is certainly important, the phenomenon I am interested in here is distinct from the concept of taste. Sociological research on taste examines how the content of aesthetic judgment is shaped by social class, boundary- and distinction-making processes, and so on (Bourdieu, 1984). Here, aesthetic judgments of taste have to do with the cultivation of legitimacy that is determined by class position. They are also part of a cultivated *habitus* inculcated in families, schools, and other socializing institutions and operate below the level of consciousness or control of the will (1984, p. 466). Taste is linked to emotions, and contributes to making and maintaining boundaries. It is a mechanism through which social class is naturalized.

But there are, on the other hand, aesthetic judgments that are not purely a product of social class and that may even be shared across historical and cultural boundaries (Haidt et al., 1997). A body of research in fields ranging from architecture to history to music to finance to mathematics to physics tries to assess whether there are any universal aesthetic properties in looking for some underlying factor that governs aesthetics (e.g., Kak, 2011; Livio, 2002; Neperud & Serlin, 1984). For instance, one review of research conducted over the 20th century suggests overall "real psychological effects associated with the golden section" (Green, 1995). The explanatory factor appealed to in such cases is evolutionary processes (Chatterjee, 2014).

For our purposes, we don't need to resolve whether there are aesthetic universals. I am also not focusing on how specific aesthetic judgments are produced and socially patterned. Instead, I simply want to draw attention to how certain kinds of aesthetic experience might move people, under certain conditions, to social action. Can such aesthetic experiences serve as a mechanism to help explain attraction and adherence to religious and political commitments? At least in terms of social movement outcomes, Jasper's work offers a suggestion; for example, when considering the role of the physical beauty of geographical terrain, he notes: "The imagination can define and defend a place more neatly when the eyes can see its parameters, especially when to see it is to appreciate it" (1997, p. 201). This phenomenon has received scant attention from scholars. In examining the relevance of experiences of beauty or "positive emotional shocks" for the study of social movements as well as the sociology of religion, I want to examine its relevance to people's commitment to justice, which constitutes a primary goal both for many religious groups as well as contemporary social and political movements.

Beauty and Justice

Beauty is a concept that eludes concise definition. As Emerson remarked, "I am warned by the ill fate of many philosophers not to attempt a definition of beauty" (1860/1988, p. 274). This difficulty has led scholars interested in the phenomenon to adopt two divergent approaches: one, to settle for the least common denominator – to define beauty simply (and unhelpfully) as "whatever is pleasing to the senses," or alternatively, to discard the term altogether and focus on smaller, more manageable phenomena, such as physical attractiveness, aesthetic pleasure, or preference (Armstrong & Detweiler-Bedell, 2008, pp. 305–306; Dickie, 1997; Danto, 2003).

What might be more helpful for our purposes is Scruton's approach: to sidestep the circularity, vagueness, or seeming mismatch with experience that definitional attempts suffer from and instead settle for a list of basic logical platitudes – a method similar to what philosophers adopt in their attempts to define truth. He presents six "comparable platitudes" about beauty, against which our theories and assertions can be tested (Scruton, 2009, pp. 5–6):

> (i) Beauty pleases us. (ii) One thing can be more beautiful than another. (iii) Beauty is always a reason for attending to the thing that possesses it. (iv) Beauty is the subject-matter of a judgment: the judgment of taste. (v) The judgment of taste is about the beautiful object, not about the subject's state of mind. . . . (vi) [T]here are no second-hand judgments of beauty. There is no way that you can argue me into a judgement that I have not made for myself, nor can I become an expert in beauty, simply by studying what others have said about beautiful objects, and without experiencing and judging for myself.

While inadequate as an "operational definition" of beauty, this gives us at least some sense of the concept we are dealing with. In most of what follows, I will be concerned with how we experience this phenomenon of beauty and what it has to do with commitments to religious faith or to justice-oriented collective action. Such a phenomenological approach might be more adequate to understanding the topic than trying to start with clearly demarcated categories. As Charles Taylor (1985, p. 41) argues:

> In philosophy typically we start off with a question, which we know to be badly formed at the outset. We hope that in struggling with it, we shall find

that its terms are transformed, so that in the end we will answer a question which we could not properly conceive in the beginning. We are striving for conceptual innovation which will allow us to illuminate some matter, say an area of human experience, which would otherwise remain dark and confused. The alternative is to stick stubbornly to certain terms and try to understand reality by classifying it in these terms (are these propositions synthetic or analytic, is this a psychological question or a philosophical question, is this view monist or dualist?).

An approach very much along these lines is taken up by Elaine Scarry (1999) in her Tanner Lecture, "On Beauty and Being Just." Using rich examples and analogies, she makes a series of claims about beauty and develops an argument about its relationship to justice. Some of these claims are about what encounters with beautiful objects and persons do to us: they exert various kinds of pressures on us – for example, the incitation to replicate, to imitate, to beget, to stay-with, to share, or to protect.

Beauty, argues Scarry, serves as a doorway of sorts, pulling us into a larger world: "Something beautiful fills the mind yet invites the search for something beyond itself, something larger or something of the same scale with which it needs to be brought into relation" (p. 29). An encounter with beauty also has an energizing or renewing effect:

> The beautiful, almost without any effort of our own, acquaints us with the mental event of conviction, and so pleasurable a mental state is this that ever afterwards one is willing to labor, struggle, wrestle with the world to locate enduring sources of conviction – to locate what is true.
>
> (p. 31)

Here we see similarities to experiences of people who join religious or political movements: being drawn out of oneself into something greater or having an experience that generates in someone the conviction and endurance to commit oneself to a cause.

Drawing on Kant, Scarry goes on to argue that the pleasure we take in beauty – unlike other pleasures such as from food or drink – is inexhaustible (p. 50). Yet, she cautions us, beauty only introduces the possibility of certainty and conviction – it does not guarantee it; there is always the possibility of making errors. "It creates, without itself fulfilling, the aspiration for enduring certitude" (p. 53). Beauty and truth are thus "allied" but not identical (p. 52).

Another pressure that beauty exerts on us, she argues, is to repair injuries and injustices. Something we perceive as beautiful incites in us "an urge to protect it, or act on its behalf" (p. 80). Here she goes on to make a strong causal claim that "it is the very symmetry of beauty which leads us to, or somehow assists us in discovering, the symmetry that eventually comes into place in the realm of justice" (p. 97). Beauty, because of its properties such as symmetry and harmony, she argues, "acts as a lever in the direction of justice" (p. 100). Because of its feature of symmetry, it serves as a call toward harmony, order, fairness, and peace: "the term that is present becomes pressing, active, insistent, calling out for, directing our attention toward, what is absent" (p. 109). Another mechanism she states – also an empirical question well worth investigating – is that

> in periods where a human community is too young to have yet had time to create justice, as well as in periods when justice has been taken away, beautiful things (which do not rely on us to create them but come on their own and have never been absent from a human community) hold steadily visible the manifest good of equality and balance.
>
> (p. 97)

In addition, she argues, natural beauty, such as in "the symmetry, equality, and self-sameness of the sky," are present to our senses in a way that these very same qualities in social relationships are not (p. 101). Unlike clear, blue skies that we can see as evenly distributed above us, we have no such concrete, visible manifestations of justice being consistently administered. Yet, she argues, this experience of beauty awakens our desire for such distributive justice. Furthermore, the equality of such beauty as manifested by nature does not depend on us to bring it about (p. 108). A final contribution of beauty to our sense of justice, she argues, citing Iris Murdoch and Simone Weil, is that it has a "decentering" and "unselfing" function – it not only pulls us out of ourselves but enables us to recognize that we are not the center of the world, and also awakens in us the desire to preserve and to share what is beautiful even if this does not serve our self-interest (pp. 110–113; 117–123). It thus serves as a "positive emotional shock" that strikes us, dislodges us, and generates emotions such as awe and wonder that can draw us out of ourselves.

Scarry's arguments are fascinating, though not entirely convincing. Critics such as Gitlin (1999) and Dutton (2000) argue that while Scarry is able to establish parallels between beauty and justice, the causal argument simply does not work, for several reasons. Experiencing or loving beauty does not necessitate that I would care about – much less commit myself to – others having equal access to it. While beauty may prepare us to pursue and commit to justice or provide the sort of "decentering" that Scarry, (with Murdoch and Weil) claims that it does, this connection is not necessary. Further, Scarry neglects to consider people's differences and disagreements about beauty. Worst of all, perhaps, is that beauty can also be compatible with grave injustices. Hitler and the Nazis, for example, found inspiration in Wagner (Meyer, 1975), and looting art was, for them, a war priority (Feliciano, 1997). Perhaps the Nazis imagined themselves to be pursuing a form of justice, but in any case, this is not the sort of argument that Scarry wants to make.

Scarry's causal argument is much stronger than the evidence she can marshal in support for it. And much of the difficulty with her argument seems to lie in its essentialism. In making claims about what beauty does or does not do, her argument makes claims about the nature of beauty or justice itself regardless of scope conditions – claims which can easily be refuted by a single piece of contrary evidence. Her arguments clump together all kinds of beauty and expect them to function in the same way – to have the same causal effect regardless of context. Such a general and totalizing account seems untenable. If we have learned anything from the studies of the last several decades, it should be that no one single explanatory factor is sufficient to account for the complexity of sociological phenomena such as religions or social movements, even if we focus on particular dimensions such as commitments to religious truth or to social justice. A more helpful approach would be to ask whether certain combinations of factors, under certain conditions, come to matter in decisive ways for particular outcomes.

There are at least two empirical approaches that could improve and clarify her argument. The first is psychological and involves examining personality-level relationships between responses to beauty and commitment to justice. One such study has already been attempted (Diessner et al., 2009), which found significant correlations between "engagement with beauty" and justice-mindedness among a sample of university students.

A second approach, which I will at least begin to undertake here, is sociological. Similar to Jasper's (1997) study of emotions, such an approach can examine, either through ethnographies, interviews, or historical/biographical analyses, whether, how, and in combination with what other factors beauty might matter for commitments to religions or social movements. This tack would modify her argument from an essentialist one (which all too easily is challenged by examples of correlations of experiences of beauty with acts of injustice) to one that posits a mechanism or tendency that works under certain scope conditions.

Towards a Phenomenology of Beauty in Social Movements

In what follows, I will consider a few examples that are suggestive of the role of beauty in shaping commitments to religion as well as social movements. These examples are primarily of leaders of religion-based social movements – Martin Luther King Jr., Hans and Sophie Scholl, Mahatma Gandhi, and Dorothy Day – and the types of accounts are different: rhetorical speeches, biographies, and autobiographical accounts. The mechanisms that these accounts suggest, however, are not necessarily restricted to leadership; some of these might well serve as factors motivating ordinary participants and adherents of movements.

Martin Luther King Jr.'s "Birth of a New Nation" speech, delivered in 1957 on the occasion of Ghanaian independence, contains a host of references to beauty. What is particularly interesting here is King's phenomenological presentation of the way thoughts and emotions arise in him, all as responses provoked by beauty.

King starts with an account of a visit to London, where he was mesmerized by the sight of the great political edifices of Buckingham Palace and the parliamentary buildings:

Look at the beauty of the changing of the guards with their beautiful horses. It's a beautiful sight.... Move into the House of Lords and the House of Commons. There with all of its beauty standing up before the world is one of the most beautiful sights in the world.

(Carson & Shepard, 2001, p. 36)

Following this, he speaks of visiting Westminster Cathedral, whose "great architecture" provokes a sense of "awe . . . about the greatness of God and man's feeble attempt to reach up for God." And yet, at the same time, the same beauty of the cathedral and the palace evoked other thoughts: the "dying system" of the British empire, the power it once held in having conquered so much of the world, its hubris and arrogance, the humiliation and exploitation wrought by colonialism, and the disastrous consequences of this empire on much of the rest of the world. King continues:

All of these things came to my mind when I stood there in Westminster Abbey with all of its beauty, and I thought about all of the beautiful hymns and anthems that the people would go in there to sing. And yet the Church of England never took a stand against this system; the Church of England sanctioned it; the Church of England gave it moral stature. All of the exploitation perpetuated by the British Empire was sanctioned by the Church of England. But something else came to my mind: God comes in the picture even when the Church won't take a stand. God has injected a principle in this universe. God has said that all men must respect the dignity and worth of all human personality, and if you don't do that, I will take charge. It seems this morning that I can hear God speaking. I can hear him speaking throughout the universe, saying, "Be still and know that I am God. And if you don't stop, if you don't straighten up, if you don't stop exploiting people, I'm going to rise up and break the backbone of your power. And your power will be no more!" And the power of Great Britain is no more.

(pp. 38–39)

It is worth noting the transition that occurs in the above passage and what it implies. We start with King's experience of beauty, provoked by a marvelous religious edifice – and it is not only the sights that move him but the imagined sounds of "beautiful hymns" that people would sing there, perhaps also the sense of community and collective pride that people would experience there. But all of this is juxtaposed with images of injustice and cruelty. The images of ugly injustices stand in stark contrast to the beauty of the religious edifices. Implied in the juxtaposition – and note that the audience has to understand this; otherwise, the effect would be lost – is the sense of dissonance or discord between the beauty of religious institutional worship and the ugliness of human exploitation that is not denounced by these institutions. Beauty seems to implicitly demand justice, which provokes indignation for King as a religious believer, who also believes that this indignation is experienced by God himself. What this awakens then is the idea that God, unlike people and institutions, will not forget or ignore injustice. Beauty thus seems to awaken a commitment both to justice and to a religious faith in which justice is protected and demanded.

Implicit in King's rhetoric is an expectation of correlation between beauty and justice, and it is this expectation that leads him to denounce the travesty that the same institution which can generate such beautiful structures was complicit in grave injustices. But why should one expect beauty and justice to go hand in hand? At least for someone like King, the answer has to do with a source that ensures consistency: God. The beauty both of religious edifices and of just social orders are constructions that are responses – for believers, both of them are experienced as responses to God and expressions of faith-commitments. As King continues with his speech, recounting the images of God's justice that are provoked by the earlier experience of dissonance, he presents two other images which suggest a resolution to the discord – images in which beauty and justice are integrated. The first is an image of a God who "struggles with you," sharing in our experience of human injustice and suffering, but also a God who will – King claims to believe with certainty – come in resplendent "glory," referring to a final day of judgment, an assurance of justice (p. 40). While the term "glory" usually has connotations of power – for example, in characterizing the glory of the colonialist British empire – the reference to God here emphasizes not power so much as radiance or resplendence, of which justice is a feature.

The second image is elaborated in the prophet Isaiah's vision – an image which has profound meaning for King and which he cites on several other occasions, such as his famous "I Have a Dream" speech – "every valley shall be exalted, and every hill shall be made low; the crooked places shall be made straight, and the rough places plain; and the glory of the Lord shall be revealed, and all flesh shall see it together." And citing this, he continues, "That's the beauty of this thing: all flesh shall see it together" (p. 40). This theme of togetherness and unity serves as another source of beauty – the beauty of an ideal worth committing one's life to. The togetherness and unity here, aspired to here are coextensive with justice as equality, made clear by the contrast to a sense of ugliness in present social arrangements: "Not some from the heights of Park Street and others from the dungeons of slum areas. Not some from the pinnacles of the British Empire and some from the dark deserts of Africa." And this theme of equality and unity resonates with Scarry's account of beauty and justice (1999, pp. 99–100).

It may seem like a pie-in-the-sky ideal when he says that the ideal they are working towards is "there waiting with its milk and honey, and with all of the bountiful beauty that God has in store for His children" (p. 40). But these ideals matter for the precise forms and means of justice pursued here and now. King ties all this into Nkrumah's nonviolent freedom-struggle in Ghana. Praising Nkrumah's "positive action" approach, King says: "And it's a beautiful thing, isn't it? That here is a nation that is now free, and it is free without rising up with arms and with ammunition. It is free through nonviolent means" (p. 31). The themes of togetherness, unity, and harmony present an ideal of justice as peace and reconciliation rather than as vengeance. They allow certain approaches and modes of action and prohibit others. King notes that as a result of Nkrumah's approach, "when the British Empire leaves Ghana, she leaves with a different attitude than she would have left with if she had been driven out by armies." This example of beauty had clear implications for the vision King wanted his followers to live by: "We've got to revolt in such a way that after revolt is over we can live with people as their brothers and sisters. Our aim must never be to defeat them or humiliate them" (pp. 41–42). Revenge may be sweet, but at least according to King's conception of justice, it is not beautiful.

Another example comes from the diaries of members of the White Rose movement, a resistance movement in Nazi Germany. The account of the Scholl siblings, who were part of this movement, suggests conditions under which beauty can serve ends that are antithetical to justice in the sense in which Scarry (1999) envisions. Inge Scholl speaks of herself and her siblings having been mesmerized by the unity and purpose of the Hitler Youth. And yet an engagement with beauty can serve as one of the conditions that also enables people to undergo conversions. She also speaks of how her brother, Hans, belonged to a boys' club where he was nurtured by the pursuits of hiking, camping, music, sports, literature, and so on, until the group was arrested by the Nazis. She also speaks of how she and her sister Sophie found themselves drawn to the Jewish people the more the Nazis denigrated them: "We felt attracted to people we had been commanded to spurn, and the harder we tried to spurn them, the more intensely they attracted us" (Scholl, 1970/1983, p. 43). Sophie, in one of her letters, speaks as well of experiencing and being sustained by the beauty of nature and God, which was in stark contrast to the ugliness of the atrocities being committed by their country (Vinke, 1984, p. 94):

> Isn't it a tremendous enigma and, if we know the reason, almost frightening, that everything is so beautiful? In spite of all the terrible things that are going on. A great unknown has burst into my simple enjoyment of things beautiful, a faint vision of their creator, whom the innocent, created beings glorify with their beauty. Only man can be ugly.

Hans and Sophie became active members of the Resistance movement, publishing and circulating flyers that attempted to raise the awareness of their fellow citizens to the ugliness of the Nazi regime, until they were caught and beheaded.

A further set of examples comes from Dorothy Day, founder of the Catholic Worker movement. She writes in her newsletter about how the recognition of beauty in the simple things and people around her enables her to serve them better.

> I look back on my childhood and remember beauty. The smell of sweet clover in a vacant lot, a hopeful clump of grass growing up through the cracks of a city pavement. A feather dropped from some pigeon. A stalking cat. Ruskin wrote of

"the duty of delight," and told us to lift up our heads and see the cloud formations in the sky. I have seen sunrises at the foot of a New York street, coming up over the East River. I have always found a strange beauty in the suffering faces which surround us in the city. Black, brown and grey heads bent over those bowls of food, that so necessary food which is always there at St. Joseph's House on First St., prepared each morning by Ed Forand or some of the young volunteers. We all enter into the act of hospitality, one way or another. So many of those who come in to eat return to serve, to become part of the "family."

(1974)

"Beauty will save the world," Dostoevsky wrote. I just looked up this quotation in Konstantin Mochulsky's *Dostoevsky, His Life and Work* . . . In a paragraph on page 224, in speaking of art, Dostoevsky is quoted as saying, "It has its own integral organic life and it answers man's innate need of beauty without which, perhaps he might not want to live upon earth." When a man is in discord with reality, conflict . . . the thirst for beauty and harmony appears in him with its greatest force. Art is useful here because it pours in energy, sustains the forces, strengthens our feeling of life . . . Man accepts beauty without any conditions and so, simply because it is beauty, with veneration he bows down before it, not asking why it is useful and what one can buy with it . . . Beauty is more useful than the simply useful, for it is the ultimate goal of being. On this height, the way of art meets with the way of religion.

(1974)

She also notes how "the thirst for beauty and harmony appears in [people] with its greatest force" when they experience a sense of discord with reality and how art "pours in energy, sustains the forces, strengthens our feeling of life." She continues to spell out what for her is the relationship between beauty and religious faith:

Man accepts beauty without any conditions and so, simply because it is beauty, with veneration he bows down before it, not asking why it is useful and what one can buy with it . . . Beauty is more useful than the simply useful, for it is the ultimate goal of being. On this height, the way of art meets with the way of religion.

(cited in Zwick & Zwick, 2000)

Mahatma Gandhi also speaks of how art and the beauty of nature foster adherence to his religious convictions: "I see and find Beauty in Truth or through Truth. All Truths, not merely true ideas, but truthful faces, truthful pictures or songs are highly beautiful" (1958/2004, p. 68).

These beauties ["a sunset or a crescent moon that shines amid the stars at night"] are truthful, inasmuch as they make me think of the Creator at the back of them. How else could these be beautiful, but for the Truth that is in the center of creation? When I admire the wonder of a sunset or the beauty of the moon, my soul expands in worship of the Creator. I try to see Him and His mercies in all these creations.

(1958/2004, p. 379)

We see in his words a link between experiences of beauty and notions of truth. These articulations resonate with Murdoch's notion of "unselfing" experiences, and in this case, these seem to foster attachment to God as well as causes of truth and justice, to which Gandhi dedicated his life.

Discussion and Conclusion

In this chapter, I have tried to address a gap in the sociological study of both religion and social movements by examining the potential role of aesthetic experience in shaping social action. Building on social movement theory (Jasper, 1997, 2018) and aesthetic theory (Scarry, 1999), I have identified ways in which "positive" emotional shocks or experiences of beauty may drive commitments to justice. To illustrate such mechanisms, I have drawn on the work of prominent religious activists who articulate their perceived relationship between aesthetic experience (beauty in particular) and justice.

Drawing on discourse analysis of religious activists like King, Scholl, Day, and Gandhi, I have tried to suggest that this relationship between aesthetics and justice holds at least under some conditions. For example, beauty can be experienced as a precursor to a sense of injustice or disharmony in the world that one is moved to commit oneself to rectifying (such as in the case of the example from King). Experiences of beauty could be precursors to the desire to protect and not lose something valuable (such as one's home or way of life – for example, in the case of the Scholls under Nazi occupation). Experiences of beauty could also serve as sources of resilience in everyday life – in meeting one's commitment to service in facing the ordinary day-to-day struggles of poverty (as in the case of Dorothy Day), or in reawakening one's confidence in and love of the Divine during times of intense struggle and hardship (such as in the examples from Gandhi).

What mechanisms can aesthetic experience trigger that enable such commitment? Scarry, as we have seen, drawing on Plato, Kant, Murdoch, and others, has outlined several: an energizing and renewing capacity, its capacity to "unself" us and draw us out of ourselves, a certain inexhaustibility in the pleasure it brings, and the symmetry and equality which evoke in us a desire to preserve and perpetuate them. Such mechanisms are not universal laws; they are activated in some social contexts and not others and may be counteracted by other mechanisms, and the task of analysis here would be similar to studying the effects of phenomena such as moral outrage.

An objection someone could raise here is that these accounts, particularly the speeches, are merely rhetorical – mere strategic constructions to evoke certain emotions among constituents. But even if such a cynical reading were accurate, it would still raise the question as to why symbols and arguments that evoke *beauty* are resorted to rather than, for example, fear or anger – the emotions most often considered in the social movements literature. In other words, even if one were to argue that all such speeches, letters, or biographical material were merely rhetorical attempts to provoke certain emotions, it is still worth looking at what precise emotions are evoked and what mechanisms evoke them. Here, I propose we examine whether and how aesthetic experience can evoke emotions that foster commitments to religious and political movements.

Such considerations of beauty involve a return to certain elements of early approaches to religion and social movements – the possibility that people can be susceptible to being moved or overwhelmed by certain "irrational" forces, particularly by the way in which aesthetic experiences can catch us unawares, as it were, and pull us out of ourselves. I argue that considering them as "positive emotional shocks" akin to the way in which "moral outrage" has been considered as a negative emotional shock (Jasper, 1997, 2018) can help us make sense of this phenomenon.

The discourse analysis undertaken here suggests additional possibilities for future research. For example, it might be worth examining whether this expected correlation between beauty and justice holds more strongly for people with religious or spiritual commitments compared to those without. Another possibility might be a priming study to assess whether exposure to images of beauty or harmony presented before images of injustice make a difference in people's responses. Such experiments could compare people who are religious vs. non-religious (e.g., to assess whether presenting images of ornate religious edifices prior to images of oppression would lead primed religious respondents to express stronger condemnations of injustice than non-primed religious respondents would. Alternatively, studies could assess whether religious respondents, upon exposure to images of injustice, would express disapproval towards ornate religious artifacts), or minorities vs. non-minorities, to assess whether a connection between beauty and justice is contingent upon whether subjects are likely to have experienced injustice themselves.

This initial pull of aesthetics, however, cannot be sufficient to determine outcomes. The explorations and data in this chapter thus only get at a very small part of the story. A more thorough consideration would have to examine, in addition to when beauty can foster justice commitments of activists, when and why it does not. Several questions can be considered here:

First, when and how might experiences of beauty coexist with and even contribute to perpetuating oppression? A clear example to consider is the forms of beauty, such as Wagner's music, that were enjoyed by the Nazis. Does this mean that aesthetic experiences fail to activate commitments to justice here? Or are conceptions of justice themselves fraught – i.e., did the Nazis understand themselves as actually furthering a just cause, to which aesthetic experience served as a support? To put it differently, do aesthetic experiences support a commitment to some standard of justice about which there could be universal agreement (which is what Scarry's account seems to suggest), or can such experiences simply be marshaled in support of whatever cause a person is already committed to, however unjust others may judge it to be?

Second, when and how might experiences of beauty inhibit justice commitments? For instance, can they distract or defuse the anger and outrage that can fuel activism? Is the "unselfing" in such cases a distraction from one's immediate goals, which could include the goals of a movement one is committed to? Alternatively, if such cases do occur empirically, should they be seen as furthering the possibility of peace over violence and hatred?

Third, can beauty be experienced as irrelevant to one's justice-commitments? Certainly all sorts of aesthetic experiences can be simply consumed in ways that seem to have no perceptible effect on their consumers' lives. Is some sort of active agency required on the part of the person to evaluate or acknowledge the experience as meaningful, as evoking a commitment to something? What are the conditions under which people might be receptive to such effects? In other words, what does it take for an aesthetic experience to be meaningfully connected to a commitment to justice?

Fourth, can commitments to justice or perpetrations of injustice alter what experiences strike someone as beautiful? Certain kinds of art can begin to be perceived as offensive or threatening *after* one has been involved in a social or political or religious movement (*Danto, 2003*). Certainly, attention needs to be paid to how this process happens by which past experience can shape even those future experiences which "shock" people or which, on the other hand, inhibit people's capacity to be shocked. Such considerations are absent from essentialist accounts such as Scarry's.

All the above outcomes are very much possible, and serious empirical investigation is needed into the conditions under which these different outcomes might be obtained.

References

Allport, F. (1924). *Social psychology*. Boston: Houghton Mifflin.
Armstrong, T., & Detweiler-Bedell, B. (2008). Beauty as an emotion: The exhilarating prospect of mastering a challenging world. *Review of General Psychology*, 12(4), 305–329.
Benford, R. D. (1997). An insider's critique of the social movement framing perspective. *Sociological Inquiry*, 67(4), 409–430.
Blumer, H. (1969). Collective behavior. In A. M. Lee (Ed.), *New outline of the principles of sociology* (pp. 166–222). New York: Barnes & Noble.
Bourdieu, P. (1984). *Distinction: A social critique of the judgement of taste* (R. Nice, Trans.). Cambridge, MA: Harvard University Press.
Carson, C., & Shepard, K. (Eds.). (2001). *A call to conscience: The landmark speeches of Dr. Martin Luther King Jr.* New York: Warner Books.
Chatterjee, A. (2014). *The aesthetic brain: How we evolved to desire beauty and enjoy art*. Oxford University Press.
Collier, A. (1994/1998). Explanation and emancipation. In M. Archer, R. Bhaskar, A. Collier, T. Lawson, & A. Norrie (Eds.), *Critical realism: Essential readings* (pp. 444–472). London: Routledge.

Collins, R. (2004). *Interaction ritual chains*. Princeton, NJ: Princeton University Press.
Comte, A. (1896). *The positive philosophy* (2 vols., H. Martineau Ed. and Trans.). London: Geroge Bell and Sons.
Danto, A. C. (2003). *The abuse of beauty: Aesthetics and the concept of art*. Chicago: Open Court.
Davis, K. (1949). *Human society*. New York: Macmillan.
Day, D. (1974, September). On pilgrimage. *The Catholic Worker*, Retrieved from https://catholicworker.org/543-html/
de la Fuente, E. (2000). Sociology and aesthetics. *European Journal of Social Theory*, 3, 235–247.
Dickie, G. (1997). *Introduction to aesthetics*. New York: Oxford University Press.
Diessner, R., Davis, L., & Toney, B. (2009). Empirical relationships between beauty and justice: Testing Scarry and elaborating Danto. *Psychology of Aesthetics, Creativity, and the Arts*, 3(4), 249–258.
Durkheim, E. (1912/1915). *The elementary forms of religious life*. London: George Allen and Unwin.
Dutton, D. (2000). Mad about flowers: Elaine Scarry on beauty. *Philosophy and Literature*, 24, 249–260.
Emerson, R. W. (1860/1988). *The conduct of life*. Boston: Mifflin.
Evans-Pritchard, E. E. (1965). *Theories of primitive religion*. Oxford: Clarendon.
Ezzy, D. (2016). Religion, aesthetics and moral ontology. *Journal of Sociology*, 52(2), 266–279.
Feliciano, H. (1997). *The lost museum: The Nazi conspiracy to steal the world's greatest works of art*. New York: Basic Books.
Feuerbach, L. (1841/1957). *The essence of Christianity*. New York: Harper Torchbooks.
Freud, S. (1927/1961). *The future of an illusion*. New York: Doubleday.
Gandhi, M. K. (1958/2004). *All men are brothers: Autobiographical reflections*. New York: Continuum.
Gitlin, T. (1999). Elaine Scarry's on beauty and being just. *The American Prospect*, 11(3), 61–63.
Goodwin, J., & Jasper, J. M. (Eds.). (2004). *Rethinking social movements: Structure, meaning, and emotion*. Lanham, MD: Rowman and Littlefield.
Goodwin, J., & Jasper, J. M. (Eds.). (2006). Emotions and social movements. In J. Stets, & J. H. Turner (Eds.), *The handbook of social emotions* (pp. 611–630). New York: Springer.
Green, C. D. (1995). All that glitters: A review of psychological research on the aesthetics of the golden section. *Perception*, 24(8), 937–968.
Haidt, J., Rozin, P., McCauley, C., & Imada, S. (1997). Body, psyche and culture: The relationship between disgust and morality. *Psychology and Developing Societies*, 9(1), 107–131.
Hirschman, A. (1977). *The passions and the interests: Political arguments for capitalism before its triumph*. Princeton, NJ: Princeton University Press.
Hobbes, T. (1956). *Leviathan, Part I*. Chicago: Regnery and Co.
Hoffer, E. (1951). *The true believer*. New York: Harper and Row.
Iannaccone, L. (1994). Why strict churches are strong. *American Journal of Sociology*, 99, 1180–1121.
Iannaccone, L. (1997). Skewness explained: A rational choice model of religious giving. *Journal for the Social Scientific Study of Religion*, 36, 141–157.
Jasper, J. M. (1997). *The art of moral protest: Culture, biography, and creativity in social movements*. Chicago: University of Chicago Press.
Jasper, J. M. (2018). *The emotions of protest*. Chicago: University of Chicago Press.
Jenkins, J. C., & Perrow, C. (1977). Insurgency of the powerless: Farm worker movements (1946–1972). *American Sociological Review*, 249–268.
Jerolmack, C., & Porpora, D. (2004). Religion, rationality, and experience: A response to the new rational choice theory of religion. *Sociological Theory*, 22(1), 140–160.

Johnston, H., & Klandermans, B. (Eds.). (1995). *Social movements and culture.* Minneapolis: University of Minnesota Press.
Kak, S. (2011). The golden mean and the physics of aesthetics. In B. S. Yadav, & M. Mohan (Eds.), *Ancient Indian leaps into mathematics.* Basel: Birkhauser.
Kornhauser, W. (1959). *The politics of mass society.* Glencoe, IL: Free Press of Glencoe.
Lasswell, H. D. (1930). *Psychopathology and politics.* Chicago: University of Chicago Press.
Le Bon, G. (1895/1960). *The crowd.* New York: Viking.
Livio, M. (2002). *The golden ratio: The story of Phi, the world's most astonishing number.* New York: Broadway Books.
McAdam, D. (1982). *Political process and the development of black insurgency, 1930–1970.* Chicago: University of Chicago Press.
McCarthy, J. D., & Zald, M. N. (1977). Resource mobilization and social movements: A partial theory. *American Journal of Sociology,* 82, 1212–1241.
Melucci, A. (1982). *L'invenzione del presente: Movimenti, identità, bisogni individuali.* Bologna: Il Mulino.
Meyer, M. (1975). The Nazi musicologist as myth maker in the Third Reich. *Journal of Contemporary History,* 10, 649–665.
Neperud, R. W., & Serlin, R. C. (1984). The Fibonacci sequence: Proportional and semantic bases of children's aesthetic preferences. *Studies in Art Education,* 25(2), 92–103.
Oberschall, A. (1973). *Social conflict and social movements.* Englewood Cliffs, NJ: Prentice-Hall.
Olson, M. (1965). *The logic of collective action: Public goods and the theory of groups.* Cambridge, MA: Harvard University Press.
Piven, F. F., & Cloward, R. (1977). *Poor people's movements.* New York: Pantheon.
Piven, F. F., & Cloward, R. (1992). Normalizing collective protest. In A. Morris, & C. Mueller (Eds.), *Frontiers in social movement theory* (pp. 301–325). New Haven, CT: Yale University Press.
Pope, L. (1942). *Millhands and Preachers.* New Haven, CT: Yale University Press.
Scarry, E. (1999). *On beauty and being just.* Princeton, NJ: Princeton University Press.
Scholl, I. (1970/1983). *The white rose: Munich 1942–1943* (A. R. Schultz, Trans.). Hanover, NH: Wesleyan.
Scruton, R. (2009). *Beauty.* New York: Oxford University Press.
Simmel, G. (1905/1959). *Sociology of religion.* New York: Wisdom.
Smelser, N. J. (1962). *Theory of collective behavior.* New York: Free Press.
Smith, C. (2007). Why Christianity works: An emotions-focused phenomenological account. *Sociology of Religion,* 68(2), 165–178.
Smith, C. (2008). Future directions in the sociology of religion. *Social Forces,* 86(4), 1561–1589.
Snow, D. A., & Benford, R. D. (1988). Ideology, frame resonance, and participant mobilization. *International Social Movement Research,* 1(1), 197–217.
Stark, R. (2003). *For the glory of god: How monotheism led to reformations, science, witch-hunts, and the end of slavery.* Princeton, NJ: Princeton University Press.
Stark, R., & Finke, R. (2000). *Acts of faith.* Berkeley: University of California Press.
Swidler, A. (2003). *Talk of love: How culture matters.* Chicago: University of Chicago Press.
Taylor, C. (1985). *Human agency and language: Philosophical papers 1.* New York: Cambridge University Press.
Thompson, E. P. (1964). *The making of the English working class.* New York: Pantheon.
Tilly, C. (1978). *From mobilization to revolution.* Reading, MA: Addison-Wesley.
Trenchard, J. (1709). *The natural history of superstition.* London: A. Baldwin.
Turner, J. H., & Stets, J. E. (2006). *The sociology of emotions.* New York: Cambridge.
Turner, R., & Killian, L. M. (1957). *Collective behavior.* Englewood Cliffs, NJ: Prentice-Hall.

Vinke, H. (1984). *The short life of Sophie Scholl*. New York: Harper and Row.
Walder, A. G. (2009). Political sociology and social movements. *Annual Review of Sociology*, 35, 393–412.
Wallace, A. F. C. (1966). *Religion: An anthropological view*. New York: Random House.
Wuthnow, R. (1987). *Meaning and moral order: Explorations in cultural analysis*. Berkeley and Los Angeles: University of California Press.
Zuber, D. (2006). Flânerie at ground zero: Aesthetic countermemories in Lower Manhattan. *American Quarterly*, 58(2), 269–299.
Zwick, M., & Zwick, L. (2000). Dorothy day and the light from the east: Eastern Christianity, fathers of the desert, Dostoevsky. *Houston Catholic Worker*, 20(3). http://www.cjd.org/paper/roots/reast.html

Chapter 14

The Beloved Community as Aesthetic Theory
Intimations From Josiah Royce, Martin Luther King Jr., and Erich Fromm

Nahanni Freeman

A Sorrow Song

When anchored in authentic presence and witness, creativity that makes contact with suffering can magnify the potentialities and endowments of the human spirit. Lingering in the edges of a Cimmerian forest, propinquity permits view of a midnight where resilience, mourning, and remodeling encounter destructiveness. Both wild places and manicured arboretums can contain, amplify, nourish, and question the organic processes of survival, luminous vision, and self-definition. This story, which examines the aesthetic impulse within a redemptive community, begins with "the voice of exile" (Du Bois, 1903/2018, p. 192). Slave songs spoke as veiled messages, shadow "figures as a river of death" (Du Bois, 1903/2018, p. 194). The sorrow songs brought the misty visage of wandering, passage, separation, and the "cradle song of death" (Du Bois, 1903/2018, p. 194). Yet there was also a hope in the songs for an inevitable justice, a spirit borne home, a crossing over from the body, hovering over the waters, returning to ancient woods, for the "'wilderness' was the home of God" (Du Bois, 1903/2018, p. 194). The eloquence of these songs is also meted out in their omissions, their ominous lack and segregation from the brotherhood of a new land – this Other country where unrelenting toil could never beat back the weeds of injustice.

Awakening: Consciousness, Art, and Lost Presence

One could imagine a township where beauty is essential to existence, art is not desecrated by capitalistic gain, and creative work harbors in the Sound, not alienated from economic and social realities, nor subjugated to "ideological appropriation" (Payne, 1996, pp. 5, 11). Perhaps aesthetic work contains a transcendent structure, beyond and within the social, yet still longs for "lost presence" (Innes, 1996, pp. 515–516). Royce's (1916/2005, p. 1158) "Holy City of the community of mankind" is prophesied outside of politics, the non-solution. The refulgent call, a prophetic image of the Beloved augured by Martin Luther King Jr., deploys an aesthetic model.

DOI: 10.4324/9781003598107-18

The dawn of the beloved community remains elusive. In his call to religious communities to engage in reconciliation, Nilson (2010) begins with consciousness of racism as well as the mutations that hide behind overt expressions (p. 83). One may envisage and yearn for the ideal of Dr. King's vision of the Kingdom of God, "a society where all live lives that befit their dignity as children of God; a society where everyone is accepted, everyone belongs" (Nilson, 2010, p. 84). Nevertheless, the shadowy history that defended, masked, and legitimized slavery remains lodged in memory. While a sacramental unity is a compelling ecclesiastical mission, the church has often operated as a vessel of hegemony (Nilson, 2010, p. 84). An aesthetic model intimates of a prophetic vision, with warnings to resist "rapacious individualism" (West, 1982, p. 132) and fragmentation based on territorial specialization and hierarchies of class, emergent from the murky projections of sexism, racism, and political alterity. Post-traumatic art as reappropriation of a history of displacement offers a method of resilience and sociocultural transformation. A visionary, Dr. King "made his home in the promised land like a stranger in a foreign country" (Hebrews 11:9, NIV).

Personalism and the Irreducible

Functioning beyond swarm conformity, aesthetic renaissance incubates in a chrysalis of personalism. The uniqueness of the person, not submerged in an undifferentiated matrix of symbiotic ego (Bowen, 1978/1992, p. 440), allows for the "superpersonal" (Royce, 1913/1968b, p. 352), where interior intuition and connection to transcendent epiphenomena can conceive art. The eclectic set of ideologies that fall under the auspices of personalism are cohesive in their counter to depersonalization, materialism, and determinism (Williams & Bengtsson, 2022). For personalists, humankind has an inviolable quality, an inescapable dignity, and a subjectivity that anchors the person in both uniqueness and relationality. When personalism coexists with idealism, reality is constructed in an irreducible consciousness, intuited with self-awareness and pointing towards a transcendent quality that revivifies art.

A layered aesthetic ecology will review the chaotic, the inexplicable, and the struggle for meaning, attempting to represent the ineffable. Dr. King's province adumbrated a non-amnestic place beyond migration and exile, above a diaspora, where hegemonies were quieted by an alternative story (Inwood, 2009). This counter-narrative was inspired by Royce's (1913/1968a) personalism (p. 80), which was indicative of a "live unity of knowledge and of will, of love and deed" (p. 197), a recognition of the purposiveness of each human, a vineyard attachment where the infinite worth of the individual was also celebrated. The transcendent quality is expressed with Royce's contention that the "Community of the Kingdom of Heaven . . . is at once within you, and above you, a human life, and yet a life whose tabernacles are built upon a Mount of Transfiguration" (Royce, 1913/1968a, p. 197).

The beloved community is seen as the fulfillment of the church and the parables, a creative country where transcendence is both within and above the individual, and loyalty as devotion and volition manifests "the Eternal, the conscious and superhuman unity of life, in the form of the acts of an individual self" (Royce, 1908/2005, p. 996). The sense of a transcendent grace is shown by Royce's (1913/1968b) reference to the father of the prodigal son, who delights in the mere presence of the young man. The father represents "the incarnation of the spirit of this community" (Royce, 1913/1968b, p. 353). Royce argues that the parable of the lost sheep also implies the value and irreplaceable quality of the individual person, which "has its infinite meaning in and through the unity of the Kingdom" (1913/1968b, pp. 353–354).

Liberation Psychology: Freedom and the Contextualized Aesthetic

Emancipatory aesthetics will also serve localized botanical and untamed spaces. In his construction of liberation psychology, Alsup (2009) accesses Dr. King's metaphor of the beloved community to organize a creative response built from humanistic, transpersonal, and developmental models (p. 388). Liberation psychology offers a study of creativity that is contextual, ecological, and social (Alsup, p. 391), where dialogue serves to advance altruism and growth, fostering relational repair. Dialogue between the creative cosmos, the individual, and the neighborhood of earth engages conversations about ethics, personal commitment, interconnectedness, and pursuit of the biophilous illumination. In his work *The Montgomery Story: Strides towards Freedom* (1958/2010), Dr. King emphasized the importance of Christ as a model for nonviolent resistance, suggesting that this work "avoids not only external physical violence but also internal violence of spirit. The nonviolent resister not only refuses to shoot his opponent but he also refuses to hate him" (King, 1958/2010, p. 92). Conscientious creation will seek to preserve the individual with many possible selves and those who encircle them, affirming life.

Martin Luther King, the Beloved Community, and Art as Non-Hate

A transformative aesthetic will permit art as contrition and cultural dynamism, curation, and preservation. In his chapter that contrasts the civil rights movement with the religious new right, Rhys Williams (2002) explores the symbolic tools and rhetoric that are used as cultural frames to promote collective change. While the civil rights movement sought to open access to political process and economic opportunity, the new right uses religious symbols and authority to legitimate claims for closure and restraint (Williams, 2002, p. 251). The message of nonviolence in Dr. King's work is conjoined with a representation of the good built from reversals in social status that are replete in New Testament language, foreshadowing a beloved community where "every valley shall be exalted, every hill and mountain shall be made low" (King, 1967/1986, p. 242).

These reversals are suggested in Matthew 20:16 as a future kingdom where "the last shall be first, and the first last" (KJV). Art as reversal will perplex, authoring an inquiry into capacity.

Art as Spatial Reconstruction, Paradox, and Openings

A sacred aesthetic, a sanatorium, is both an expanse and a room, a library and a thicket. Dr. King's beloved community sought a "complete re-creation of space" (Inwood, 2009, p. 491). This sense of the beyond, this prophetic Shangri-La, did not connote a phantasm but rather a future to strive towards. Burrow (2012, p. 46) infers that Dr. King conceived of the beloved community in language that Reinhold Niebuhr once attributed to Christian love, namely as the "impossible possibility" (Niebuhr, 1935/2013, p. 120). This was described in Niebuhr's (1935/2013) chapter, *The Relevance of an Impossible Ethical Ideal*.[1] Niebuhr concludes that a moral theory must contain both the optimism of the possible and the contrition and awareness of finiteness that attaches to the impossible, which is grounded in spiritual transcendence rather than limitless "progressive approximations" (Niebuhr, 1935/2013, pp. 135, 117). Niebuhr transforms Freud's notion of "the cultural superego," which implies unlimited power, aggressively issuing commands for moral perfectionism (Freud, 1930/1961, pp. 106–109). Slavish obedience to the cultural superego is both personal and collective. In contrast, Niebuhr anticipates equity discussions with his allusion to "imaginative justice" which exceeds equality, and rather than grounding his ethic in rational universalism, which holds life at the core, he offers a "transcendent source of unity" (Niebuhr, 1935/2013, pp. 113, 109). The potency of an aesthetic of social justice is augmented when the artistic content is not sacrificed to messaging, commodification, or posturing, which may serve the demands of superiority striving rather than offering vineyard husbandry.

Art as Barrier Deconstruction, Depolarization, and Justice

Aesthetic work moves with a confluence that can leverage subtlety and flow to prevent anxious-avoidant resistance to change, taming masochism, the seduction of compensatory superiority, and sadistic impulses. The barriers between people restrict the "full revelation of divine love" (Williams, 2002, p. 255), which would be expressed in the beloved community through shared experience, creativity, superordinate goals, and mutual sacrifice. Boundaries based on social class, rejection, and judgment are broken in a country of unified vision where "There is neither Jew nor Gentile, neither slave nor free, nor is there male and female" (Gal 3:28, NIV). The power of commitment to the beloved community is demonstrated in Dr. King's words about polarization in the midst of social struggle when he states,

> With this faith we will be able to transform the jangling discords of our nation into a beautiful symphony of brotherhood. With this faith we will be able to

work together, pray together, struggle together, go to jail together, stand up for freedom together . . . This will be the day when all of God's children will be able to sing with new meaning.

(King, 1963b/1986, p. 219)

Nonviolence: Arts as Moral Courage and the Refusal of Hatred

An aesthetic of abnegation will offer self, redefining and reappropriating chivalry outside of gender and conquest, as a form of courage-in-humility, wielded in spite of the darkening skies. In his sermon at the Riverside Church, one year prior to his assassination, Dr. King critiqued the war in Vietnam and the policies of the Johnson administration, stating "a time comes when silence is betrayal" (King, 1967/1986, p. 231). King calls for increasing awareness of a transformative spirit with the power to help humankind to transcend the darkness of violence. With a transcendentalist ethical viewpoint, King elevates a universal moral ethic above nationalism, arguing that the time has come to "move beyond the smooth patriotism to the high grounds of firm dissent based upon the mandates of conscience and the reading of history" (King, 1967/1986, p. 231).[2] Calling for a revolution of values that can defend against communism, King's work parallels that of Erich Fromm (1955), identifying the alienating role of mechanism, technology, greed, and materialism, which tend to perpetuate militarism and racism. In contrast, King can envision a country where "the radiant stars of love and brotherhood will shine over our great nation with all of their scintillating beauty" (King, 1963b/1986, p. 302).

Movement From Self-Interest: Art as Reconciliation

Aesthetics, framed as reconciliation, will move slowly with a confluence of deep self-reflection. While he sought to address economic inequality, Dr. King's beloved community was not built from an ethic of self-interest, but served the goal of "reconciling the oppressor with the oppressed" (Williams, 2002, p. 256). In addition, Inwood (2009) describes Dr. King's search for the beloved community as an aspect of a more expansive anti-colonial striving (p. 487). The potential for art to move beyond self-interest is also enhanced by a dialectical method, where self-critique, contradiction, and perspective taking facilitate humility (Royce, 1897/2005, pp. 309–314). Dialectical aesthetics will surrender consciousness and the hidden nature to the "great whole of life" (Royce, 1882/2005, p. 270), supplying rich engagement with the present moment and portending something greater than the impersonal Absolute of Kant (Royce, 1897/2005, p. 306).

Syncretism and Art as Prophetic Vision

Transformative aesthetics will form a lattice, a network of roots in the copse of alpine aspens. In his analysis of Dr. King's pursuit of the beloved community,

Inwood (2009) builds on the work of Cornel West (1999), pointing out the foundation of King's prophetic vision that included Gandhi's methodology, the cultural voice of the Black church, and an American civil responsibility. Indeed, West (1999, p. 426) describes several influential forces in the ideologies of Martin Luther King Jr., which reveal the syncretism of philosophy, theology, historical context, and social activism. West (1999, p. 426) discusses the complexity and hybridization of the "prophetic black church tradition," which developed when Afro-Americans internalized Christianity and transformed it as an expression of autonomous creativity. West (1999) identifies the impact of confinement and commodification of persons on the formation of the black church, stating, "The black church signified and signifies that collective effort of an exploited and oppressed, degraded and despised, dominated . . . people of African descent to come to turns with the absurd in America" (p. 427). In West's (1999) view, the black church was an attempt at sensemaking and meaning construction, "a communal response to an existential and political situation" (p. 427). Art as sense-making is an attempt, a commitment.

A transpersonal aesthetic will be anchored in intellectual ancestors, with a resplendent library as its harbor. West (1999) describes the "prophetic liberal Christianity" that Dr. King encountered in higher education (p. 426). From this tradition, Dr. King extracted principal Christian themes, including the primacy and transformative power of love, social responsibility to resist institutionalized racism, the dignity and sacredness of all humans, and the hope of personal immortality (West, 1999, p. 430). King was exposed to the teaching of George Davis, whose personalism reflected the concept of divine intervention through individuals, beloved to God in pursuit of an eventual brotherhood of humankind (West, 1999, p. 430). Furthermore, the influence of L. Harold DeWolf amplified King's understanding and application of personalism and its implications for a social gospel, allowing for the integration of themes of imperfection, forgiveness, hope, and the strength to wrestle for freedom (West, 1999, p. 431).

Transformation of the Representation of the Other

Metamorphosis in aesthetics will integrate darkness, oppression, and awareness of the rage of the Other. In his interpretation of the beloved community, Simpson (2008, p. 58) asserts that "King discovered an entire way of life in Jesus' 'Love your enemies,' and he named that life 'the beloved community.'" Possibly King's construction of the beloved community was influenced by the work of Harvard professor Josiah Royce (1913/1968a, pp. 218, 219), although the lack of egalitarianism in Royce's perspective has been challenged, and King's exposure to Royce may have been derivative, through DeWolf or Brightman (Burrow, 2012, pp. 48, 49). Dr. King presented a beloved community as a call with universal appeal; he presented the civil rights movement as a collective action which empowered the African American "to transmute hatred into constructive energy, to seek not only to free himself but to free his oppressor from his sins. This transformation, in turn, had the marvelous effect of changing the face of the enemy" (King, 1964/2010, p. 35). The living energy of the victim will also transplant hatred in a luminary aesthetic. Witness the art of transfiguration, which exposes the radiance in the face of Stephen as he stood before the Sanhedrin, for an aura of light surfaced as he was murdered (Acts 6–7, NIV).

The Black Atlantic as an Aesthetic Model of Movement

An aesthetic of spiritual deliverance will also expose, and the darkness will be a testimony. One way that projection may be transformed is through the recognition of the "dislocation, hidden transcripts and cultural ruptures that characterized the middle passage and the experience of slavery" (Inwood, 2009, p. 489), which are described in Gilroy's (1993) identification of transculturalism (p. 4). Gilroy's (1993) description of the "middle passage" included double consciousness, as well as cross-pollination between cultures, borrowing, and dynamic assimilation, with artifacts, beliefs, values and narratives that interact, restrict, and redeem in ways that go beyond any single culture. Double consciousness can be considered as duality in awareness, with experiences of hybridization between cultures, an adopted space which promotes assemblage. In Gilroy's (1993) employment of the term "Black Atlantic world," he seeks to capture the ways that Janusian experience interacts with memory (both personal and collective, historically situated and intergenerational), language structures, emotion, and initiation (p. 3). Gilroy (1993) uses the metaphor of a ship to describe a chronotope, or an analysis lodged in space and time, as a "living, micro-cultural, micropolitical system in motion" (p. 4). The ship is a symbol to organize the movement across spaces and time, with features that include fractal structures, like interior latticework or a snowflake crystal, with complex microcosms. The cross-pollination between spaces is also pictorialized like a rhizomorph, which both absorbs and translates nutrition, serving as a root or mycelium.

The irreducible quality of the Other, affirmed in artistic representation, lies beneath an understanding of dispersion, slavery, migration, and exile, with the branching out of countercultural and intergenerational forces (Subramaniam, 1996, p. 144). Hybrid cultures[3] that result from a diaspora contain transnational connections and histories, revealing a "spectrum of displacements, revivals, and reconfigurations of identities and traditions" (Subramaniam, 1996, p. 144). The African diaspora is irreducible and untraceable to a single origin, and the Black Atlantic is an ineffable geography that can be envisioned but not tangibly reconstructed. The cartographies of racial experience and hierarchy reveal cramped spaces, retreats for hiding when one's bodily self and agency have been transparent and violated (McKittrick, 2006). These attics for fugitives take on the "shape of mystery," and yet the longing for emancipation comes as "glimpses of control and agency" (McKittrick, 2006, p. 39). Power, as "spatially organized," encodes the bodily geography of both the oppressor and subjugated; the former may remain lodged in "self-captivity and a loophole of retreat" (McKittrick, 2006, p. 37).

Diaspora and Art, Fragmentation and Unification

Aesthetic perspective taking will incorporate prismatic consciousness. The diversity of experiences of diaspora and its contextualized, situated particularities that represent experiential complexities (Sucharov, 2015) include reversals in time and space, compression, and landlessness, with pathologies that yield fragmentation (McKittrick, 2006, p. 36). Engaging with the "discourses of ownership" (McKittrick, 2006, p. 37), resistance becomes manifest in the psychology of double consciousness as described by Du Bois (1903/2018), where the self is as a revelation to another world. The struggle to construct a self, constrained by projection and yet also with second sight, is conveyed in Du Bois's (1903/2018, p. 9) assertion that the person of color is caged in a "sense of always looking at one's self through the eyes of others, of measuring one's soul by the tape of a world that looks on." Burrow (2012) has also pointed to the paradoxical way that Dr. King engaged with the topic of gender, suggesting that King's doctrine of personalism was limited and contradictory in this respect (p. 49). The personalistic theory of King grounded ultimate reality in both finite and infinite personality (King, 1958/2010). The concept of reality as an interconnected love structure, sacrificial, reconciliatory, and sublime, may also radiate in forms of "nature mysticism" (Andrus, 2021, pp. 81, 82, 86). The mystical affordance of art is affirmed as revelatory.

Art as Transcendent to Materialism

An aesthetic world is a *more-than*, a beyond territory. King's call for a humanitarian vision was influenced by the work of the Jewish philosopher Martin Buber (1923/1996), whom King quotes in the *Letter from the Birmingham City Jail,* stating that "segregation substitutes an 'I-it' relationship for the 'I-Thou' relationship, and ends up relegating persons to the status of things" (King, 1963a/1986, p. 293). In his call for a transformation of values in his sermon to the Riverside Church, King states that the time has come for to "shift from a 'thing-oriented' society to a 'person-oriented' society" (King, 1967/1986, p. 240).

The transformation of the face of the Other occurs through love for one's enemy, for as Dr. King argued, "hate distorts the personality of the hater" (King, 1957, p. 321). Simpson (2008) describes the way that nonviolent direct action and love may change "the face of the oppressed, the face of the oppressor, and the face of the oppressive system" (p. 60). When justice arrives, the enemy of the people, an unjust system, is transfigured (Simpson, 2008, p. 62).

Restoration, Destiny, Solidarity, and Divine Otherness

Aesthetic exodus also imagines entry, migration into a region of succorance, a place of honey, fortification for the journey, and maternal transmission for the newly reborn. Dr. King envisioned the beloved community as a place of mutual responsibility and respect, "tied in a single garment of destiny" (King, 1963a/1986, p. 290). This destiny attached to interrelatedness of humanity and was part of King's critique of the restraining message sent by eight white, liberal Alabama clergymen. In contrast, King imagined a "true ecclesia," a place beyond conformity and fear, where one may find that those with moral courage have "carved a tunnel of hope through the dark mountain of disappointment" (King, 1963a/1986, p. 300). This would be an inclusive and comprehensive moral community, where recognition of "the complete 'otherness' of the divine" (Williams, 2002, p. 262) could permit a form of openness to the vast uncertainty of knowledge.

While art's survival does not require democracy, a broad-based flourishing of creators may find greater expansion in this habitat. In order for a democracy to achieve some kind of shared vision, "cultural resonance" must be examined (Williams, 2002, p. 264). With a faith that exceeded hope, Dr. King called for an entry into a heavenly country more than material space, an exodus built on a sacred covenant, for "I will give your descendants all this land I promised them, and it will be their inheritance forever" (Exodus 32:13). On the other hand, Inwood (2009) emphasizes the notion of the beloved community as "a geographic space where all people have the opportunity to share in the riches of society" (p. 489). Creating a decolonialized space, reimagined and fashioned selectively to transcend hegemonic templates of community, may have been fundamental to the promised land.

Art can be a location that is also an immaterial ontology, a kingless monarchy where all can partake in the royal feast. Influences on Dr. King could have included Benjamin Mays, who quoted a sermon that had been preached and transcribed in 1914 about the kingdom of God and presented this ideology in his co-authored work, *The Negro's Church* (1933). The kingdom vision prophesied not only the elimination of artificial impediment, greed, and racism but personalistic values aimed towards human potential and individual self-actualization. Mays and Nicholson (1933/2015) imagine that "at the center of our lives would be the sacredness of human personality" (p. 64). Unification of disparate elements renders a more original aesthetic. The transformation towards the beloved community included a transcendent dimension that expanded the notion of brotherhood where the hidden tensions are brought to light, as Dr. King professed,

> Whether we call it an unconscious process, an impersonal . . . or a Personal Being of . . . power and infinite love, there is a creative force in this universe that works to bring the disconnected aspects of reality into a harmonious whole.
> (King, 1958/2010, p. 95)

Art as Redemptive Transfiguration, Atonement, and the Personal Absolute

An aesthetic sublime can thrive in the context of personal relationship, imitating divine Otherness and receiving dynamic reform. The possible influence of Josiah Royce on

Dr. King, whether derivative or direct, synthesizes both the sense of imminence and eventuality of the beloved community as well as the transcendent nature of the ideal. Jensen (2016, 2019) seeks to place the beloved community within the context of Royce's description of a "transfiguring experience" which serves to be both a "saving absolute" and an "infinite atonement" (Jensen, 2016, p. 240, 2019, p. 123). The Absolute includes mediated structure, dynamic systems, a collaboration of interpreters, and the Logos as the "soul of the natural order," which serves as the ground of personhood, in which individual selves partake (Smith, 1950, pp. 17–18). The gathering of interpreters has infinite qualities; the limitless social field is self-representative as a system, yet the Other remains mysterious (Smith, 1950, pp. 32, 137).

A redemptive artistic society is conceived as a victory of love and forgiveness that transforms hostility (Marsh, 2005, p. 3), functioning as a divine gift, an instrument of liberation, and an "eschatological hope" (Marsh, 2005, p. 50). To be won over by community is "to be saved" (Royce, 1913/1968a, p. 207), and the world has access to an interpreter with an infinite array of processes and possibilities through community (p. 362). Yet the superlative in Royce's (1913/1968a) narrative is revealed in Christ, who "ascended to the level of the Spirit, and had become . . . the spirit of a community where boundaries were coextensive with the world" (p. 140). Incarnation unified the material and ineffable, for "the mystery of loving membership is a community whose meaning seems divine" (p. 140). The transcendent quality of community is embodied in the contention that "the individual soul has infinite meaning in and through the unity of the kingdom" (Royce, 1913/1968a, p. 198). An aesthetic of unification and particularity, universalism and salvation, ascension and descent can become a kingdom-generative art-path.

Art and responsibility co-mingle, for there are purposive and random features entertained. Royce (1913/1968b) describes the transcendent ideal of the beloved community in language of responsibility with the words "the kingdom of heaven is a perfectly lived unity of individual men joined in one divine chorus" (p. 350). The salvific element is expressed in his contention of the desperation emanating from isolation and the moral obligation to view others as living members of the kingdom of God. For Royce (1913/1968b), the "Doctrine of Life" is represented through creation, regardless of difference and in the midst of enemies, of a regal space – "the community of God's beloved" (p. 351).

The Muse as Incarnation of the Spirit of Truth

The muse has been relegated in modernity to an oddity, an artifact of Elizabethan prose and poetry. Royce (1913/1968b) implores the reader to act to precipitate and create that which does not exist – a form of spiritual communion that is rooted in the unification with the Spirit. The preeminence of this communion is noted when Royce (1913/1968b) states, "the principle of principles in all Christian morals remains this: 'Since you cannot find the universal and beloved community, – create it'" (p. 359). Yet art is also discovered, a form of grasping before it disappears into obscurity. Royce (1913/1968b) conveys a connection between the beloved community and "the way of salvation," which also connects to atonement, and remains in tension with sin (pp. 361, 362). The climactic atonement arrives in the person of Christ, who Royce (1913/1968b) identifies as the magnification towards the infinite of the story of Joseph's open forgiveness of his brothers (pp. 367–368). Atonement is a place of "expanded being," requiring the honesty of the transgressor and the regeneration of a social reality that was formerly unrealized (Proudfoot, 1976, p. 157). Art will acknowledge, report truth, as witness to the dying, precarious self.

Loyalty as Devotion, Art, and the Superpersonal

Royce (1908/2005) defines loyalty very differently from the stereotypical connection to warfare and the brotherhood of soldiering. In his model, loyalty is defined as devotion to a cause that is "larger than [the] private self" (Royce, 1908/2005, p. 874). In this way, loyalty is superpersonal – it links several selves into a "social unity" (p. 874). The spiritual union of loyalty is expressed in Royce's work as a metaphysical and revelatory experience, which manifests "the eternal . . . the conscious and superhuman unity of life, in the form of the acts of an individual self" (Royce, 1908/2005, p. 996). Loyalty unifies the plan of a life, permitting fragmentary connection to consciousness that transcends the individual (Royce, 1908/2005, p. 978). The communion with the conscious lives of others is revealed in both devotion and full presence in gratitude and awareness, for "devotion . . . to universal conscious life itself . . . or self-surrender of each conscious moment to the great whole of life" is teleological, producing meaning and sense that "This life is my life: It is a rich moment" (Royce, 1882/2005, p. 270). Art bears witness to evanescent existence in its full and magnificent tragedy.

The Saving Absolute in Pluralistic Aesthetic Spaces

Salvific otherness is imagined in artistic representation. Nagl (2012) discusses Royce's high view of the beloved community as invisible and pluralistic, transcendent and transformative to the self, extending beyond the finite, towards "a saving absolute" (p. 110). Nagl (2012) argues that loyalty in Royce's model is the "will to believe in something eternal . . . to express that belief in the practical life of a human being" (p. 109). This sense of the possibility is reckoning in authentic communities, which function with a vision of infinity (Nagl, 2012, p. 110). Jensen (2016, p. 254) points out that in Royce, King, and civil rights leader and philosopher Howard Thurman, the notion of the expansion of the beloved community includes the discovery that there are expanded boundaries that include new brothers and sisters, whose unassailable humanity must be acknowledged.

Temporal Existence, Art, and Co-Creation

Musical and visual art will be encountered in various subjectivities of time, meter, epoch, remembrance, and season. Scored into the annals, organized into compositions, the art object seeks immortality. The stagnant artist seeks liberation, often requiring an internal psychic champion, an internalized benefactor, and economic means. The integration of time into Dr. King's call is described by Simpson (2008), who emphasized the human responsibility to co-create a divine kingdom (p. 59). The urgency and connection to basic human needs is expressed in King's (1955/1987) address at Holt Street Baptist Church, when he states,

> There comes a time when people get tired of being trampled over by the iron feet of oppression. There comes a time, my friends, when people get tired of being plunged across the abyss of humiliation, where they experience the bleakness of nagging despair. There comes a time when people get tired of being pushed out of the glittering sunlight of life's July and left standing amid the piercing chill of an alpine November. There comes a time.
> (King, 1955/1987, p. 72)

The artist needs a motive. The urgency and temporally bounded features of social change arrive with a weathering, but King speaks to the power of dialogue and persistence, for "some of us who have already begun to break the silence of the night have found that the calling to speak is often a vocation of agony, but we must speak" (King, 1967/1986, p. 231). When justice is pursued in courageous nonviolence, the potential for transformation of an inequitable system is optimized (Simpson, 2008). The geography of the beloved community is prismatic belongingness, a territory outside of dualities of exclusion and divided consciousness (Inwood, 2009, p. 490). These regions are the beginning of a new aesthetic epoch.

Art as Transdisciplinary Re-Examination: Erich Fromm and a Vision of Solidarity

Liberatory aesthetics are responsive, with both individual and collaborative transmutation. Fromm's concept of solidarity includes a form of radical humanism that focuses on potential, seeking to apprehend a basic human essence (Wilde, 2004). Fromm's "ethically-driven communitarianism" is transdisciplinary and seeks to produce a just society (Wilde, 2004, p. 1). Influenced by the notion of "ethical reawakening: and Rabbinical "critical-interpretive pedagogy," Fromm sought to apply reason, wonder, and concern for ultimate human questions about meaning and freedom to his understanding of reality while remaining engaged in a process of re-examination (Wilde, 2004, p. 3). Steering towards the goal, art will deconstruct oppression, classism and exploitation by exploring love as filial devotion and rootedness.

Transformative aesthetics refuse the popular. Solidarity, in Fromm's view, diverges from, and rejects, a conformist mentality. The individual seeks escape from domination, determinism, and submission in a region where equality presumes awareness of the uniqueness of the individual (Wilde, 2004, p. 4). The alienation produced by oppressive economic structures must give way to love and movement from self-interest, yet the market functions as regulator, inhibiting a compassionate society (Wilde, 2004, pp. 5, 12). The deadness and objectification of the fetish for consumerism supports mechanistic views of personhood and subjugation (Wilde, 2004, p. 12). Factories of production enslave artistic fruitfulness and impoverish the *what-could-be*.

Aesthetic Alienation and the Productive Society

Artistic bankruptcy adopts a superficial subject in a sham of aesthetic freedom. Fromm (1950/1978) identifies the form of alienation that has surfaced in psychology as it emulates the natural sciences, becoming preoccupied with "insignificant problems" rather than its central human subject matter (p. 6), adopting a mechanism concerned with measurement precision. Fromm (1941/1964, 1955/1990) argues that modernity has created a form of pseudo-freedom that terminates in detachment from the pursuit of meaning, reason, and love; individuals will attempt to escape this state through destructiveness, submission, and attraction to authoritarianism. An alternative is to pursue the need for rootedness, which is founded in unconditional maternal love, through filial devotion, transcending passivity and the thrownness of existence through creativity and affirmation of identity as a subject with agency (Fromm, 1955/1990, pp. 36–63).

A Generative Moral Aesthetic

Virtue, when not entombed, may exercise epistemic growth in action, a culture's art forms, and generative ontology. In Fromm's (1947/1990) work, *Man for Himself*, a productive existence is creatively spontaneous, enlivens existence, and shows imagination transcendent to literal reality but not in opposition to it (pp. 82–92). The generative capacity does not merely reproduce or chronicle what exists but accesses power that is connected to virtue, reason, and an "activity of the soul" (p. 92). The productive creator is not dominated by anxiety, automaton activity such as blind allegiance to culture or science, nor encumbered by the desire to enact what one is "supposed" to do or feel (p. 87). In his posthumous publication of writings produced between 1974 and 1976, Fromm (1976/1993) identifies factors that can alienate art and existence, including the commodities of a fully commercialized civilization, insincere usage of language, and pursuit of expediency and profit as first values, with the renunciation of suffering (pp. 11–26). In contrast, the awakening of a vivified moment of consciousness can allow two individuals to "see each other in their unique suchness" (Fromm, 1976/1993, p. 37), and the countenance of the Other is apprehended as an entirely new creation, freed from the constraints and fog of illusion. The creative state is observed in sleep, a country exterior to the perimeter of common sense, with its sedating automaticity.

"Productivity" is a word hemmed in with semantic differentials. Varied permutations of freedom will inform artistic *productivity-as-aliveness*, counter to the eminent focus in modernity on production, consumption, assembly lines, convenience, and technocratic simulation. D'Agostino and Lake (2014) review Erich Fromm's practice of being, as revealed in several of his works written between 1941 and 1976. This collection addresses the alienation of the modern human being in a technological and competitive society. Fromm distinguished two types of freedom which are relevant to the quest for the beloved community. Freedom that allows movement, transcendent to oppression and constraints, was termed negative freedom. In contrast, positive freedom propels the individual to attach to community and the world without eliminating the individual into a herd-like automaton conformity. While both freedom *from* and freedom *towards* strengthen the beloved community, the former in its most radical permutations may produce rootlessness and fear, depriving the person of the security that arrives from intimate attachment bonds. When freedom *from* is also expressed in a cultural surround of materialism, technological obsession, competition, and extreme individualism, a sense of meaninglessness can create a readiness for aggression, moving society away from rational discussion of difference. When discussing the dehumanization of modern life in his work *Escape from Freedom*, Fromm (1941/1964, p. 110) surmised, "Man became a cog in the vast economic machine . . . to serve a purpose outside of himself."

Centralization as Aesthetic and Personal Death

Centralization in aesthetics strengthens the readiness for dehumanization. Erosion of the beloved community presents with shifts from local to centralized agriculture, trade, and governance, serving the interests of monopolies, mechanistic journalism rendered from artificial intelligence, and ravenous corporations. Alienation from the racial, political, and gendered Other intersects with a society that is built on corporatism, a work ethic that obscures familial attachments, and an identity-formation process built on individual achievement, social comparison, and economically motivated cyber-control. The automaton conformity that Fromm warns about is connected to a rising distance between creative works and local production, for a corporatist society causes the individual to become "estranged from the products that he makes with his own hands" (D'agostino & Lake, 2014, p. 21). In *Escape from Freedom*, Fromm (1941/1964, p. 119) concludes, "Man does not only sell commodities, he sells himself and feels himself to be a commodity."

Resonance and Space

Collaborative aesthetics and connection to inter-historical beacons can facilitate living art. Peters (2017) reviews the work of Fromm in relation to sonority and the central quest to overcome isolation, rooting his understanding of both resonance and reflection in the writings of Kierkegaard. He understands alienation as a gap, a space between the self and the context or the Other, which results in a foreign experience. Peters understands resonance within Fromm to represent the warmth that arrives with connection to others and the world and the coherence between the self and the body (p. 3). The evolution of society is expressed by Fromm as a developmental emergence which is tied to self-conscious awareness. The process of changing from an embedded state with the mother to an autonomous or isolated state is fundamental to the human experience of separation and division within the self. There remains an interest in returning to the state of unity with the Other (the resonance), and yet there is also freedom; both of these elicit fear. In Fromm's work, it is the consciousness of separateness and the reflection on the need for connection which prompt inauthentic expressions of love. Human beings take on an atomistic quality within a society where instrumental relationships are chief (Peters, 2017, p. 8).

Diffusion in the Orchard: Agenesis of the Artistic Core

One form of alienation in Fromm's work could be the aspect of artistic self-estrangement that disconnects the individual from a felt sense of meaning, leading to a diffuse perspective on one's future (Grey, 1975, p. 124). Such alienation is termed uncommitted by Grey (1975). In contrast, there is another form of alienation assisted by the conformist path; in this manifestation, termed "overconformist," self-awareness is impeded by the thrust to seek to reduce isolation. Attempts to find a clear governmental or ethnographic linkage to outcomes would be more difficult to come by than what Grey's analysis seems to imply. In a politicized aesthetic economy, the "undifferentiated family ego mass" (Bowen, 1978/1992, p. 440) incarcerates the creative impulse. Pseudo-resonance, a reverberation of imitation, will impede living art.

Inclusion, Attachment, and Aesthetic Families of Becoming

Aesthetic *becoming* is an attachment-seeking enterprise. King's notion of the beloved community may offer healing for the lack of attachment that drives authoritarian aggression within Fromm's work. Smith and Zepp (1974) describe King's vision of the beloved community as an ideal of total inclusion, relatedness, justice, and integration. This community would be based on radical reconciliation and redemption, a collective expression of a Christian ethic. Smith and Zepp identify Dr. King's expression of the solidarity of the human family, a location where our indebtedness to one another and the preceding generations is made conscious. Those who participated in the civil rights movement revealed a microcosm of the beloved community (Smith & Zepp, 1974, p. 362). King was careful to avoid both naive optimism and unfettered pessimism in his understanding of the prophetic vision that sought justice and economic inequality. The beloved community in King's vision retained a "not-yet" quality, as described in Smith and Zepp (1974, p. 363), yet the pilgrimage was felt to be expressed in approximations that were leading towards an eventuality. Creative intimations sense the emergent qualities.

Both Fromm and King present constructive aesthetic possibilities. Areas of overlap between King and Fromm include humanism, a restorationist love, and an aspiration towards transcendent ethics that allows for social critique. Miri (2014) evaluates Fromm's comparison of authoritarian versus humanistic religion, derived from Fromm's (1950/1978) work, *Psychoanalysis and Religion*. While Fromm characterized the authoritarian religious form as an expression of obedience and surrender, the humanistic variety explores the pursuit of human strength and reason within a context of love and awareness of limitation. Self-realization, connectedness to others, and joy were outgrowths of a humanistic religious orientation. The central existential questions will be asked in such spaces, a forum of dialogue for art.

An Environmental Surround for Organismic Art

Habitats and their dynamic ecologies allow artistic epiphenomena. Fromm allows for dialogue between the subjectivity of culture and the normative strivings of ethics (Thompson, 2014); his biophilous perspective emphasized the inherent value of living organisms and the environment, justice, security, and freedom (Gunderson, 2014). The importance of establishing stewardship over the natural world is revealed in Fromm's model, which also points to the meaninglessness that can arise when the person fails to resolve the existential dichotomy of both living within the world and also transcending it (Gunderson, 2014, pp. 185–186). Within Fromm's construction, pathological socialization may contaminate the development of identity in ways that contribute to the formation of a pseudo-self, prone to authoritarian conformity and the internalization of legislators (Fromm, 1947/1990, p. 144). Artistic work is an epigenetic "I" phenomenon.

The Pseudo-Self as the Delimiter, the Barricade to Latitudes of Acceptance

A continuum of belief and experience permeates the aesthetic membrane. In *Man for Himself* (1947/1990), Fromm argues that the authoritarian conscience is the Freudian Superego, but there are also other manifestations of conscience. This internalization of the fear of those with the power to punish also contains a projected ideal rooted in the need to admire. The pseudo-self emerges with feelings of powerlessness and resignation, as the original self is submerged below an expected role, repressed and automatized when the person fears punishment or ridicule (Fromm, 1941/1964, pp. 205–206). Authoritarianism, often inextricable from political agenda, renders the organic features of art into leaden artifacts – the "it" quality.

Reversals, Power Distance, and the Aesthetic Democracy

Democratic artistic communities are learning retreats, townships of cooperative equality. A transposition of hierarchical structures in organizations, education, and government can prompt potential for progress towards decentralized communities, offering a revival of local culture, intergenerational cross-pollination, and city governance. Casey Nelson Blake (1990) provides a broad historical analysis of the concept of the beloved community, examining the cultural critiques offered by Randolph Bourne, Van Wyck Brooks, Waldo Frank, and Lewis Mumford. He begins his work with the contention that the beloved community embodies broad-based participation, rooted in early-twentieth-century critiques of the harmful effects of industrialization and the importance of democratic engagement for human actualization. In his discussion of the "latter day Emersonians," Blake (1990) explores a movement that adopted some of the vision of the New England transcendentalists, rejecting consumerism in favor of an aesthetic and humanistic worldview, critiquing classism without adopting a Marxist view (p. 3).

An ideal community in the young American view would include intimate, local groups that find solidarity with shared cultural traditions, commitment to the Other, and prosocial orientation within a system that values the individual's pursuit of self-actualization. The critique of political and economic forms that are "lethal to the human spirit" were contrasted with creativity, imagination, and idealism, with realization that corporate control of the individual and industrial suppression curtails the artisan, taxing small communities (Blake, 1990, p. 4).

While the transcendentalists sought purity in idealism, solitude, and the higher law, they have also been critiqued for their deism, referred to by Royce (1885/2005) as a commitment to "Deus absconditus" (p. 140). The form of idealism practiced and the separation from urban needs, conjoined with a distant and uninvolved deity, is viewed by Royce as an extravagance (p. 141), which is limiting for the one who is "born with the infinite soul" (p. 140). Perhaps the abstraction is also illuminated by Dr. King's insistence on real economic, structural, and political change, which he juxtaposed with a prophetic vision of a transcendent deliverance.

Social Engineering and the Dismembering of the Beloved Community

Progress, especially in the realm of techno-genesis, can be construed as the antithesis of a personalistic thesis of aesthetics. A cyber-controlled society runs the risk of "technocratic social engineering," which is a form of imperialism linked to power stalking (Blake, 1990, p. 6), potentially rooted in self-interest, unfettered greed, corporate monopolization, and cultural narcissism. The hollow technocratic society uses algorithms aligned with the confirmation bias and the human urgency to reduce uncertainty and fear despite the individual's need for diverse perspectives, productive dialogue, rational debate, symbols of compassion, and interdependence. A beloved community will search for a shared vision yet be open to reconstruction and iteration, pursuing transcendence through the arts and sciences. A movement beyond "technological determinism" and the feudal rise of "commercial mass culture" will require an orbit above self-aggrandizement, atomism and disconnection, mega-politics, uniformity, and anonymity; in this heavenly country, transfiguration includes the spiritual restoration of the individual towards wholeness within an organic space (Blake, 1990, pp. 267–269).

A technological society also has the potential to contaminate art with authoritarian aggression, submission, sexism, conventionality, and infatuation with symbols of power. In his vision for a new democratic ideal, Philip Slater (1991) examines the morbidity associated with authoritarianism, which glamorizes death, conquest, secrecy, deflection, and submissiveness, using dichotomous marketing to vilify the Other (pp. 19, 27, 32, 33). The insidious onset of authoritarianism subjugates women, enslaves the conquered, and rapidly replicates a narrative of evil as "an organized entity, a kind of cosmic conspiracy" (Slater, 1991, pp. 37, 39, 85). In contrast, he offers a perspective of a democracy orthogonal to mega-culture, a place where complexity, playfulness, creativity, and self-organization can thrive.

Although markedly different in his approach, Cornel West (1982) discusses a prophetic-deliverance model of Afro-American Christianity, pointing out that specialization and rigid workplace hierarchies contribute to fragmentation among socioeconomic groups (p. 133). The deliverance aesthetic model intuits pending illumination, as observed in Martin Luther King Jr., planting a "cultural potency" that took root from the black churches in the South (West, 1982, pp. 142–143).

The Corruptible Corpus, a Fragile Art

Aesthetic morbidity, the insidious fixation with destruction, is a neurotic infirmity, a mutation of the fragility of the human condition. In his discussion of the sick society, Fromm (1962/2001) discusses psychic pathology and fixation on self-interested wish fulfillment as well as the influence of Hegelian thought on alienation from nature, self, and humanity (pp. 43–44). The oppressive features of alienated labor in Fromm's work, influenced by the writings of Marx, are assumed to prompt an "impoverished inner life," with a cavernous distance between the body, mind, natural productivity, and freedom. While self-aware, the individual represses awareness of the great social need, declining the cognitive strength that comes from communion (p. 127). Therefore, while the individual dreads separation from conscience, the overwhelming terror is of social ostracism, which capsizes artistic potential.

Conclusions

A transformative aesthetic will find its ground in redemptive atonement, an ineffable compassion that permits individual personhood and community, dynamic spiritual progress, and historical preservation. King's construct of the beloved community includes an incorporation of Agapic love and moral law (Herstein, 2009, p. 93). The limitless nature of Agapic love is characterized by the "oceanic, other-oriented, and all-redeeming love which flows unchecked" (Herstein, 2009, p. 93). Royce (1913/1968a) emphasized loyalty as teleological and self-evident – devotion as the primary aim of existence (p. 42). King's promised land may have been nourished in part from Royce's view of communitarian loyalty (Royce, 1908/2005, p. 874), expressed as sacrificial commitment to a cause in ways that unify disparate groups around the common good (Herstein, 2009, p. 97). This unification moves from belief to the agentic pursuit of discovering and fulfilling basic human needs during a process of reparation, where love is the core of creative activity. The idea of loyalty as devotion to a cause beyond the individual self and oriented towards social unity is fundamental to Royce's development of the beloved community, the "pearl of great price" (Royce, 1908/2005, p. 916). However, Royce also presents the importance of discovering one's personal cause.

Like Dr. King, Fromm offers a normative humanism and a prescription, a view of health and pathology which evokes a vision of a sane society. Erich Fromm's positive freedom connotes a region where individuality and authentic love redress the alienation between and within persons, adrift from nature in a technology of powerlessness and fear (D'Agostino & Lake, 2014). The beloved community may be considered as an organizing axiom as well as a transcendental life-world, where the self, the community, and consciousness co-create a collective and energizing call.

Political and religious frames ignite social classifications, goals, behaviors, and economic outcomes in ways that mobilize human emotion; within the modern American society, such movements are cyber-orchestrated and controlled. Rhetorical and cognitive frames for social movements can galvanize agency, although a linguistic or political edifice is constrained by culture and bias (Williams, 2002). Religious symbols and language games are often recruited for malevolent political aims; nevertheless, adaptive modes of spiritual and aesthetic inquiry can drive progressive forces, anchoring capacious fields for interracial dialogue and democratic participation.

Emancipatory aesthetics are also life-affirming. Liberation psychology, which builds on Dr. Martin Luther King's vision of the beloved community as an organizing principle, articulates the relationship between basic need fulfillment and social creativity beyond a position of "soul-destructive othering" (Alsup, 2009). Liberation theology, with its disavowal of the idols of the market and the idols of death, offers a decolonized mission (Andrade, 2017). As a collection of writings, liberation theology supports consciousness of injustice, visibility of poverty, and a response to "structural sin" that moves beyond a developmental metaphor (Andrade, 2017, p. 621).

Dr. King's vision for the beloved community included equality, reversal, and the revelatory product of divine love, for "every valley shall be exalted, every hill and mountain shall be made low, the rough places will be made plains . . . and the glory of the Lord shall be revealed" (King, 1963b/1986, p. 219). The countenance of this love illuminates a "divine otherness" (Williams, 2002, p. 262) and exemplifies a world where the humanity of each person is elevated above representations, projections, and political reductions. In the promised land, needs for safety, security, and competence are met, power serves the cause of justice, and belongingness and uniqueness find balance with freedom and self-determination (Alsup, 2009).

The aura of the Beloved is restorationist, a "call to return to the moral community" (Williams, 2002, p. 265). Redemptive love, rooted in the power of suffering and forgiveness of adversaries, must be nonviolent in spirit, language, and physical expression, for "he who loves is a participant in the being of God"[4] (King, 1956/1992, p. 419). A reconciling community, seeking unity and humanitarian mission, must be pursued as a sacramental commitment, for "we are still far from the dawning of the 'Beloved Community'" (Nilson, 2010, p. 84). From Erich Fromm we arrive with a structure for art that includes being, loving, and mindful consciousness rather than having, hoarding, controlling, and legislating. This art emerges in the space of relationships that allow for individuality. This is an art that is both communal and free, with dignity as its principle. The metamorphosis of hatred into tolerance, nonviolence, and unity is observed in Dr. King's call for transformation, which has "the marvelous effect of changing the face of the enemy" (King, 1964/2010, p. 35).

Notes

1 See this chapter in R. Niebuhr, *An Interpretation of Christian Ethics* (John Knox Press, 1935).
2 Also note King's discussion of the law of humanity towards the Jewish community, which transcended the unjust laws in Hitler's Germany. He contrasts this with the Hungarian resistance. (M. L. King, "Letter from the Birmingham Jail," in *A Testament of Hope: The Essential Writing and Speeches, MLK*, ed. J. M. Washington (Harper One, 1963), 295).
3 See S. Hall, "Cultural Identity and Diaspora," in *Identity: Community, Culture, Difference*, ed. J. Rutherford (London: Lawrence & Wishart, 1990), 222–237; A. Appadurai, "Disjuncture and Difference in the Global Cultural Economy," *Theory, Culture & Society*, 7(2–3) (1990), 295–310.
4 King refers to I John 4:16.

References

Alsup, R. E. (2009). Liberation psychology: Martin Luther King, Jr.'s beloved community as a model for social creativity. *Journal of Humanistic Psychology*, 49(4), 388–408.
Andrade, L. M. (2017). Liberation theology: A critique of modernity. *Interventions*, 19(5), 620–630.
Andrus, M. (2021). *Brothers in the beloved community: The friendship of Thich Nhat Hahn and Martin Luther King, Jr.* Parallax Press.
Blake, C. N. (1990). *Beloved community: The cultural criticism of Randolph Bourne, Van Wyck Brooks, Waldo Frank, and Lewis Mumford.* Univ of North Carolina Press.
Bowen, M. (1978/1992). *Family therapy in clinical practice.* Rowman & Littlefield Publishers, Incorporated.
Buber, M. (1923/1996). *I and thou.* (W. Kaufmann, Trans.). Touchstone.
Burrow, Jr., R. (2012). The beloved community: Martin Luther King, Jr. and Josiah Royce. *Encounter*, 73(1), 37.
D'agostino, V., & Lake, R. (2014). Fromm's dialectic of freedom and the praxis of being. In S. J. Miri, R. Lake, & T. M. Kress (Eds.), *Reclaiming the sane society: Essays on Erich Fromm's thought* (pp. 17–29). Springer.

Du Bois, W. E. B. (1903/2018). *The souls of black folk* (P. H. Hinchey, Ed.). Myers Education Press.
Freud, S. (1930/1961). *Civilization and its discontents* (J. Strachey, Trans. and Ed.), with a biographical introduction by P. Gay. W.W. Norton & Co. Printed in 1989.
Fromm, E. (1941/1964). *Escape from freedom*. Farrar & Rinehart, Inc.
Fromm, E. (1947/1990). *Man for himself: An inquiry into the psychology of ethics*. Henry Holt and Company.
Fromm, E. (1950/1978). *Psychoanalysis and religion*. Yale University Press.
Fromm, E. (1955). *The sane society*. Holt, Rinehart and Winston.
Fromm, E. (1955/1990). *The sane society*. Henry Holt & Company.
Fromm, E. (1962/2001). *Beyond the chains of illusion: My encounter with Marx and Freud* (R. Funk, Foreword). Continuum.
Fromm, E. (1976/1993). *The art of being*. Continuum.
Gilroy, P. (1993). *The black Atlantic: Modernity and double consciousness*. Harvard University Press.
Grey, A. L. (1975). Modern alienation and the good old days. *American Journal of Psychoanalysis*, 35, 123–133.
Gunderson, R. (2014). Erich Fromm's ecological messianism: The first biophilia hypothesis as Humanistic social theory. *Humanity & Society*, 38(2), 182–204.
Herstein, G. (2009). The Roycean roots of the beloved community. *The Pluralist*, 4(2), 91–107.
Innes, P. (1996). Structuralism. In M. Payne (Ed.), *A dictionary of cultural and critical theory* (pp. 513–517). Blackwell Publishers.
Inwood, J. F. (2009). Searching for the promised land: Examining Dr. Martin Luther King's concept of the beloved community. *Antipode*, 41(3), 487–508.
Jensen, K. E. (2016). The growing edges of beloved community: From Royce to Thurman and King. *Transaction of the Charles S. Peirce Society*, 52(2), 239–258.
Jensen, K. E. (2019). *Howard Thurman: Philosophy, civil rights, and the search for common ground*. University of South Carolina Press. https://doi.org/10.2307/j.ctvgs0bx9
King, M. L. (1955, December 5/1987). Speech to the first mass meeting of the Montgomery Improvement Association at the Holt Street Baptist Church, Montgomery, AL. In C. Carson, D. J. Garrow, G. Gill, V. Harding, & D. C. Hine (Eds.), *The eyes on the prize civil rights reader: Documents, speeches, and firsthand accounts from the Black Freedom Struggle, 1954–1990*. Penguin Books.
King, M. L. (1956, November 4/1992). Paul's letter to American Christians, sermon delivered at Dexter Avenue Baptist church. In S. Burns, S. Carson, P. Holloran, & D. L. H. Powell (Eds.), *The papers of Martin Luther King, Junior, Vol. III, December 1955 to December 1956* (pp. 414–420). University of California Press.
King, M. L. (1957, November 17). Loving your enemies: Sermon delivered at the Dexter Avenue Baptist Church. Montgomery, AL. In C. Carson, S. Carson, A. Clary, V. Shadron, & K. Taylor (Eds.), *The papers of Martin Luther King, Junior, Vol. IV, Symbol of the movement, January 1957 to December 1958* (pp. 315–324). University of California Press.
King, M. L. (1958/2010). Pilgrimage to nonviolence. In M. L. King, & C. Carson (Eds.), *Stride toward freedom the Montgomery story* (pp. 77–95). Beacon Press.
King, M. L. (1963a/1986). Letter from the Birmingham jail. In J. M. Washington (Ed.), *A testament of hope: The essential writing and speeches, MLK* (pp. 289–302). Harper One.
King, M. L. (1963b/1986). I have a dream. In J. M. Washington (Ed.), *A testament of hope: The essential writing and speeches, MLK* (pp. 217–220). Harper One.
King, M. L. (1964/2010). *Why we can't wait*. Beacon Press.
King, M. L. (1967/1986). A time to break silence. In J. M. Washington (Ed.), *A testament of hope: The essential writing and speeches, MLK* (pp. 231–244). Harper One.

Marsh, C. (2005). *The beloved community: How faith shapes social justice from the civil rights movement to today.* Basic Books.

Mays, B. E., & Nicholson, J. W. (1933/2015). *The negro's church.* Wipf & Stock. First published by the Negro University Press.

McKittrick, K. (2006). *Demonic grounds: Black women and the cartographies of struggle* (1st ed.). University of Minnesota Press.

Miri, S. J. (2014). Humanism and sociological imagination in a Frommesque perspective. In *Reclaiming the sane society* (pp. 31–35). Brill.

Nagl, L. (2012). Loyalty: Royce's post-Kantian, pragmaticist conception of ethics. In K. Parker, & K. Skowronski (Eds.), *Josiah Royce for the twenty first century.* Lexington Press.

Niebuhr, R. (1935/2013). The relevance of an impossible ethical ideal. In *An interpretation of Christian ethics* (pp. 101–135). Westminster John Knox Press.

Nilson, J. (2010). Towards the "beloved community": The church's role in the struggle against racism. *US Catholic Historian, 28*(1), 83–91.

Payne, M. (1996). Introduction: Some versions of cultural and critical theory. In M. Payne (Ed.), *A dictionary of cultural and critical theory* (pp. 1–12). Blackwell Publishers.

Peters, M. (2017). Erich Fromm on resonance and alienation. In Fromm Forum (English Edition – ISBN1437-1189), 20/2016, Tuebingen (Selbstverlag), 19, 24–34. *Erich Fromm Document Center for Fromm Online.* https://fromm-online.org/wp-content/uploads/secondary-titles/Peters_M_2017.pdf

Proudfoot, W. (1976). *God and the self: Three types of philosophy of religion.* Bucknell University Press.

Royce, J. (1882/2005). Pessimism and modern thought. In J. J. McDermott (Ed.), *The basic writings of Josiah Royce, Vol. I: Culture, philosophy, and religion* (pp. 249–272). Including an annotated bibliography of the publications of Josiah Royce, Prepared by Ignas K. Skrupskelis. Fordham University Press.

Royce, J. (1885/2005). An episode of early California life: The squatter riot of 1850 in Sacramento. In J. J. McDermott (Ed.), *The basic writings of Josiah Royce, Vol. I: Culture, philosophy, and religion* (pp. 119–158). Including an annotated bibliography of the publications of Josiah Royce, Prepared by Ignas K. Skrupskelis. Fordham University Press.

Royce, J. (1897/2005). The place of will in the conception of the absolute. [The concept of the Absolute and the dialectical method]. In J. J. McDermott (Ed.), *The basic writings of Josiah Royce, Vol. I: Culture, philosophy, and religion* (pp. 299–318). Including an annotated bibliography of the publications of Josiah Royce, Prepared by Ignas K. Skrupskelis. Fordham University Press.

Royce, J. (1908/2005). The philosophy of loyalty. In J. J. McDermott (Ed.), *The basic writings of Josiah Royce, Vol. II: Logic, loyalty, and community* (pp. 855–1014). With an annotated bibliography by I. K. Skrupskelis. Fordham University Press.

Royce, J. (1913/1968a). *The problem of Christianity.* University of Chicago Press. First published by MacMillan.

Royce, J. (1913/1968b). *The problem of Christianity* (Vol. 1. The Christian doctrine of life; J. A. Mann, Foreword). A Gateway Edition. Henry Regnery Company.

Royce, J. (1916/2005). The hope of a great community. In J. J. McDermott (Ed.), *The basic writings of Josiah Royce, Vol. II: Logic, loyalty, and community* (pp. 1145–1164). With an annotated bibliography by I.K. Skrupskelis. Fordham University Press.

Simpson, G. M. (2008). "Changing the face of the enemy": Martin Luther King, Jr., and the beloved community. *Word & World, 28*(1), 57.

Slater, P. (1991). *A dream deferred: America's discontent and the search for a new democratic ideal.* Beacon Press.

Smith, J. E. (1950). *Royce's social infinite: The community of interpreters.* The Liberal Arts Press.

Smith, K. L., & Zepp, Jr., I. G. (1974). Martin Luther King's vision of the beloved community. *Christian Century*, 91(13), 361–363.
Subramaniam, R. (1996). Diaspora. In M. Payne (Ed.), *A dictionary of cultural and critical theory* (p. 144). Blackwell Publishers.
Sucharov, M. S. (2015). Historical and cultural narratives: Confessions of a Diaspora Jew. *International Journal of Psychoanalytic Self Psychology*, 10(4), 305–317.
Thompson, M. J. (2014). Normative humanism as redemptive critique: Knowledge and judgment in Erich Fromm's social theory. In *Reclaiming the sane society* (pp. 37–58). Brill.
West, C. (1982). *Prophecy deliverance: An Afro-American revolutionary Christianity*. The Westminster Press.
West, C. (1999). *The Cornel West reader*. Basic Civitas Books, Perseus Books Group.
Wilde, L. (2004). *Erich Fromm and the quest for solidarity*. Palgrave Macmillan.
Williams, R. H. (2002). From the "beloved community" to "family values": Religious language, symbolic repertoires, and democratic culture. In D. S. Meyer, N. Whittier, N., & B. Robnett (Eds.), *Social movements: Identity, culture, and the state* (pp. xvi–xvi, 247–265). Oxford University Press, Incorporated.
Williams, T. D., & Bengtsson, J. O. (2022, Summer). Personalism. In E. N. Zalta (Ed.), *The Stanford encyclopedia of philosophy*. Stanford University.

Chapter 15

Radical Empathy
Socially-Engaged Art as Democratic Tool

Diana Boros

As a political philosopher, I have often been asked how we could revitalize the American political landscape – how we could start to heal the many broken aspects of our democracy. Various international bodies have, since 2017, termed the U.S. a "flawed" or "backsliding" democracy, or as existing in a "downward trajectory" of democratic quality (Kleinfeld, 2022). Still, before 2025,[1] this conversation was less frantic, but once 2025 was off to its chaotic political start in the United States, the questions about the country's democratic health naturally became more urgent and more anxious. Peers and strangers alike have commented (with great upset) on the significance of constitutional (not to mention human rights) violations by the executive branch and on the particular tragedy that is the governmental attack on arts, culture, and the public domain broadly. Alongside these fearful discussions, I've thankfully also repeatedly engaged with inquiries about how citizens themselves could strengthen democratic norms and build a more responsive citizenry. And while at the time of this writing, 2025 has barely completed its first quarter, and it is still unclear what lasting harm will stick to our delicate system of checks and balances, my answers now do not stray far from the methods I have long advocated for.

Whether a country is determined to be at risk for elements of illiberalism or veering, even careening towards it, community life can always be strengthened by thoughtful acts of citizenship and inclusive and provocative public spaces and experiences. Our public selves, us as community members and civic actors, require empathetic exercises by which we can exercise and strengthen our ability to see others well, to be able to actively, in full spirit and mind, feel the joys and traumas of those around us, especially those we do not know, the strangers in our communities. It is these "strangers" who make up our communal fabric, who are the other components of the human oneness that we are inextricably sewn within. We walk alongside so many, and so many more we can only imagine physically sharing space with, all of whom are nonetheless reflections of our humanness.

The Crisis of Apathy and Exclusion

American democracy is in many ways a beautiful system, one filled with great possibility. Yet we know that multitudes of people in this country choose not to participate in the system, and while some may say they feel uninterested and/or lacking relevant knowledge, many others will tell you that they feel excluded, alienated, and disappointed by the system. This is a crisis in and of itself.

Whenever I am asked about this crisis, I first answer the expected – that we need to increase voter turnout (whether due to voter apathy or structural barriers that disenfranchise voters, the U.S. consistently trails other developed countries in voter turnout (this is true even after the upswing in voter turnout in the last few elections, most notably in the presidential election of 2020)) and that this is especially true in midterm elections (the elections in which we vote for our direct representatives to government). I will add that we need to better limit partisan gerrymandering and the direct exclusion of minority voices, and even that we need to insist that the obligations of citizenship be in balance with the rights afforded to us by the U.S. Constitution – in other words, that all Americans should be educated in what is required of them as citizens to aid in the health of the democratic system.[2]

Underlying all of this, though, is, I believe, a general need to increase participation in the public sphere. Accordingly, in order to heal democracy, to start the process of making it more accountable and less estranging, we need to find ways to encourage citizens to associate more actively and consistently in their communities – to not only join civic and political associations of all stripes but to make a habit of experiencing the diversity and the inherent spontaneity and unpredictability of public spaces.

Wealth in this country allows us to buy our way out of public experiences across many arenas of life. If we can afford it, we can buy a home in a gated community, send our children to private schools, visit private parks, buy box tickets at the ballgame, buy books online rather than visit a public library, watch movies in our home theater rather than visit our local cinema, and stay in our private cars rather than wait in a public bus stop or train station. With enough material success, it is possible to almost completely abandon public experiences in favor of comfortable and predictable experiences in our homes, places of work, and neighborhoods. Add to this that we can curate our news feeds (and the algorithms of social media reinforce this) – our information about the public – so that they can become echo chambers – and taken collectively, this avoidance of the public (and I might add, fear of the public) can be seen as a particular crisis within the greater crisis of the ill health of democracy.

Without regular public experiences and the diversity and unpredictability that go along with that, it is far easier to consider your own beliefs and experiences above those of others. It is far easier to lack knowledge of human experiences that you do not have a firsthand account of. It is far easier to hold political beliefs that favor people who are most like you. And it is far easier to hold political beliefs that disregard or diminish the needs of people most unlike you in social or economic condition.

"Radical Empathy"

To combat this, which I think we consciously need to do, we need to add a concept to our language of responsible citizenship, and I call it "radical empathy". I believe that we need to educate citizens in this concept, in much the same way that we educate citizens about, say, being more "eco-conscious" in our daily lives. Yes, some can and do ignore these calls to recycle and reuse, but many understand that such responsibility is the duty of the citizen and will make adjustments to their habits in this direction. In much the same way, we can advise our children, our students, our peers, and our communities to consciously engage in such radical empathy as a habit of political life.

I designate the term "radical empathy" to mean the regular and consistent use of empathy in the process of determining political opinions and solutions to common problems. I argue that it is a term that should be added to our civic vocabulary and taught as a pillar of civic responsibility. It relies on regular and consistent experience with the public, with the diversity of others in the world.

Empathy, by definition, is a feeling whereby we can relate to the feelings of others, in which we can imagine the experiences and the emotions those experiences might yield. The more vividly we can envision another's situation – the more keenly we can "walk in another's shoes", the more empathy is enlarged. The closer we can get to a feeling that is not our own, the more it temporarily becomes our own, and the more we can relate to and understand the choices and decisions made by those experiencing that feeling(s).

We are often raised to consider empathy in our lives, as part of the moral education that we gain from caregivers and educators who hope that by encouraging us to empathize, they are encouraging the development of kinder, more understanding human beings. This is no doubt true, but empathy can also assist in achieving more overtly political goals. That regular experiences of empathy create kinder, more understanding people – and that such moral benefit contributes directly to a more equitable and just world – is an underlying assumption of this argument. This being treated as a starting point of the argument, radical empathy can increase the speed, quantity, *and* quality of inclusive and understanding public interactions.

So what do I mean by engaging in radical empathy as political practice? A call for an education in radical empathy goes several steps further than expressing a vague desire for increased empathy in our political affairs. I see radical empathy as the notion, put quite simply, that when contemplating political issues, we first try to imagine if we were in another's situation, and that we do this deliberately and consistently – that we make such empathy a habit of action.

I say action because although we commonly think of empathy as a feeling, and we tend to conceive of feelings as something internal, something private, something that we are regularly instructed by society to keep inside and hold in our intimate realms, radical empathy must maintain a fundamentally public, outward-reaching, and active exercise. It asks that we consciously attempt to feel a connection to strangers. It conjures a series of questions to be repeated to oneself whenever facing a question of political life – what if that were me? What if that was my child? What if that was my mother, my father, or my grandparent? What if that was my street, my neighborhood, my town? The idea is that rather than to lead solely with one's own already determined beliefs when deciding on the solution to a political quandary, one should also consider if and how one's opinion shifts once faced with the notion that it could be happening to you and yours.

I also say habit because it is the regular and consistent use of empathetic techniques that lends itself well to supporting a healthy political life. Aristotle wrote in *The Politics* (Aristotle, 1996) that justice must be a habit, that we become just as we act justly. That as humans, we are most easily able to reach our full potential as members of a political community, and that as citizens of a state pursuing the good life, we must make ethical choices as part of our mode of existence. He believes that we need help to accomplish this – the help provided by laws and education, he argued – but that ultimately, we must choose to make just actions a habit.

Just as Aristotle believed about ethics, I too believe that we can be *taught* to be empathetic in such a deliberate and thoughtful way, in the interest of a healthier and more just state. We can be taught this, as part of a civics education, from an early age. And if we are not, we can relearn our relationship to empathy at any age so that we associate it as much with political deliberation as we do with the sort of spontaneous and personal moments that commonly give rise to feelings of empathy. Radical empathy relies on a proactive approach versus a reactive one – to say to oneself, I will readily consider how X must feel, regardless of what it is and who it is happening to, versus now that I am in the position of being faced with a loved one experiencing a difficult situation, I feel for them.

Empathy, or compassion (pitié), as Rousseau had called it in his *Discourse on Inequality* (Rousseau, 1993), has long been thought to lead to ethical behavior. Rousseau actually based much of his understanding of the human condition on this empathy – on what he calls (one of) the first instinct(s) – this compassion (the other primary instinct being that of self-preservation). He tells the story of his "savage man", navigating the state of nature, and how, when confronted by a fellow member of his species in a state of pain, injury, or death, his impulse is to feel immediate and overwhelming distress, he feels natural "repugnance", as he calls it, upon witnessing this pain, he *shares* the pain, as he instantly imagines that the pain could be his own. This instinct prevented natural man from harming others, said Rousseau; it imbued him with a "gentle" nature by which he lived in peace with those around him.

Rousseau also argues that we are never distant from this natural compassion. That despite a political culture that favors the individualism of liberalism and the competitive nature of capitalism, we are always within reach of our inherent urge for empathy. The trouble is, as he saw it, that the human-created inequalities and oppressions of society are so vast and ingrained that we too often have trouble connecting to our natural selves. If indeed Rousseau is right, and I like to believe that he is, then it is our duty to human nature, and to justice everywhere, to work towards a more deliberate attention to the value of empathy in society.

The reasoning often goes that if we can imagine the feelings of others, share in the feelings of others, *truly* share, then this newfound connection can pave the way for compassionate action – in much the way that Rousseau describes. It is this possibility that I take as a foundational assumption of my arguments here. I very much believe that increased understanding of the very different situations of others can assist in more inclusive and equitable political decisions and, ultimately, public spaces and institutions.

Still, I am aware that to achieve empathy in public, and to achieve it in the face of the glaring *otherness* that makes up our public worlds, is not an easy task. When in our shared spaces, especially those outside of our comfort zones of familiarity, there are a multitude of visual reminders we are confronted with that tell us that we are in some evident or notable way different from many of those around us. Sadly, it is often these visual reminders that compel people to look away, resist connection, and exclude. So how and what can encourage us to see sameness more frequently than otherness? It is clear that both are true – we are indeed different, but we are also startlingly similar in our shared humanness.

Aristotle's philosophy reminds us that people need to be taught to do "justice as habit". Similarly, radical empathy can, and should, be a learned civic virtue. But beyond doing this work in civics classes in schools or through the announcements and advertisements of a national public service campaign – both of which would hold great value – there is yet another way to encourage such empathy among citizens, and that is through the vehicle of artistic experience, and specifically through participation in collective creative practices.

I believe there are a multitude of ways that art and politics intersect to important and useful ends. Art, by its nature, transforms and transcends – both the medium it employs and the everyday reality in which it exists. In this transformative capacity, transforming material and idea, art encourages critique and introspection, self-awareness, and connection to oneself as well as to those around us.

Perhaps most importantly for pursuing radical empathy, art reveals moments of human unity – it highlights the universal truths that exist within the multitude of particular moments. This capacity of art to articulate our common emotions – of love, joy, sorrow, grief – makes it directly and profoundly valuable for encouraging empathetic practice.

Socially-Engaged Art Practices

To this end, there is a form of public artmaking that has grown increasingly more visible on the arts landscape over the past few decades, and that is what is known as social practice or socially engaged artmaking. This sort of art practice is uniquely situated to be a teacher of empathy.

Such approaches in public art encompass a vast diversity of works that are created in response to social and political problems and possibilities and that create transcendent experiences via collaborative solutions to these problems. These projects dance on the edge of art and political protest or art and civic organization or art and community initiative. They challenge traditional norms of art and have even been accused of not being art at all. The shared ethos of these works, though, is that they invite people to join in and take part, they transform audiences into participants, and they empower individuals and communities to take action and to be a part of a collective and collaborative public experience. In that active engagement, collaboration, and dialogue, they help people to see and feel experiences outside of their own, inherently enabling possibilities for empathy.

These projects – enacted all over the world – are not so much a movement or a style in art but rather a belief about the power of art itself. Many of these projects do not produce a material art object or a resulting commodity. Rather, they make a transformation – they create an effect, a moment, a memory, and sometimes, new community processes and/or brick-and-mortar facilities. They all aim, in some way, to change the communities in which they are created. The medium of this sort of art is always human interaction itself – participants are required to complete the artistic vision. Rooted in 20th-century movements such as performance, conceptual, and community arts, and brought to global prominence in the 1990s and the 2000s, there are a multitude of examples of such socially engaged artworks.

Public and social art can be an integral part of a healthy and welcoming community. It is an essential part of a layered and diverse environment, helping us to make connections with those around us, with our shared histories, and with the issues of the day. Beyond this, it simply, importantly, and majestically brings creativity and aesthetic emotions into our everyday lives. Art maintains a profound ability to activate conversations, to present new ways of seeing and understanding, and to create profound experiences of wonder, awe, and joy. Public art allows for opportunities for artists to share their ideas with the public through outdoor, freely accessible works. These public artworks can become places to chat or rest or connect – with others, with ourselves, and with the space itself. Spaces, both permanent and ephemeral, where we want to linger, that captivate us, that sustain us, that calm us, and that educate us, rarely just happen. They need to be thoughtfully created, and the many artists leaving their studios and creating work on the street aids in transforming, project by project, our public lives.

Social practice, or socially engaged art (both terms derive from the early 2000s), is also known as, or inclusive of, new genre public art (coined by Suzanne Lacy in 1991), relational aesthetics (coined by Nicolas Bourriaud in 1998), community art, interventionist art, participatory art, collaborative art, civic art, and dialogical art, among other terms. These artistic creations – many activist or engaging directly in social and political issues, and made in public spaces – are completed by the "audience", who become participants and collaborators. These projects rely on the interactive experience that takes place within and because of the artwork. It is the act of creating them that is important; that becomes the art itself. The interaction, the collaboration, the dialogue, and the sharing that take place are the key to this approach in artmaking.

This form of artmaking has, since its upbringing, been a source of controversy for art critics who debate the artistic value of this largely 21st-century medium. Some argue it is a form of interactive participatory art, but some believe these sorts of projects should not be termed artworks, that they are in fact political and cultural initiatives. Either way, more and more artists are bypassing galleries, entering community hubs, collaborating with residents, adding to their neighborhoods, and working to change the status quo. Nato Thompson once argued that he would refrain from engaging in a discussion that decides whether to qualify social practice art as indeed being art and rather focus on the reality – that artists are doing this work, and the related practices are spreading quickly and diversely (Thompson, 2017).

I believe it is important, though, to defend and provide support for the artistic value of such projects. Accordingly, I argue that socially engaged art is a method of artmaking, no matter if the result is a fully functioning bus depot or a more overtly aesthetic creation. Regardless of the outcome of the works and the various extents to which they provide care and resources within the community, it is the intention and perspective that matter most. If it is made by an artist, with the belief that connecting people in interaction, conversation, and mutual aid is the goal, then the creation is an artistic venture. Artists have always felt compelled to act in an oversight role over society, and it is important to this discussion that the very fact that an artist chooses to do work in a way that might resemble a political action or provision of a social service is telling of a world troubled enough that artists feel a call to intervene in the traditional landscape of solutions to municipal problems.

There are new socially engaged projects being developed every day. Many approach interventions in our daily worlds by creating unexpected moments of awe or spirited conversation among strangers – they intervene in the everyday landscape by placing in public spaces an invitation to pause, participate, and reflect. Some are intended to be ephemeral experiences of joy and connection, temporary exhibits that launch for an hour or a day or a week. Others are formed with the intention to adapt to the longer-term needs of their communities and work to become part of the ongoing landscape. Still others provide not only an experience or a burst of inspiration or beauty but work to fulfill a tangible need present in the community. They might provide food or transportation or safety or child or elderly care. Projects have included everything from community gardens and food libraries to bike loan initiatives and after-school programs for children. These projects can sometimes become institutionalized, remaining as permanent additions to a neighborhood.

One well known example of such a project is Rick Lowe's Project Row Houses (1993–). Project Row Houses began decades ago when an area in Houston's Historic Third Ward, one of the city's oldest African-American neighborhoods, was on the verge of being demolished by the city, and Lowe, along with other artists, purchased several derelict row houses and began transforming them into places for cultural collaboration and community togetherness. The site now encompasses five city blocks and houses thirty-nine buildings that collectively create an enclave within the larger city and are home to a variety of community-enriching initiatives, art programs, and neighborhood development activities. Over the years, programs have been developed that assist under-resourced neighbors, mothers and their children (providing, for example, childcare and housing so the mothers could attend school), small enterprises trying to grow, and artists interested in using their talents to enrich the lives of others.

In a similar vein, Theaster Gates created the Dorchester Projects (2009–; an early example of the work of his non-profit The Rebuild Foundation), which likewise transformed abandoned buildings in a distressed neighborhood, this time on Chicago's South Side, into vibrant gathering spaces for culture, crafting a model for community building. What began as the reconceptualization of a single building (housing a library, an archive, and a kitchen) that aimed to preserve, honor, and activate Black cultural forms grew into a thirty-two-building collective that supplies locals not only with affordable housing and employment opportunities but also with performances and exhibitions. Gates writes that, "We leverage the power and potential of communities, buildings, and objects that others have written off".

Another project that comes to mind as an example of one where life needs are being supplied directly by the work is Mary Mattingly's Swale (2015–2020) (a new iteration is being designed now), which was a collaborative food project that aimed to reimagine how we might provide nutrition to those in need. It consisted of a steel barge (floating in New York City's East and Hudson rivers) that housed a community garden. When Mattingly discovered that you cannot legally forage or grow food in public spaces in New York City, she decided to create a "food forest" of edible plants out on the water to circumvent those laws and let people gather food for free. The project served as an education and advocacy platform for public food sources as well as a place to be a part of performances, exhibits, and community meetings. Mattingly explains, "Swale has become a tool . . . for envisioning forms of food sovereignty in public space".

There are also those social works that use the artistic process of transformation to change what the artists perceive as a negative or harmful part of society into a beautiful or life-nourishing one. Pedro Reyes's Palas Por Pistolas (2011–) is a compelling example of this. *Palas Por Pistolas* (Shovels for Guns) was initially created for the Botanical Garden in Culiacán, a city in western Mexico with the highest rate of handgun deaths in the country. Helped by a campaign organized by the Culiacán city government, Reyes collected 1,527 guns from civilians (more than 40% of which were issued by the military). These were first publicly steamrolled and then melted down to create shovels that were then used to plant trees in urban areas affected by violence (through schools and community groups). Since then, these shovels/recycled weapons have been used to plant trees in many major cities, in honor of local people and communities harmed by gun violence. The shovels have also been exhibited worldwide, and every time they are, they are also used to plant more trees.

Taking a different creative approach, French artist JR has also created many such transformative projects. One he titled *Carrying Valeriia Through Lviv* (2022), where he traveled to Lviv – the Ukrainian city by which a five-year-old girl named Valeriia and her mother escaped the war (and one flooded by refugees since the beginning of the war) – and took a now-famous photograph of little Valeriia. He then created a photographic installation using a 148-foot-tall print of Valeriia's photo on a massive tarp. He unwrapped the image in a central Lviv square, and many – well over 100 convened in mere minutes – local residents offered to help. They walked through the city together, groups of men and women holding up this giant tarp. His intention was to call attention to the alarming rate at which children in Ukraine had become refugees (almost one child per second in April 2022) and to revive the spirits of the Ukrainian people through a creative collective action of hope.

A few years earlier, he planned another project that shed light on a very different group of underserved people, this time prisoners. JR created Tehachapi, The Yard (2019), in a maximum security prison where the majority of the incarcerated population had been imprisoned for nearly a decade, with many sentenced to life with no chance of parole. JR and his team photographed the men, one by one, and they were also given a chance to tell their story in front of a video camera. JR also photographed former prisoners and prison staff, collecting a total of forty-eight portraits and stories from the prison system, resulting in 338 strips of paper. The prisoners then worked closely with guards, former inmates, and members of JR's studio to paste these portraits onto the ground of the prison yard. When the final image is viewed from above, one can see the incarcerated and the prison staff standing close together, looking out onto the world. The installation, intended to be temporary, faded away in days under the footsteps of the prison's inhabitants, but you can still listen to each of the participants' stories on the artist's app.

A project that also employs digital public space in inspiring ways is Richard Kearney and Sheila Gallagher's Guestbook Project (2009–), a cross-disciplinary multimedia network of creative approaches to inspiring peace around the world through the exchange of stories. The initiative's website serves as an archive for these narratives. In one aspect of the project, young people in divided communities exchange powerful narratives for the purpose of better understanding each other's communities across political conflict and turn them into creative video projects, which can then encourage change all over the world. In another aspect of the project called "Storybites", space is created "for people to share transformative moments in which 'the other' becomes a guest. Overcoming violence and facilitating conflict resolution means hosting a radical and surprising shift in perspective".

Yet another approach to socially engaged work is embraced by artists who design projects that bring joy and invite creative expression and emotional connection in public spaces. A brilliant example of this, Luke Jerram's Street Pianos: Play Me I'm Yours (2008–) has reached millions of people worldwide. Over two thousand street pianos have been installed by Jerram and his team in over seventy cities across the globe, all bearing the simple instruction to 'Play Me, I'm Yours". This project encourages community members to create interactive performance venues out of everyday spaces. By making it free and accessible to enjoy the fruits of a piano – a large, heavy, and generally cost-prohibitive instrument – passersby can share together in a love of music and all manner of the arts (as dancing and singing often accompany the piano playing). Located on street corners, in public parks, markets, train stations, and airports, the pianos are available for everyone to play and enjoy. Donated and then decorated and cared for by local artists and community groups, the street pianos create a place for creative exchange and an opportunity for people to connect and commune together.

Ronni and Dany Abergel, Asma Mouna, and Christoffer Erichsen founded The Human Library (2000–) to create a safe space to engage in conversations that you likely wouldn't have otherwise. Real people – and their experiences and histories – are the "books" that can be "borrowed" by participants, so that the "readers" can sit down with the people/books they choose and listen to their stories. The idea is for people to be able to have conversations with those they may not meet in their everyday lives. This project has been enacted all over the world in a variety of different settings, but the original event took place in Copenhagen at an outdoor cafe over the course of four days, spanning eight hours each day, with over a thousand participants and over fifty "books" "read" in that first enactment alone. The creators call themselves a "hands-on learning platform" and explain that they aim to "better our understanding of diversity in order to help create more inclusive and cohesive communities across cultural, religious, social and ethnic differences". Their slogan is "unjudge someone".

Candy Chang's Before I Die (2011–) After the death of someone she loved dearly, Chang painted an abandoned house in her New Orleans neighborhood with chalkboard paint and titled it with the prompt, "Before I die I want to ___". It was her intention to restore perspective by finding consolation in her grief not alone but rather with her neighbors, those both known and unknown to her. Anyone walking by was able to pick up a piece of chalk and share their hopes, dreams, regrets, and vulnerabilities in public. By the next day, that original wall was entirely filled, and the project has only grown since then. Chang then created online resources so that the project could be easily replicated by anyone wishing to create their own wall. As of this writing, over five thousand *Before I Die* walls have now been created by communities in over seventy-five countries.

In a similar vein, and begun just a year after Before I Die, Chang's Confessions (2012–) is inspired both by Japanese Shinto shrine prayer walls as well as the Catholic practice of entering a confessional to voice one's sins to a priest. In Chang's words, "It creates a secular space for catharsis and consolation" and "examines the relationship between public space and emotional communion". Passersby become active participants when they choose to enter the private booths – as you would in a Catholic church (or perhaps a voting booth) – and write a confession on a wooden plaque that is then hung on a wall, alongside many others, just outside the booths. Enacted in a variety of cities, the project has now totaled over 20,000 confessions.

Conclusions

From these examples, one can see that these sorts of artistic projects directly serve the creation of empathetic ties between people in public. It is especially in response to thinking about public and participatory artworks like these that I invite you to host art in your lives – to reconsider its political value and its democratic possibilities, and to recognize its capacity to engage individuals in empathetic connection and interaction. Artistic communication and collaboration can create and deepen ties between people and within communities, and socially engaged projects can serve as welcoming vehicles for "hosting" interactions, dialogues, and relationships.

I believe deeply that empathy is needed in and among individuals to support a healthy political life, and I also believe that the realm of art is naturally well-suited to encouraging such empathy. This is particularly true of socially-based artworks that rely on the participation of community members, on their interactions and collaborations, and on their willingness to be, in various ways, open and vulnerable to each other and to the public world in general.

When thinking about empathy as an element of civic life, the oft quoted Cornel West line about justice being love in public (West, Howard University, 2011) comes to mind. I have always been moved by this way of phrasing. As we come of age, we are socialized to keep emotions, love included, behind the closed doors of our rooms and our homes. Public life, culture teaches us, is for reason – for rational decisions, for controlled behaviors, and for restrained communications. Yet West's quote reminds us that when we care for others, no matter how public or formal or distant, it is ultimately emotional, it is a form of love. Just as justice is love in public, justice is also empathy in public. We should embrace radical empathy as a political good and as a civic virtue – we should talk about it, we should educate about it, we should practice it.

This work examines the rich relationship between art and political life, focusing specifically on the lessons of citizenship, most notably habitual empathetic exercises, that can be learned from collaborative interactive art experiences. It argues that "radical empathy" should be an essential component of our civic language and that it can be developed and aided by participating in shared artistic experiences as provided by the vast diversity of social practice art projects.

I have examined how art – and specifically public and socially engaged art – can serve as a host for dialogues, connections, and relationships. I have described the many possibilities inherent to art practice and experience and made a case for why we all would benefit from hosting art more centrally, both in our everyday lives and in our self-understandings. Specifically, I have argued that empathy, via the vehicle of shared creative experience, can and should serve as an ethos for contemporary political life and be viewed as a form of civic responsibility. Further, the definition of empathy I put forward here does not focus exclusively on sameness (believing oneself to be like another) but rather on empathy as recognition of the human and of the inevitable human experience of fundamental emotions like the joy of creation and the grief of loss. "Radical empathy" implies the intentional and habitual act of working to understand, and ultimately accept, others across differences. When viewed as an integral component of citizenship, empathy becomes essential to democracy and helps to inform a healthy relation between the individual psyche and society writ large.

Notes

1 In March 2025, the U.S. was also added to the Civicus monitor watchlist due to "threats to civic freedoms" (https://monitor.civicus.org/watchlist-march-2025/USA/).
2 Universally mandatory and rigorous, well-designed civics courses in public education would help, yet sadly, civics education in American public schools has notably been in decline since the 1960s. https://oconnorinstitute.org/research2024/; https://www.brookings.edu/articles/the-need-for-civic-education-in-21st-century-schools/; https://www.aft.org/ae/summer2018/shapiro_brown.

Works Cited

Abergel, R., Abergel, D., Mouna, A., & Erichsen, C. (2000–). The Human Library.
Aristotle. (1996). *The politics and the constitution of Athens* (S. Everson, Trans.). Cambridge, UK: Cambridge University Press.
Chang, C. (2011–). Before I Die.
Chang, C. (2012–). Confessions.
Gates, T. (2009–). Dorchester Projects.
Jerram, L. (2008–). Street Pianos: Play Me I'm Yours.
JR. (2019). Tehachapi, the Yard.
JR. (2022). Carrying Valeriia through Lviv.
Kearney, R., & Gallaghers, S. (2009–). Guestbook Project.
Kleinfeld, R. (2022, September 15). *Five strategies to support U.S. democracy*. https://carnegieendowment.org/2022/09/15/five-strategies-to-support-u.s.-democracy-pub-87918
Lowe, R. (1993–). Project Row Houses.
Mattingly, M. (2015–2020). Swale.
Reyes, P. (2011–). Palas Por Pistolas.
Rousseau, J.-J. (1993). *The social contract and the discourses.* New York: Everyman's Library (Random House).
Thompson, N. (2017). *Living as form*. Boston, MA: MIT Press.
West, C. (2011). Speech, Howard University.

Index

Note: Page numbers in *italic* indicate an image or figure on the corresponding page.

Absolute, the 241–242, 243
absurdity 111–112
acute shame 94–97
aesthetic: alienation 245, 246; becoming 247–248; Black Atlantic as an aesthetic model 239;centralization as aesthetic death 246; democracy 248–249; Divine Otherness 241; emancipatory 251; generative moral aesthetic 245–246; liberatory 244; life-affirming 251; metamorphosis 238; muse, as Incarnation, Spirit of Truth 242–243; pluralistic aesthetic spaces 243; politicized aesthetic economy 247; prophetic deliverance as an aesthetic model 250; resonance and space in 246–247; sublime 241; transpersonal aesthetic 238
aesthetic alienation 245
aesthetic articulations 29–30, 37–38; aesthetic holding 35–36; case if Ilyas 36; creating resonance 33–35, *34*; critical engagement 37; potency of articulation 32–33; psychological paradigms 30–32
aesthetic death 246
aesthetic democracy 248–249
aesthetic families of becoming 247–248
aesthetic holding 35–37
aesthetic knowing 42–56, *48*
aesthetic model of movement 239–240
aesthetic motivation 211–212, 227–229; beauty and justice 219–222; emotional turn 215–219; irrationality 212–213; phenomenology of beauty in social movements 222–227; rationalism 213–215

aesthetics 1–2, 15–17; beauty and goodness 22–25; becoming "better" 19–21; contextualized 235; dialoguing towards beautiful justice 10–11; divorce of ethics and aesthetics 2–4; ethics as encounter 4–6; generative moral aesthetic 245–246; psychological humanities and ethics 25–27; reimagining beauty 17–19; Western philosophical divorce of ethics and 2–4
aesthetic spaces 243
aesthetic vertex 58–60
aisthetikos 181
Alexander the Great 79–87
alienation, aesthetic 245; as gap 246
Alsup (2009): liberation psychology 235; soul-destructive Othering 251
ancestral voice 200
Andrade (2017): decolonized mission 251
Andru (2021): nature mysticism 240
Angelou, M. 196–197, 199
anxiety 94–97
apathy 256–257
arcs 84
Aristotle 2, 5, 79–88, 259–260
Aristotle With a Bust of Homer (Rembrandt) 79–80, 84–89, *88*; arcs, lines, and fluid motion 84; attire 81; countenances 82; fame 82–83; first impressions 77–79; hands 81–82; impact of lived experience 85–86; learning to see 75–76; legacy of influence 80; moral and existential inquiry 86–87; painting as inquiry 80–81; phenomenological approach to art 77; schooling of desire 76–77; wisdom 82–84

Index

art/art practices 79–80, 84–89, *88*, 101–102, 116–117, 233–234, 256, 258–266; agenesis of artistic core 247; apathy and exclusion 256–257; arcs, lines, and fluid motion 84; as atonement 241–242; attire 81; as barrier, deconstruction, depolarization 236–237; bears witness 243; as co-creation 243–244; and consumerism 245; countenances 82; as courage-in-humility 237; and diaspora 240; environmental surround for organismic art 248; fame 82–83; first impressions 77–79; fragile 250; and fragmentation 240; hands 81–82; impact of lived experience 85–86; kingdom-generative art path 242; language of 106–114, *109*, *112*; learning to see 75–76; legacy of influence 80; loyalty as 243; message of 114–116, *116*; as moral courage 237; moral and existential inquiry 86–87; as movement from self-interest 237; as non-hate 235–236; obligation of 102–106; organismic 248; painting as inquiry 80–81; phenomenological approach to 77; as prophetic vision 237–238; as reconciliation 237; as redemptive 241–242; redemptive artistic society 241–242; as reversal 236; as sacred 236; schooling of desire 76–77; as sensemaking 238; and soul-making 124–152, *130–133*, *135*, *137–140*, *142*, *144–151*; as spatial reconstruction 236; and syncretism 237–238; and temporal existence 243–244; as transcendent to materialism 240–241; as transdisciplinary re-examination 244–245; as transcendent to materialism 240–241; as transfiguration 241–242; wisdom 82–84
articulation, potency of 32–33; *see also* aesthetic articulations
artistic epiphenomena 248
atonement 241–242
attachment 247–248
attention 126, 136–137, 141–144; decreative 164–165
attire 81
authoritarianism 248
automaton conformity 246

Bachelard, G. 58–9, 67, 72
backward glance 64–68, 70–71

barrier deconstruction 236–237
beauty 1–2, 15–17, 219–222; becoming "better" 19–21; dialoguing towards beautiful justice 10–11; divorce of ethics and aesthetics 2–4; ethics as encounter 4–6; and goodness 22–25; phenomenology of 222–227; psychological humanities and ethics 25–27; reimagining 17–19
becoming, aesthetic families of 247–248
becoming "better" 15–17, 19–21; beauty and goodness 22–25; psychological humanities and ethics 25–27; reimagining beauty 17–19
beloved community 233–255 234–238, 241–252; as atonement in Royce 2431 as call, civil rights, changing the Face of the Other 239; devotion to something larger than self 243; Divine Otherness 251; as geographic space 241; Holy City of community of mankind 233; imminence 242; Kingdom of God 234; love as organizing axiom 251; promised land 234; Prophetic Deliverance 250; reconciling community 252; reconciliation of oppressor to oppressed 237; redemptive society 242; reparation 251; revelation of divine love 236; reversal (1963) 251; sacredness of the person 241; saving absolute 242; total inclusion, justice, integration 247; transcendent conscious, ethics 237; as transcendent self-actualization 243; transfiguring experience 242; transformation of the representation of the Other 238–239
Bernini: *St. Teresa in ecstasy* 131, *133*
Bion, W. R. 58–60, 63, 68–69, 136, 156
Black Atlantic 239–240; geographical 239; ineffable 239
Blake (1990): commercial mass culture 249; corporatism 249; industrialization and the beloved community 249; technocratic social engineering 249; technological determinism 249
body 101, 110–111, 113
Bowen (1978): symbiotic ego 234; undifferentiated family ego mass 247
brokenness 113–114
Buber, M. (1923): *I and Thou* 240
Burrow (2012): beloved community 236; MLK's view of gender 240

Index

Celan, P. 164, 167–174
centralization 246
Cézanne, P.: *La maison du pendu* 115–116, *116*
clarity *see* denotational clarity
co-creation 243–244
complicated mourning 94
consciousness 233–234
contextualized aesthetic 235
corruptible corpus 250
countenances 82
courage, moral 237
crisis 256–257
critical engagement, aesthetic articulation as 37
cultural potency 250
cyber-control 246

Davis, G. 238
D'Agostino & Lake (2014) 246; alienation 250; estrangement 247; on Fromm's (1941–1976) work on alienation 246
Day, D. 222, 225, 227
death 106–108, 246
decolonized 241
decreative attention 164–165
decreative hermeneutics 166–169, 173–174
democracy 241, 256, 258–266; aesthetic 248–249; apathy and exclusion 256–257
denotational clarity 30–32, 34, 35–36
depolarization 236–237
desire 76–77
despair 108–111
destiny 240–241
devotion 243
DeWolf, H. 238
dialogue 10–11
diaspora 240
diffusion in identity 247
dissociated 156, 161
divine otherness 240–241, 251
DuBois (1903): double consciousness 240; self as revelation to another world 240; voice of exile 233
dying of the unharmed self 93–99

education 75–77, 80–81, 85
emotions 211–213, 215–219, 221–222, 227–228
empathy *see* radical empathy
environment 248
ethical obligation 101–102; language of art 106–114, *109*, *112*; message of art 114–116, *116*; obligation of art 102–106
ethics 1–2, 15–17; beauty and goodness 22–25; becoming "better" 19–21; dialoguing towards beautiful justice 10–11; divorce of aesthetics and 2–4; as encounter 4–6; psychological humanities and 25–27; reimagining beauty 17–19; Western philosophical divorce of aesthetics and 2–4; *see also* ethical obligation
excellence 4–6
exclusion 256–257
existential inquiry 86–87
experience of beauty 15–17; beauty and goodness 22–25; becoming "better" 19–21; psychological humanities and ethics 25–27; reimagining beauty 17–19

fame 82–83
Fanon, F. 181–190
fluid lines 77, 84
fragmentation 240
Francesca, P. della: *Baptism of Christ* 137, *137*; *Resurrection of Christ* 140
freedom 235
Freud, S. (1930) 3, 30–31, 65, 71, 95, 125–129, 136, 143, 152, 155–157, 182–188, 236, 248; conscience and superego 248; cultural superego 236
Fromm, E. 237, 244–248, 250–252; alienation, mechanism, automaton conformity 237; authoritarianism (1947) 248; conscience and superego (1941, 1947) 248; freedom from or towards; negative vs positive freedom 245; Hegelian thought and impoverished inner life 251; humanistic religious orientation (1950) 248; mechanism (1950) 245; productive existence (1950) 245; pseudo freedom (1941) 245; pseudo-self (1947) 248; rootedness (1955) 244; Sick Society (1962) 250

Gandhi, M. 222, 226–227, 238
gaze 76–77, 79–80, 82, 84–89, 134, 138, 141
generative moral aesthetic 245–246
Gilroy (1993): double consciousness 239; transculturalism 239
goodness 22–25

Gray (1975): overconformist 247; self-estrangement 247; uncommitted 247
grief 108, 113
Gunderson (2014): biophilous 248; meaninglessness 248

hands 81–82
hatred 64, 174, 215, 229, 237–239, 252
healing 195–197
hermeneutics: decreative 166–169, 173–174; of suspicion 159; of trust 155
Herstein (2009): agapic love 250; oceanic, all-redeeming love 250
history 157–160
Hogarth, W.: "Marriage A-la-Mode" *48*, 49
Holocaust 158, 164, 166–168, 170, 173–174
Homer 80–84, 86–87, 160; see also *Aristotle With a Bust of Homer* (Rembrandt)
humanities, psychological 25–27

iconic representations 83–84, 86
idols of the marketplace 251
Ilyas 36–38
image 42, 44–50, 53–56
imagination: reimagining beauty 17–19; see also moral imaginations
impossible: "impossible/necessary" 94–97
inclusion 247–248
influence 80
injustice *see* social injustice
Innes (1996): lost presence 233
inquiry, painting as 80–81
intergenerational transmission of trauma 67–68
Inwood (2009): anticolonial striving 237; beloved community as geographic space 24; counternarratives 234; influence of Gandhi on MLK 238; middle passage 239; prismatic belonging 244; spatial reconstruction 236
irrationality 186, 212–213; the irrational 114, 215–219; irrationalist perspective 213, 215
irreducible, the 234–235

Jensen (2016): humanism 243; saving absolute 242; transfiguring experience 242
justice 233, 240, 244, 247–248, 251; art as 236–237; and beauty 219–222; dialoguing towards beautiful justice 10–11

King, M. L. Jr. 233–244, 247–248, 249–252; beloved community as call, civil rights, changing the Face of the Other 239; brotherhood (1963) 236; changing the face of the enemy 252; Creative Force—synthesis (1958) 241; courage to speak (1955; 1967) 244; I vs it language 240; infinite personality (1948) 240; Kingdom of God 234; letter from the Brimingham Jail (1963) 240; love as transformative 238; Montgomery Story (1958) 235; nonviolent resistance (1958) 235, 236; participant in Being of God (1956) 252; Personal Immortality 238; promised land 234; reversal (1963) 251; silence as betrayal (1967) 237; transcendent conscious, ethics 237

language 42–43, 53; of art 106–114, *109*, *112*
latitudes of acceptance 248–249
Latter-Day Emersonians 249
legacy 80–87, 95, 196–197, 200, 206
Levinas, E. 4, 19–20, 37, 40n10, 111–112, 163–164, 182–186, 189–192; and Celan 167–174; and decreative hermeneutics 166–167; and Weil 164–165
liberation 4–6
liberation psychology 235, 251
Lieu, C. 40n8; *Falling* 34
light 68–70, 84–85
lines 84
lived experience 85–86
logic 42, 44, 52–56
lost presence 233–234
loyalty 243

marginalization 62–65
Marsh (2005): eschatological hope 242; redemptive society 242
materialism 240
Mays, B. (1933): Kingdom of God 241; sacredness of the person 241
McKittrick (2006): cartography of racial experience 239
meaning 58–60, 62–72
message of art 114–116, *116*
metamorphosis of hatred 252
Michelangelo: *Pietà* 108, *109*, 114
Miri (2014): humanistic religious orientation 248
MLK *see* King, M. L. Jr.

moral aesthetic 245–246
moral courage 237, 241
moral imaginations 1–2, 30, 32–37, 78; dialoguing towards beautiful justice 10–11; divorce of ethics and aesthetics 2–4; ethics as encounter 4–6
moral inquiry 30, 79, 86–87
morality 58–61, 72
motivation *see* aesthetic motivation
mourning 93–99
movement, aesthetic model of 239–240
movement from self-interest 237, 245
Murdoch, I. 20–27, 221, 227
muse, as Incarnation, Spirit of Truth 242–243

nachleben 156
Nachträglichkeit 65–67, 70–71
Nagl (2012): beloved community as transcendent self-actualization 243
necessary: "impossible/necessary" 94–97
Niebuhr, R. (1935): imaginative justice 236; impossible possibility 236; spiritual transcendence 236; transcendent unity 236
Nilson (2010): consequences of racism 233; sacramental unity 252
non-hate, art as 235–236
nonviolence 237

obligation 101–102; of art 102–106; language of art 106–114, *109*, *112*; message of art 114–116, *116*
oblivion of history 157–158
openings 236
organismic art 248
Other/other, the 21, 24–25, 37, 61–66, 155–161, 163–164, 165–169, 170–174, 190–191, 238–241, 245–249; as irreducible 239
otherness 4–6, 18, 64, 164–167, 169–170, 172–173, 243, 260; divine 240–241, 251
ox-herding pictures *146–150*, 151

paradox 236
Payne (1996): ideological appropriation 233
personal Absolute 241–242
personal death 246
personalism 233, 234–235
Peters (2017): Kierkegaard's influence on Fromm 27
phenomenology 79–80, 84–89, *88*; arcs, lines, and fluid motion 84; attire 81; of beauty 222–227; countenances 82; fame 82–83; first impressions 77–79; hands 81–82; impact of lived experience 85–86; learning to see 75–76; legacy of influence 80; moral and existential inquiry 86–87; painting as inquiry 80–81; phenomenological approach to art 77; schooling of desire 76–77; wisdom 82–84
pluralistic aesthetic spaces 243
poetic image 42, 44–50, 53–56
poetics of formation 29–30, 38; aesthetic holding 35–36; case if Ilyas 36; creating resonance 33–35, *34*; critical engagement 37; potency of articulation 32–33; psychological paradigms 30–32
poetry 195–196; disruptive 204–209; psychological depths of 198–200; reclaiming ancestral voice 200–204; transformative power of 196; trauma and healing 196–197
power-distance 248–249
presence, lost 233–234
primary process 58–60
productive society 245
prophecy 195–197, 199, 202, 204, 206–209, 237–238
Proudfoot (1976): expanded being 243
pseudo-resonance 247
pseudo-self 248
psychic reality 58–59
psychoanalysis 155–157, 158, 160–161; and soul-making 124–152, *130–133*, *135*, *137–140*, *142*, *144–151*
psychology: liberation psychology 235; and poetry 195–196, 198–200, 207–209; psychological humanities 25–27, 29; psychological paradigms 30–32

Rabelais, F. 157, 161n13
radical empathy 256, 257–266; apathy and exclusion 256–257
rationalism 43, 49, 211, 213–217
reclaiming 11, 29, 62, 198–200, 207–208
reconciliation 237
reconciling community 252
reconstruction, spatial 236
redemptive transfiguration 241–242
refusal of hatred 237
regret 97–99
religious activism 211–212, 227–229; beauty and justice 219–222; emotional

Index   273

turn 215–219; irrationality 212–213; phenomenology of beauty in social movements 222–227; rationalism 213–215
Rembrandt 79–80, 84–89, *88*, 134, *135*; arcs, lines, and fluid motion 84; attire 81; countenances 82; fame 82–83; first impressions 77–79; hands 81–82; impact of lived experience 85–86; learning to see 75–76; legacy of influence 80; moral and existential inquiry 86–87; painting as inquiry 80–81; phenomenological approach to art 77; schooling of desire 76–77; wisdom 82–84
reparation 251
representation of the Other 238–239
resonance 33–35, *34*; as aesthetic holding 35–36; and space 246–247
restoration 240–241
reversals 248–249
Ricoeur, P. 34, 58–59
Royce (1908): communitarian loyalty 250; loyalty as devotion to something larger than self 243; Pearl of Great Price 251
Royce (1913): community of God's beloved 242; devotion 250; doctrine of life 242; kingdom of heaven 242; mount of transfiguration 234; prodigal 235; Superlative Spirit 242; superpersonal 234; transcendence (also in 1908) 235
Royce (1916): Holy City of community of mankind 233
Royce (1883): teleology 243
Royce (1995): Deus Absconditus 249; infinite soul 249
Royce (1897): dialectical method and perspective-taking 237; Impersonal Absolute (Kant) 237

Saving Absolute 242, 243
schooling of desire 76–77
Schörghofer, G. 130; *To be in Limbo 130–131*
seeing 79–80, 84–89, *88*; arcs, lines, and fluid motion 84; attire 81; countenances 82; fame 82–83; first impressions 77–79; hands 81–82; impact of lived experience 85–86; learning to see 75–76; legacy of influence 80; moral and existential inquiry 86–87; painting

as inquiry 80–81; phenomenological approach to art 77; schooling of desire 76–77; wisdom 82–84
self-interest 237
Sengai: *Circle triangle square* 138, *138*
shame 94; acute 94–97
Simpson (2008): beloved community as loving one's enemies 238; co-create the Kingdom of God 244; nonviolent action 421
Slater (1991): authoritarianism 250
Smith (1950): collaboration of interpreters 242; logos 242
Smith & Zepp (1974): total inclusion, justice, integration as beloved community 247
social engineering 249–250
social injustice 62–65
socially-engaged art 256, 260–266; apathy and exclusion 256–257; "radical empathy" 257–260
social movements 222–227
society, productive 245
solidarity 240–241, 244–245
sorrow 94, 233
Sosno, S.: *Vénus oblitérée* 112, *112*
soul-making 124–152, *130–133, 135, 137–140, 142, 144–151*
space 246–247
spatial reconstruction 236
Subramaniam (1996): dispersion and hybrid cultures 239; intergenerational 239; transnational 239
Sucharov (2015): prismatic consciousness 240
suffering 101–102, 252; language of art 106–114, *109, 112*; message of art 114–116, *116*; obligation of art 102–106
superpersonal 234, 243
syncretism 237–238

temporal existence 243–244
thinking Otherwise 15–17; beauty and goodness 22–25; becoming "better" 19–21; psychological humanities and ethics 25–27; reimagining beauty 17–19
Thompson (2014) 248
time 58–61, 63–65, 67–69, 72
transcendental life-world 251
transcendent deliverance 249
transcendent ethics 248

transfiguration, redemptive 241–242
transformation of the represetnation of the Other 238–239
trauma 155, 158, 160–162; intergenerational transmission of 67–68; and poetry 196–197, 199
trust, hermeneutic of 155
truth, spirit of 242–243
truthtelling 198–200
turbulence 60–62

unconscious, the 64–66, 155, 157–158, 198
unharmed self 93–99
unification 240

Vermeer: *The Milk Maid* 142, *142*, 151

Weil, S. 16–17, 19–21, 27, 141, 143, 164–167, 170–173, 174, 221

West, C. (1982): imperfection, forgiveness and hope 238; influence of the Black church and syncretism on MLK 238; Prophetic Deliverance 249–250; prophetic, liberal Christianity 238; rapacious individualism 233
Wilde (2004): critical interpretative pedagogy 244; Fromm's ethically-driven communitarianism 244
Williams, R. (2002): collective change 235; complete Otherness of the divine 241; cultural resonances 241; Divine Otherness 251; moral community 252; political edifice 251; reconciliation of oppressor to oppressed 237; revelation of divine love 236
Williams & Benytsson (2022): personalism 234
wisdom 80–88
witness 182–183, 190–191

For Product Safety Concerns and Information please contact our EU
representative GPSR@taylorandfrancis.com
Taylor & Francis Verlag GmbH, Kaufingerstraße 24, 80331 München, Germany